By Arina Tanemura

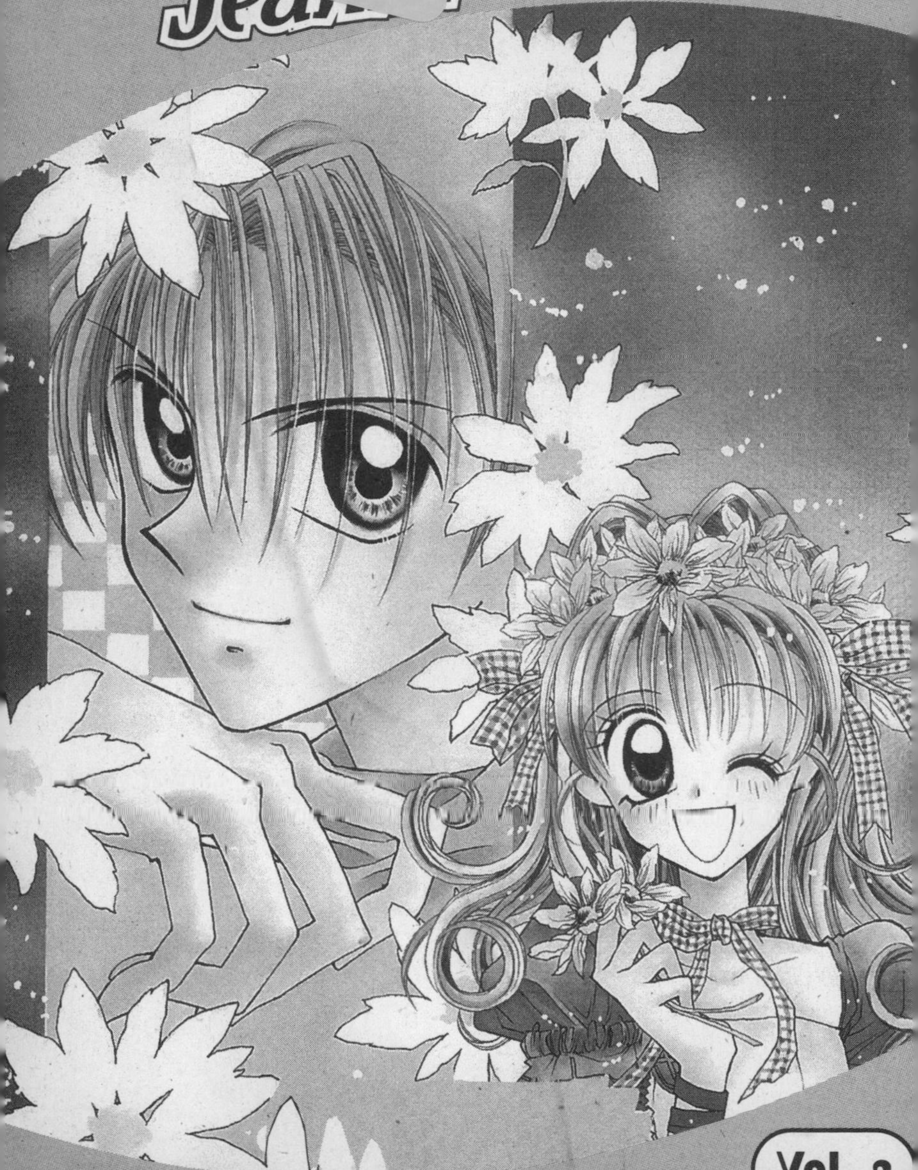

Vol. 2

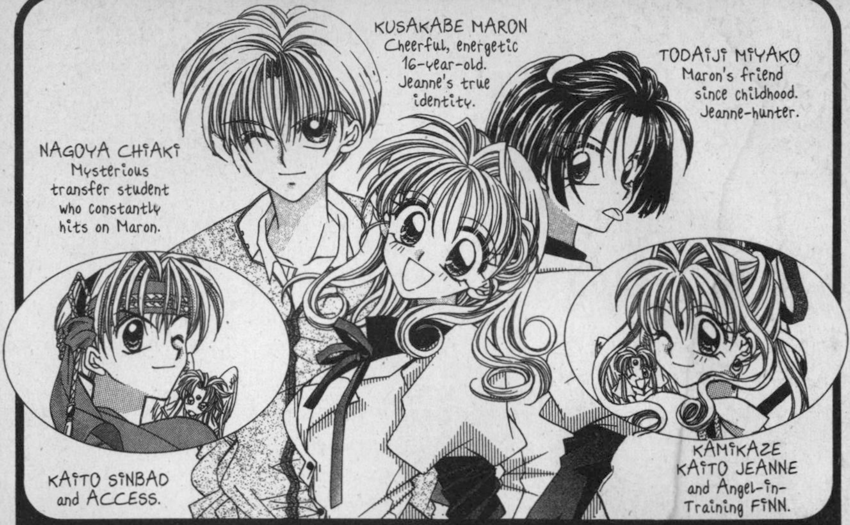
KUSAKABE MARON
Cheerful, energetic 16-year-old. Jeanne's true identity.
TODAIJI MIYAKO
Maron's friend since childhood. Jeanne-hunter.
NAGOYA CHIAKI
Mysterious transfer student who constantly hits on Maron.
KAITO SINBAD and ACCESS.
KAMIKAZE KAITO JEANNE and Angel-in-Training FINN.

Main Character Introduction

Kamikaze Kaito Jeanne

Recap of Volume One

Kusakabe Maron is an average 16-year-old girl--consumed with boys, school, and her rhythmic gymnastics club. But late at night, while the rest of her classmates are tucked away in bed, Maron's alter-ego emerges and she becomes Kamikaze Kaito Jeanne, the reincarnation of Jeanne D'Arc! Using her heavenly inherited powers, Jeanne exorcises evil demons hiding dormant inside priceless paintings. With the help of angel-in-training Finn, the duo have been very successful in their missions, despite the unwanted meddling of police detective's daughter, Miyako. But, as with most teenage girls, Maron's life is turned completely upside-down by a boy--new transfer student and seasoned Casanova, Chiaki. Just like Maron, Chiaki has a secret dual identity--Kaito Sinbad! In spite of their rivaled beginnings it seems as though Chiaki has taken to Maron. But when Sinbad rescues Jeanne after she hurts her ankle, he proposes an exchange for his services--Jeanne's retirement from phantom thieving. Will Kamikaze Kaito Jeanne give in to this ultimatum and let the demons prevail?

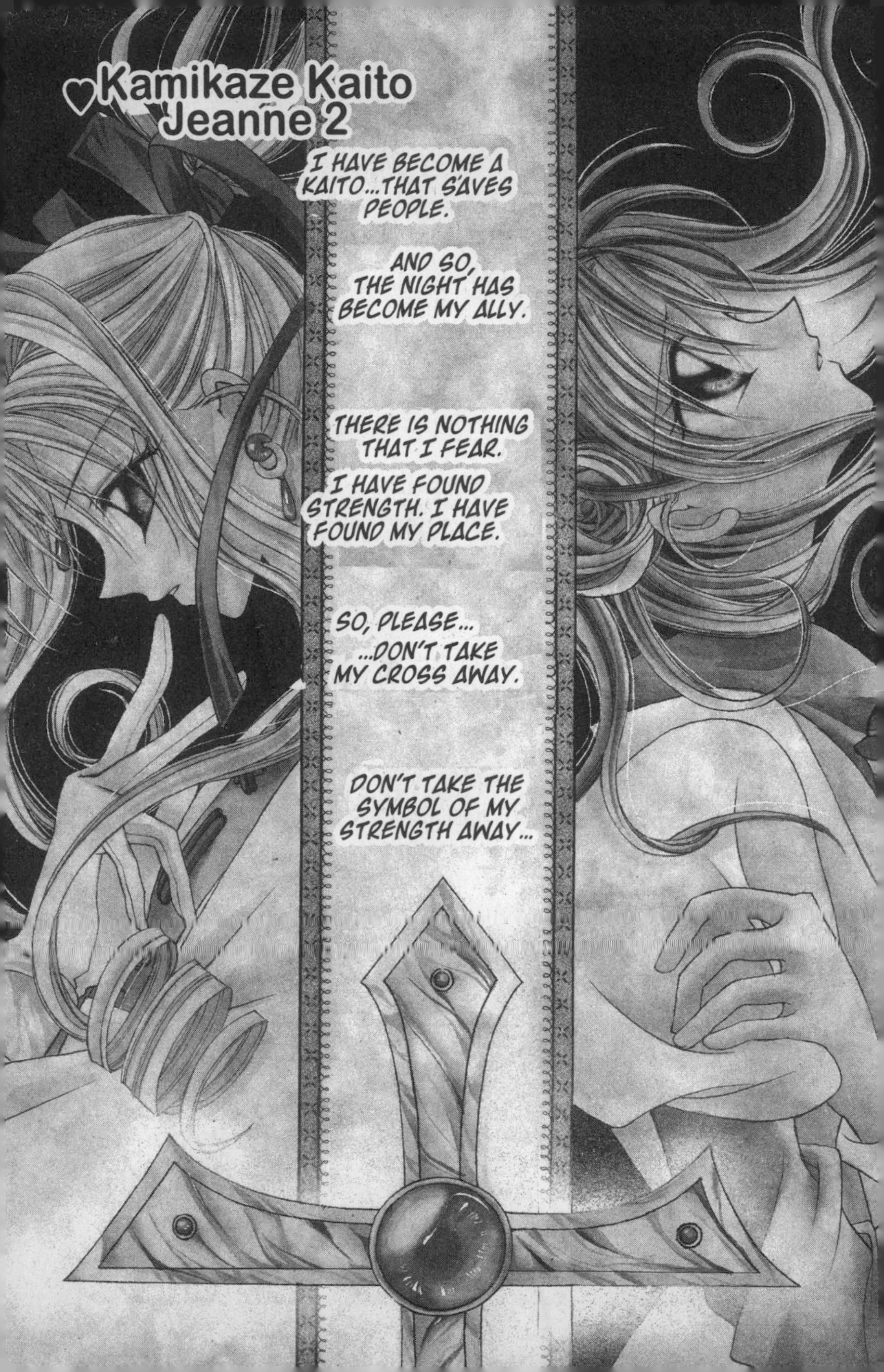
Kamikaze Kaito Jeanne 2
I HAVE BECOME A KAITO...THAT SAVES PEOPLE.
AND SO, THE NIGHT HAS BECOME MY ALLY.
THERE IS NOTHING THAT I FEAR.
I HAVE FOUND STRENGTH. I HAVE FOUND MY PLACE.
SO, PLEASE...
...DON'T TAKE MY CROSS AWAY.
DON'T TAKE THE SYMBOL OF MY STRENGTH AWAY...

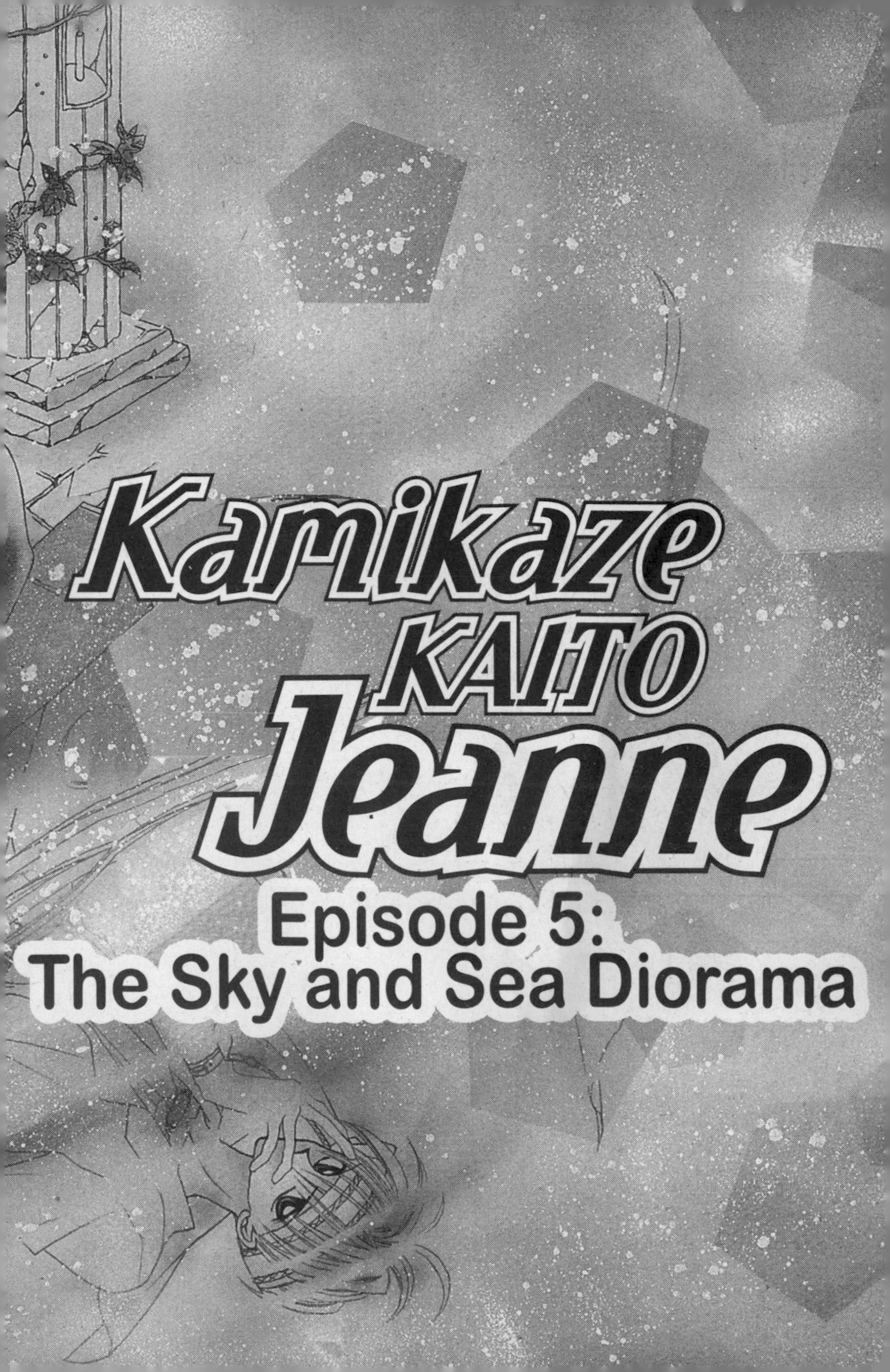
Kamikaze
KAITO
Jeanne
Episode 5:
The Sky and Sea Diorama

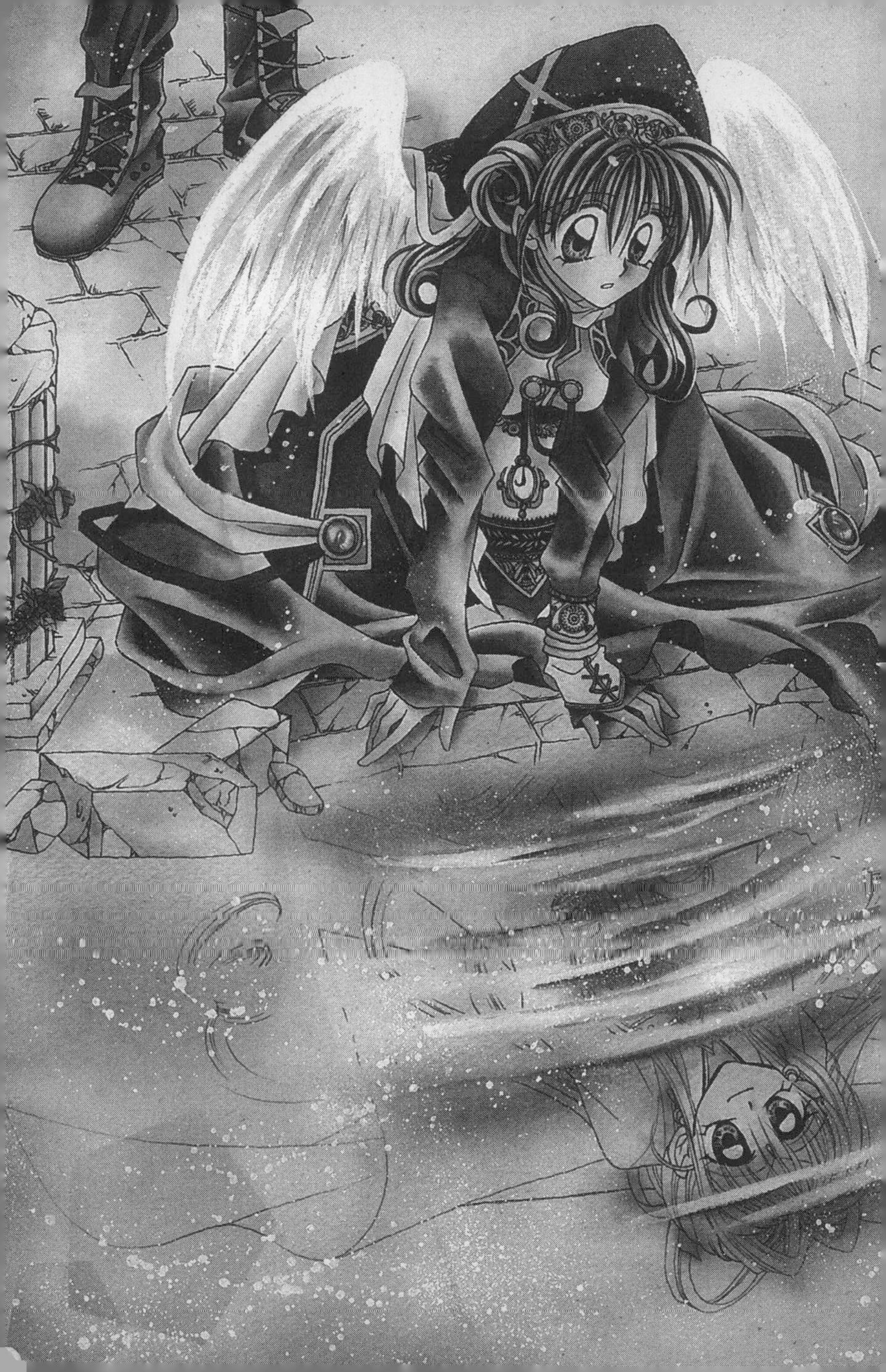

An Angel-In-Training's Duties

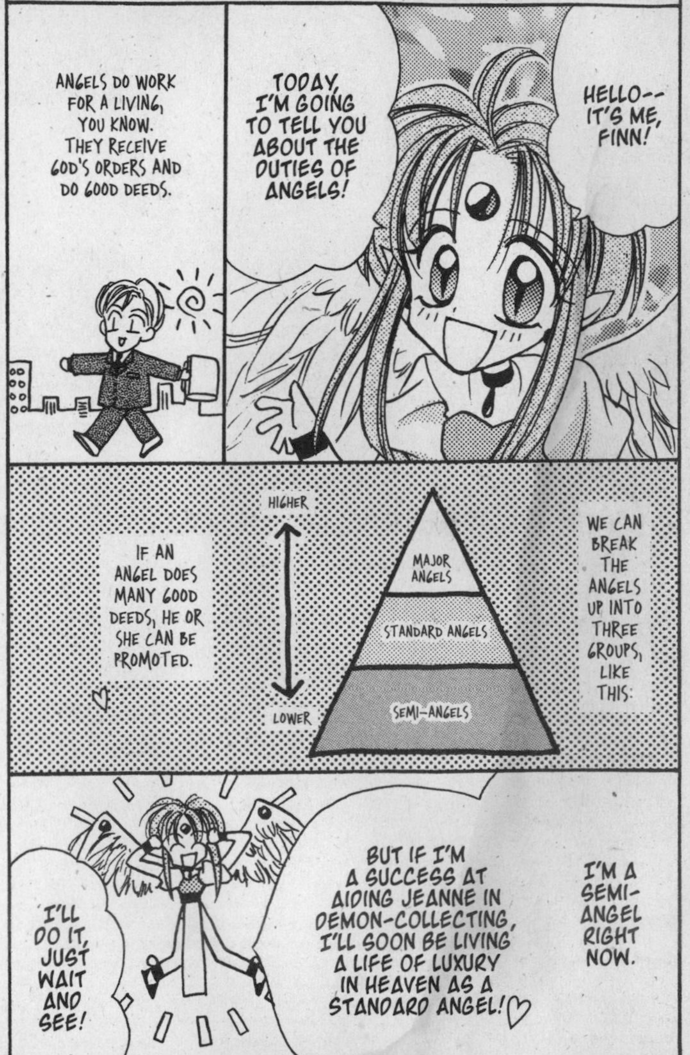
HELLO-- IT'S ME, FINN!
TODAY, I'M GOING TO TELL YOU ABOUT THE DUTIES OF ANGELS!
ANGELS DO WORK FOR A LIVING, YOU KNOW. THEY RECEIVE GOD'S ORDERS AND DO GOOD DEEDS.
WE CAN BREAK THE ANGELS UP INTO THREE GROUPS, LIKE THIS:
MAJOR ANGELS
STANDARD ANGELS
SEMI-ANGELS
HIGHER
LOWER
IF AN ANGEL DOES MANY GOOD DEEDS, HE OR SHE CAN BE PROMOTED.
I'M A SEMI-ANGEL RIGHT NOW.
BUT IF I'M A SUCCESS AT AIDING JEANNE IN DEMON-COLLECTING, I'LL SOON BE LIVING A LIFE OF LUXURY IN HEAVEN AS A STANDARD ANGEL! ♡
I'LL DO IT, JUST WAIT AND SEE!

I WANT YOU TO QUIT BEING A KAITO...

...YOU SAID YOU'D DO ANYTHING, REMEMBER?

GASP

Episode 5: GATEFOLD AND STORY COMMENTS "The Sky and Sea Diorama"

TAGLINE: "FROM THE BOTTOM OF MY HEART, I WANT TO BE STRONG..." <<<Cool!

Yep, this is the first time any of my magazine stories have had their opening pages in color. I was so, so happy. HOHOHO! However, this story has a lot of bad memories attached to it, so whenever I think about it......oooogghh! I'm still a newcomer at this game, and I want to make the story much more interesting, but my ability can't keep up with my desire. I'd been beating myself up over this for a long time, but finally, I thought I'd "arrived" somewhat at producing good manga...until my editor told me to come up with better dialogue! "Just when I thought I knew what I was doing, I discover my great flaw! I complained, falling into a funk so deep I seriously considered giving up on Jeanne. "This isn't the story I want to do!" I groused to my friends in the middle of the night. Around the same time, I was stabbed in the back by a dear friend and got a bunch of slanderous hate mail that was mixed in with the usual fan letters. Honestly, it was a terrible, terrible time for me. Ahhh, sorry to bother you with my personal problems! (About my friend's betrayal, I passed on my feelings to Maron-chan and learned my lesson, I guess...That's the sad life of a comic artist for you...) Sigh..

Anyway, on to the story. The title page is taken directly from the contents of the story. Maron-chan is peering into a lake, but the surface of the water is reflecting Jeanne back at her, with Sinbad in back...giving the hint that the person standing behind Maron may be Sinbad's real identity. This title page proved popular. Yep, I like having Maron-chan wear outfits like this, you know, old Western-style clothing. I also like the story. Despite all the hardships I went through creating it, I've got a deep love for it. I want to use Yashiro-chan again. After all, it seems like she hasn't given up on Chiaki...Actually, there is a guy who pines after her, who has already appeared in the story, but that'll remain a secret for now. Changing the subject, I was overjoyed at being able to draw the rhythmic gymnastics scene--I've loved rhythmic gymnastics for a long, long time and even now, watch it during the Olympics or on cable TV and so on♡ (I've never actually tried it myself, however.) I've been drawing like a maniac ever since I was little and give credit for my skill at drawing the human body (as well as the "movements" in my drawings) to watching gymnastics. Really, though, it was my editor who asked me, "Why don't you have Maron-chan do something like rhythmic gymnastics?" It's still a mystery to me how he hit my forte right on the head...Oh yeah! I got a letter from a reader requesting me to share my favorite Maron "moment." Okay, I'll share. (At least, the page that I like!) Turn to page 38--It's where she's apologizing. Maron-chan is too cute for words!! I love you.♡♡♡

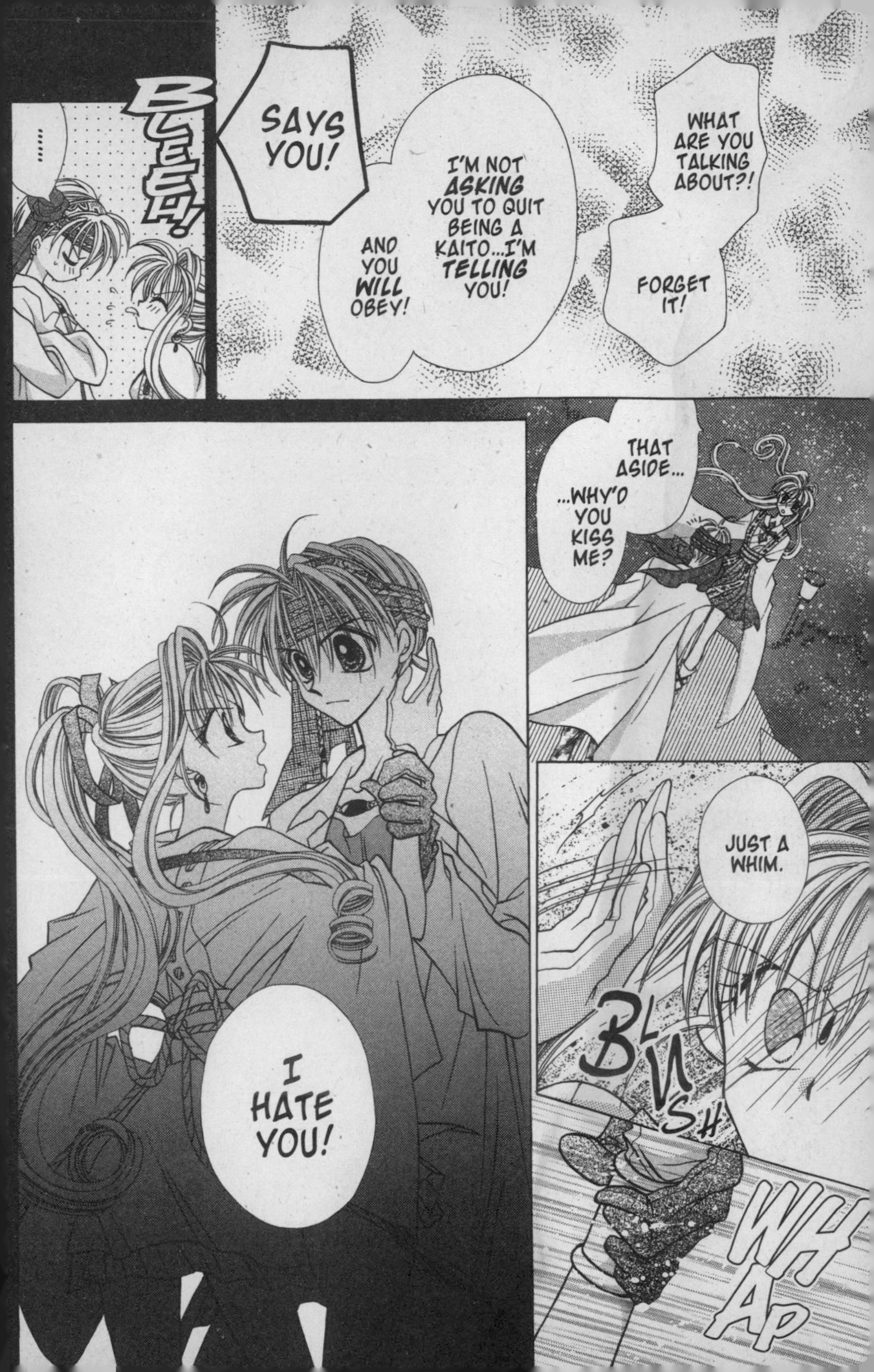
WHAT ARE YOU TALKING ABOUT?!
FORGET IT!
I'M NOT ASKING YOU TO QUIT BEING A KAITO...I'M TELLING YOU!
AND YOU WILL OBEY!
SAYS YOU!
BLEEH!
......
THAT ASIDE...
...WHY'D YOU KISS ME?
JUST A WHIM.
BLUSH
WHAP
I HATE YOU!

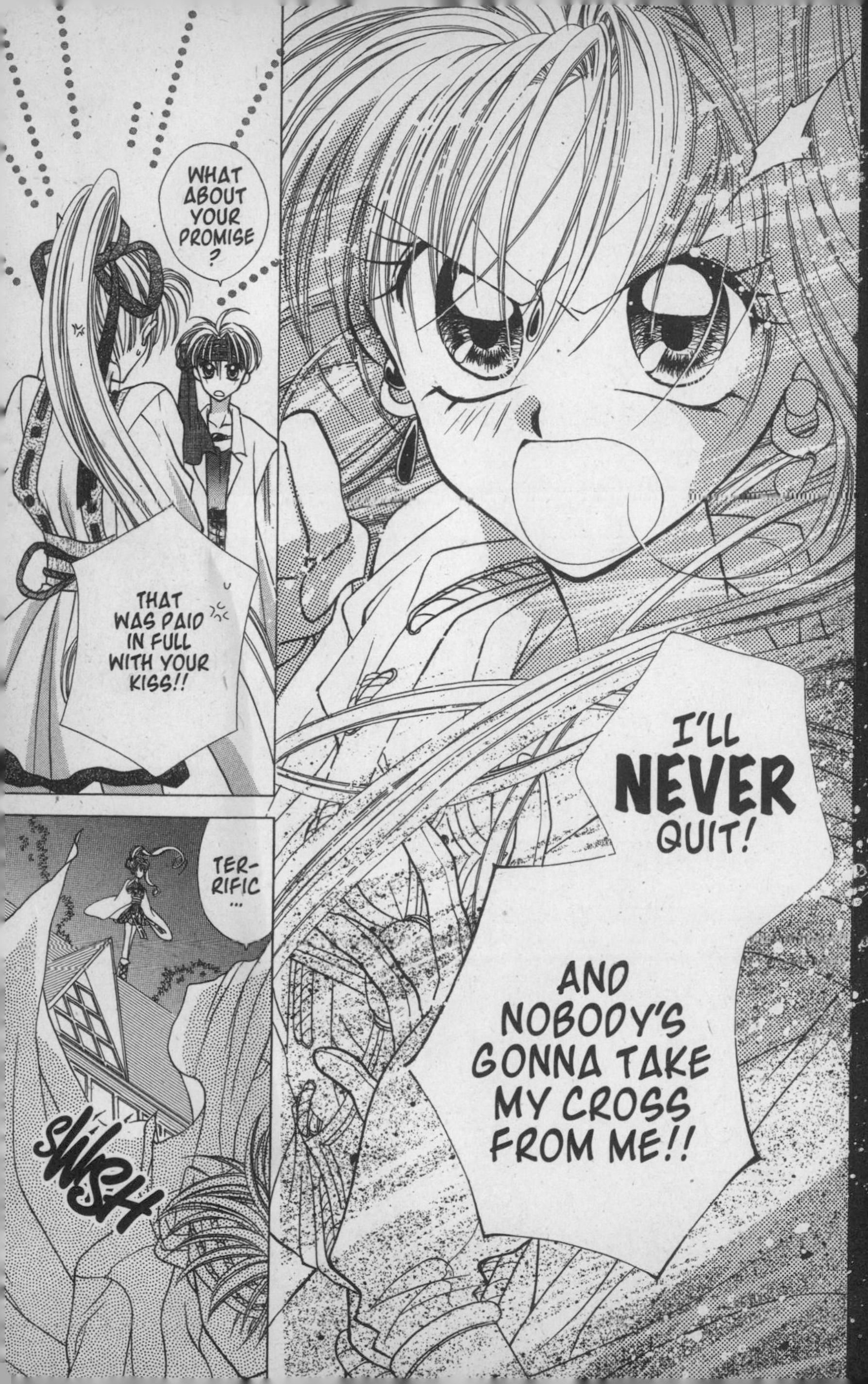
I'LL NEVER QUIT!
AND NOBODY'S GONNA TAKE MY CROSS FROM ME!!
WHAT ABOUT YOUR PROMISE?
THAT WAS PAID IN FULL WITH YOUR KISS!!
TER-RIFIC...
SWISH

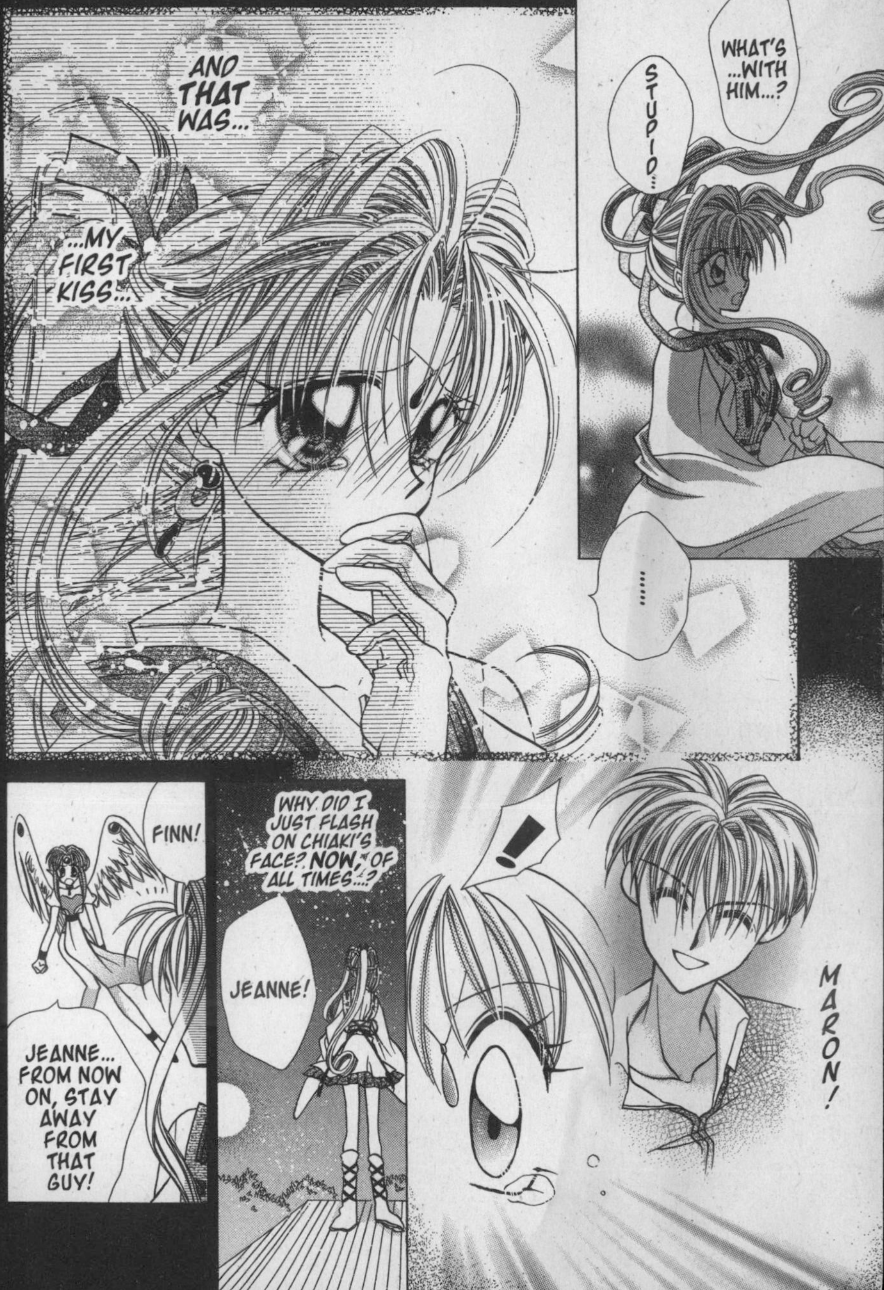
WHAT'S ...WITH HIM...?
STUPID...
......
AND THAT WAS...
...MY FIRST KISS...
MARON!
!
WHY DID I JUST FLASH ON CHIAKI'S FACE? NOW, OF ALL TIMES...?
JEANNE!
FINN!
JEANNE... FROM NOW ON, STAY AWAY FROM THAT GUY!

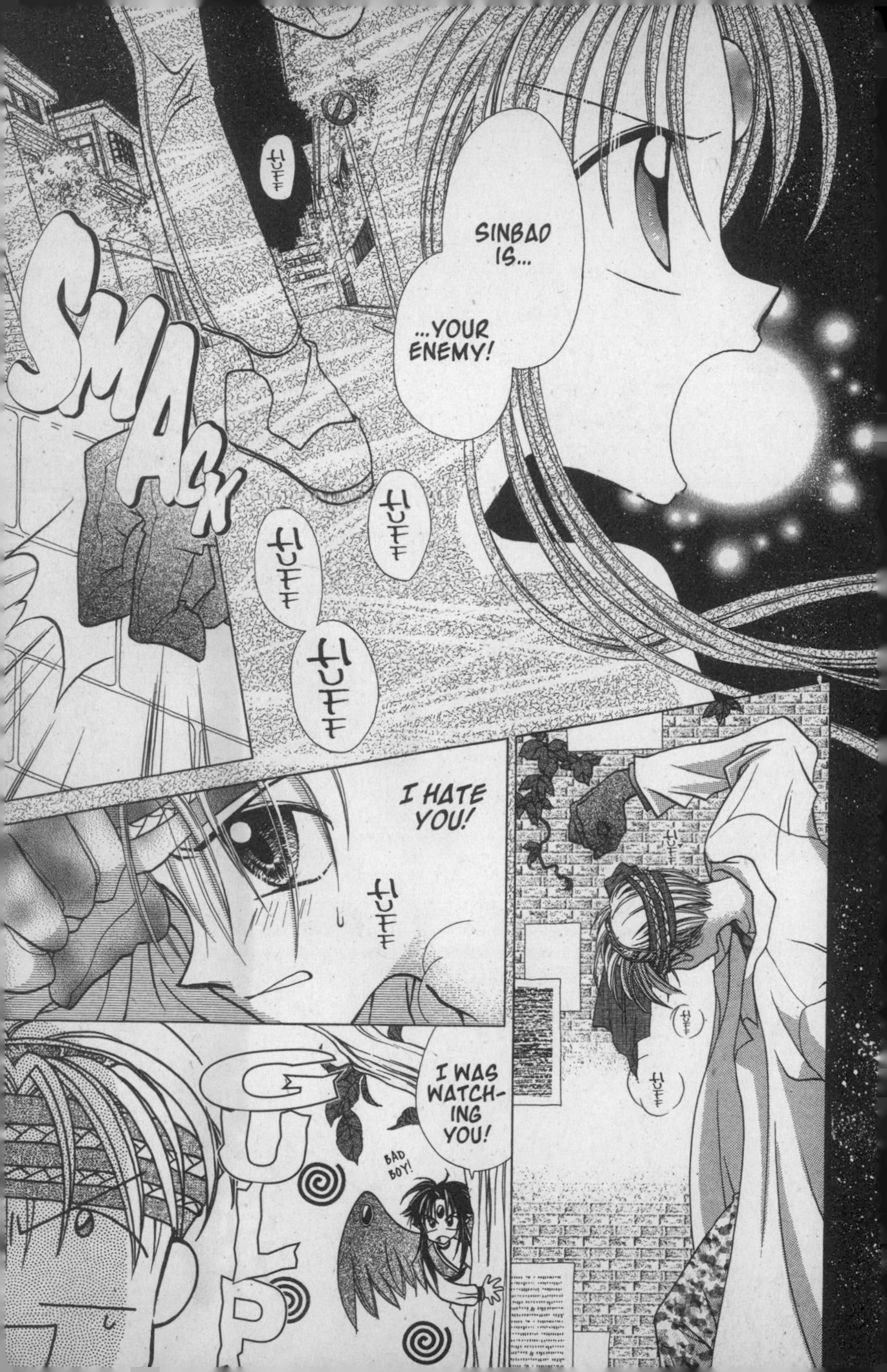
SINBAD IS...
...YOUR ENEMY!
HUFF
SMACK
HUFF
HUFF
HUFF
HUFF
HUFF
HUFF
I HATE YOU!
HUFF
I WAS WATCHING YOU!
BAD BOY!
GULP

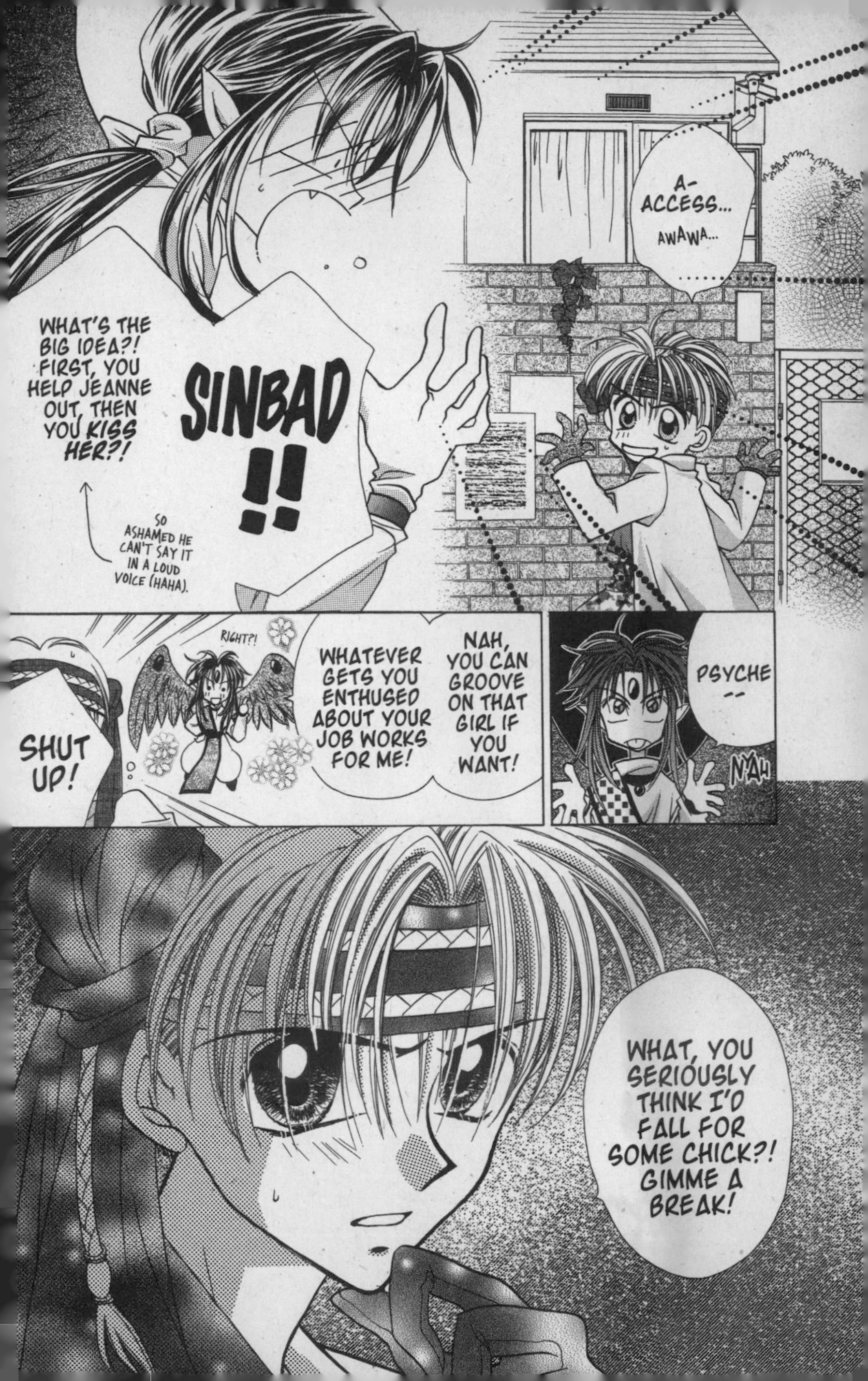
A-ACCESS...
AWAWA...
WHAT'S THE BIG IDEA?! FIRST, YOU HELP JEANNE OUT, THEN YOU KISS HER?!
SINBAD !!
SO ASHAMED HE CAN'T SAY IT IN A LOUD VOICE (HAHA).
PSYCHE --
NYAH
NAH, YOU CAN GROOVE ON THAT GIRL IF YOU WANT!
WHATEVER GETS YOU ENTHUSED ABOUT YOUR JOB WORKS FOR ME!
RIGHT?!
SHUT UP!
WHAT, YOU SERIOUSLY THINK I'D FALL FOR SOME CHICK?! GIMME A BREAK!

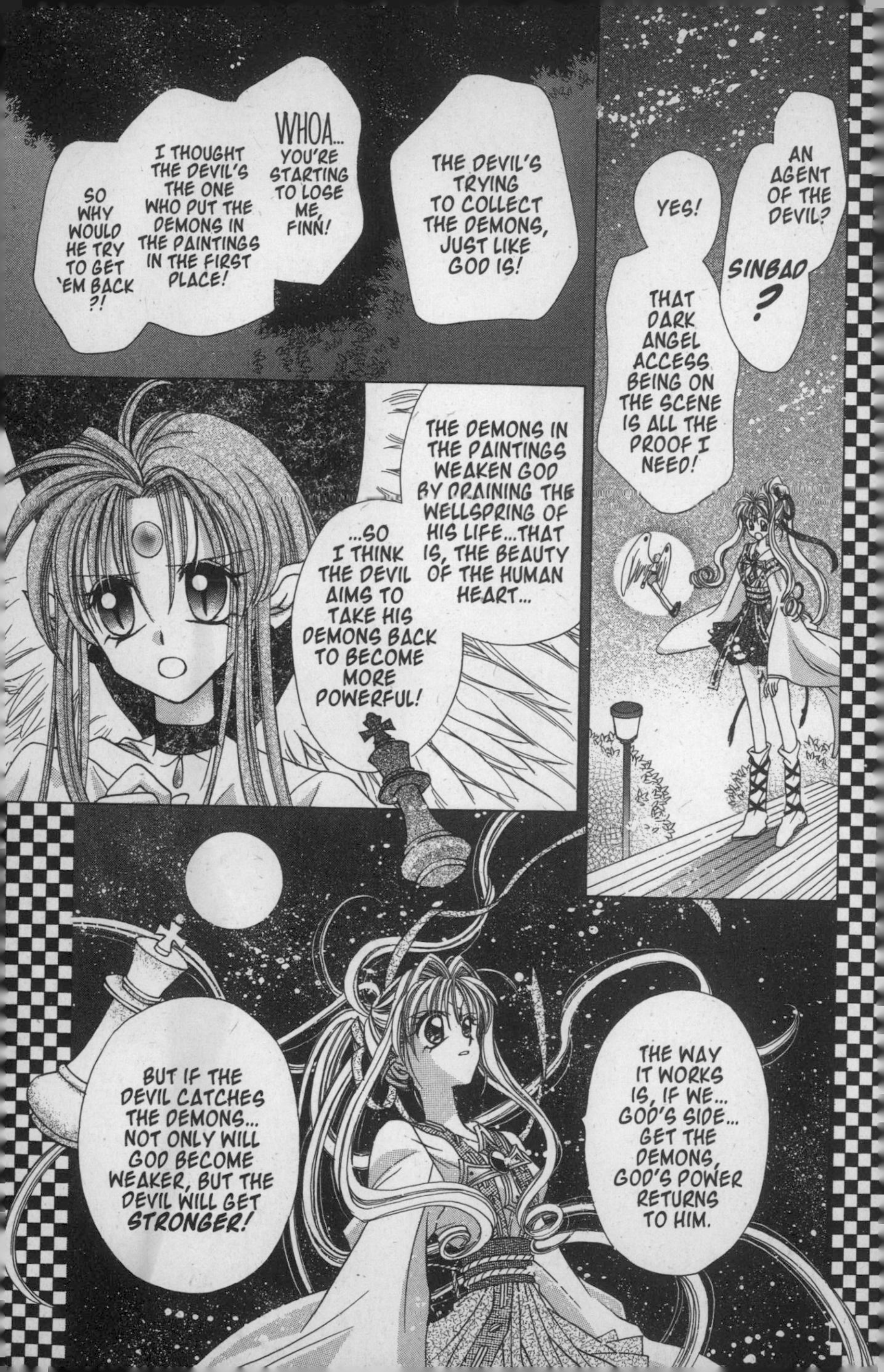
AN AGENT OF THE DEVIL?
SINBAD?
YES!
THAT DARK ANGEL ACCESS BEING ON THE SCENE IS ALL THE PROOF I NEED!
THE DEVIL'S TRYING TO COLLECT THE DEMONS, JUST LIKE GOD IS!
WHOA... YOU'RE STARTING TO LOSE ME, FINN!
I THOUGHT THE DEVIL'S THE ONE WHO PUT THE DEMONS IN THE PAINTINGS IN THE FIRST PLACE!
SO WHY WOULD HE TRY TO GET 'EM BACK?!
THE DEMONS IN THE PAINTINGS WEAKEN GOD BY DRAINING THE WELLSPRING OF HIS LIFE...THAT IS, THE BEAUTY OF THE HUMAN HEART...
...SO I THINK THE DEVIL AIMS TO TAKE HIS DEMONS BACK TO BECOME MORE POWERFUL!
THE WAY IT WORKS IS, IF WE... GOD'S SIDE... GET THE DEMONS, GOD'S POWER RETURNS TO HIM.
BUT IF THE DEVIL CATCHES THE DEMONS... NOT ONLY WILL GOD BECOME WEAKER, BUT THE DEVIL WILL GET STRONGER!

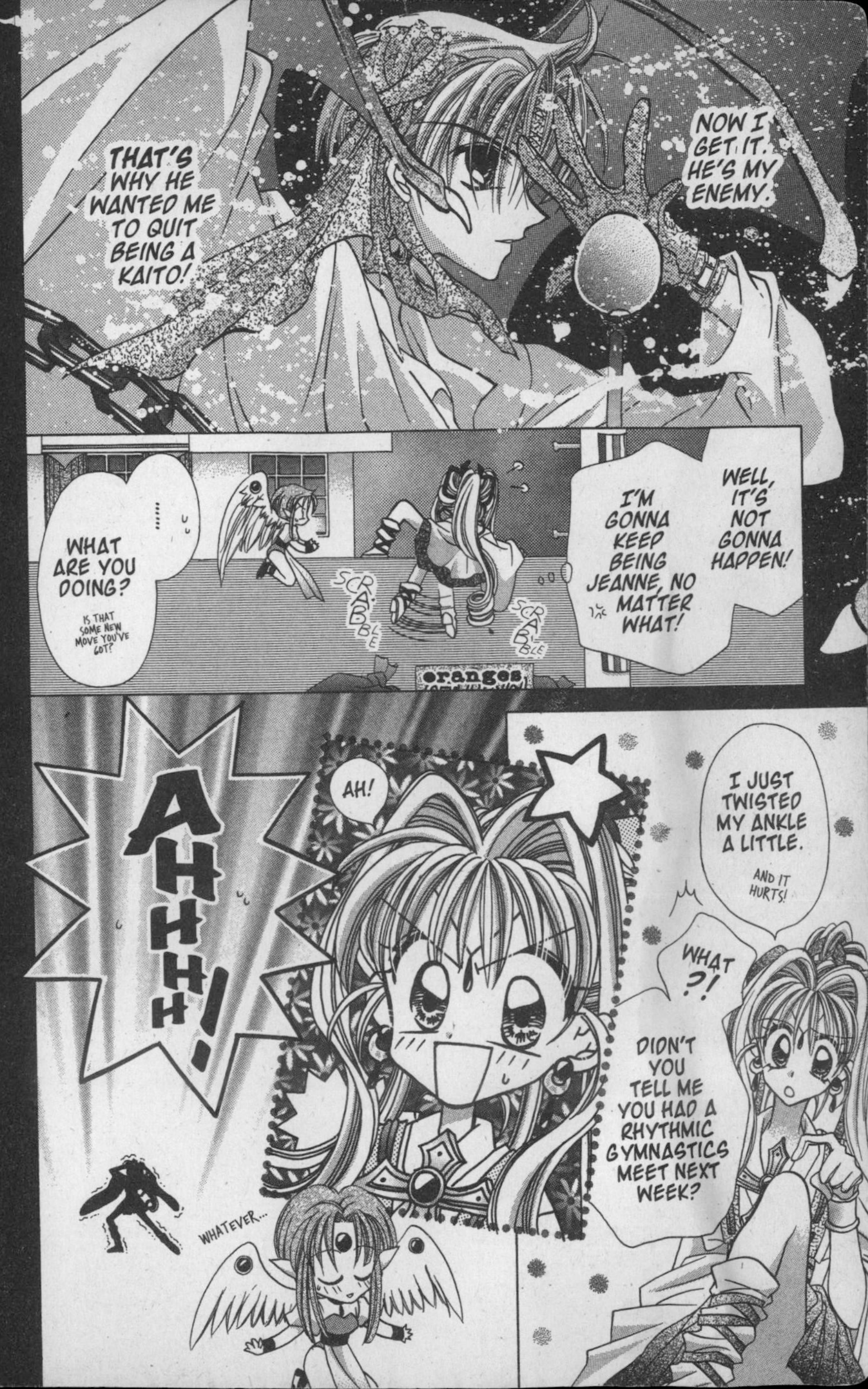
NOW I GET IT. HE'S MY ENEMY.
THAT'S WHY HE WANTED ME TO QUIT BEING A KAITO!
WELL, IT'S NOT GONNA HAPPEN!
I'M GONNA KEEP BEING JEANNE, NO MATTER WHAT!
SCRABBLE
SCRABBLE
......
WHAT ARE YOU DOING?
IS THAT SOME NEW MOVE YOU'VE GOT?
oranges
I JUST TWISTED MY ANKLE A LITTLE.
AND IT HURTS!
WHAT?!
DIDN'T YOU TELL ME YOU HAD A RHYTHMIC GYMNASTICS MEET NEXT WEEK?
AH!
AHHHHH!
WHATEVER...

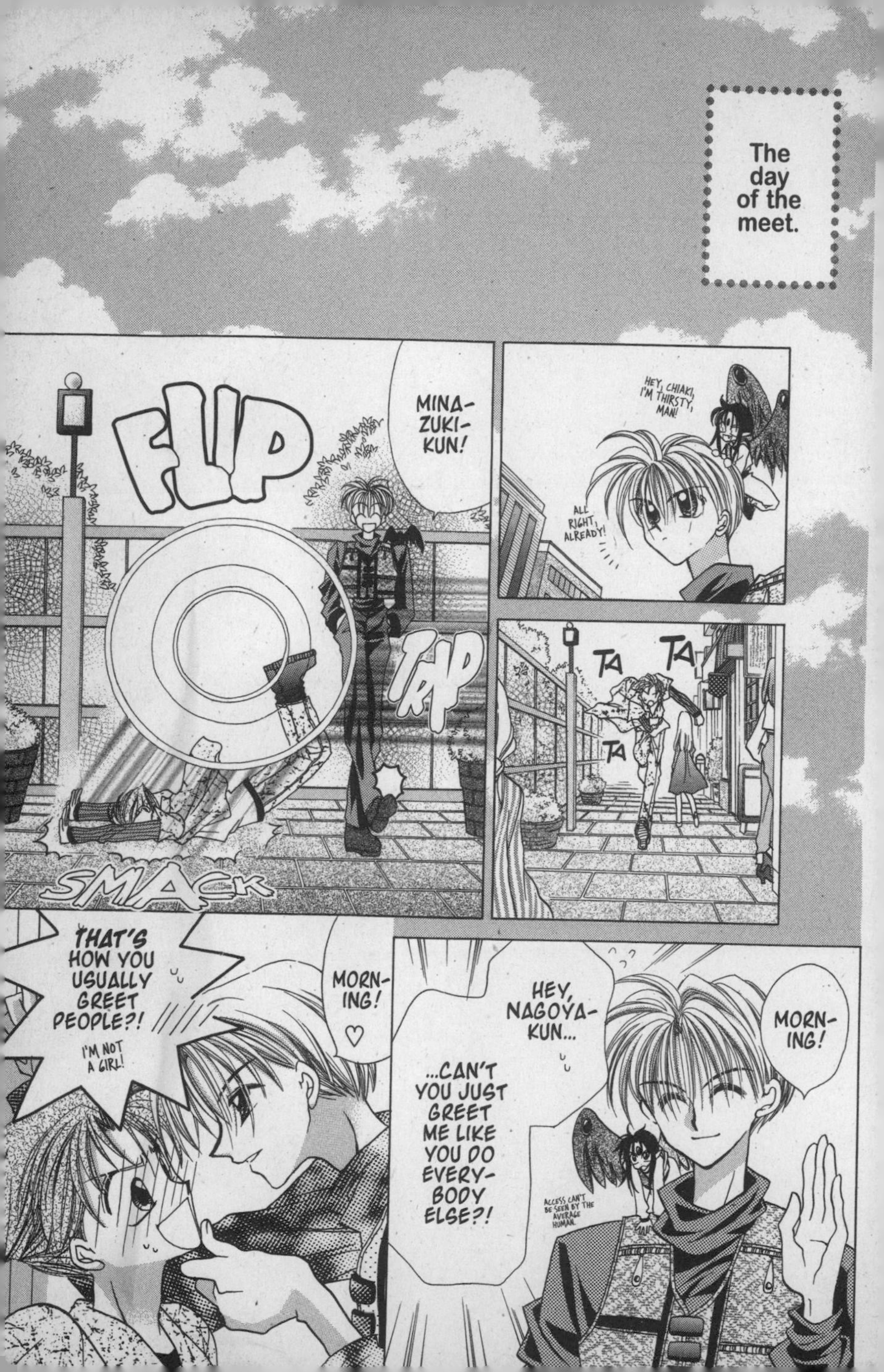
The day of the meet.
HEY, CHIAKI, I'M THIRSTY, MAN!
ALL RIGHT, ALREADY!
TA
TA
TA
MINA-ZUKI-KUN!
FLIP
TRIP
SMACK
MORN-ING!
HEY, NAGOYA-KUN...
...CAN'T YOU JUST GREET ME LIKE YOU DO EVERY-BODY ELSE?!
ACCESS CAN'T BE SEEN BY THE AVERAGE HUMAN.
MORN-ING! ♡
THAT'S HOW YOU USUALLY GREET PEOPLE?!
I'M NOT A GIRL!

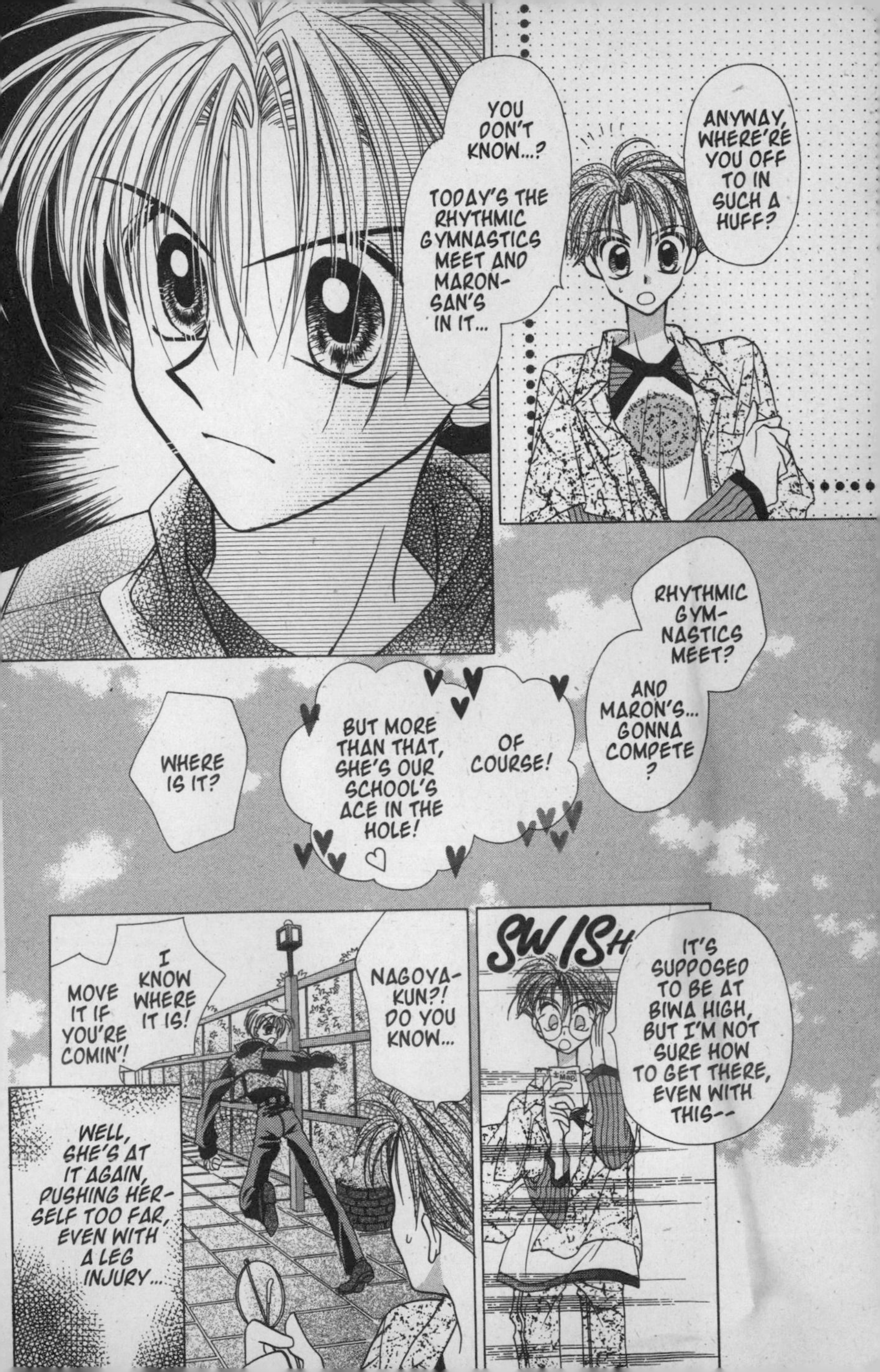
ANYWAY, WHERE'RE YOU OFF TO IN SUCH A HUFF?
YOU DON'T KNOW...?
TODAY'S THE RHYTHMIC GYMNASTICS MEET AND MARON-SAN'S IN IT...
RHYTHMIC GYM-NASTICS MEET?
AND MARON'S... GONNA COMPETE?
OF COURSE!
BUT MORE THAN THAT, SHE'S OUR SCHOOL'S ACE IN THE HOLE!
WHERE IS IT?
SWISH
IT'S SUPPOSED TO BE AT BIWA HIGH, BUT I'M NOT SURE HOW TO GET THERE, EVEN WITH THIS--
NAGOYA-KUN?! DO YOU KNOW...
I KNOW WHERE IT IS!
MOVE IT IF YOU'RE COMIN'!
WELL, SHE'S AT IT AGAIN, PUSHING HER-SELF TOO FAR, EVEN WITH A LEG INJURY...

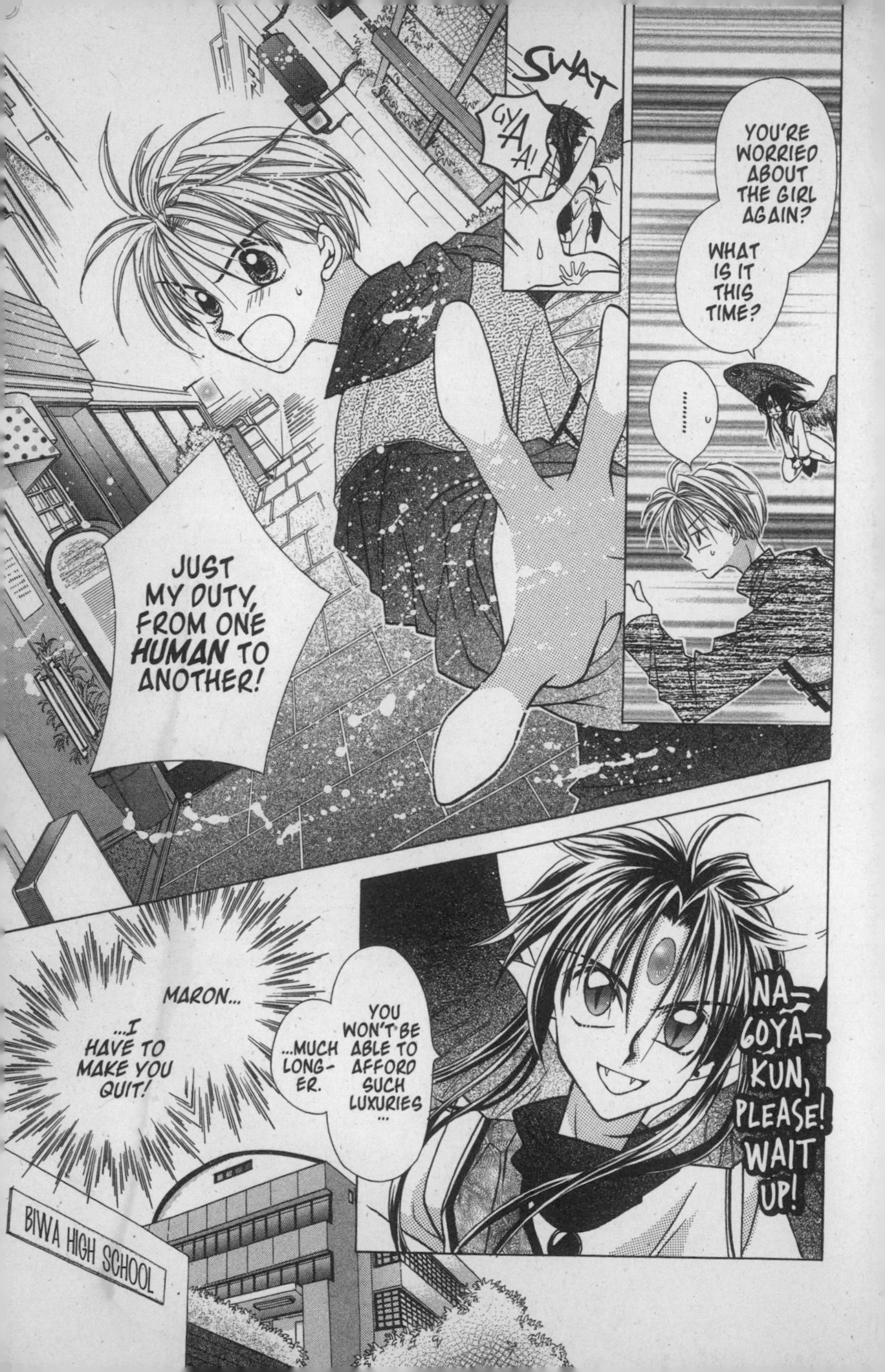
YOU'RE WORRIED ABOUT THE GIRL AGAIN?
WHAT IS IT THIS TIME?
......
SWAT
GYAAA!
JUST MY DUTY, FROM ONE HUMAN TO ANOTHER!
NA-GOYA-KUN, PLEASE! WAIT UP!
YOU WON'T BE ABLE TO AFFORD SUCH LUXURIES...
...MUCH LONG-ER.
MARON...
...I HAVE TO MAKE YOU QUIT!
BIWA HIGH SCHOOL

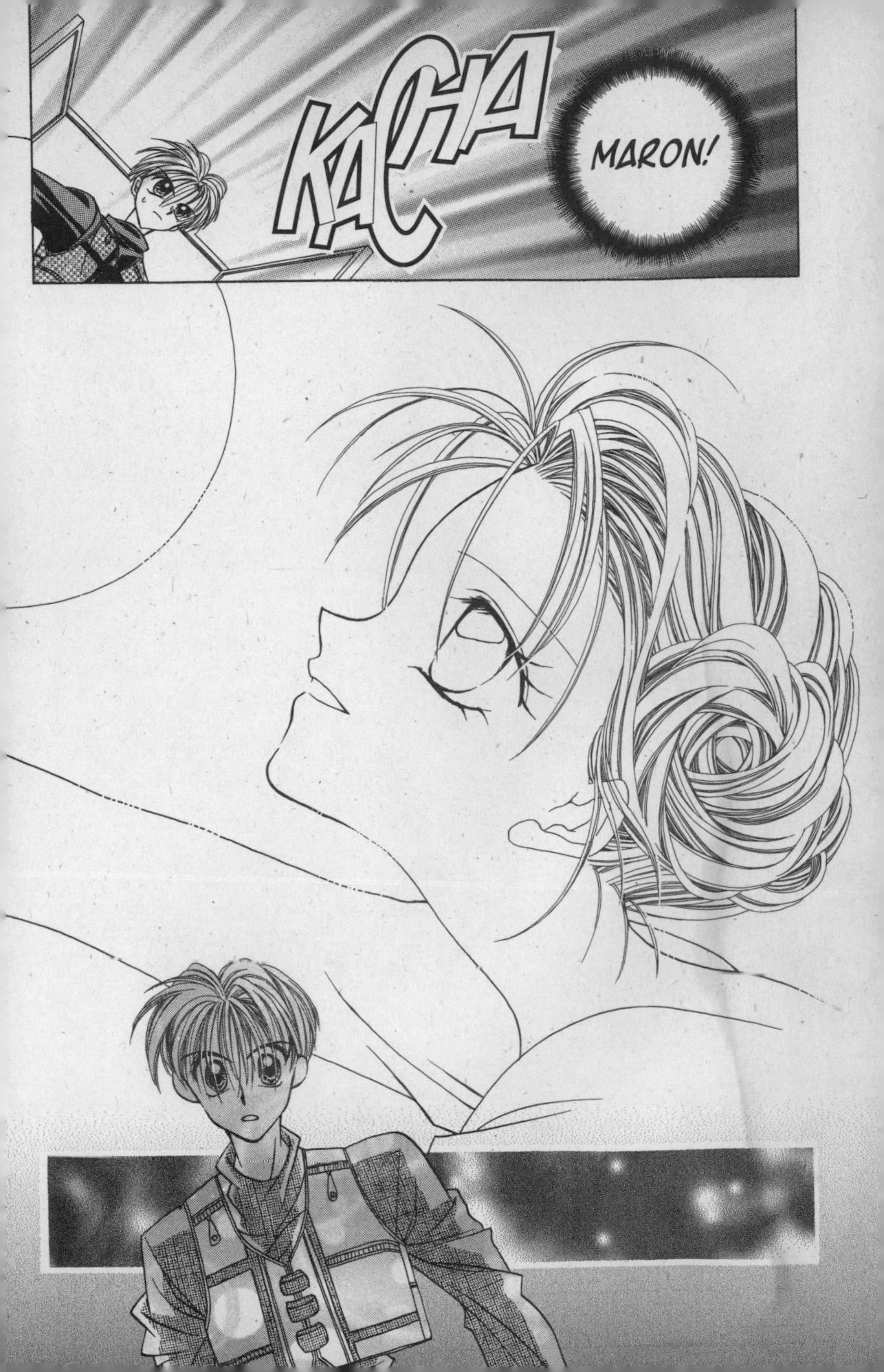
MARON!
KACHA

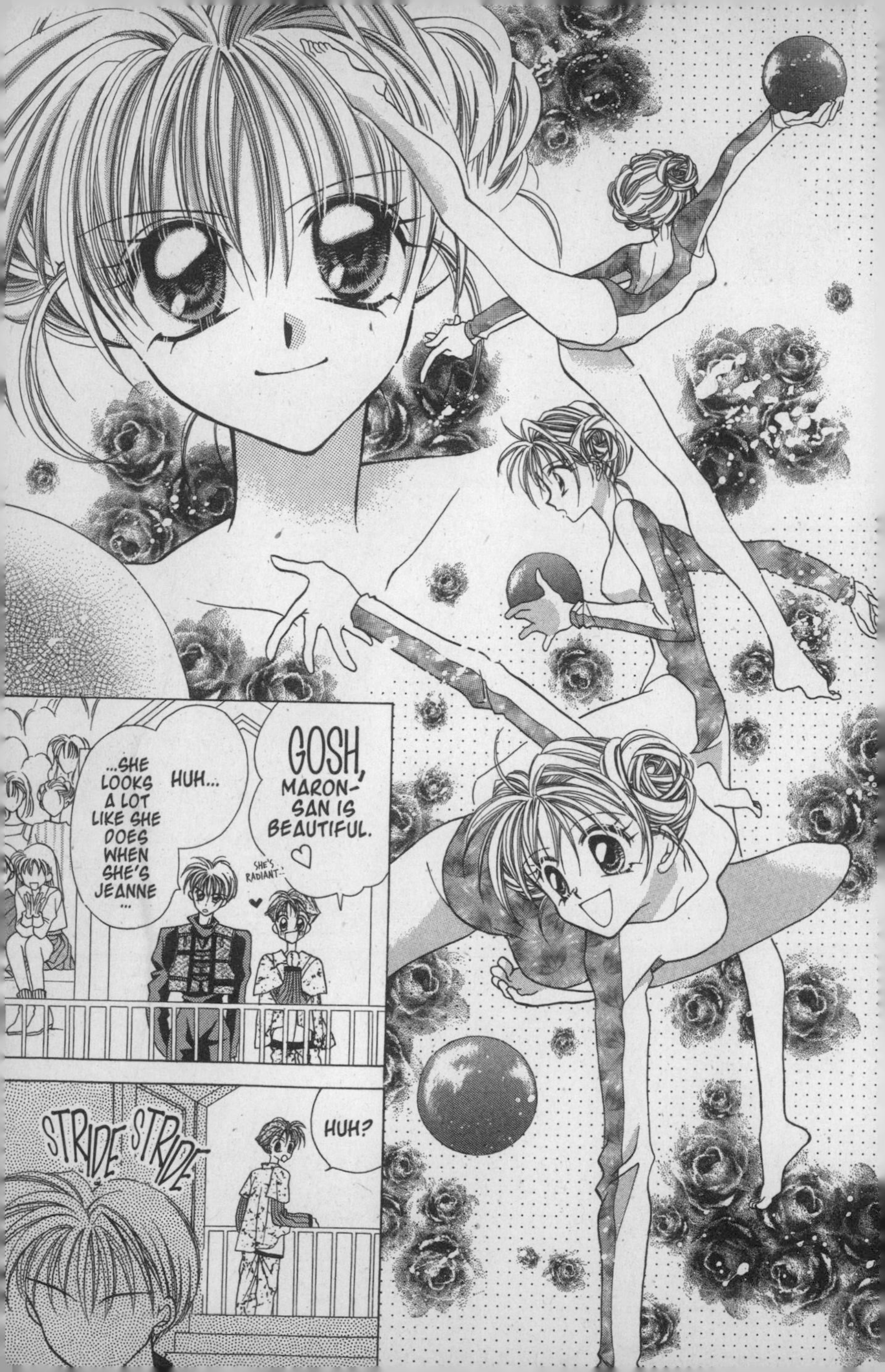
GOSH, MARON-SAN IS BEAUTIFUL. ♥
SHE'S RADIANT...
HUH...
...SHE LOOKS A LOT LIKE SHE DOES WHEN SHE'S JEANNE ...
HUH?
STRIDE STRIDE

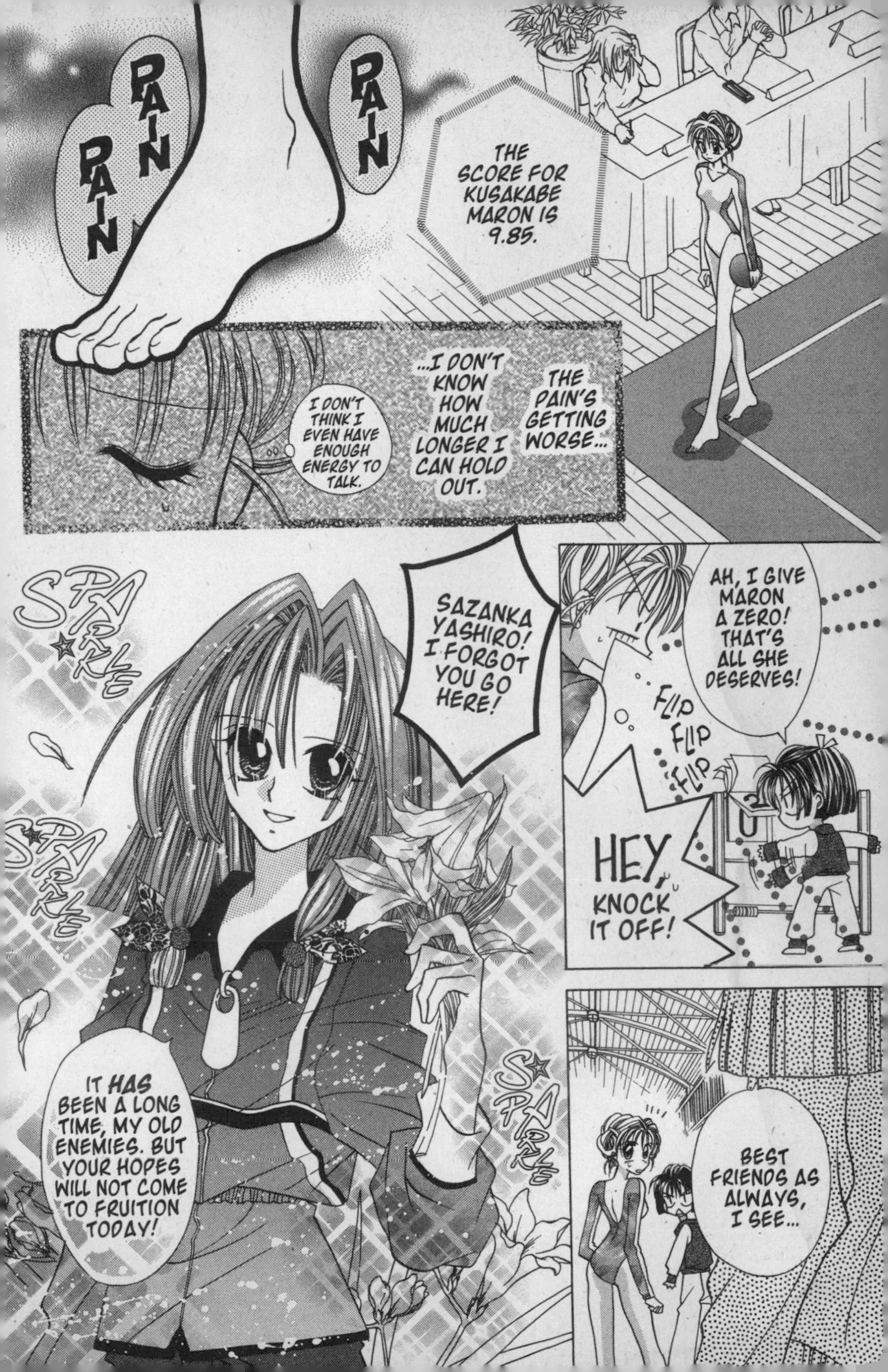
THE SCORE FOR KUSAKABE MARON IS 9.85.
PAIN
PAIN
PAIN
THE PAIN'S GETTING WORSE...
...I DON'T KNOW HOW MUCH LONGER I CAN HOLD OUT.
I DON'T THINK I EVEN HAVE ENOUGH ENERGY TO TALK.
AH, I GIVE MARON A ZERO! THAT'S ALL SHE DESERVES!
FLIP FLIP FLIP
HEY, KNOCK IT OFF!
BEST FRIENDS AS ALWAYS, I SEE...
SAZANKA YASHIRO! I FORGOT YOU GO HERE!
SPARKLE
SPARKLE
SPARKLE
IT HAS BEEN A LONG TIME, MY OLD ENEMIES. BUT YOUR HOPES WILL NOT COME TO FRUITION TODAY!

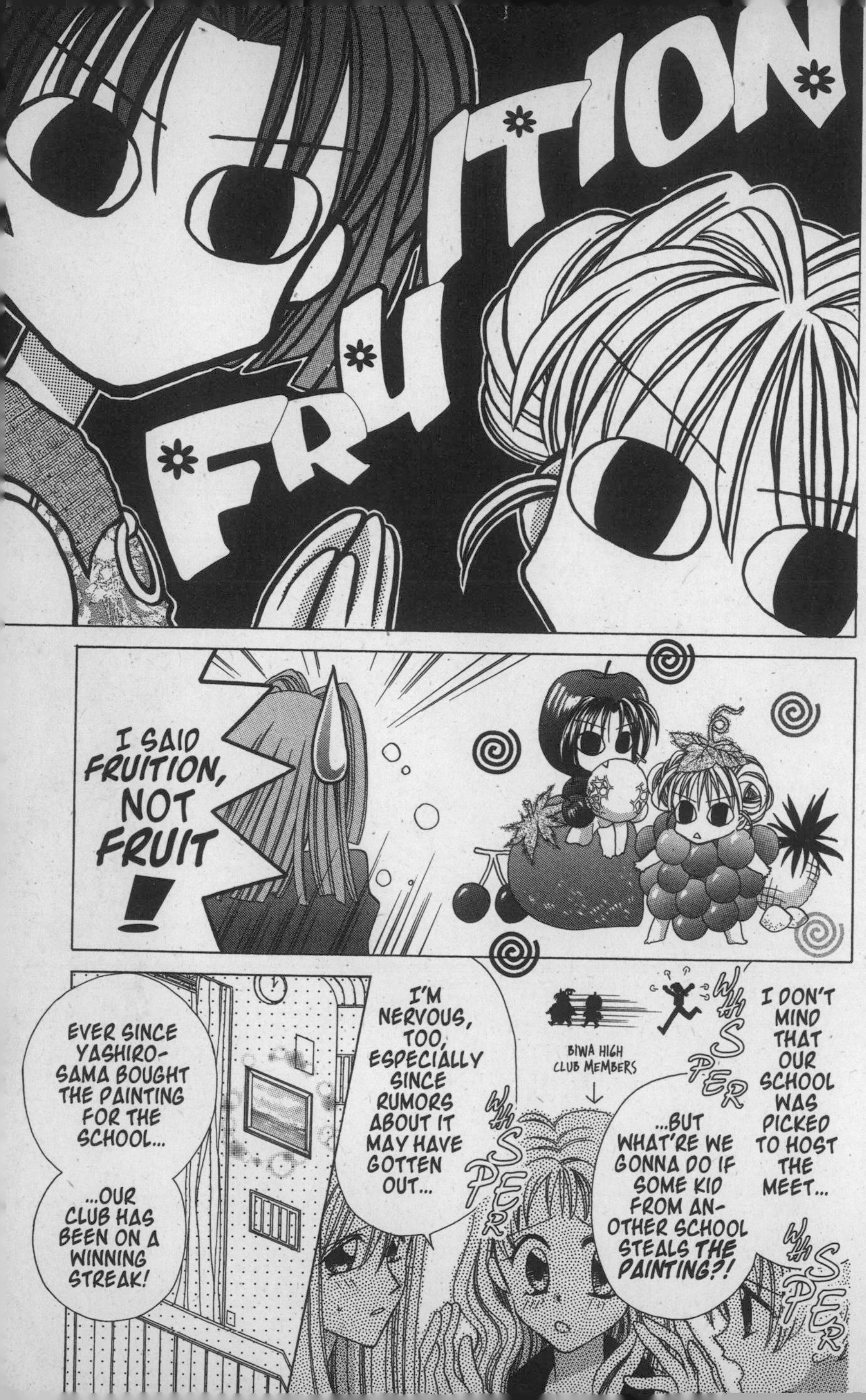
FRUITION
I SAID FRUITION, NOT FRUIT!
I DON'T MIND THAT OUR SCHOOL WAS PICKED TO HOST THE MEET...
WHISPER
WHISPER
...BUT WHAT'RE WE GONNA DO IF SOME KID FROM AN-OTHER SCHOOL STEALS THE PAINTING?!
BIWA HIGH CLUB MEMBERS
WHISPER
I'M NERVOUS, TOO, ESPECIALLY SINCE RUMORS ABOUT IT MAY HAVE GOTTEN OUT...
EVER SINCE YASHIRO-SAMA BOUGHT THE PAINTING FOR THE SCHOOL...
...OUR CLUB HAS BEEN ON A WINNING STREAK!

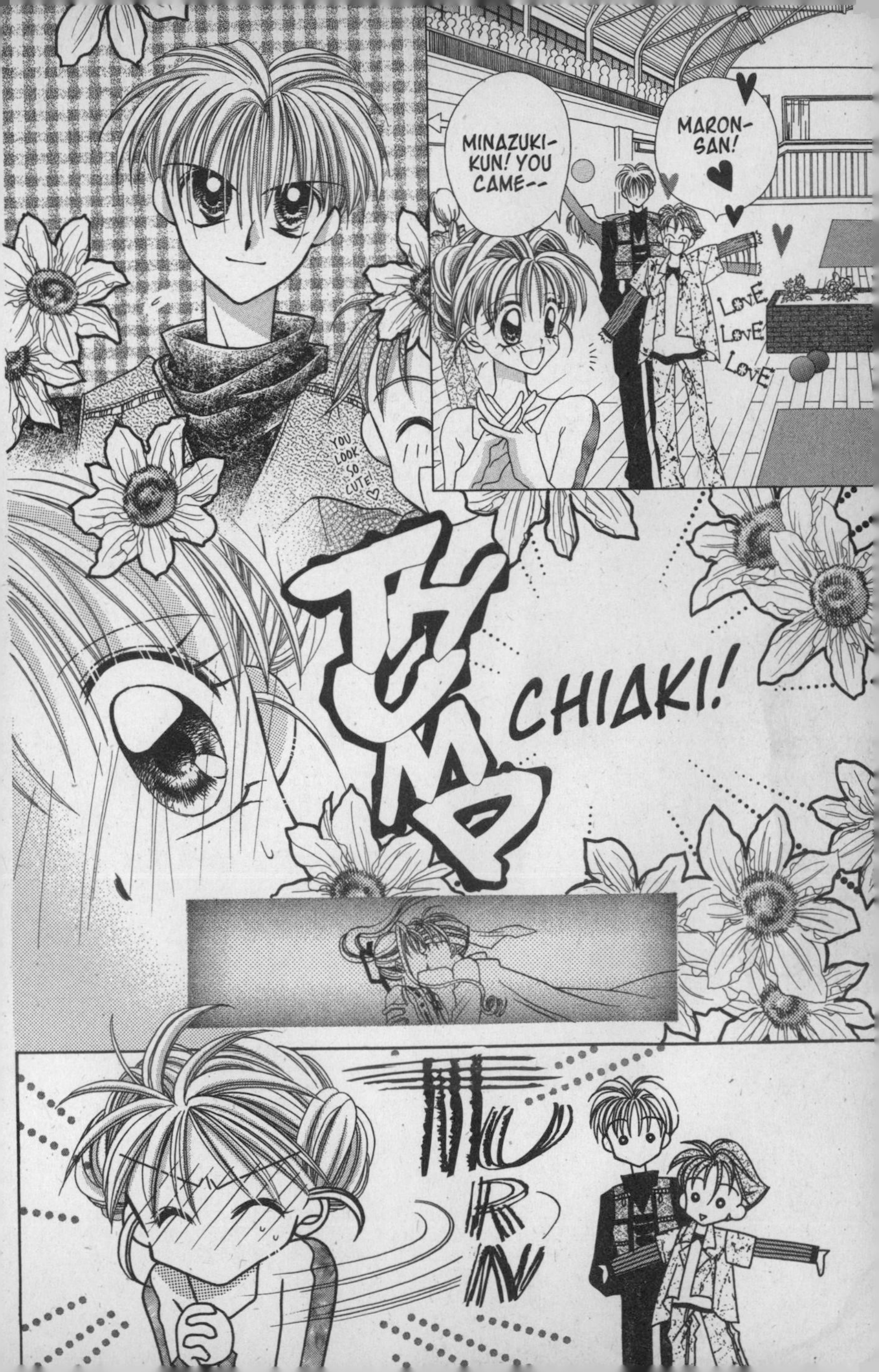
MARON-SAN!
MINAZUKI-KUN! YOU CAME--
LOVE LOVE LOVE LOVE
YOU LOOK SO CUTE!
CHIAKI!
THUMP
TURN

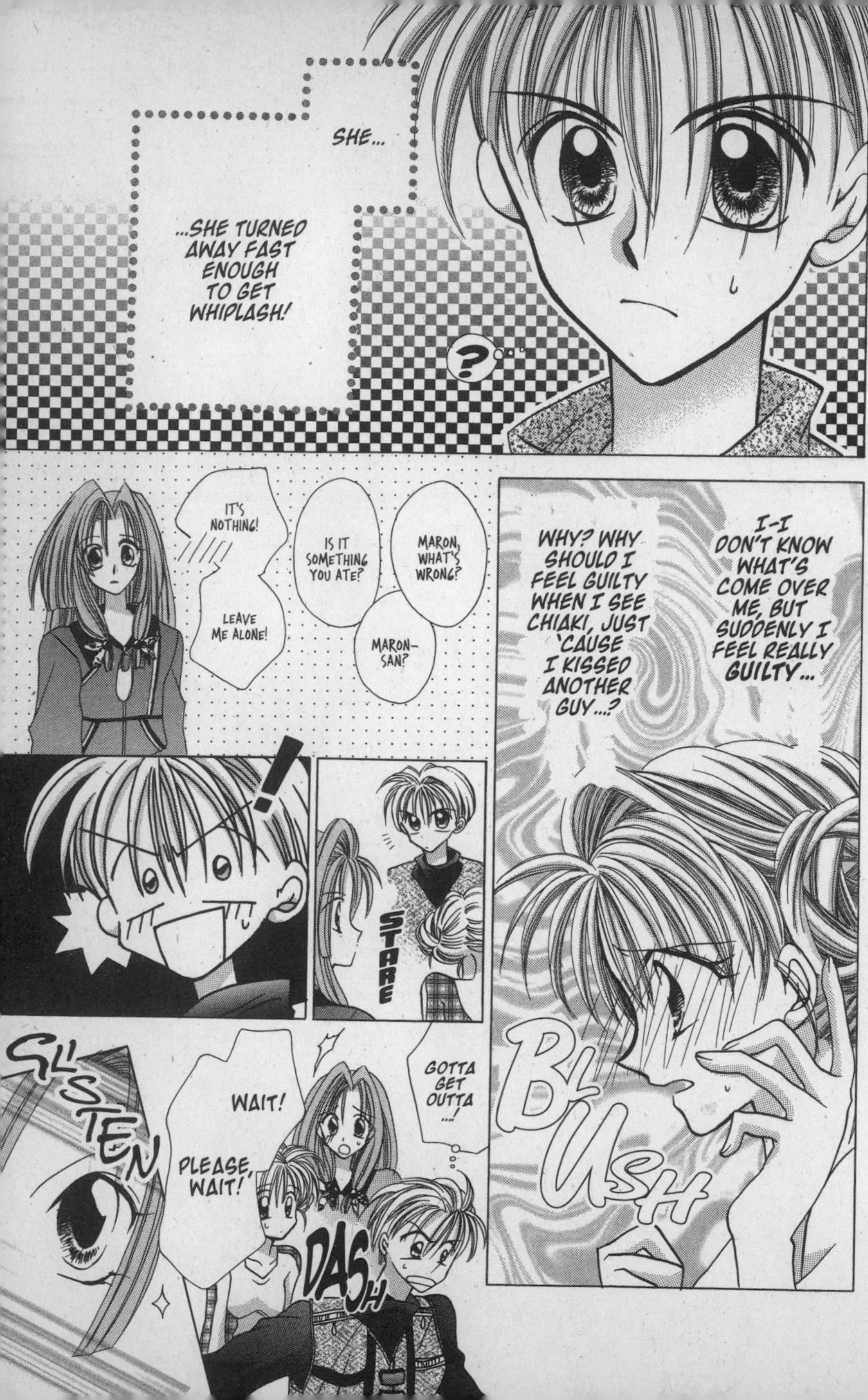
SHE...
...SHE TURNED AWAY FAST ENOUGH TO GET WHIPLASH!
?
I-I DON'T KNOW WHAT'S COME OVER ME, BUT SUDDENLY I FEEL REALLY GUILTY...
WHY? WHY SHOULD I FEEL GUILTY WHEN I SEE CHIAKI, JUST 'CAUSE I KISSED ANOTHER GUY...?
BLUSH
MARON, WHAT'S WRONG?
IS IT SOMETHING YOU ATE?
MARON-SAN?
IT'S NOTHING!
LEAVE ME ALONE!
STARE
!
GOTTA GET OUTTA ...!
WAIT!
PLEASE, WAIT!
DASH
GLISTEN

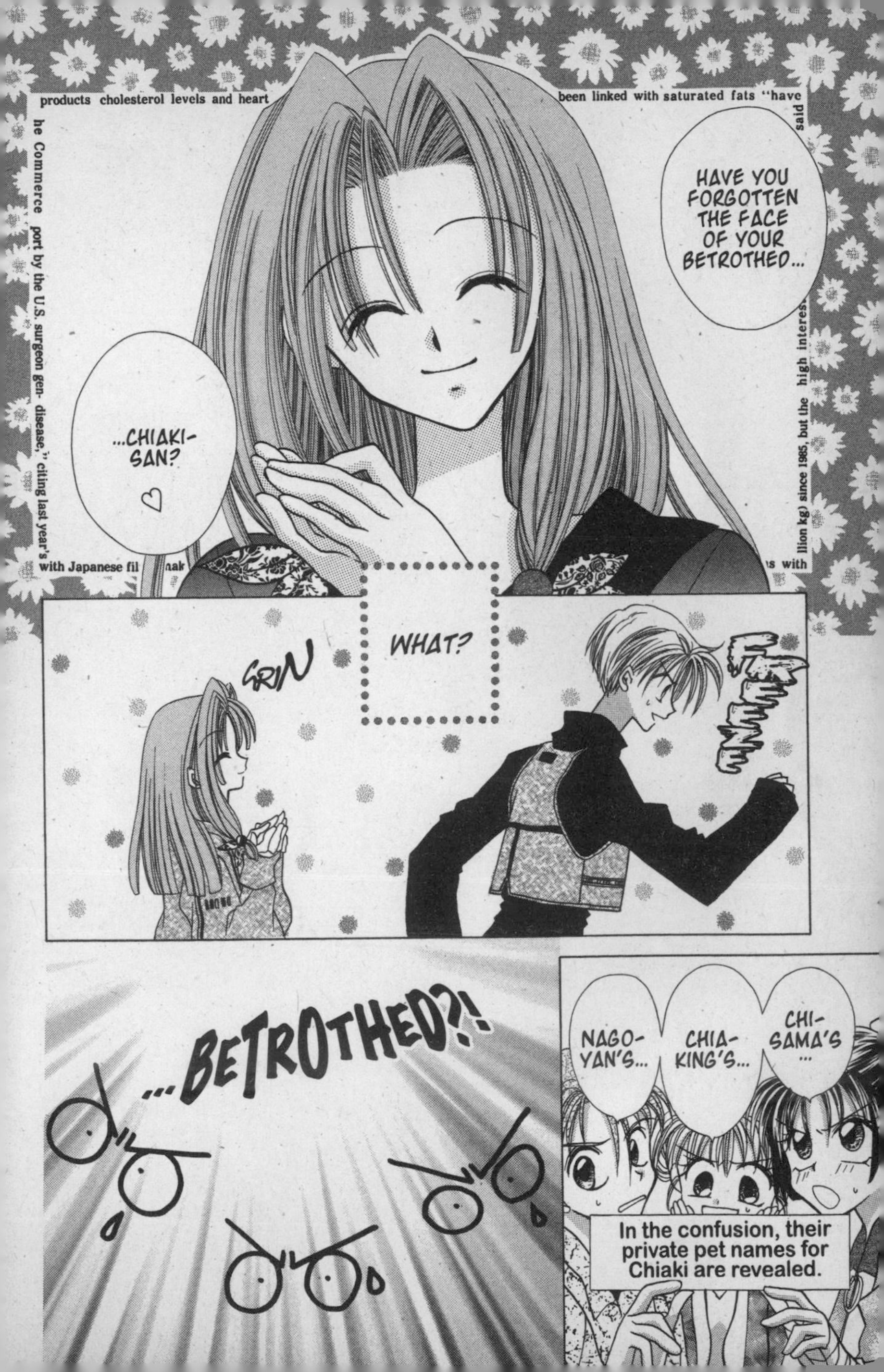
HAVE YOU FORGOTTEN THE FACE OF YOUR BETROTHED...
...CHIAKI-SAN? ♡
been linked with saturated fats "have
products cholesterol levels and heart
WHAT?
GRIN
CHI-SAMA'S ...
CHIA-KING'S...
NAGO-YAN'S...
In the confusion, their private pet names for Chiaki are revealed.
...BETROTHED?!

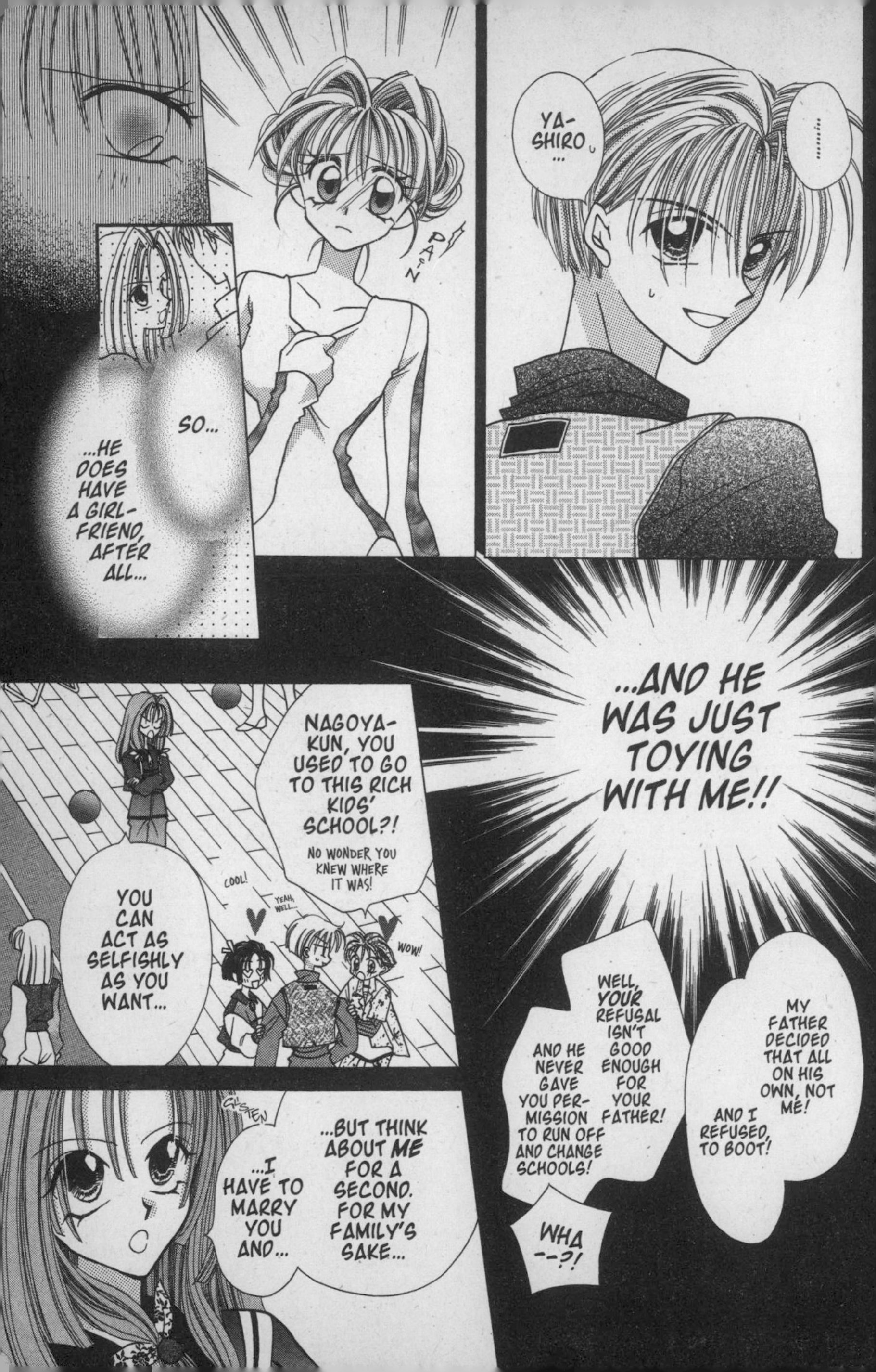
YA-SHIRO...
......
PA-N
SO...
...HE DOES HAVE A GIRL-FRIEND, AFTER ALL...
...AND HE WAS JUST TOYING WITH ME!!
NAGOYA-KUN, YOU USED TO GO TO THIS RICH KIDS' SCHOOL?!
NO WONDER YOU KNEW WHERE IT WAS!
COOL!
YEAH, WELL...
WOW!
YOU CAN ACT AS SELFISHLY AS YOU WANT...
MY FATHER DECIDED THAT ALL ON HIS OWN, NOT ME!
AND I REFUSED, TO BOOT!
WELL, YOUR REFUSAL ISN'T GOOD ENOUGH FOR YOUR FATHER!
AND HE NEVER GAVE YOU PER-MISSION TO RUN OFF AND CHANGE SCHOOLS!
WHA--?!
...BUT THINK ABOUT ME FOR A SECOND. FOR MY FAMILY'S SAKE...
...I HAVE TO MARRY YOU AND...
GLISTEN

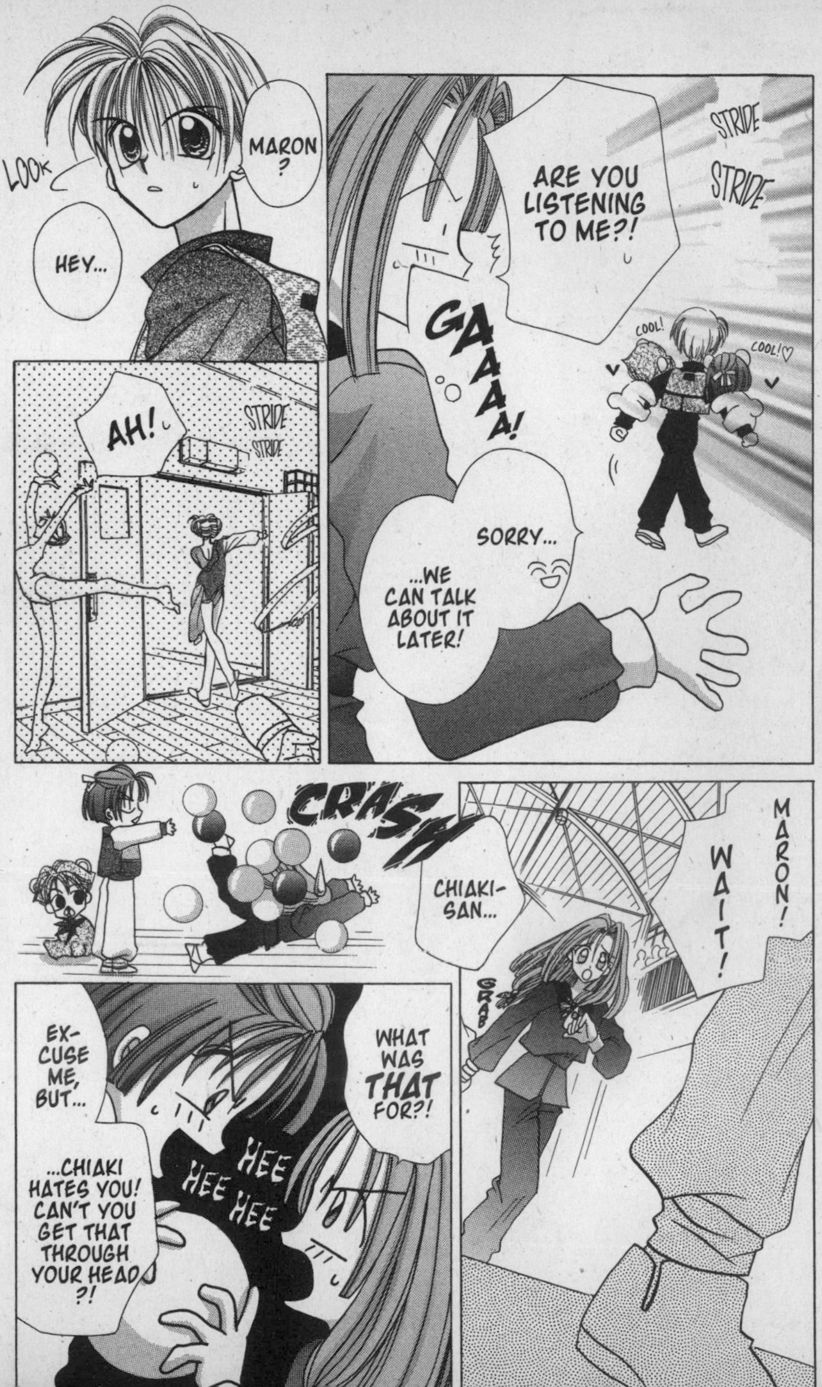
STRIDE
STRIDE
ARE YOU LISTENING TO ME?!
GAAAAA!
COOL!
COOL!♡
SORRY...
...WE CAN TALK ABOUT IT LATER!
MARON?
LOOK
HEY...
AH!
STRIDE
STRIDE
MARON!
WAIT!
CHIAKI-SAN...
GRAB
CRASH
WHAT WAS THAT FOR?!
EX-CUSE ME, BUT...
...CHIAKI HATES YOU! CAN'T YOU GET THAT THROUGH YOUR HEAD?!
HEE HEE HEE

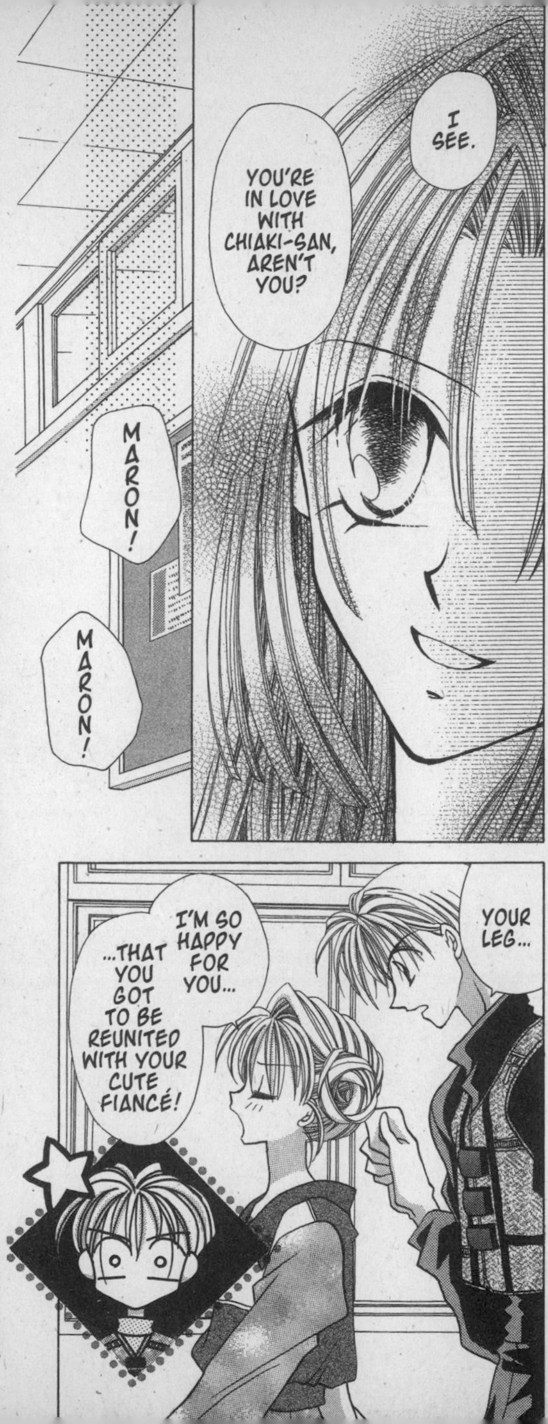
I SEE.
YOU'RE IN LOVE WITH CHIAKI-SAN, AREN'T YOU?
MARON!
MARON!
YOUR LEG...
I'M SO HAPPY FOR YOU...
...THAT YOU GOT TO BE REUNITED WITH YOUR CUTE FIANCÉ!

GREETiNGS.

HELLOOOOO! Arina here! i'm full of energy! Yay!! So here's Volume 2 of KAMiKAZE KAiTO JEANNE. Jeez, time flies. Heh. Right now, JEANNE (in magazine form) has already bypassed her first-year anniversary. YAYYYYY! Oh, yeah, around the time of this volume's publication, the current Ribon magazine (February, 1999) is giving away Jeanne-related presents, namely, a tapestry and phone cards, so for those of you who only read Jeanne here, in trade paperback form, check out the Ribon giveaway, too.♥ i have some big news, too, but i'll wait a bit for that ♥ i'll talk a lot about it in this volume's sidebars!

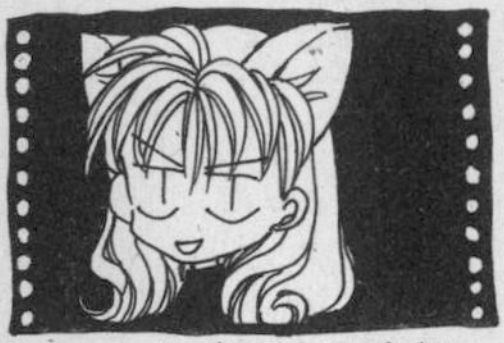

MY HAIR GREW OUT AGAIN. IT ALWAYS GROWS FAST!

Oh, another thing, in the last volume, i put out a call for homemade JEANNE comics (or comics from my other series), and i'm delighted by the response i got! Quite a few of the homemade JEANNE comics i received were sent to me on letterhead and were printed professionally or were sent in clear files...♥ Everyone who sent me one, thank you very much♥ Please keep sending! Even if the homemade comics aren't created by you, share them with me anyway, if you don't mind! No matter what kind of homemade comics they are, i don't care--just send it! That reminds me, though, of some fan letters i got a while back, asking me about my own rumored homemade anime (manga?) comics! To set the record straight, i have **never** made my own homemade comics, before or after my debut! Be careful about buying into rumors ♥ in answer to another question i get, right now, my favorite manga is that one with the angelic girl who steals stuff ♥ You know the one i mean ♥ Tee Hee ♥

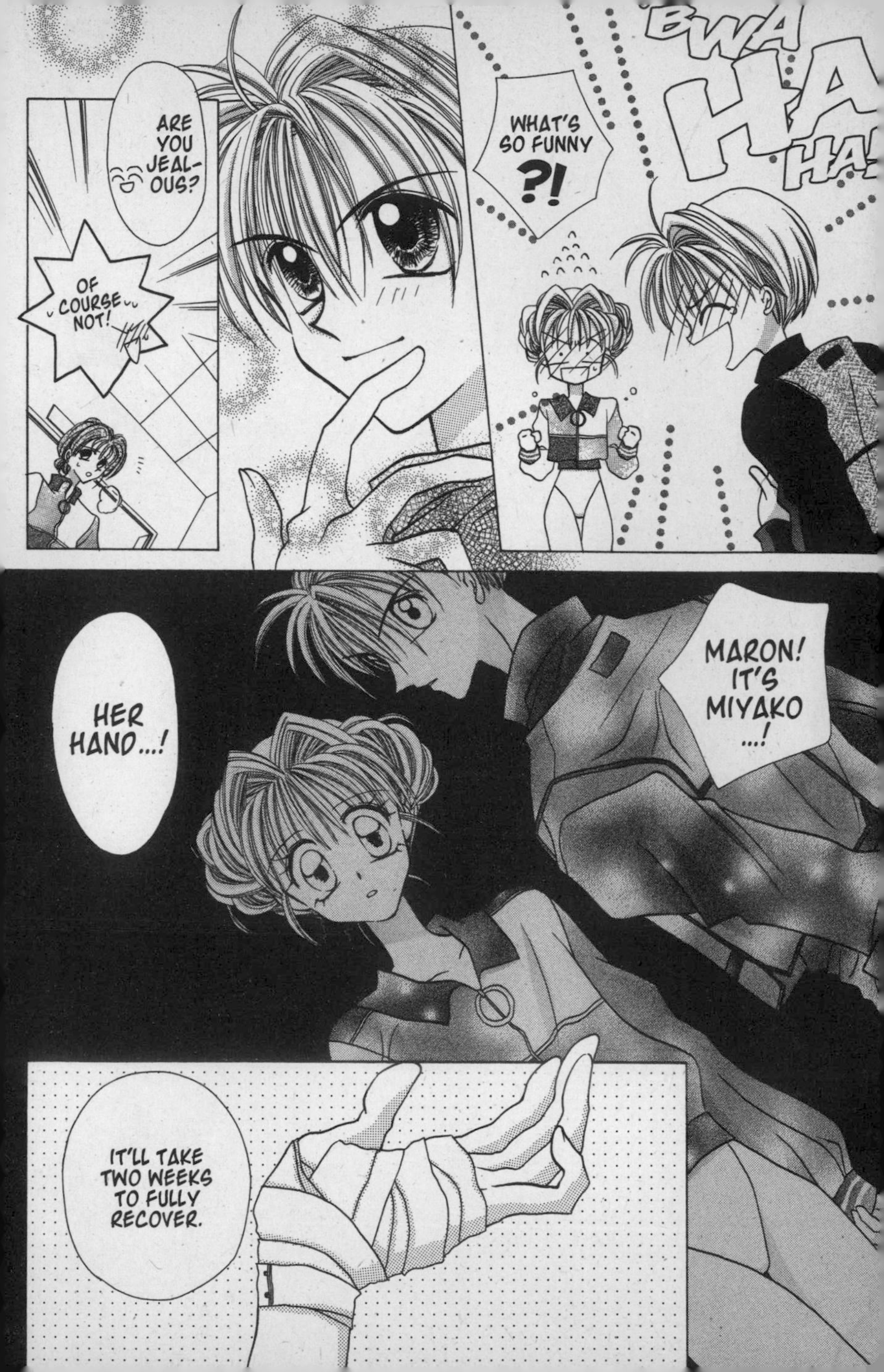
BWA HA HA
WHAT'S SO FUNNY ?!
ARE YOU JEAL-OUS?
OF COURSE NOT!
MARON! IT'S MIYAKO ...!
HER HAND...!
IT'LL TAKE TWO WEEKS TO FULLY RECOVER.

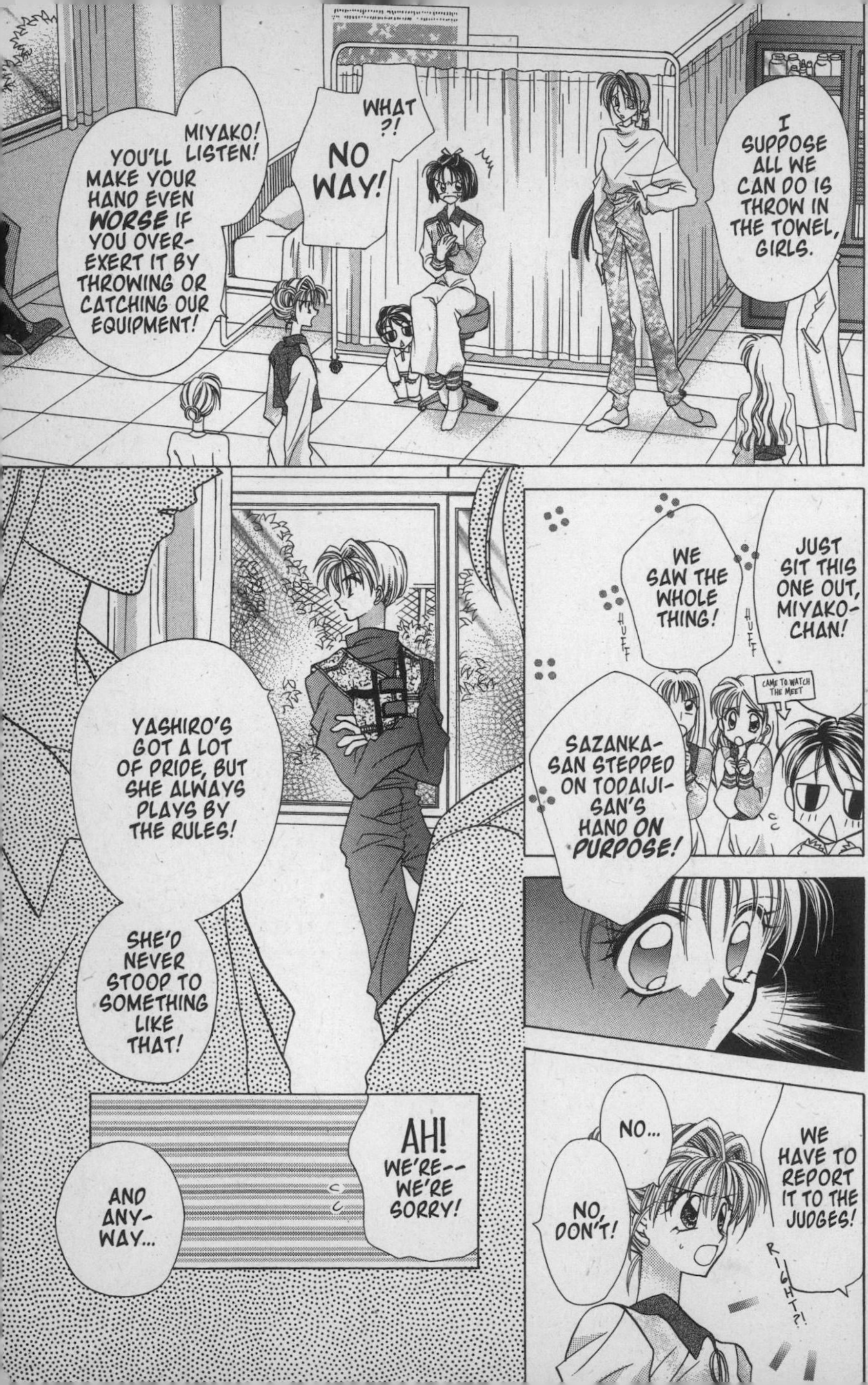
I SUPPOSE ALL WE CAN DO IS THROW IN THE TOWEL, GIRLS.
WHAT ?!
NO WAY!
MIYAKO! LISTEN!
YOU'LL MAKE YOUR HAND EVEN WORSE IF YOU OVER-EXERT IT BY THROWING OR CATCHING OUR EQUIPMENT!
JUST SIT THIS ONE OUT, MIYAKO-CHAN!
HUFF
WE SAW THE WHOLE THING!
HUFF
CAME TO WATCH THE MEET
SAZANKA-SAN STEPPED ON TODAIJI-SAN'S HAND ON PURPOSE!
WE HAVE TO REPORT IT TO THE JUDGES!
RIGHT?!
NO...
NO, DON'T!
YASHIRO'S GOT A LOT OF PRIDE, BUT SHE ALWAYS PLAYS BY THE RULES!
SHE'D NEVER STOOP TO SOMETHING LIKE THAT!
AH! WE'RE-- WE'RE SORRY!
AND ANYWAY...

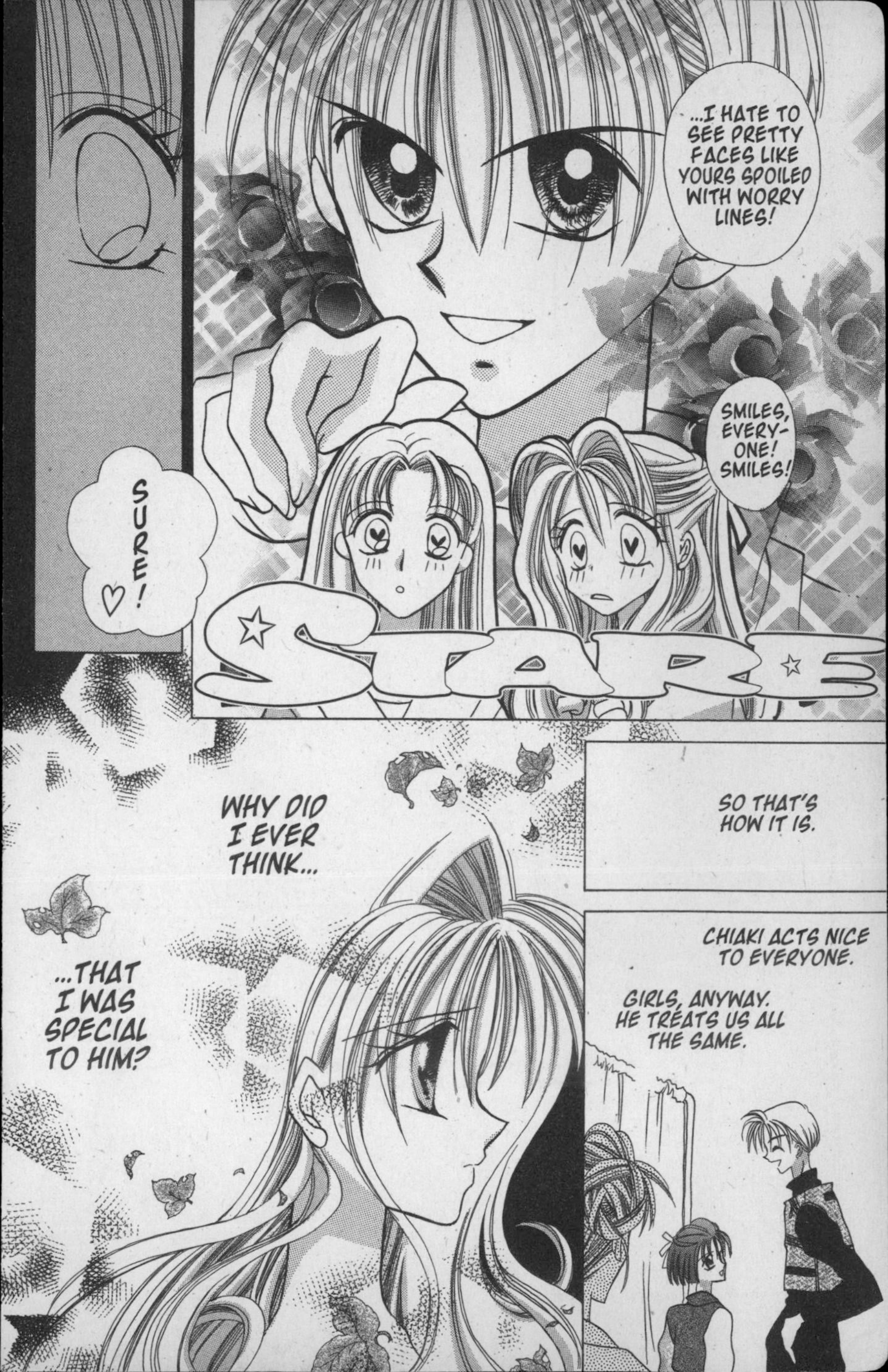
...I HATE TO SEE PRETTY FACES LIKE YOURS SPOILED WITH WORRY LINES!
SMILES, EVERYONE! SMILES!
STARE
SURE! ♡
SO THAT'S HOW IT IS.
CHIAKI ACTS NICE TO EVERYONE.
GIRLS, ANYWAY. HE TREATS US ALL THE SAME.
WHY DID I EVER THINK...
...THAT I WAS SPECIAL TO HIM?

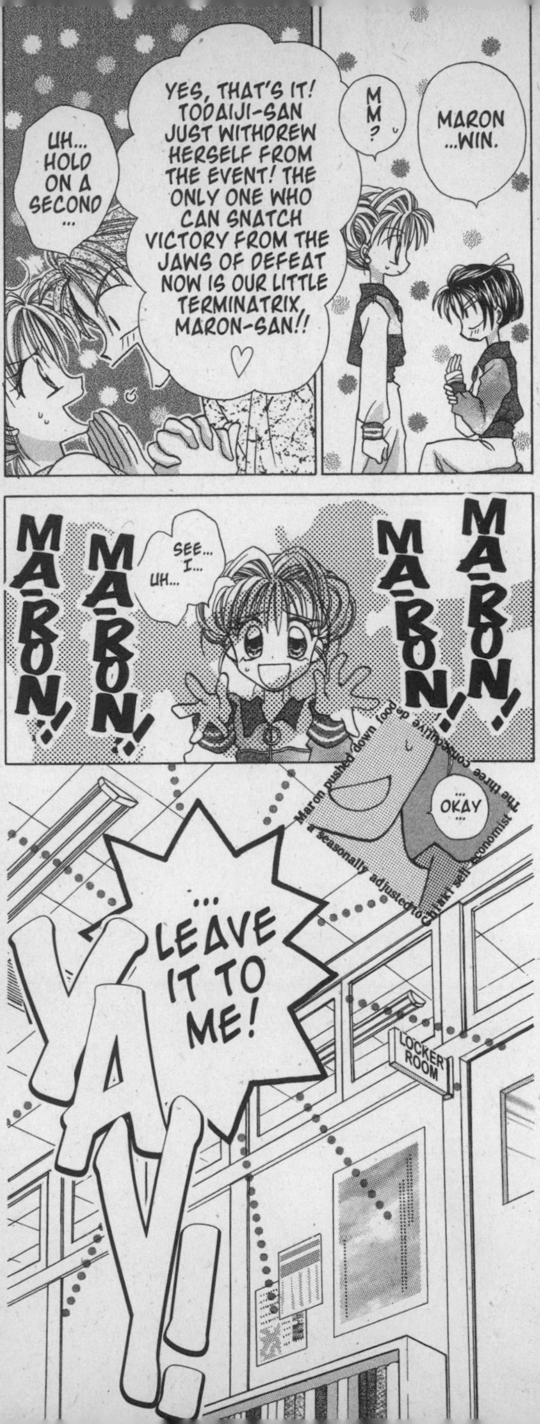
MARON ...WIN.
MM?
YES, THAT'S IT! TODAIJI-SAN JUST WITHDREW HERSELF FROM THE EVENT! THE ONLY ONE WHO CAN SNATCH VICTORY FROM THE JAWS OF DEFEAT NOW IS OUR LITTLE TERMINATRIX, MARON-SAN!!
UH... HOLD ON A SECOND ...
MARON! MARON! MARON! MARON!
SEE... I... UH...
... OKAY ...
The three consecutive
food Maron pushed down
a seasonally adjusted to Chiaki self economist
... LEAVE IT TO ME!
YAY!
LOCKER ROOM

CELEBRATE!
KAMIKAZE KAITO JEANNE
COMING SOON...
THE TV ANIME!

1

...Yep, it's true. It'll be on TV Asahi (on 24 channels across the country) starting in February 1999! HAAA...Am I nervous? Oh, yes. I first talked about it with people from the production company, Toei Animation, in the summer (just before the Nagoya signing).

Ever since JEANNE started in the magazine, I received fan letters and inquiries from friends, asking, "Aren't you going to do a JEANNE cartoon?" To be honest, I always felt it was better not to do an anime version. In the first place, one of my precepts in creating this comic was that it should be a series that "absolutely **shouldn't** be made into anime," which, I admit, is a pretty weird principle, but I can explain. See, I'm the type of person that hates losing, so when I'm challenged(?), I rise up to it. Now, before starting work on JEANNE, I couldn't decide what series to do. My friends urged me on: "I wanna see JEANNE!" "I wanna read JEANNE!" But personally, I hate imitators, so if there was a manga that debuted before mine that was even a little similar, I would lose all interest in my idea. Well, there was one, but I really, really wanted to do JEANNE by that time, so I was on the horns of a dilemma. It was solved by a reader survey in a certain manga magazine. Under the heading, "I wanna read this kind of manga!" a lot of readers wrote in that they wanted to see more series in the magazine that "didn't look like anime." And then and there, I picked up the gauntlet of that challenge (for some reason).

CONTINUED>>>

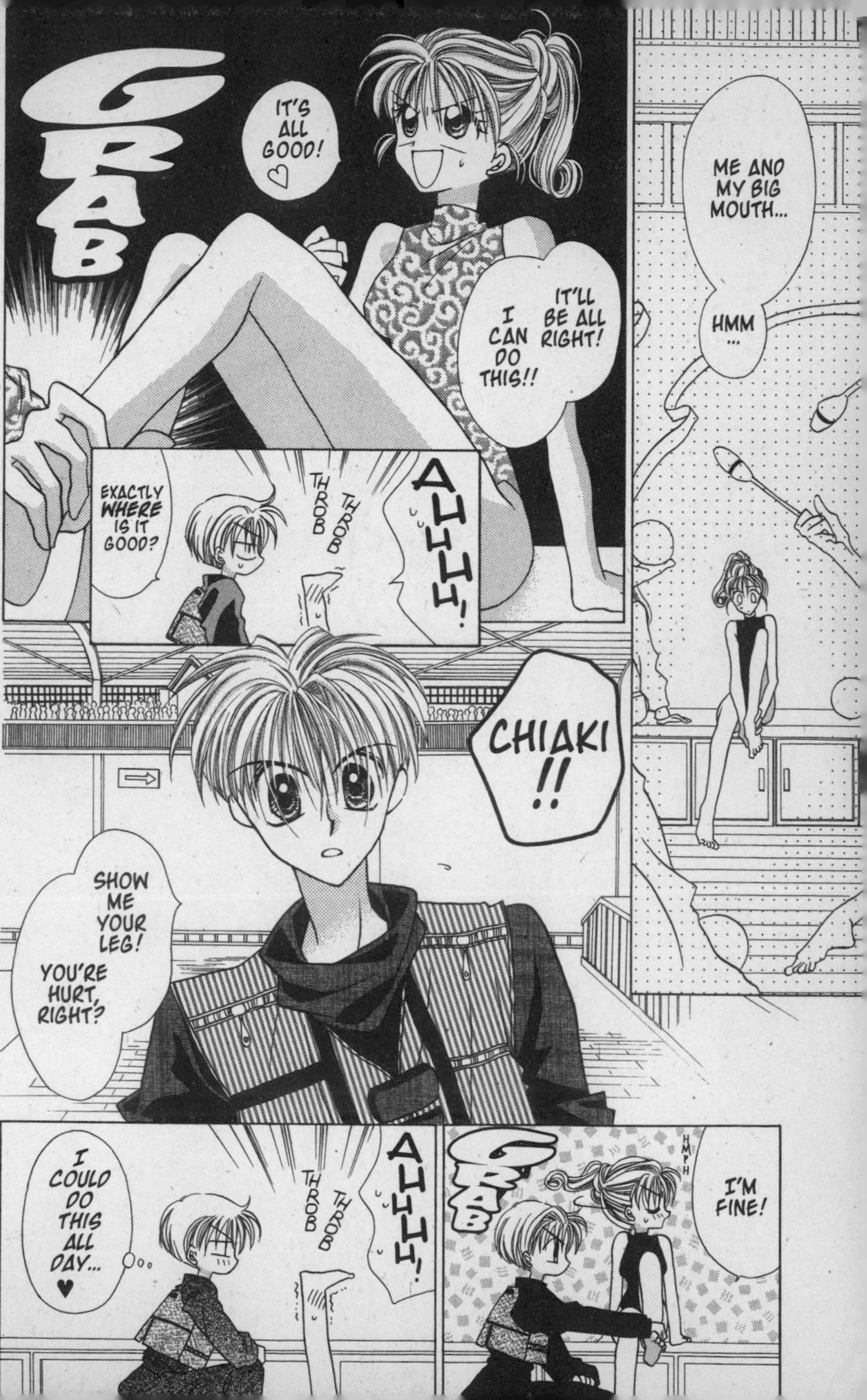

ME AND MY BIG MOUTH...
HMM...
IT'S ALL GOOD! ♡
GRAB
IT'LL BE ALL RIGHT! I CAN DO THIS!!
AHHHH!
THROB THROB
EXACTLY WHERE IS IT GOOD?
CHIAKI!!
SHOW ME YOUR LEG! YOU'RE HURT, RIGHT?
I'M FINE!
HMPH
GRAB
AHHHH!
THROB THROB
I COULD DO THIS ALL DAY... ♥

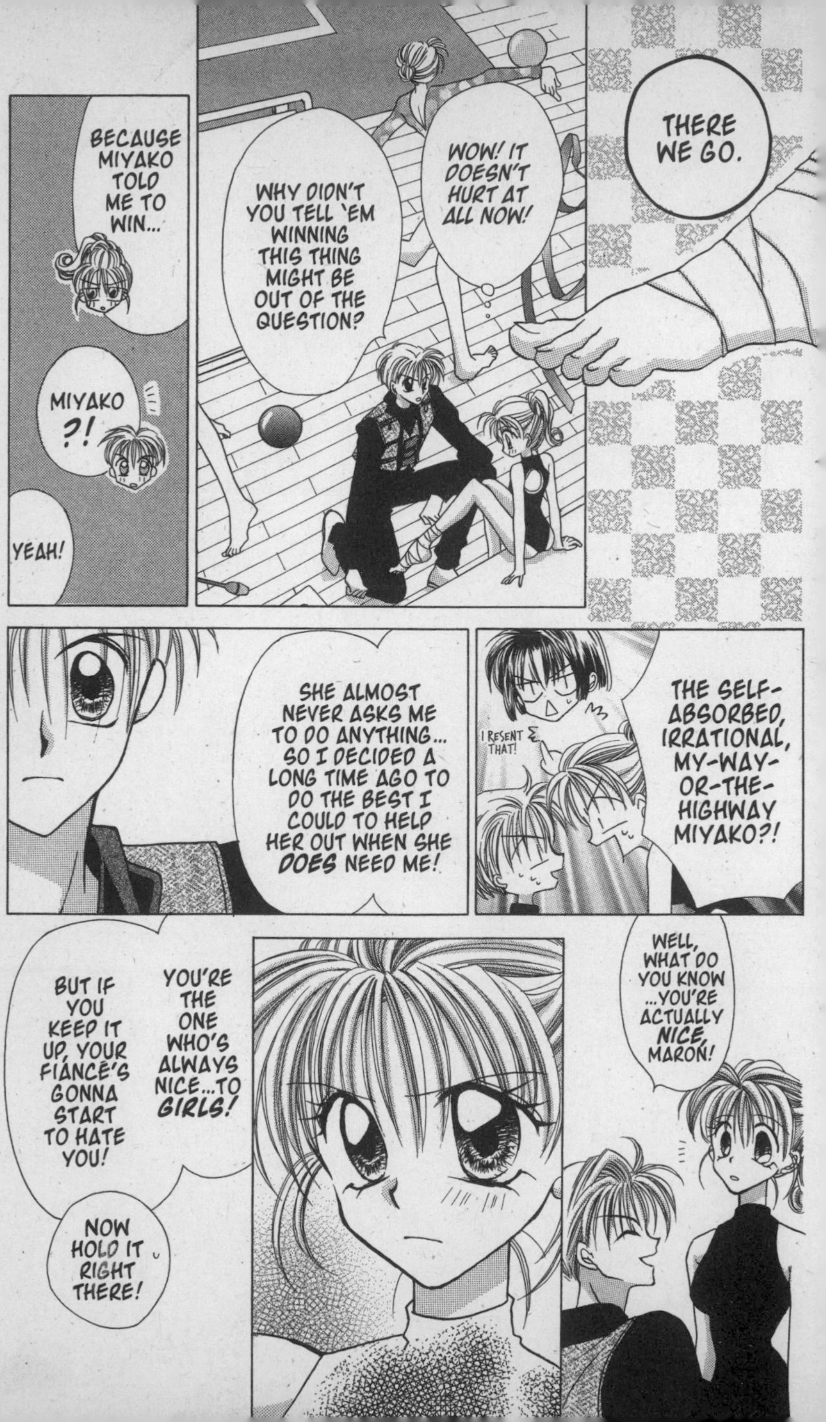
THERE WE GO.
WOW! IT DOESN'T HURT AT ALL NOW!
WHY DIDN'T YOU TELL 'EM WINNING THIS THING MIGHT BE OUT OF THE QUESTION?
BECAUSE MIYAKO TOLD ME TO WIN...
MIYAKO ?!
YEAH!
THE SELF-ABSORBED, IRRATIONAL, MY-WAY-OR-THE-HIGHWAY MIYAKO?!
I RESENT THAT!
SHE ALMOST NEVER ASKS ME TO DO ANYTHING... SO I DECIDED A LONG TIME AGO TO DO THE BEST I COULD TO HELP HER OUT WHEN SHE DOES NEED ME!
WELL, WHAT DO YOU KNOW ...YOU'RE ACTUALLY NICE, MARON!
YOU'RE THE ONE WHO'S ALWAYS NICE...TO GIRLS!
BUT IF YOU KEEP IT UP, YOUR FIANCÉ'S GONNA START TO HATE YOU!
NOW HOLD IT RIGHT THERE!

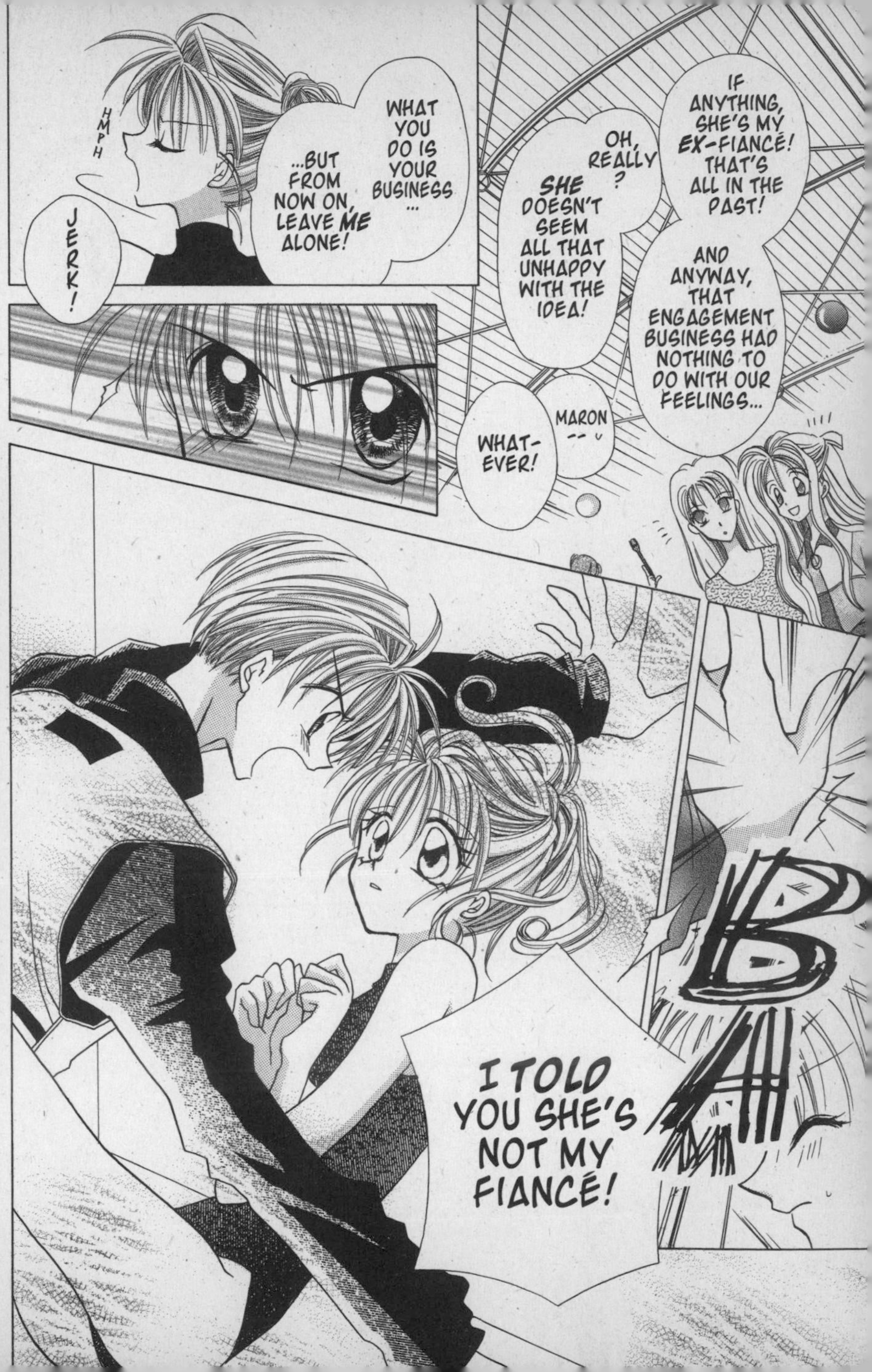
IF ANYTHING, SHE'S MY EX-FIANCÉ! THAT'S ALL IN THE PAST!
AND ANYWAY, THAT ENGAGEMENT BUSINESS HAD NOTHING TO DO WITH OUR FEELINGS...
OH, REALLY? SHE DOESN'T SEEM ALL THAT UNHAPPY WITH THE IDEA!
MARON --
WHAT-EVER!
WHAT YOU DO IS YOUR BUSINESS...
...BUT FROM NOW ON, LEAVE ME ALONE!
HMPH
JERK!
BAM
I TOLD YOU SHE'S NOT MY FIANCÉ!

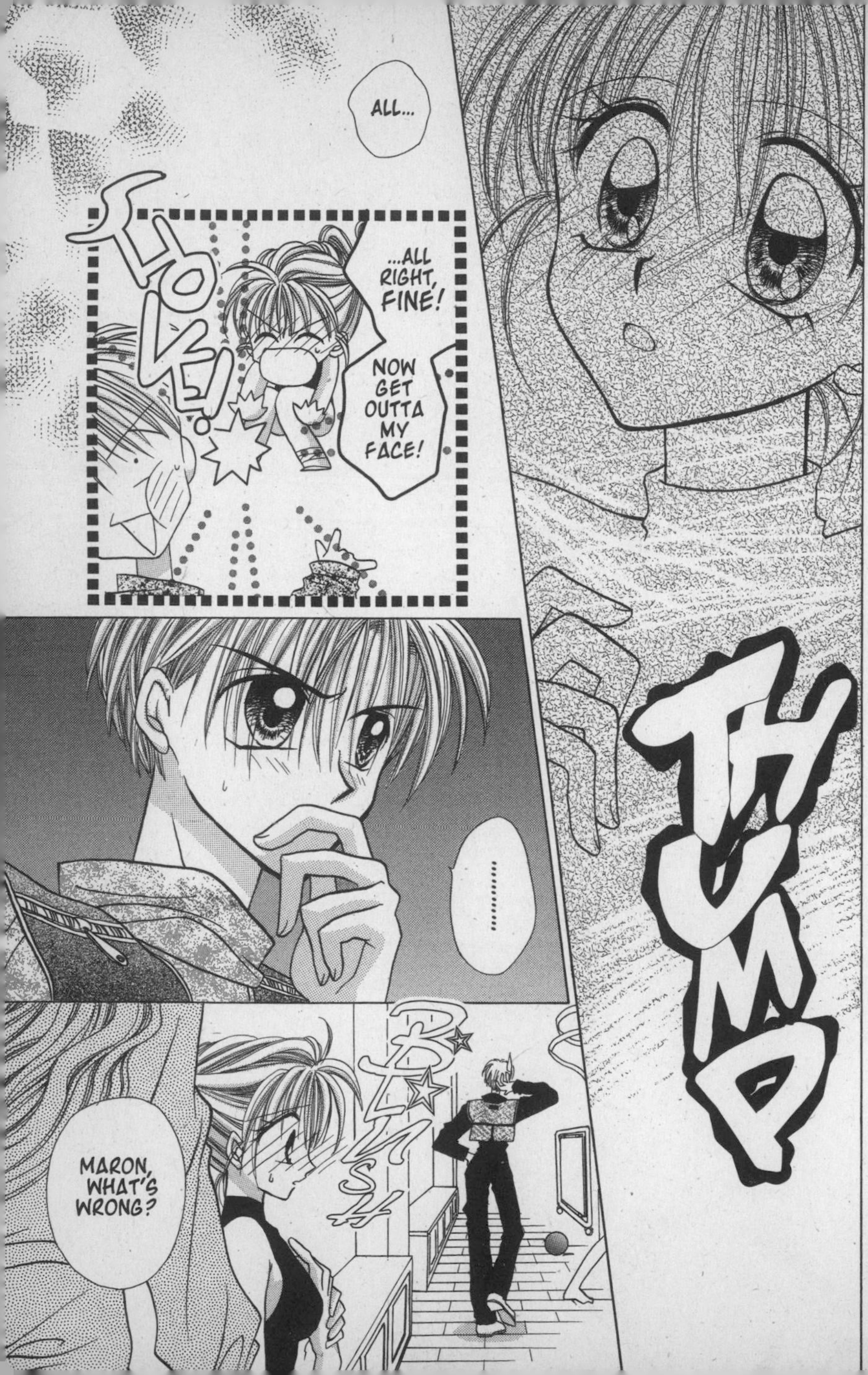
THUMP
ALL...
SHOVE!
...ALL RIGHT, FINE!
NOW GET OUTTA MY FACE!
....
BLUSH
MARON, WHAT'S WRONG?

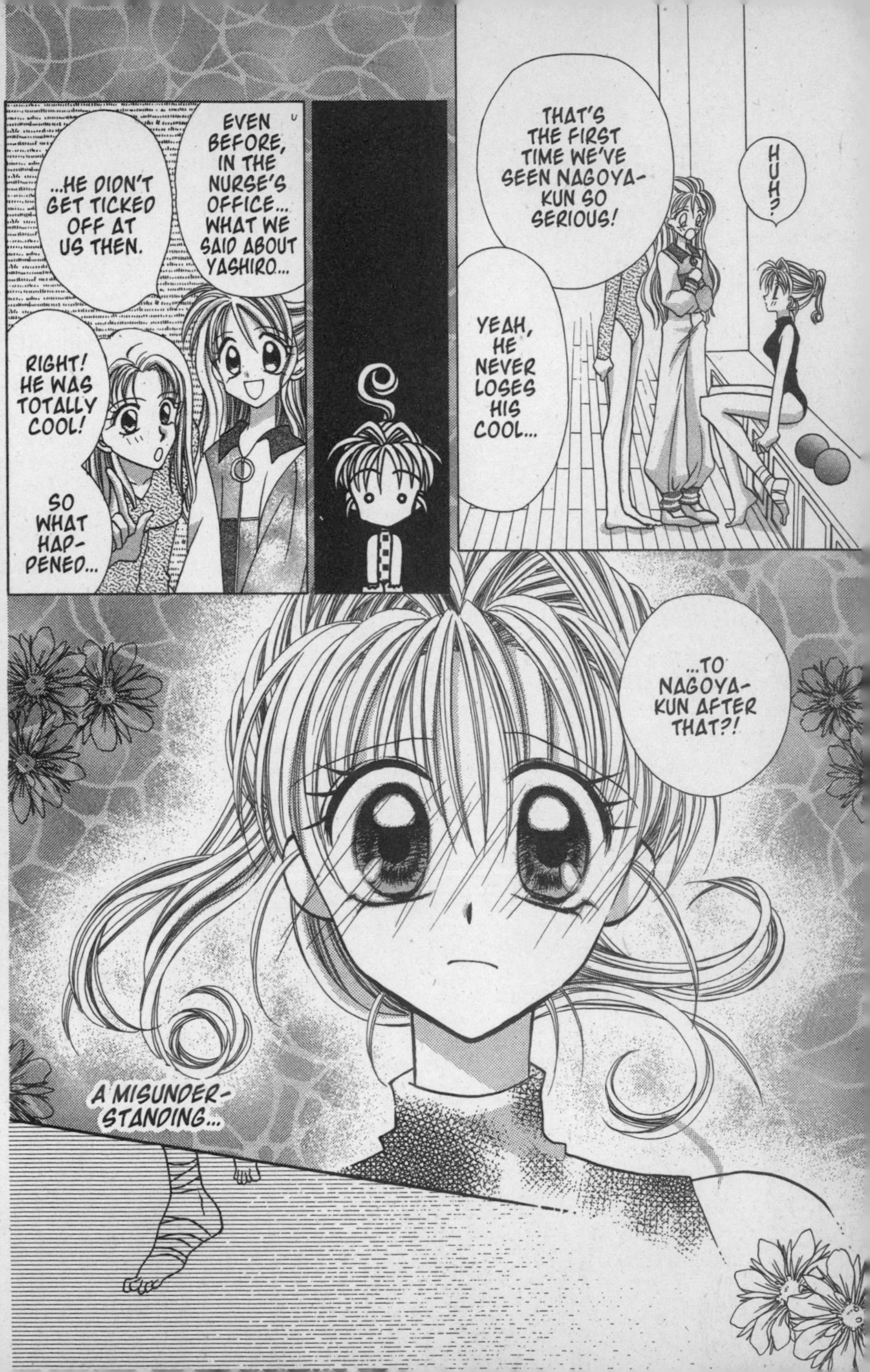
HUH?
THAT'S THE FIRST TIME WE'VE SEEN NAGOYA-KUN SO SERIOUS!
YEAH, HE NEVER LOSES HIS COOL...
EVEN BEFORE, IN THE NURSE'S OFFICE... WHAT WE SAID ABOUT YASHIRO...
...HE DIDN'T GET TICKED OFF AT US THEN.
RIGHT! HE WAS TOTALLY COOL!
SO WHAT HAPPENED...
...TO NAGOYA-KUN AFTER THAT?!
A MISUNDERSTANDING...

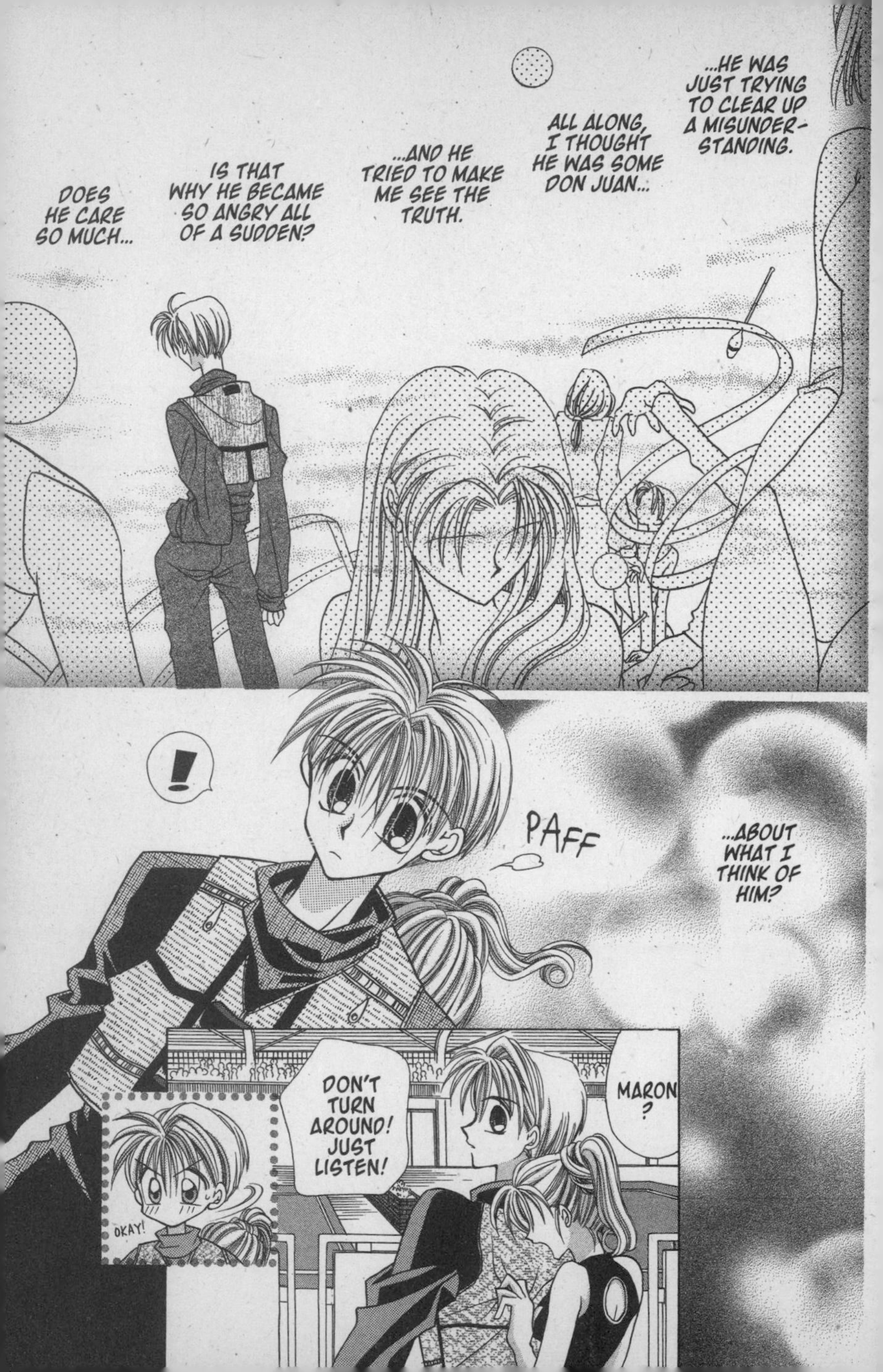
...HE WAS JUST TRYING TO CLEAR UP A MISUNDER-STANDING.
ALL ALONG, I THOUGHT HE WAS SOME DON JUAN...
...AND HE TRIED TO MAKE ME SEE THE TRUTH.
IS THAT WHY HE BECAME SO ANGRY ALL OF A SUDDEN?
DOES HE CARE SO MUCH...
...ABOUT WHAT I THINK OF HIM?
PAFF
!
MARON?
DON'T TURN AROUND! JUST LISTEN!
OKAY!

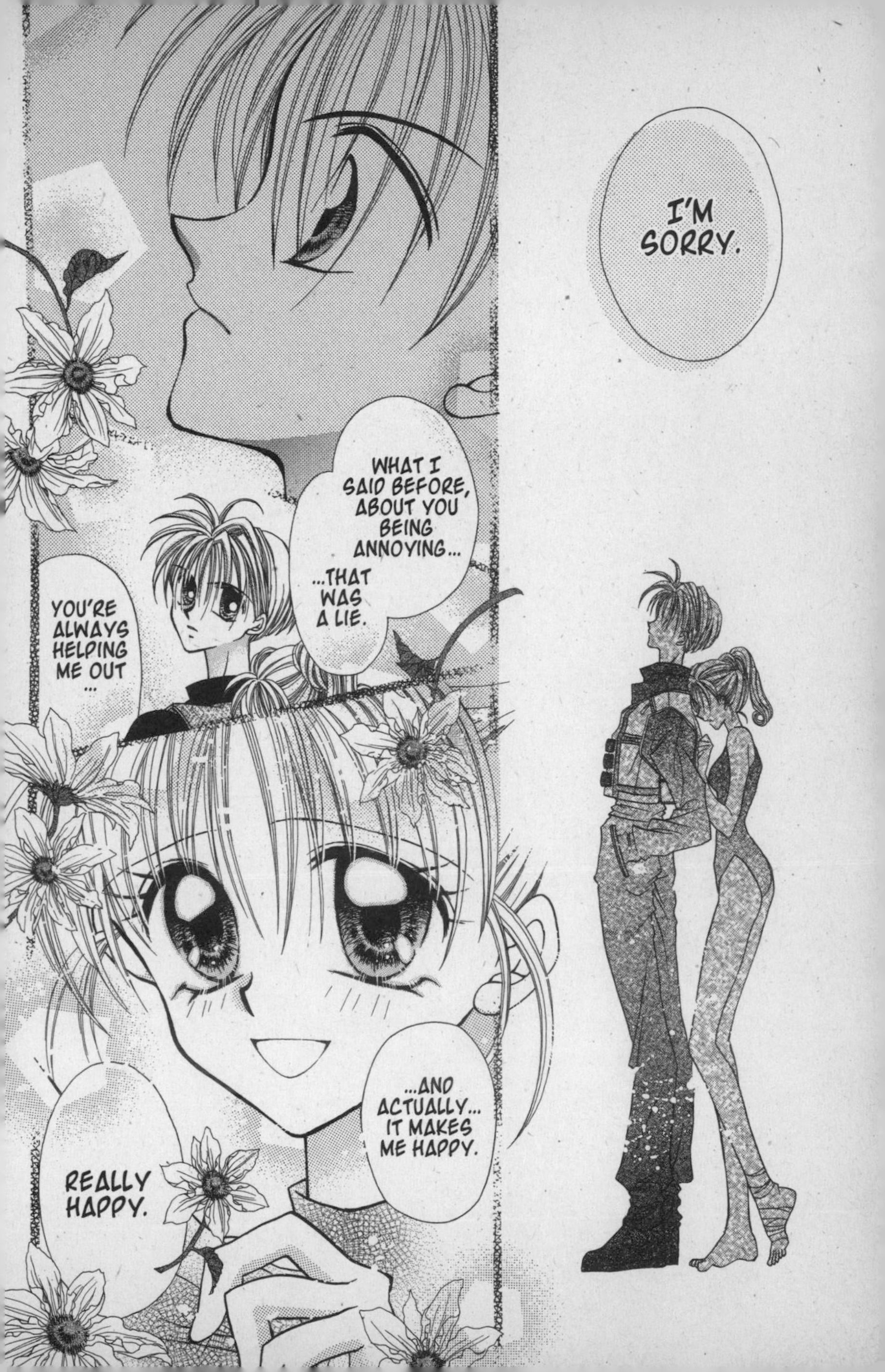
I'M SORRY.
WHAT I SAID BEFORE, ABOUT YOU BEING ANNOYING...
...THAT WAS A LIE.
YOU'RE ALWAYS HELPING ME OUT ...
...AND ACTUALLY... IT MAKES ME HAPPY.
REALLY HAPPY.

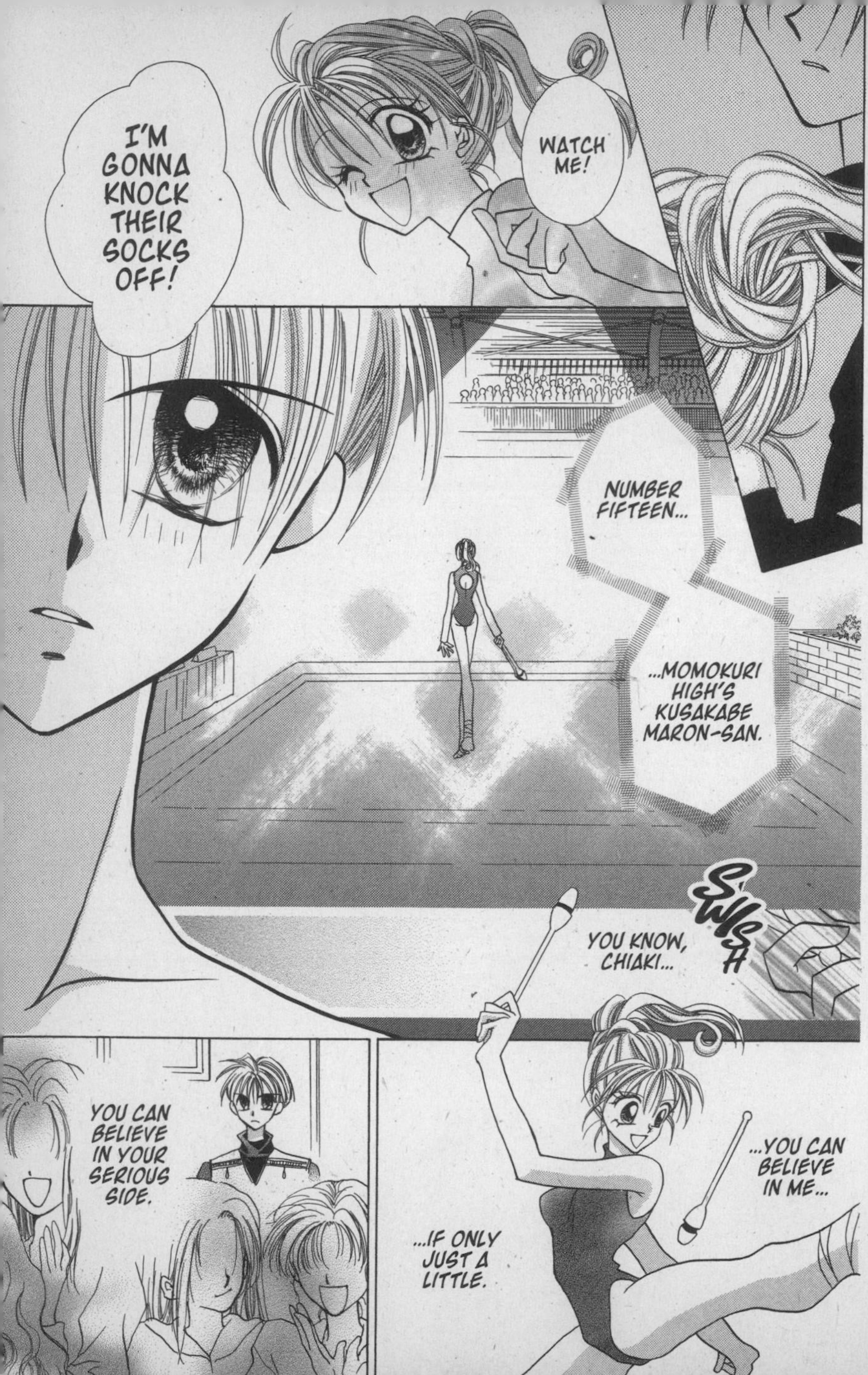
WATCH ME!
I'M GONNA KNOCK THEIR SOCKS OFF!
NUMBER FIFTEEN...
...MOMOKURI HIGH'S KUSAKABE MARON-SAN.
SWISH
YOU KNOW, CHIAKI...
...YOU CAN BELIEVE IN ME...
...IF ONLY JUST A LITTLE.
YOU CAN BELIEVE IN YOUR SERIOUS SIDE.

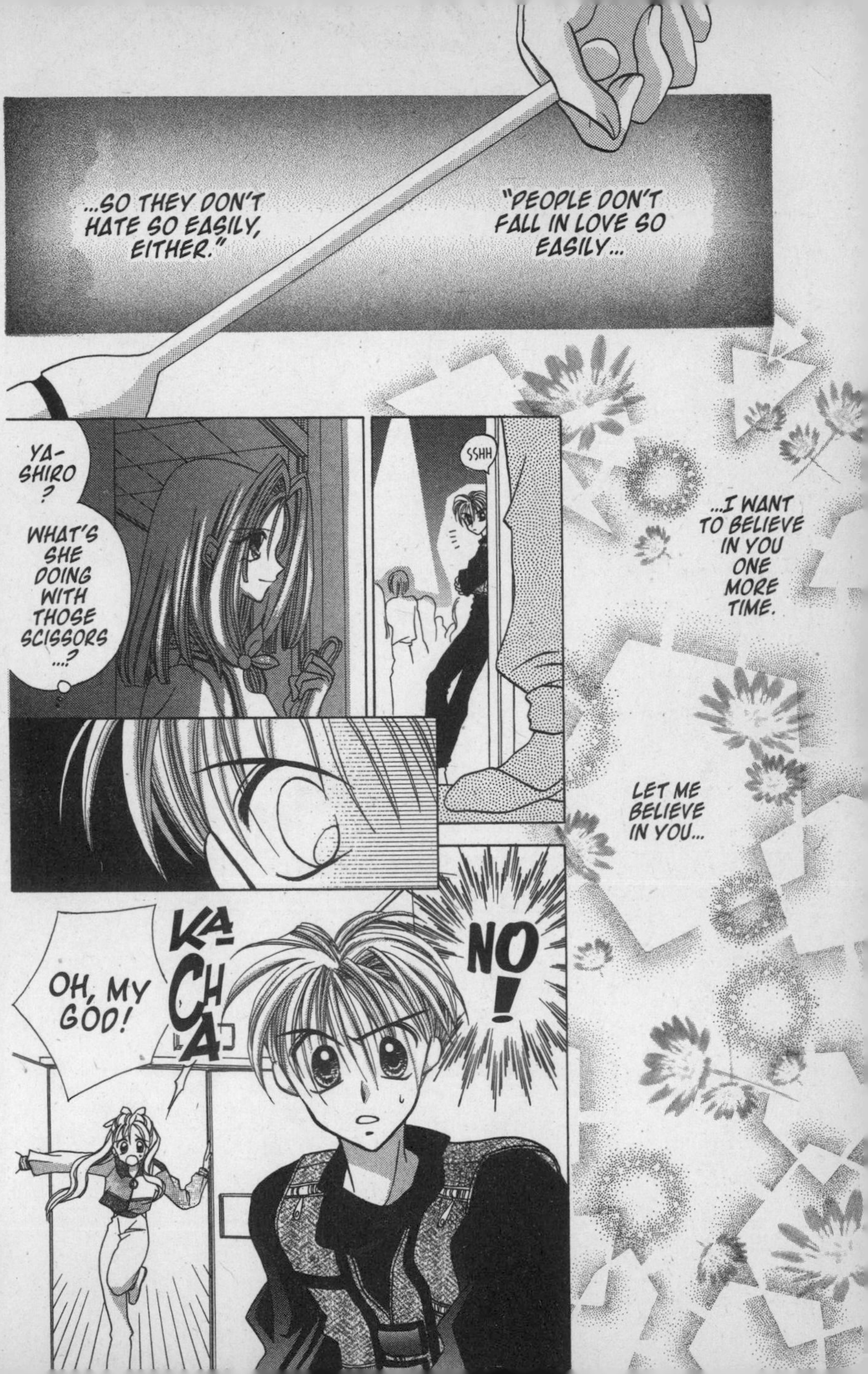
"PEOPLE DON'T FALL IN LOVE SO EASILY...
...SO THEY DON'T HATE SO EASILY, EITHER."
...I WANT TO BELIEVE IN YOU ONE MORE TIME.
LET ME BELIEVE IN YOU...
SSHH
YA-SHIRO? WHAT'S SHE DOING WITH THOSE SCISSORS...?
NO!
KA-CHA
OH, MY GOD!

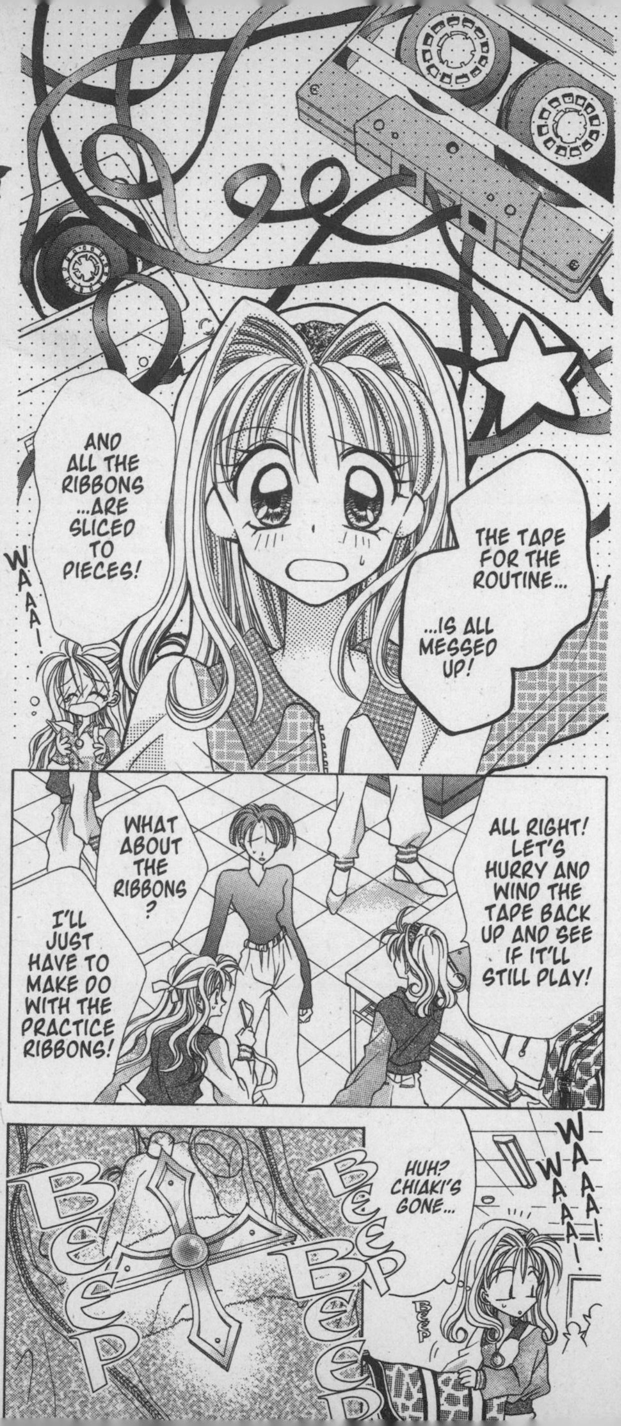
THE TAPE FOR THE ROUTINE...
...IS ALL MESSED UP!
AND ALL THE RIBBONS ...ARE SLICED TO PIECES!
WAAAI!
ALL RIGHT! LET'S HURRY AND WIND THE TAPE BACK UP AND SEE IF IT'LL STILL PLAY!
WHAT ABOUT THE RIBBONS?
I'LL JUST HAVE TO MAKE DO WITH THE PRACTICE RIBBONS!
WAAAAAI!
HUH? CHIAKI'S GONE...
BEEP
BEEP BEEP BEEP BEEP

⑧ ARINA TANEMURA'S LIKE PULLING TEETH WITH PLIERS

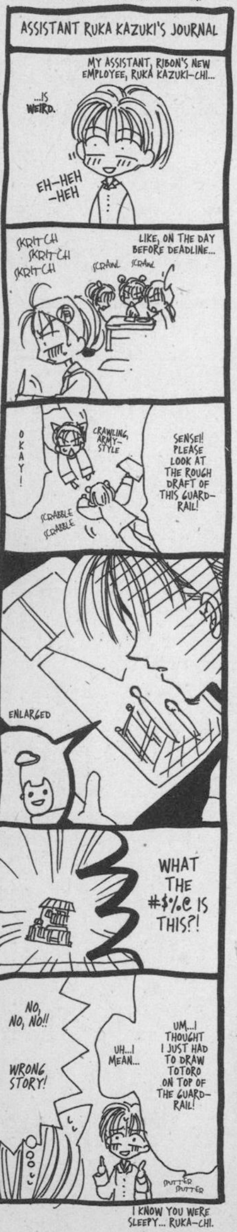
ASSISTANT RUKA KAZUKI'S JOURNAL
MY ASSISTANT, RIBON'S NEW EMPLOYEE, RUKA KAZUKI-CHI...
...IS WEIRD.
EH-HEH-HEH
LIKE, ON THE DAY BEFORE DEADLINE...
SKRITCH SKRITCH SKRITCH
SCRAWL SCRAWL
SENSEI! PLEASE LOOK AT THE ROUGH DRAFT OF THIS GUARD-RAIL!
CRAWLING, ARMY-STYLE
OKAY!
SCRABBLE SCRABBLE
ENLARGED
WHAT THE #$%@ IS THIS?!
UM...I THOUGHT I JUST HAD TO DRAW TOTORO ON TOP OF THE GUARD-RAIL!
UH...I MEAN...
NO, NO, NO!!
WRONG STORY!
SPUTTER SPUTTER
I KNOW YOU WERE SLEEPY... RUKA-CHI.

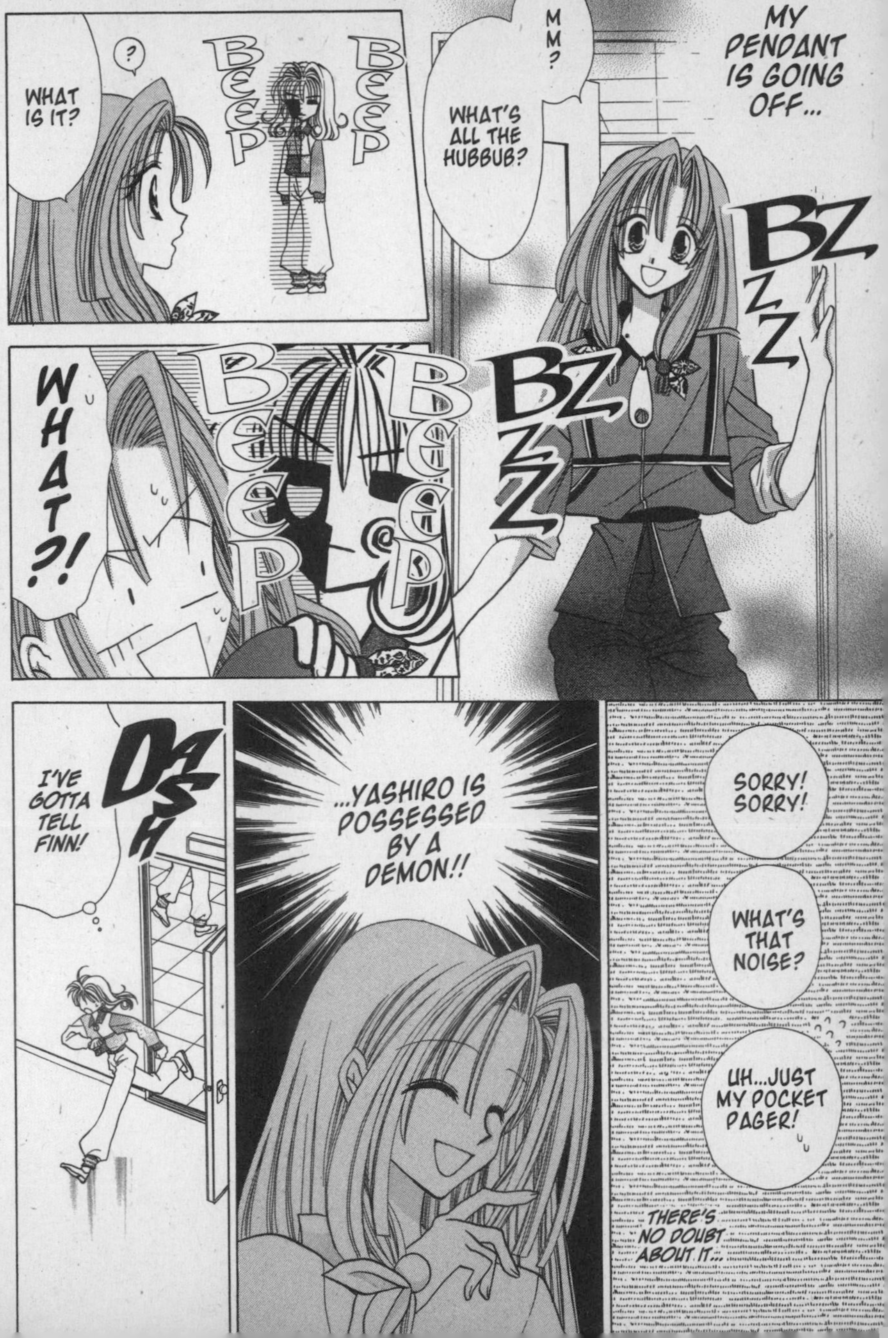
MY PENDANT IS GOING OFF...
MM?
WHAT'S ALL THE HUBBUB?
BZZZ
BZZZ
WHAT IS IT?
?
BEEP
BEEP
WHAT?!
BEEP
BEEP
SORRY! SORRY!
WHAT'S THAT NOISE?
UH...JUST MY POCKET PAGER!
THERE'S NO DOUBT ABOUT IT...
...YASHIRO IS POSSESSED BY A DEMON!!
I'VE GOTTA TELL FINN!
DASH

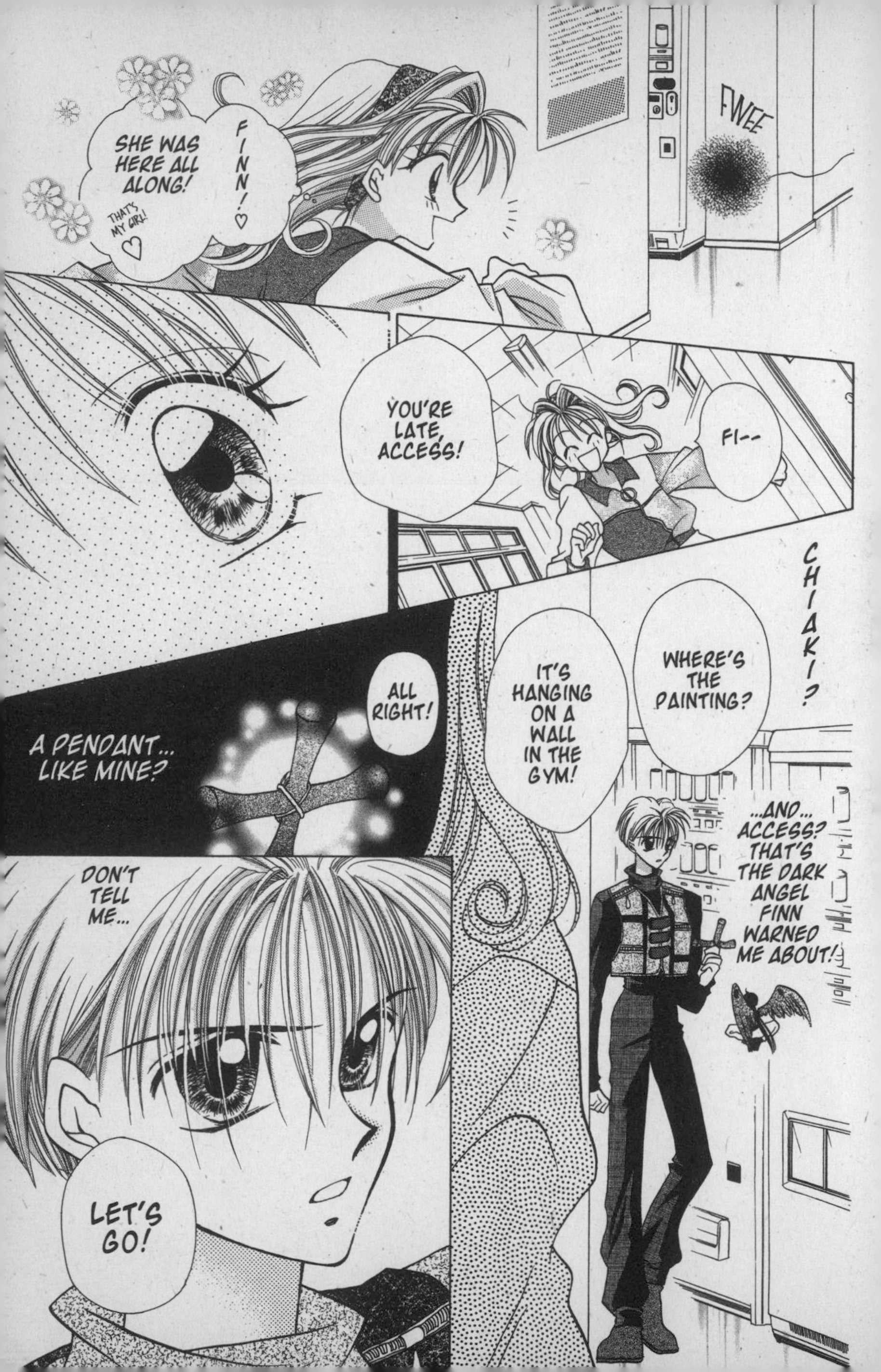
FWEE
FINN! ♡
SHE WAS HERE ALL ALONG!
THAT'S MY GIRL! ♡
FI--
YOU'RE LATE, ACCESS!
CHIAKI?
WHERE'S THE PAINTING?
IT'S HANGING ON A WALL IN THE GYM!
...AND... ACCESS? THAT'S THE DARK ANGEL FINN WARNED ME ABOUT!
ALL RIGHT!
A PENDANT... LIKE MINE?
DON'T TELL ME...
LET'S GO!

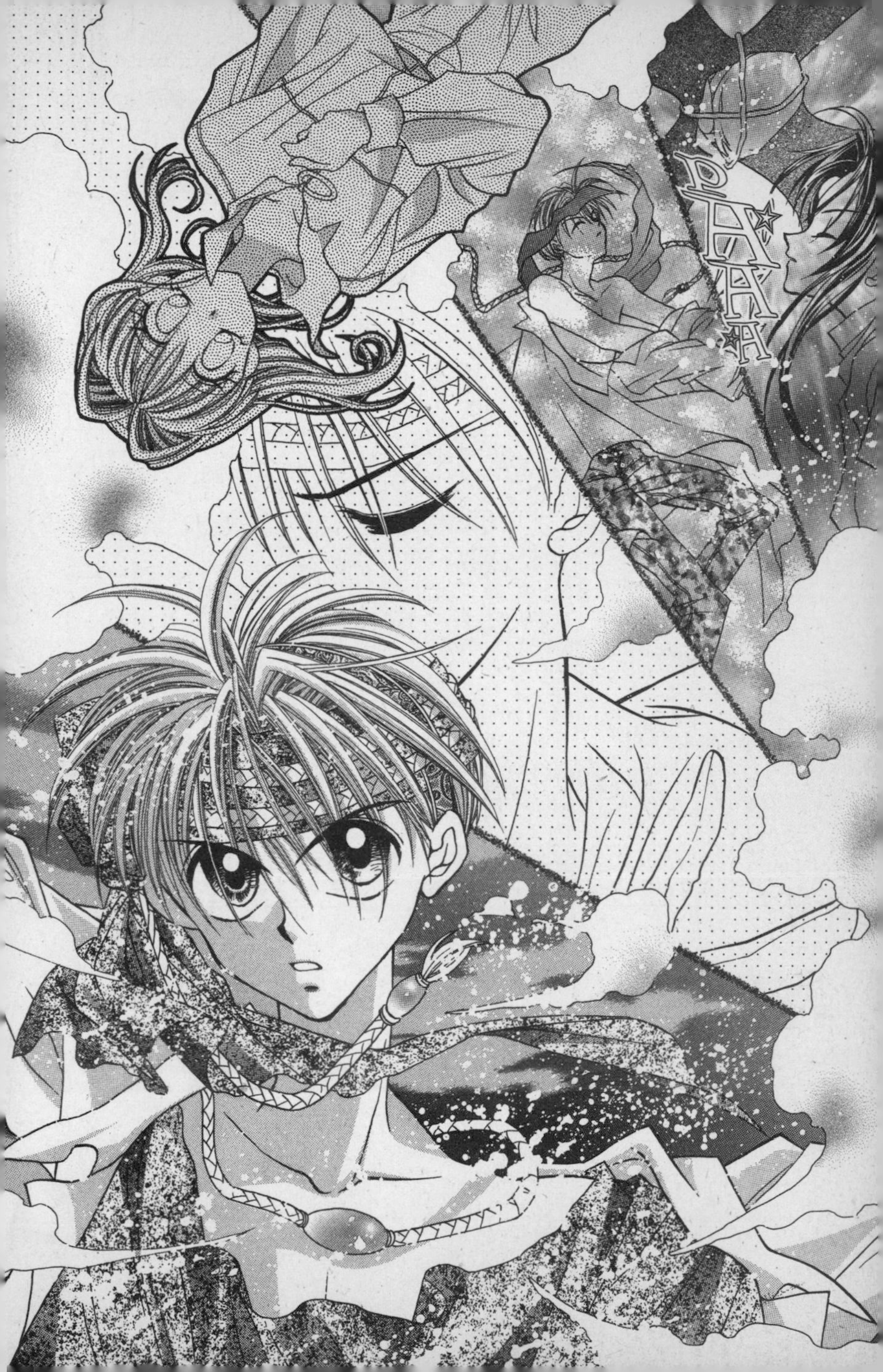
PA☆A☆A

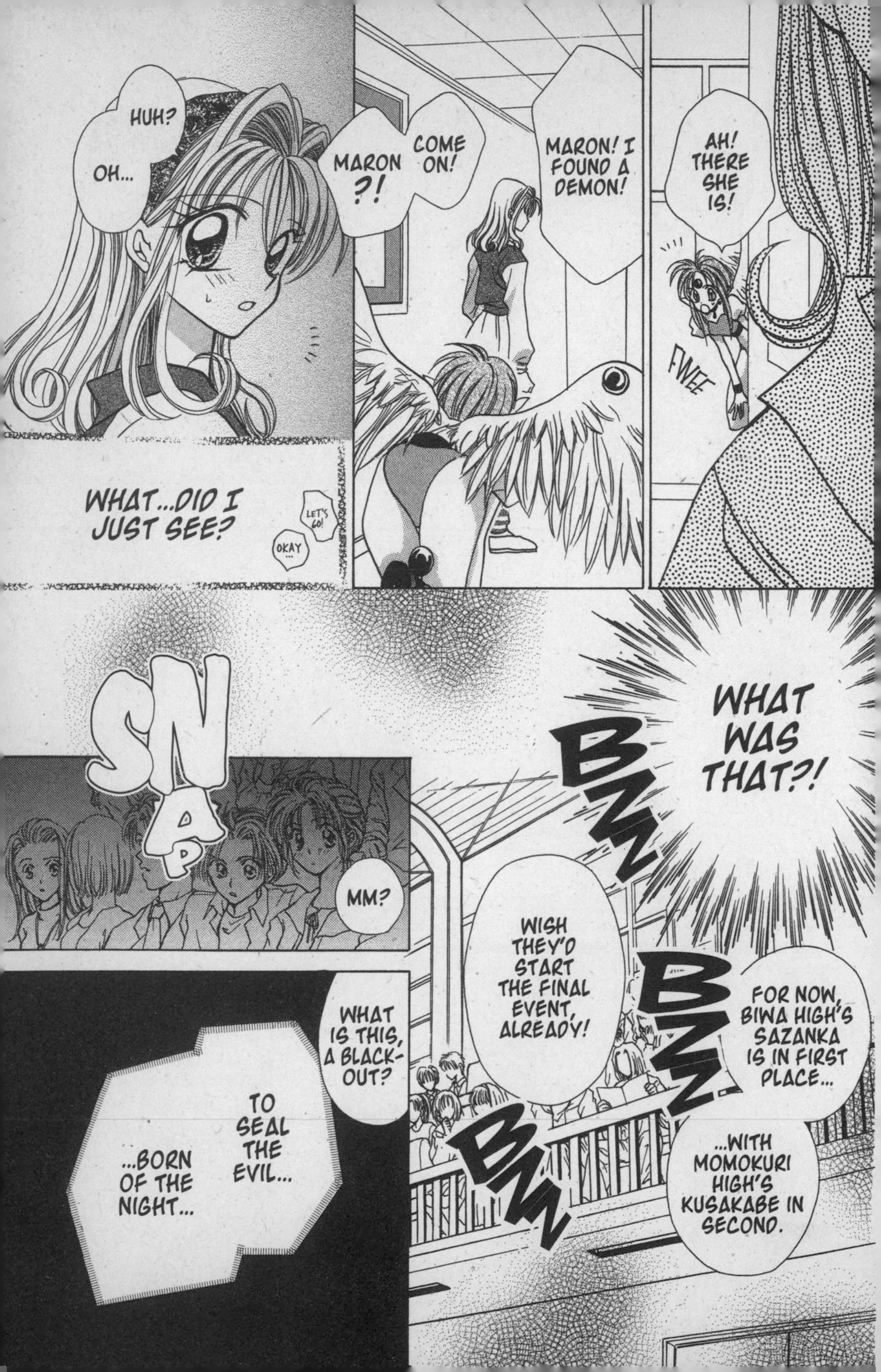
AH! THERE SHE IS!
FWEE
MARON! I FOUND A DEMON!
COME ON!
MARON ?!
HUH?
OH...
WHAT...DID I JUST SEE?
LET'S GO!
OKAY...
WHAT WAS THAT?!
FOR NOW, BIWA HIGH'S SAZANKA IS IN FIRST PLACE...
...WITH MOMOKURI HIGH'S KUSAKABE IN SECOND.
WISH THEY'D START THE FINAL EVENT, ALREADY!
SNAP
MM?
WHAT IS THIS, A BLACK-OUT?
TO SEAL THE EVIL...
...BORN OF THE NIGHT...

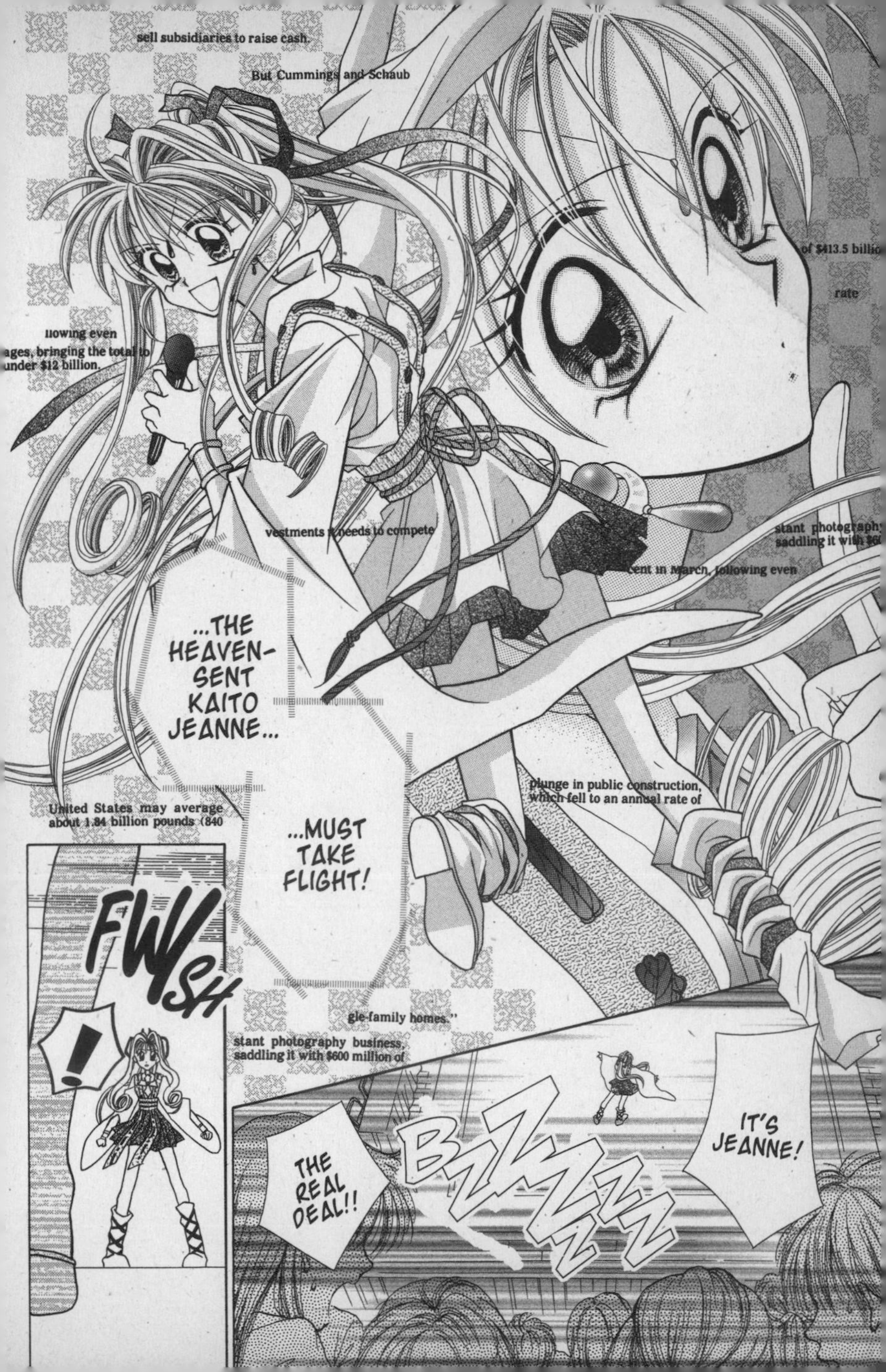
...THE HEAVEN-SENT KAITO JEANNE...
...MUST TAKE FLIGHT!
IT'S JEANNE!
BZZZZZ
THE REAL DEAL!!
FWISH
!

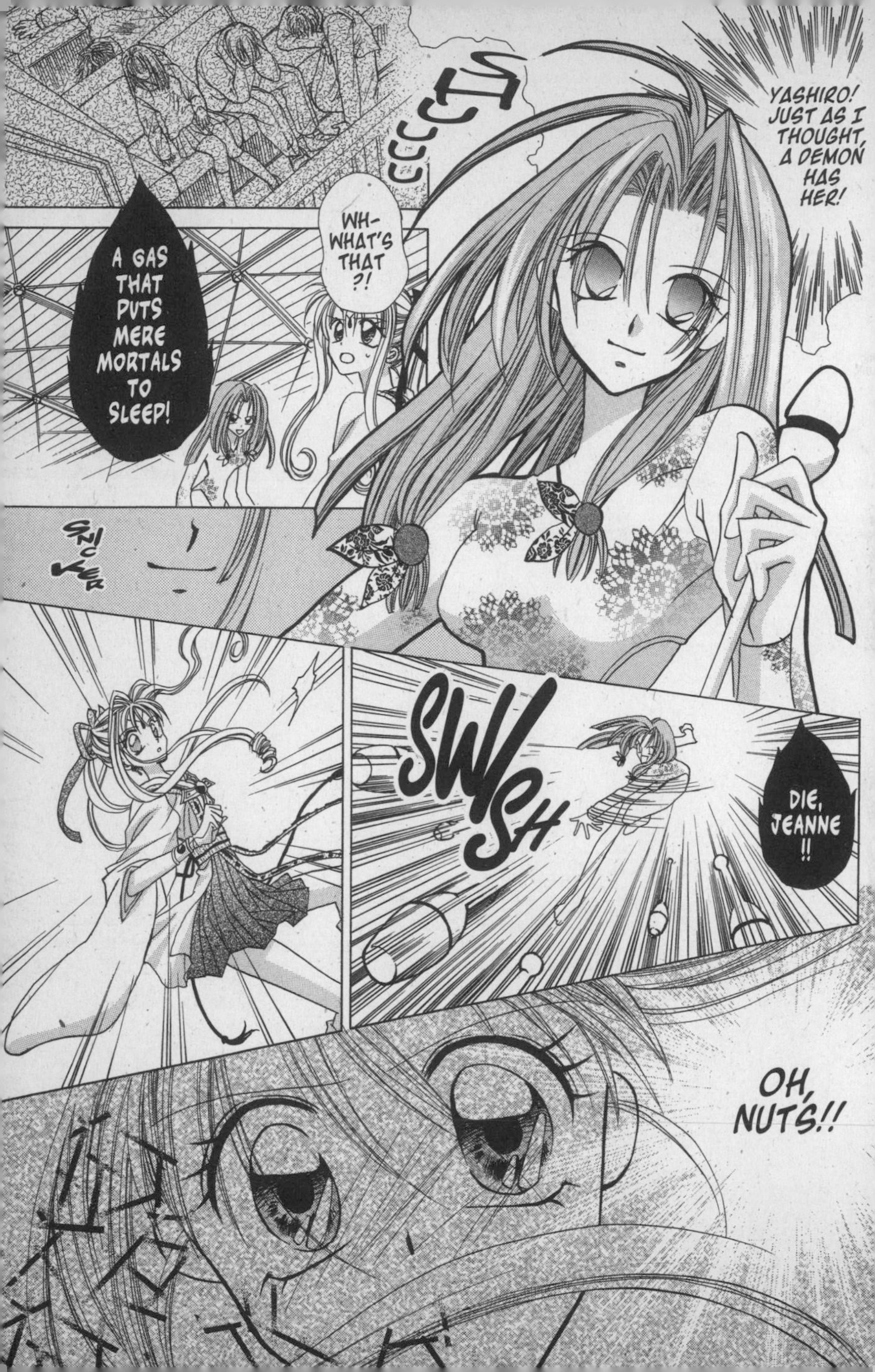
YASHIRO! JUST AS I THOUGHT, A DEMON HAS HER!
SHUUUU
WH-WHAT'S THAT?!
A GAS THAT PUTS MERE MORTALS TO SLEEP!
SNICKER
DIE, JEANNE!!
SWISH
OH, NUTS!!

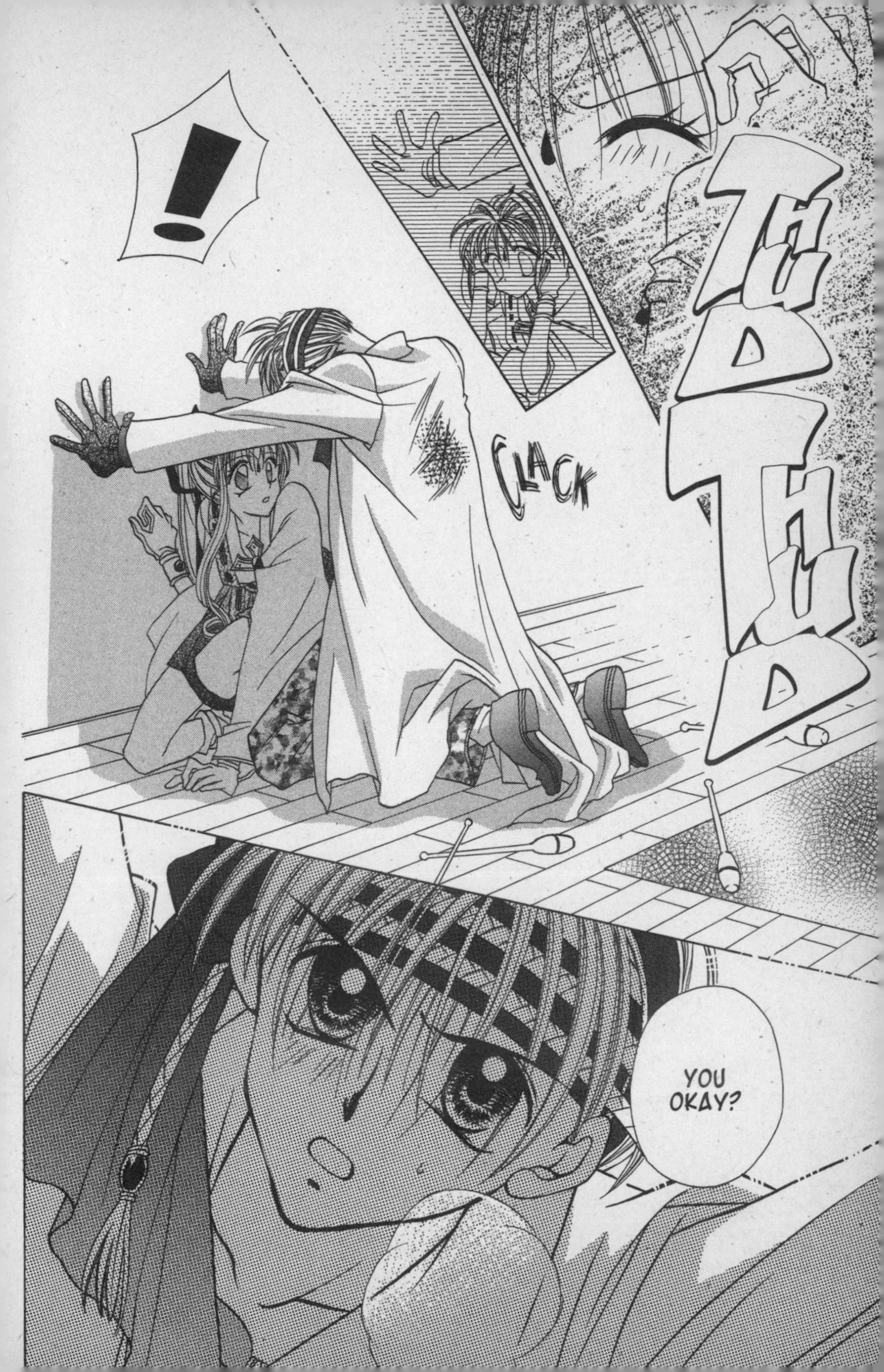
THUD THUD
CLACK
!
YOU OKAY?

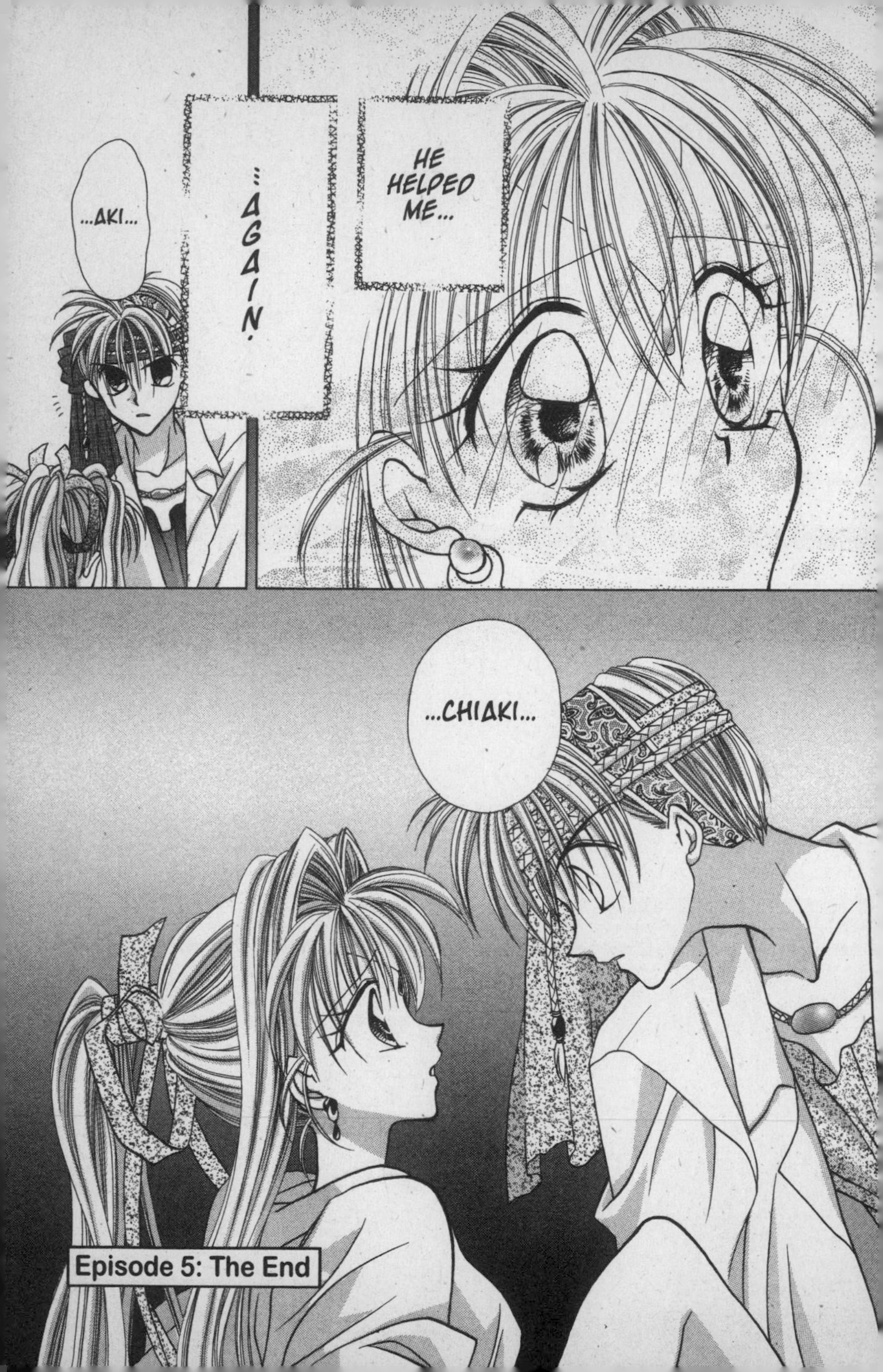

HE HELPED ME...
...AGAIN!
...AKI...
...CHIAKI...
Episode 5: The End

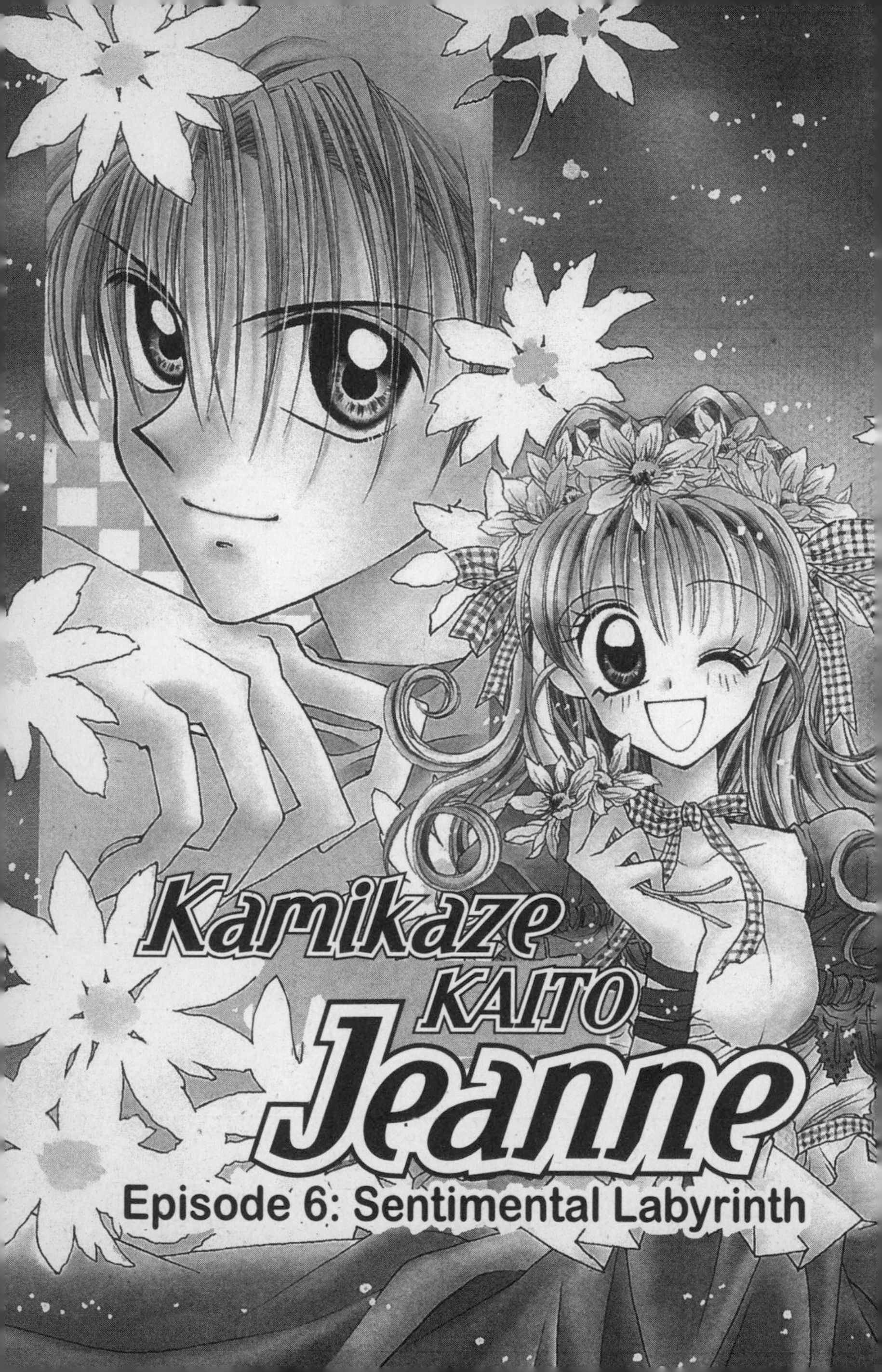
Kamikaze
KAITO
Jeanne
Episode 6: Sentimental Labyrinth

What's the deal with the chess pieces?

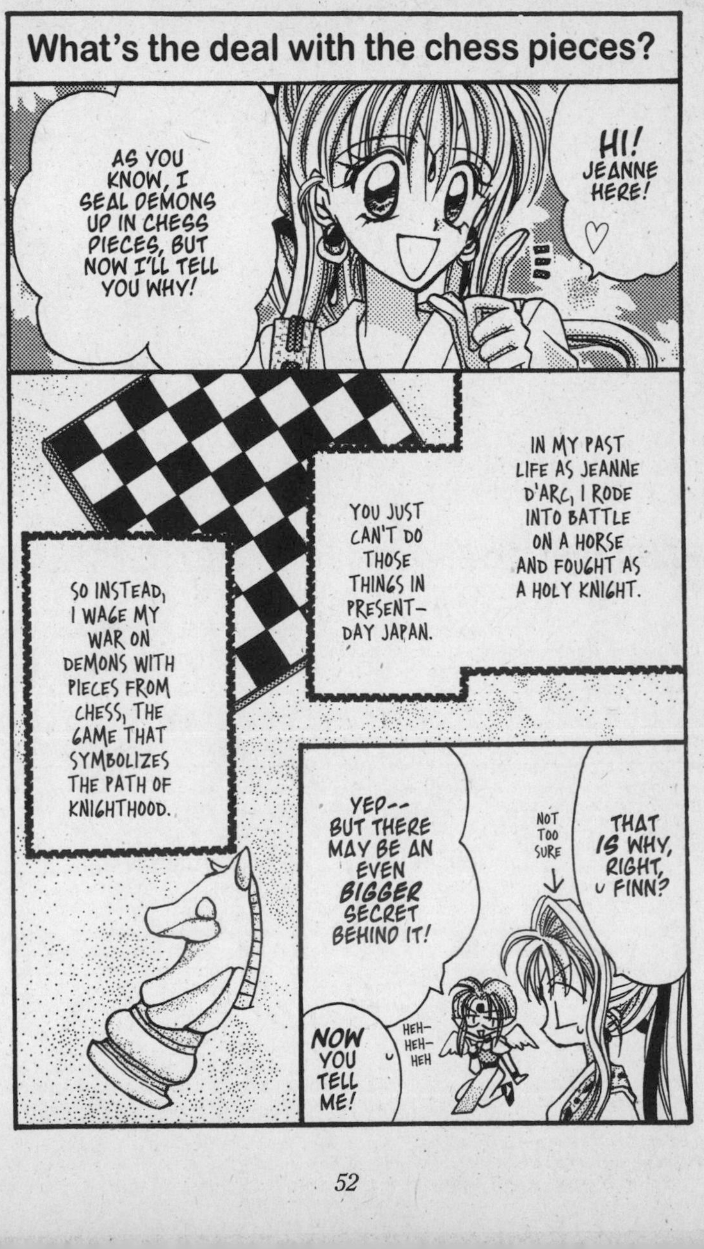
HI! JEANNE HERE! ♥
AS YOU KNOW, I SEAL DEMONS UP IN CHESS PIECES, BUT NOW I'LL TELL YOU WHY!
IN MY PAST LIFE AS JEANNE D'ARC, I RODE INTO BATTLE ON A HORSE AND FOUGHT AS A HOLY KNIGHT.
YOU JUST CAN'T DO THOSE THINGS IN PRESENT-DAY JAPAN.
SO INSTEAD, I WAGE MY WAR ON DEMONS WITH PIECES FROM CHESS, THE GAME THAT SYMBOLIZES THE PATH OF KNIGHTHOOD.
THAT *IS* WHY, RIGHT, FINN?
NOT TOO SURE
YEP-- BUT THERE MAY BE AN EVEN *BIGGER* SECRET BEHIND IT!
HEH-HEH-HEH
NOW YOU TELL ME!

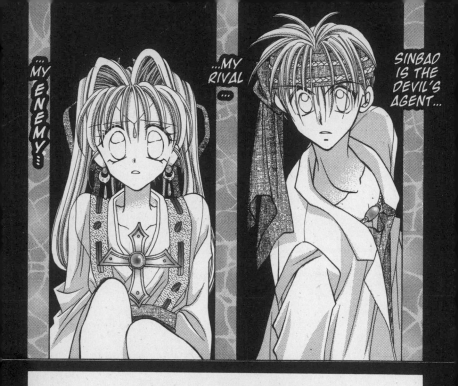

"...MY ENEMY..."

"...MY RIVAL..."

SINBAD IS THE DEVIL'S AGENT...

Episode 6: SENTIMENTAL LABYRINTH
CATCH COPY: "LET'S ALL GET HAPPY..."

The title page artwork for this story was on sale at Ribon's Summer Caravan (which I talked about in volume one's sidebars) as reproduced original artwork, and it sold like hotcakes! Actually, it nearly sold out, which pleases me to no end. ♡ (And episode three's title page art was used as the art on a desk pad, while episode two's was made into a phone card!) My goal is to change the atmosphere of the title page art for every episode, so a lotta time and effort goes into the title page each time. Of all the work that I get to do in color, that's gotta be my fave. ♡ This time around, my line of thinking while drawing the title page was, "Aim for SuperRibon!!" and "Ribonesque" artwork. Maron-chan is cute here, right? I just wanna give her a hug. ♡KYAAA! (By the way, the overall concept for the picture was to have the guy look so cool, you want to be embraced by him, and to have the girl look so cute, you wanna reach out and give her a hug!!) And the concept behind the story and the art together (i.e. the manga) this time out was, "If you're cool, anything is okay!" (LOL) Even so, Chiaki (Chi-sama) as depicted on this title page seems to be flashing us an indecent smile. Creating the story was fun, as it finally feels like the relationship between the two of them is moving forward. At first, Maron-chan feels betrayed by him and I got a lot of feedback from Chi-sama's fans about that. I did feel a little sorry for him...Who knows how they feel about each other now? It's not like confessing his feelings to her still can make up for lying to her in the first place! Actually, I was angry at him, too...Oh yeah, I also have fun drawing the back-and-forth between Minazuki-kun and Chi-sama, because Chi-sama sees Minazuki as a "cute toy." (LOL) I almost forgot! At first, I hadn't even planned on writing Minazuki into the series, but my editor, who doesn't care for the apparently womanizing Chiaki, suggested I intro a young male character who's the exact opposite of Chiaki, namely, who has a pure heart, which will somehow make the readers see Chiaki in a softer light. Fine, except that whenever the episodes run on too long, my editor is always quick to order me to cut the "Minazuki pages!" Such is life...The pages that I like best here are...hmm...there are a lot of 'em! Okay, I like the page with, "...I command thee, in God's name..." and the one with, "...another piece of bogus beauty..." Hmm...Oh! And, page 82's "Liar!" I think it took me about four hours to do that♡(So what?! HIYAAA! Daruma doll) Sorry about that...I'm sleepy. ZZZ...Okay, one more thing. Recently, I've been getting fan letters saying things like, "It must be fun working on a monthly magazine like Ribon, rather than a weekly!" Believe me, all of us serial manga artists are busy!! Granted, serialized weekly stories have a higher total page count than the monthlies, but Ribon, in any case, makes up for it by making me do special original artwork for prizes, sidebars, covers, story preview art, etc. It's a lot of work!

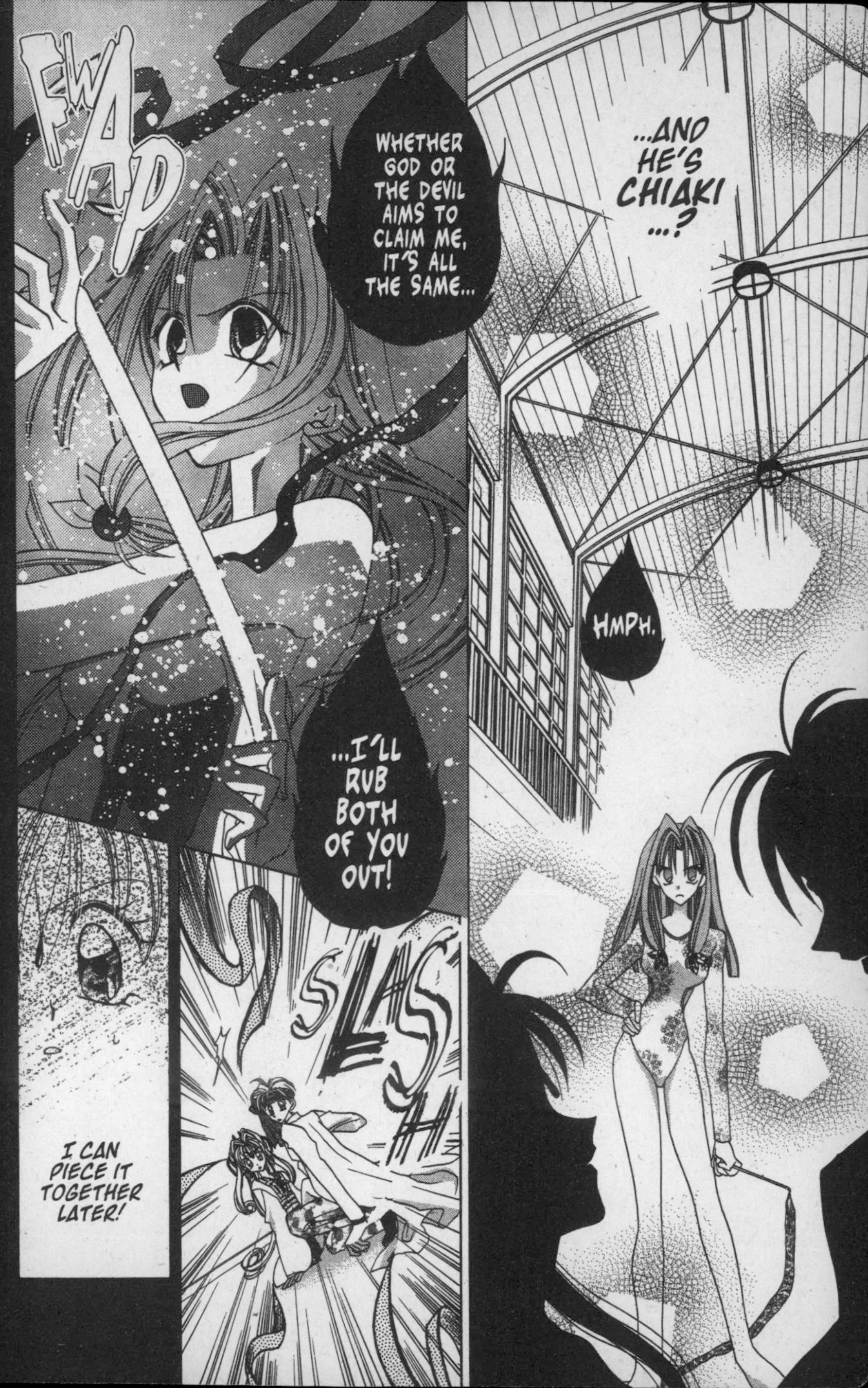
...AND HE'S CHIAKI ...?
HMPH.
FWAP
WHETHER GOD OR THE DEVIL AIMS TO CLAIM ME, IT'S ALL THE SAME...
...I'LL RUB BOTH OF YOU OUT!
SLASH
I CAN PIECE IT TOGETHER LATER!

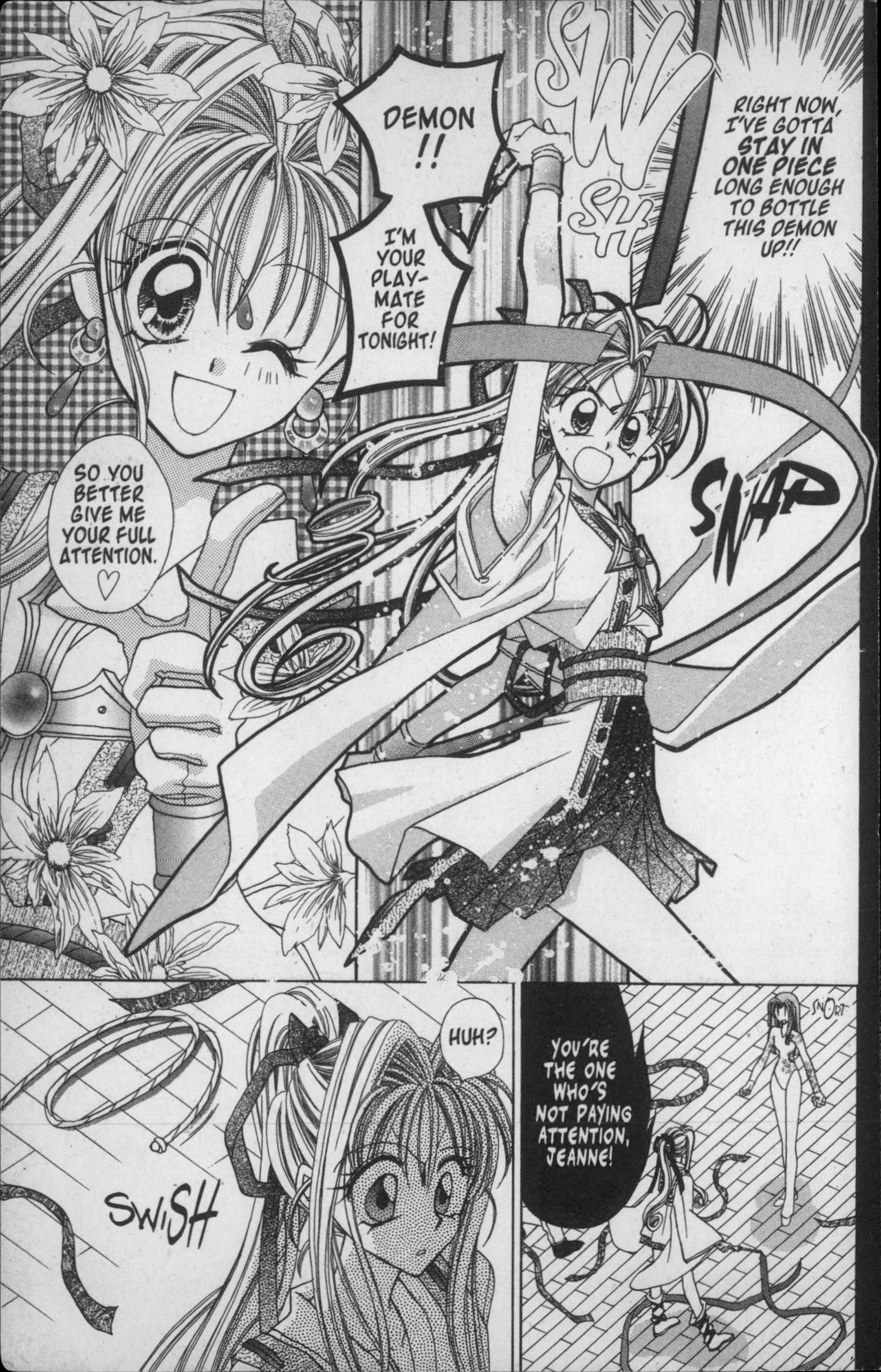
RIGHT NOW, I'VE GOTTA STAY IN ONE PIECE LONG ENOUGH TO BOTTLE THIS DEMON UP!!
SWISH
DEMON !!
I'M YOUR PLAY-MATE FOR TONIGHT!
SNAP
SO YOU BETTER GIVE ME YOUR FULL ATTENTION. ♡
SNORT
YOU'RE THE ONE WHO'S NOT PAYING ATTENTION, JEANNE!
HUH?
SWISH

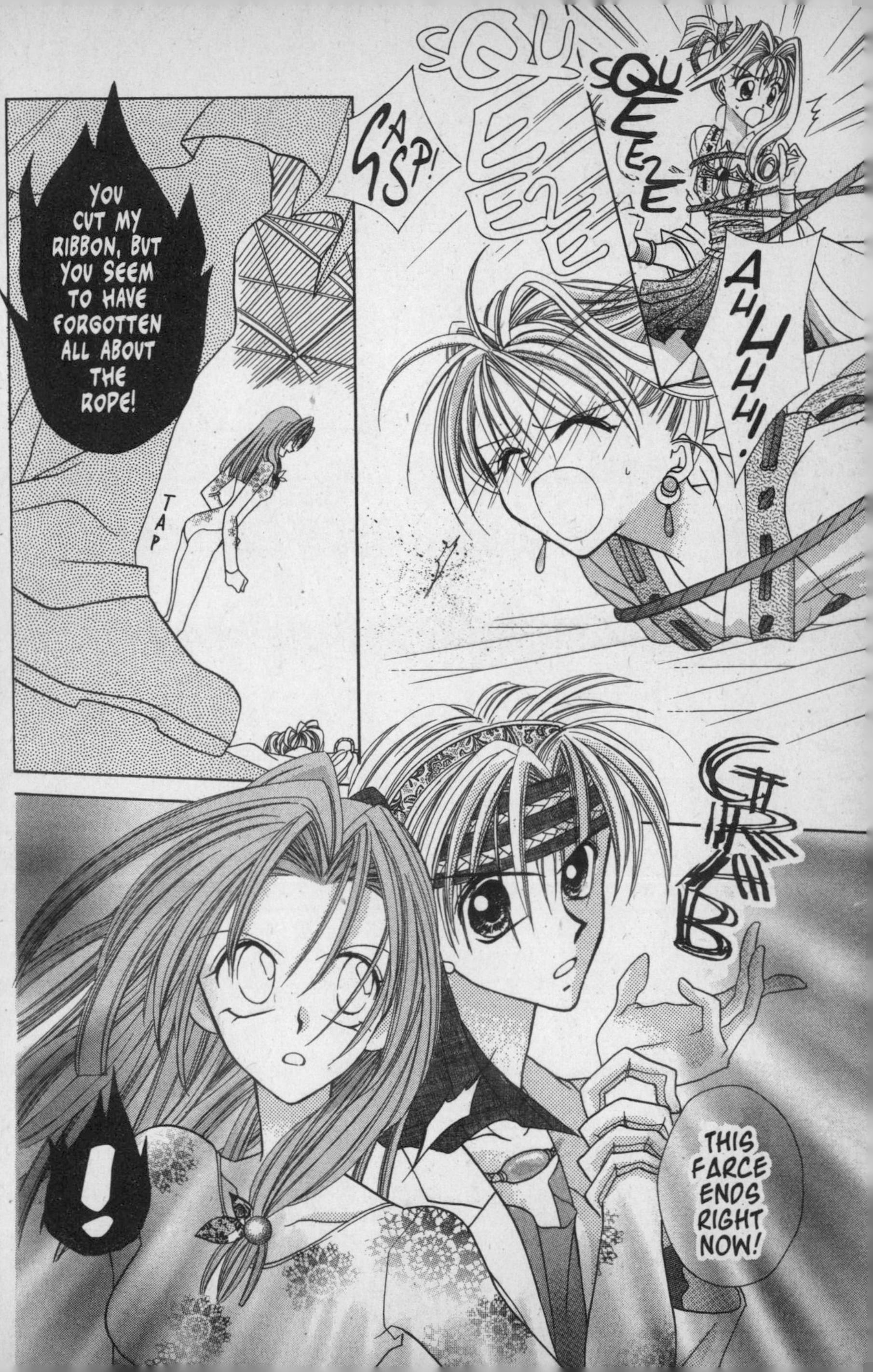
SQUEEZE
SQUEEZE
GASP!
AUHHHH!
YOU CUT MY RIBBON, BUT YOU SEEM TO HAVE FORGOTTEN ALL ABOUT THE ROPE!
TAP
GRAB
THIS FARCE ENDS RIGHT NOW!
!

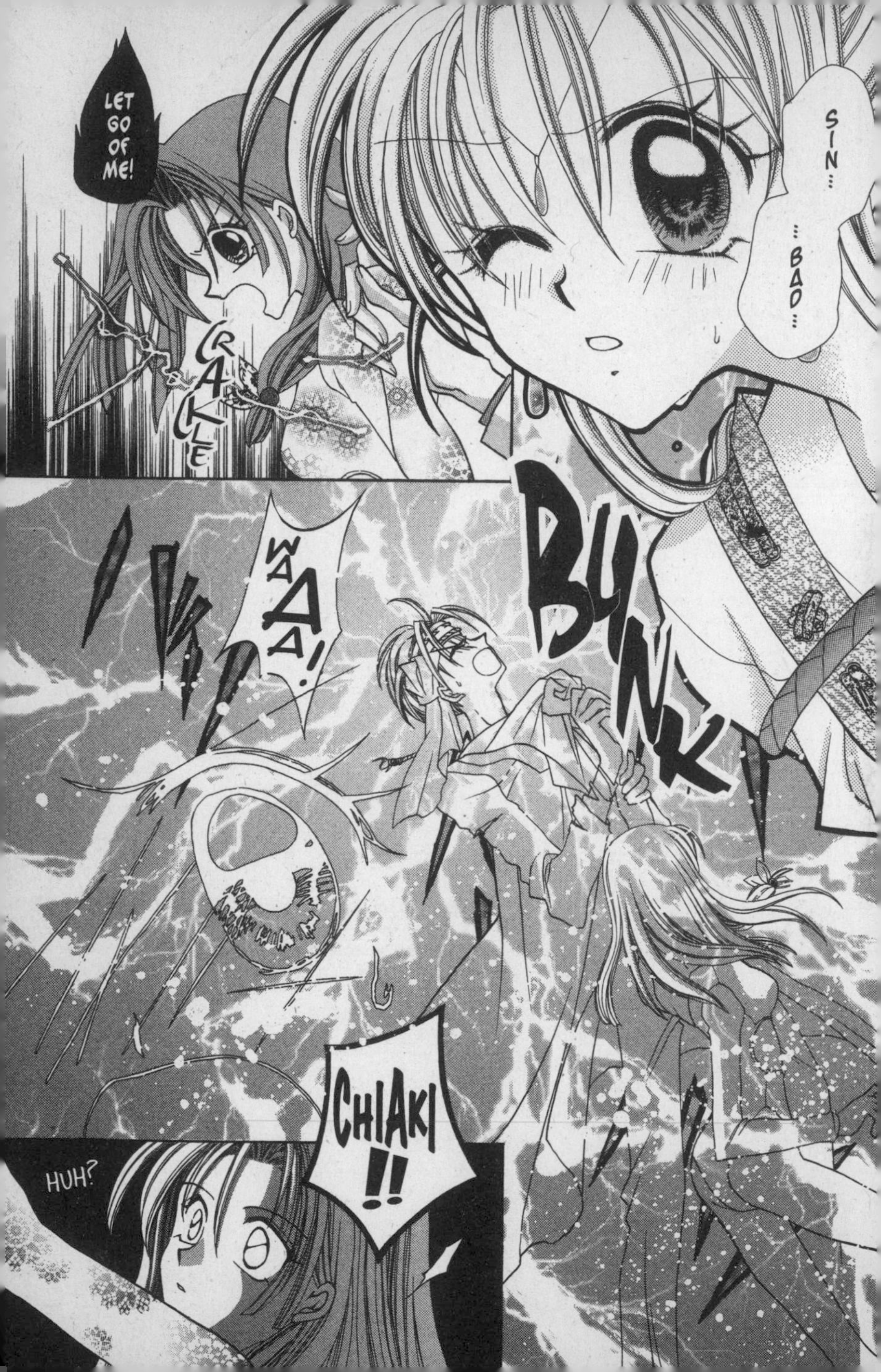
SIN...
...BAD...
LET GO OF ME!
CRACKLE
BUNK
WAAA!
CHIAKI!!
HUH?

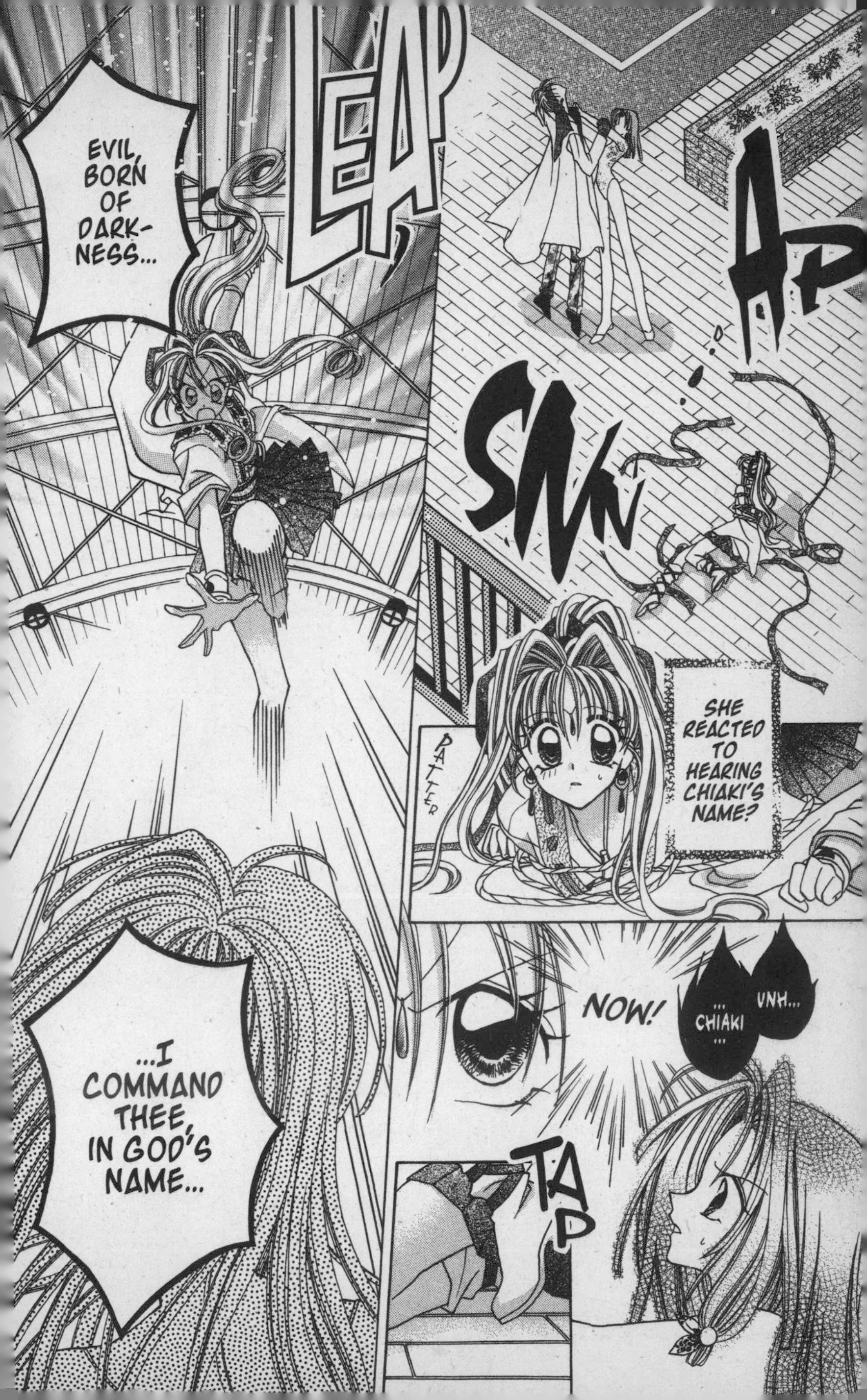
SN
AP
RATTER
SHE REACTED TO HEARING CHIAKI'S NAME?
UNH...
...CHIAKI...
NOW!
TAP
LEAP
EVIL, BORN OF DARK-NESS...
...I COMMAND THEE, IN GOD'S NAME...

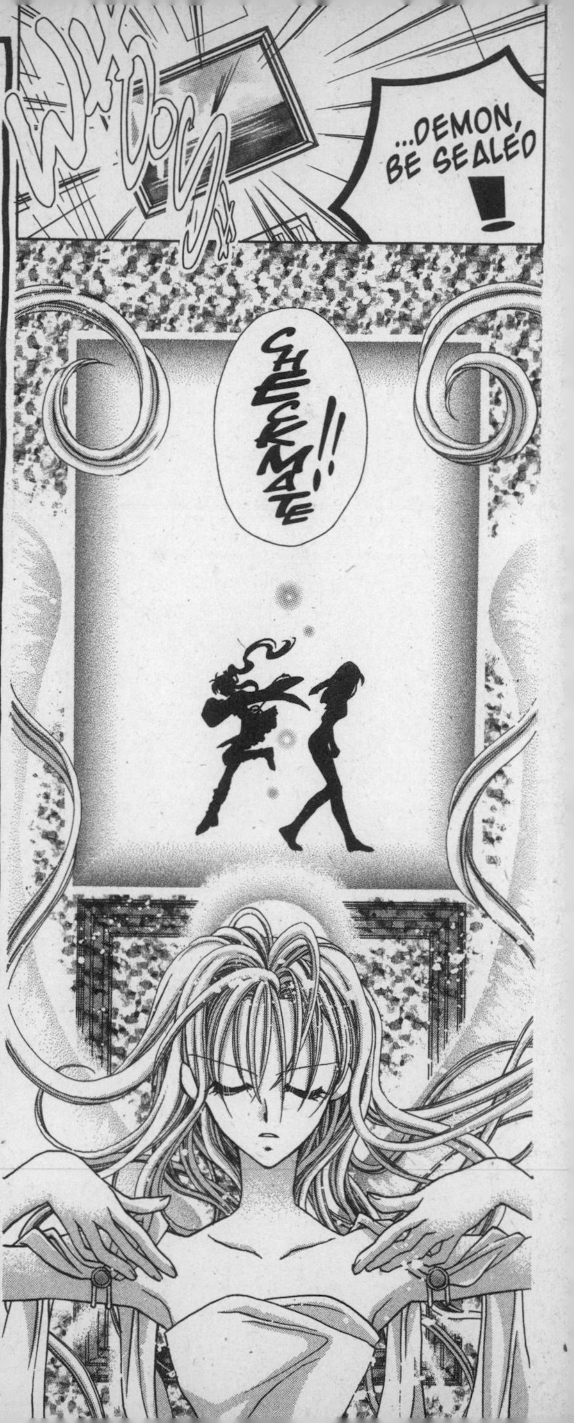
...DEMON, BE SEALED!
CHECKMATE!!

2

To be honest, though, I'm really happy that JEANNE is popular. It lets me keep the story going, I get to write these columns, I get to work in color, etc. But all that aside, I did think, for some reason...for some reason... "I'm gonna make a story so serious, they'll never be able to do an anime version of it!!" At the time, I was under the impression that anime just consisted of a lot of fight scenes strung together. (I don't watch much TV anime...but the ones that I do like, I **love**. ♡ I am, after all, a manga artist!) I also thought, "Maybe I'll make this story into a real fantasy piece!" like in other manga which share slight similarities to JEANNE (as I mentioned in the first sidebar), but I would put a whole new spin on it. But the thing is...hmm...actually, I don't read much fantasy manga. I like it, but I just don't read it much. Why, I wonder? So for now, anyway, when I try doing straight fantasy, even if I do my best, it...well, it kinda stinks. So I've gotta try even harder! (Ah! But don't misunderstand! I don't particularly hate any manga that bears a resemblance (as I've been told about two or three different series) to mine. As a matter of fact, I actually like one of the titles in question...which makes it even more frustrating that I can't really kick out the jams when it comes to doing my own fantasy piece! Sorry...Anyway, there's one title that I've read and enjoyed, but it came out after JEANNE started being published, so there's no way I could've imitated or been influenced by it. See, I told you I can't stand losing! So anyway, when I was first approached about turning JEANNE into anime, I was in a bind, to be honest, about whether to allow it. But between the staff at Toei, who gave me the reassuring feeling during negotiations that the original material would be treated with respect and TLC, and the director-to-be, Umezawa-san, who told me, "I'm aiming for an anime that's never been done before, a story about a beautiful young girl that busts all the clichés we know about the genre," I was persuaded. Those may not have been Umezawa-san's exact words, but you get the point...Yes, the people from Toei won me over with their enthusiasm and I decided to entrust them with JEANNE.

CONTINUED>>>

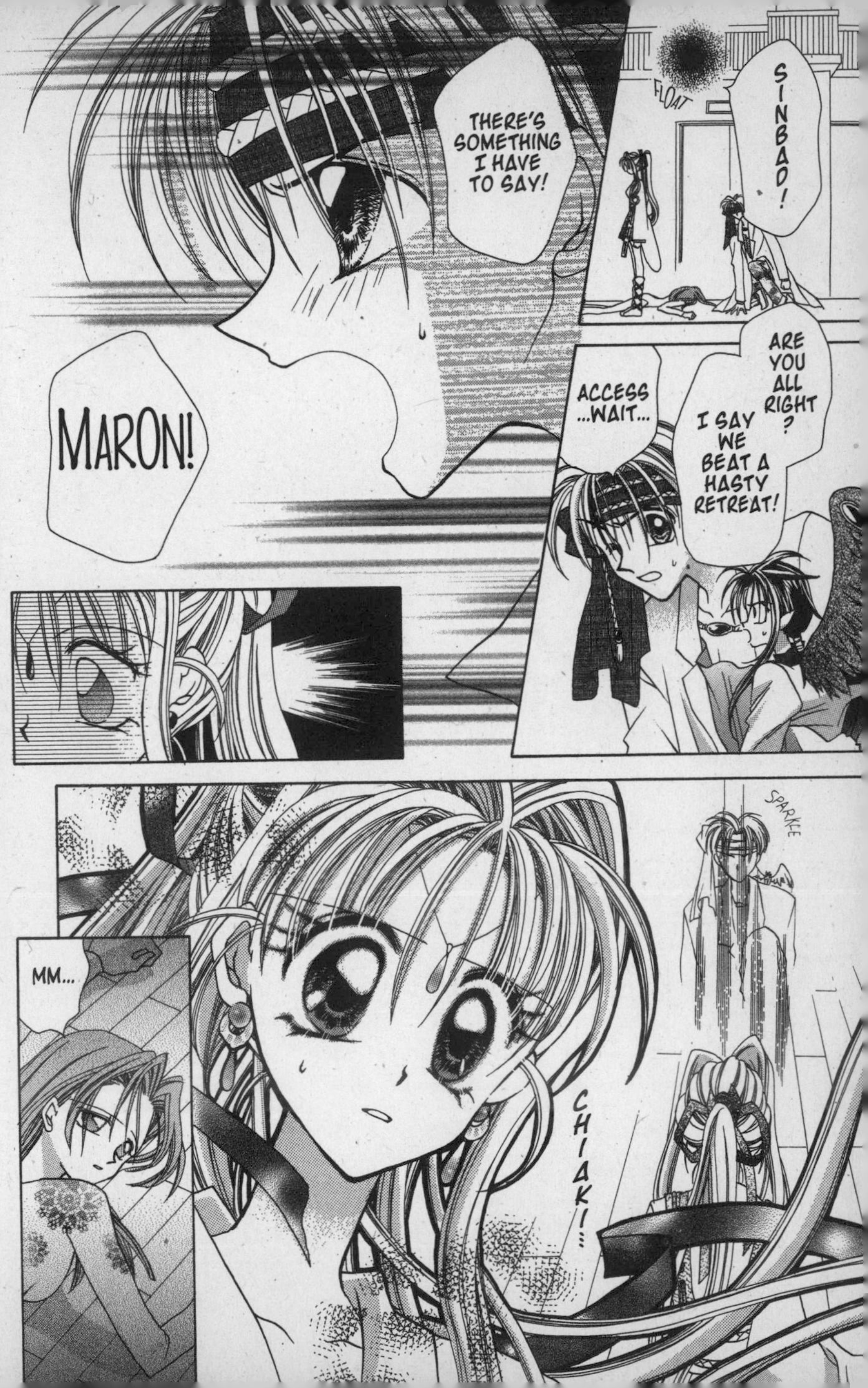
FLOAT
SINBAD!
ARE YOU ALL RIGHT?
I SAY WE BEAT A HASTY RETREAT!
ACCESS ...WAIT...
THERE'S SOMETHING I HAVE TO SAY!
MARON!
SPARKLE
CHIAKI...
MM...

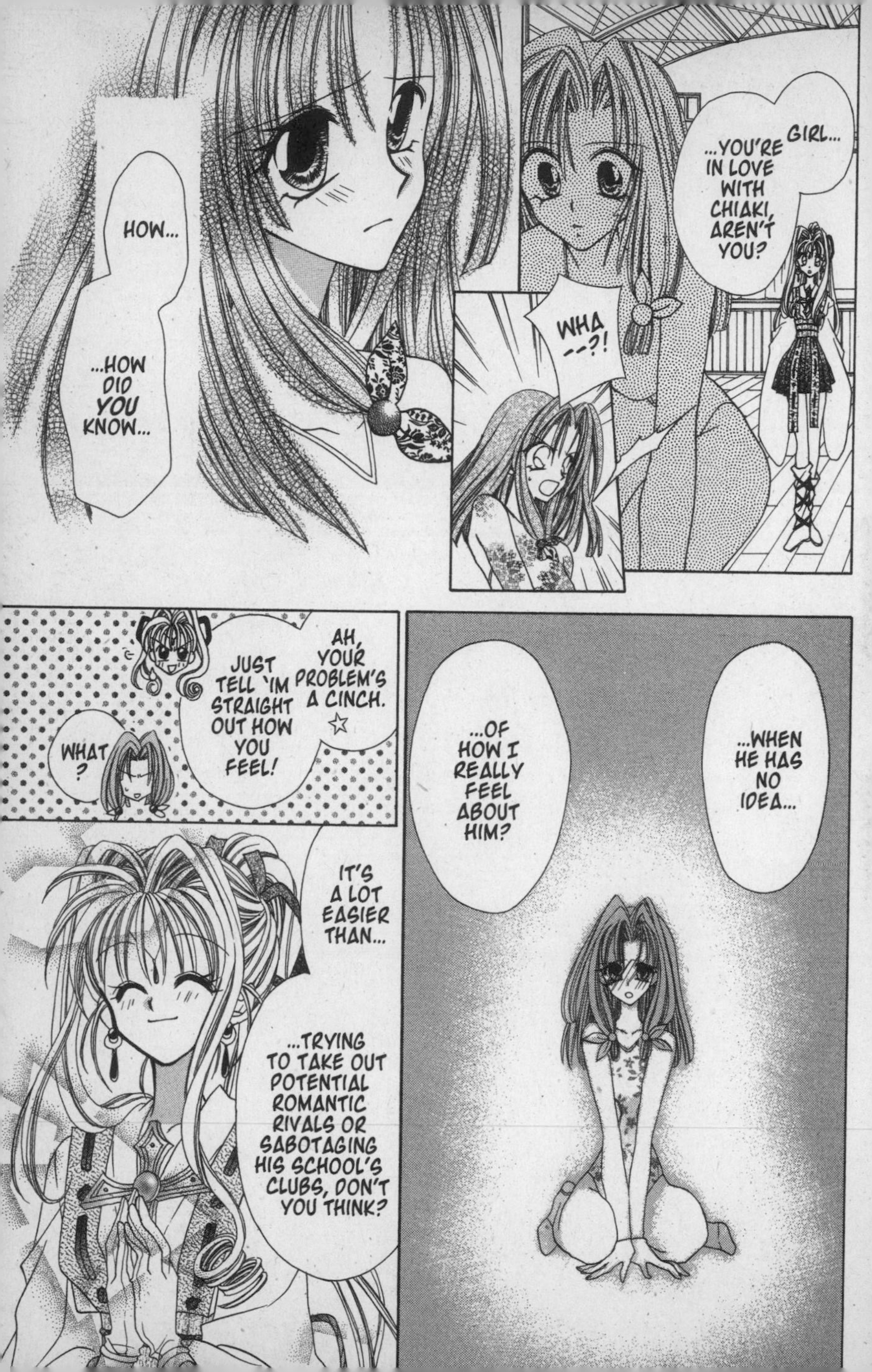
GIRL...
...YOU'RE IN LOVE WITH CHIAKI, AREN'T YOU?
WHA--?!
HOW...
...HOW DID YOU KNOW...
...WHEN HE HAS NO IDEA...
...OF HOW I REALLY FEEL ABOUT HIM?
AH, YOUR PROBLEM'S A CINCH. ☆
JUST TELL 'IM STRAIGHT OUT HOW YOU FEEL!
WHAT?
IT'S A LOT EASIER THAN...
...TRYING TO TAKE OUT POTENTIAL ROMANTIC RIVALS OR SABOTAGING HIS SCHOOL'S CLUBS, DON'T YOU THINK?

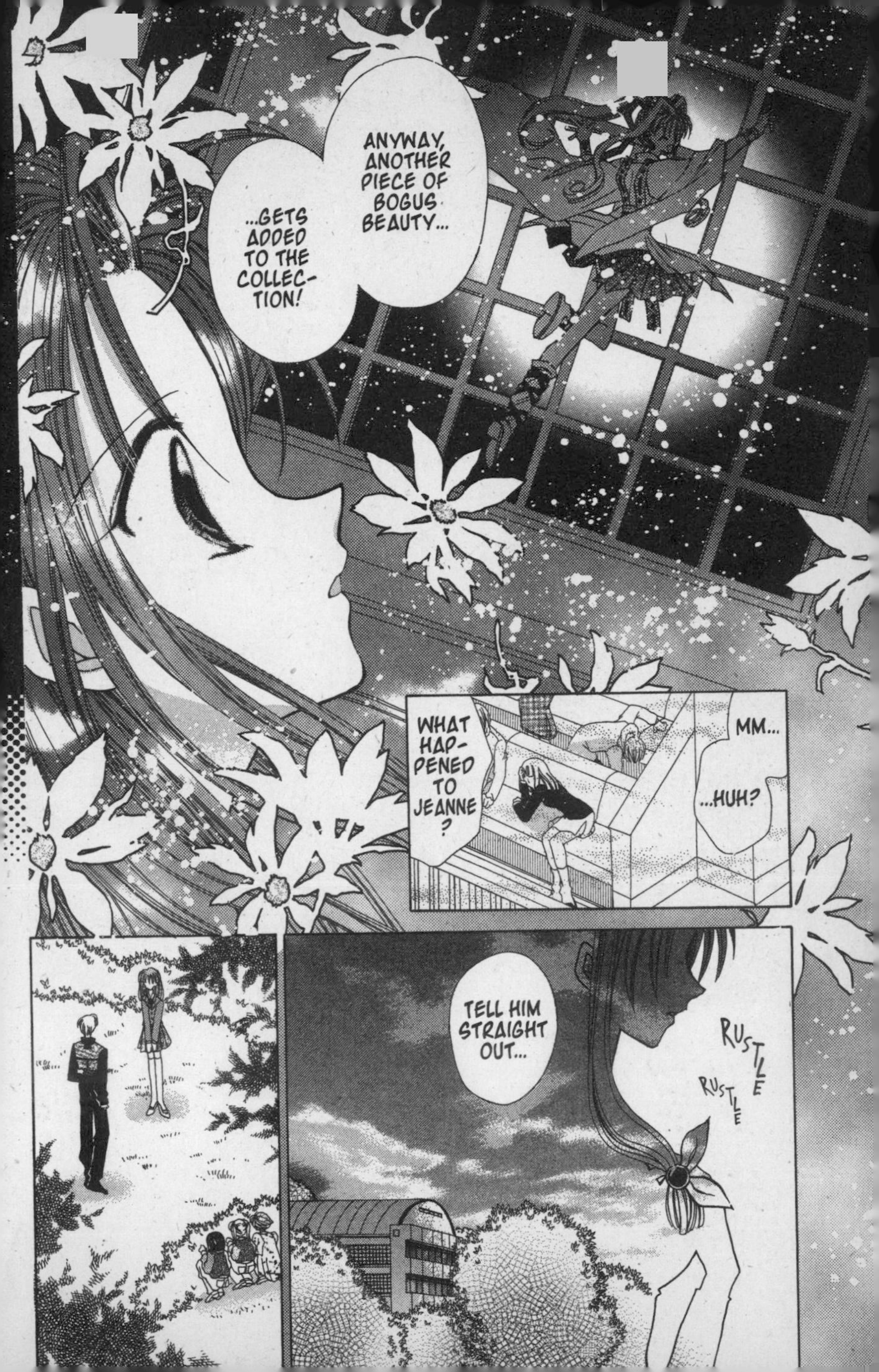
ANYWAY, ANOTHER PIECE OF BOGUS BEAUTY...
...GETS ADDED TO THE COLLEC-TION!
MM...
...HUH?
WHAT HAP-PENED TO JEANNE?
RUSTLE
RUSTLE
TELL HIM STRAIGHT OUT...

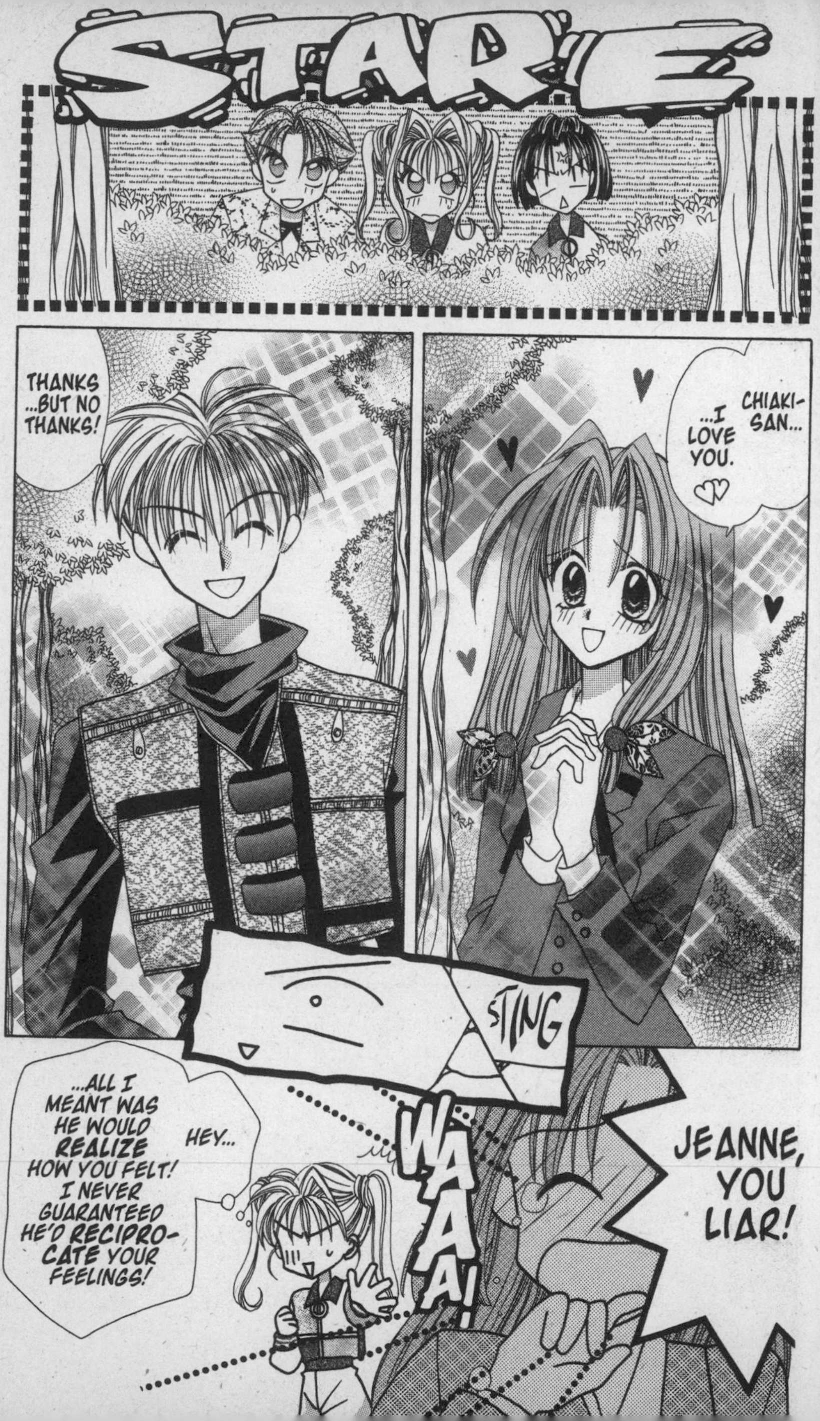
STARE
CHIAKI-SAN... ...I LOVE YOU.
THANKS ...BUT NO THANKS!
STING
JEANNE, YOU LIAR!
WAAA!
HEY...
...ALL I MEANT WAS HE WOULD REALIZE HOW YOU FELT! I NEVER GUARANTEED HE'D RECIPROCATE YOUR FEELINGS!

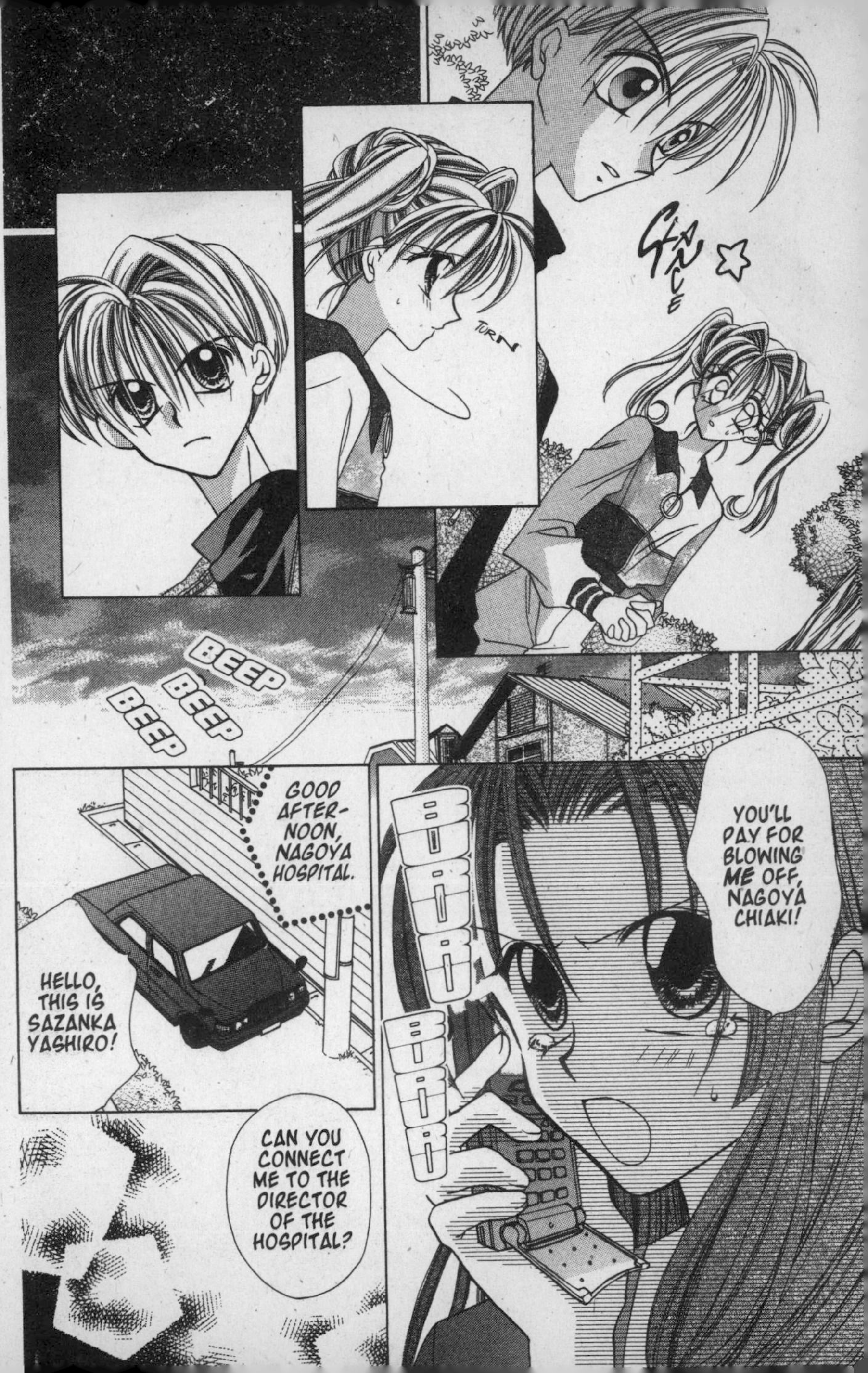
GLANCE
TURN
BEEP
BEEP
BEEP
YOU'LL PAY FOR BLOWING ME OFF, NAGOYA CHIAKI!
BURURU
BURURU
GOOD AFTERNOON, NAGOYA HOSPITAL.
HELLO, THIS IS SAZANKA YASHIRO!
CAN YOU CONNECT ME TO THE DIRECTOR OF THE HOSPITAL?

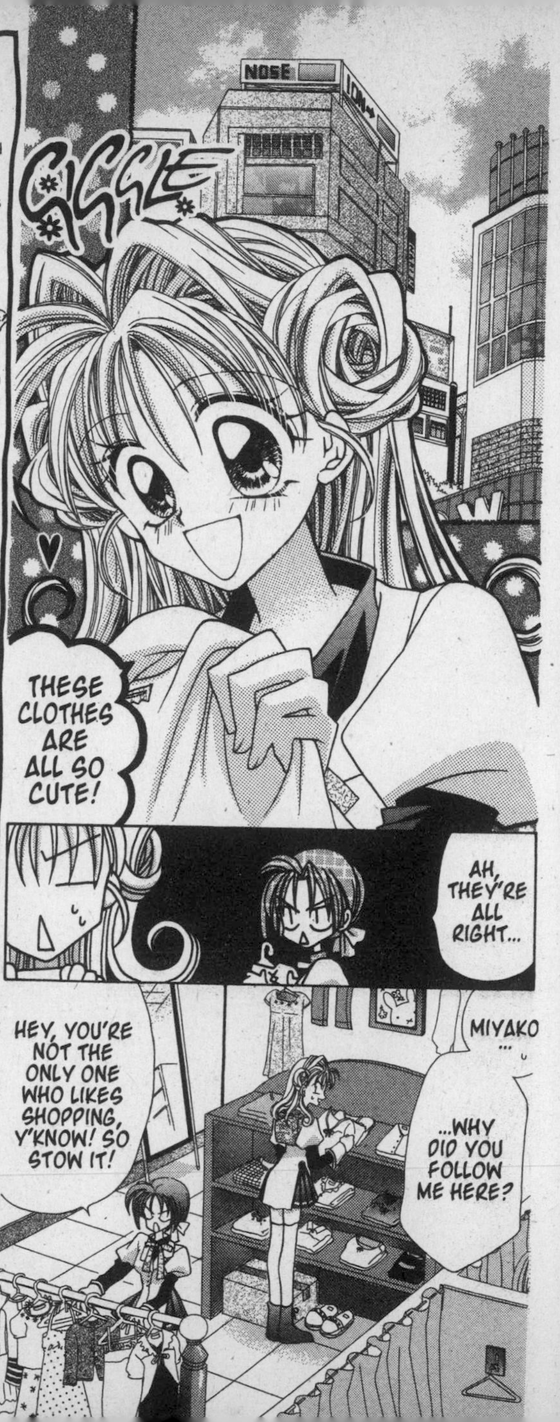
NOSE
GIGGLE
THESE CLOTHES ARE ALL SO CUTE!
AH, THEY'RE ALL RIGHT...
MIYAKO ...
...WHY DID YOU FOLLOW ME HERE?
HEY, YOU'RE NOT THE ONLY ONE WHO LIKES SHOPPING, Y'KNOW! SO STOW IT!

3 Even my editor once told me that, "JEANNE isn't really suited for anime," but one particular Toei employee (I'll call him "Toei-san"), like me, can't stand losing and likes taking on a good challenge. And I can get into that! What a cool guy! KYAAAA! Also, the director, Umezawa-san, has a daughter who's a JEANNE fan.♡(She sent me two letters before)<<I mean, before production on the anime began.

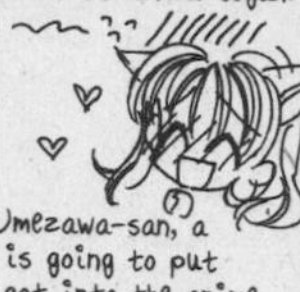

I'm sure that Umezawa-san, a real gentleman, is going to put everything he's got into the anime to satisfy his daughter as well as everyone else! He directed the popular anime, "Neighborhood Tales."

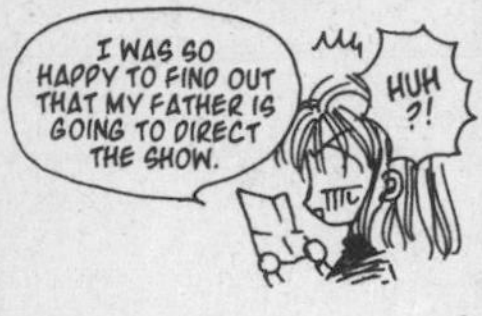
I WAS SO HAPPY TO FIND OUT THAT MY FATHER IS GOING TO DIRECT THE SHOW.
HUH ?!

THANK YOU FOR THE LETTERS.♡

WOW! Okay, so what I'm trying to say is that for even those of you who are opposed to an animated JEANNE, check it out, anyway! It'll be a lotta fun! The scripts, the character designs, etc. are really great, I mean, great enough for me to get a warm, tingly feeling all over! Sure, there are a few minor alterations in characters and so on, but these differences are due to the anime staff's focusing on making the story easier to follow and even more interesting.

But I think most fans will be really pleased by this adaptation. (It's even occasionally moving.) I am sooo lucky. When people say, "Finally, it's here!" and the like, I think, "Yep. I'm glad I okayed it." 'Cause when everyone's happy, I'm totally thrilled. Thank you so much. And a special thank you goes out to everyone who sent me congratulatory presents to mark JEANNE's foray into anime! Takanashi Kirika-sama, I was overjoyed when I received the bouquet. I love you! KYAAA! Good luck on your new series! I'll be your fan forever! The yellow roses were beautiful.

CONTINUED>>> →

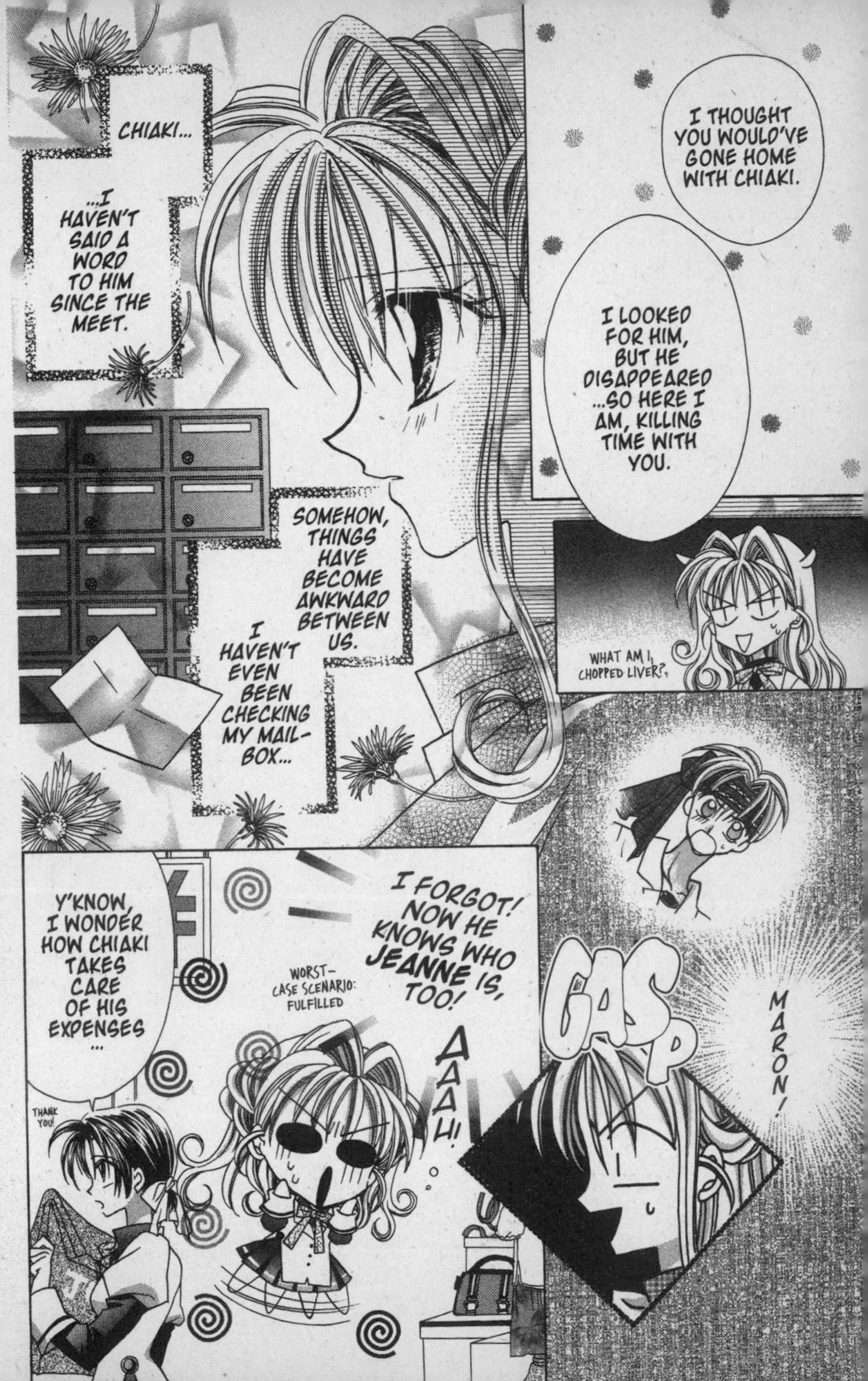

I THOUGHT YOU WOULD'VE GONE HOME WITH CHIAKI.
I LOOKED FOR HIM, BUT HE DISAPPEARED ...SO HERE I AM, KILLING TIME WITH YOU.
WHAT AM I, CHOPPED LIVER?
CHIAKI...
...I HAVEN'T SAID A WORD TO HIM SINCE THE MEET.
SOMEHOW, THINGS HAVE BECOME AWKWARD BETWEEN US.
I HAVEN'T EVEN BEEN CHECKING MY MAIL-BOX...
MARON!
GASP
I FORGOT! NOW HE KNOWS WHO JEANNE IS, TOO!
AAAH!
WORST-CASE SCENARIO: FULFILLED
Y'KNOW, I WONDER HOW CHIAKI TAKES CARE OF HIS EXPENSES...
THANK YOU!

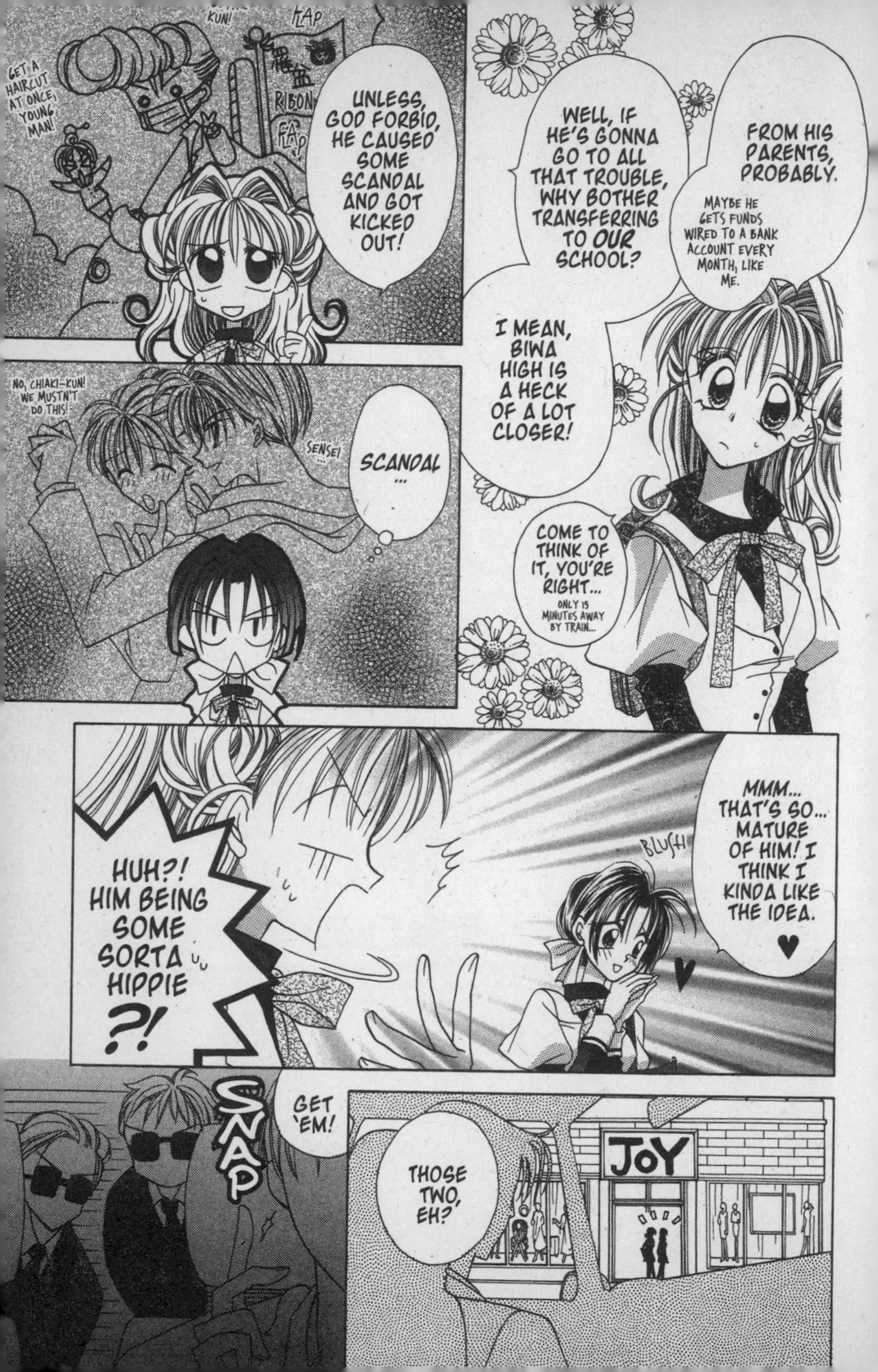
FROM HIS PARENTS, PROBABLY.
MAYBE HE GETS FUNDS WIRED TO A BANK ACCOUNT EVERY MONTH, LIKE ME.
WELL, IF HE'S GONNA GO TO ALL THAT TROUBLE, WHY BOTHER TRANSFERRING TO OUR SCHOOL?
I MEAN, BIWA HIGH IS A HECK OF A LOT CLOSER!
COME TO THINK OF IT, YOU'RE RIGHT...
ONLY 15 MINUTES AWAY BY TRAIN...
KUN!
FLAP
RIBON
FLAP
GET A HAIRCUT AT ONCE, YOUNG MAN!
UNLESS, GOD FORBID, HE CAUSED SOME SCANDAL AND GOT KICKED OUT!
NO, CHIAKI-KUN! WE MUSTN'T DO THIS!
SENSEI...
SCANDAL...
MMM... THAT'S SO... MATURE OF HIM! I THINK I KINDA LIKE THE IDEA. ♥
BLUSH
HUH?! HIM BEING SOME SORTA HIPPIE ?!
JOY
THOSE TWO, EH?
GET 'EM!
SNAP

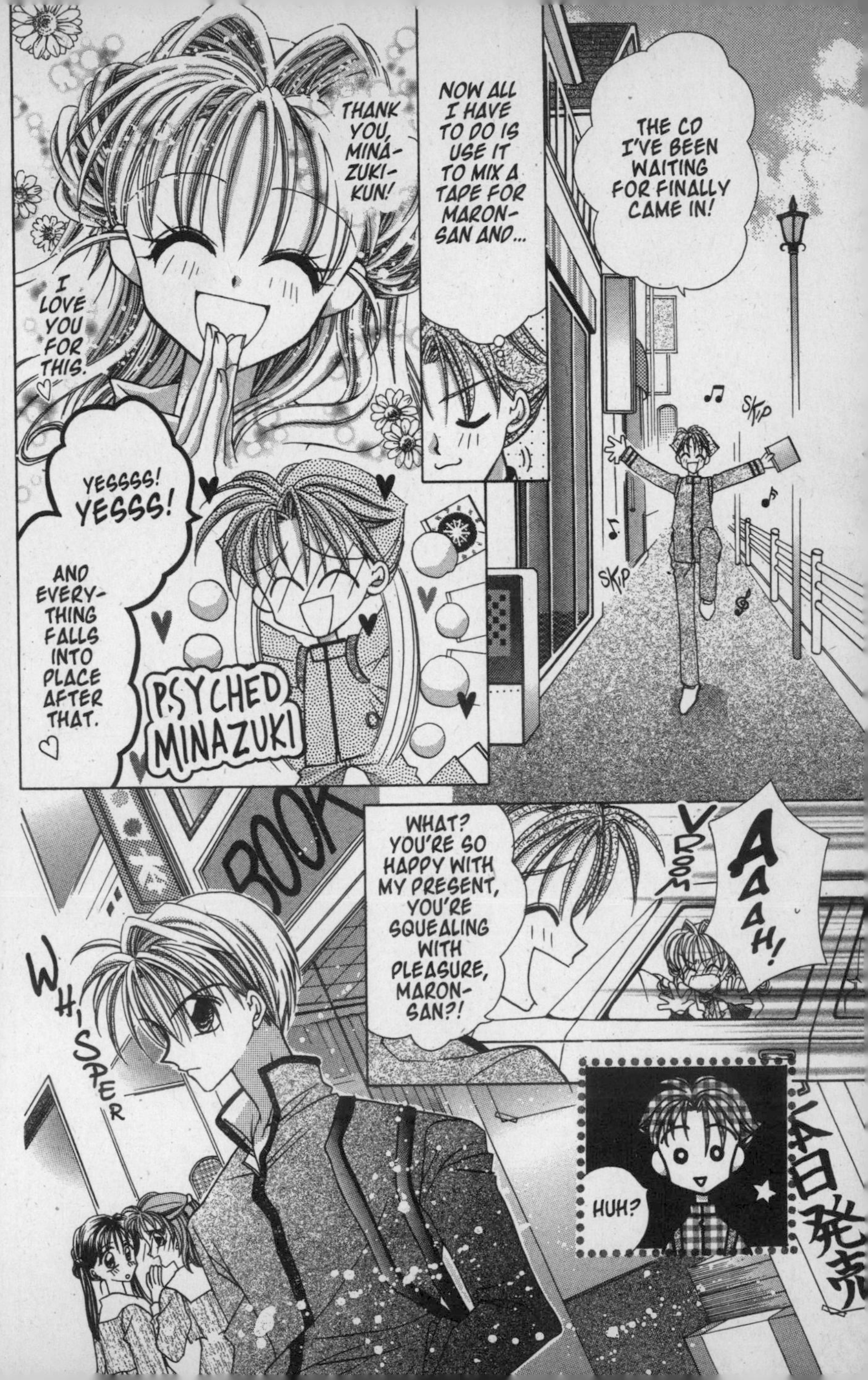
THE CD I'VE BEEN WAITING FOR FINALLY CAME IN!
SKIP
SKIP
NOW ALL I HAVE TO DO IS USE IT TO MIX A TAPE FOR MARON-SAN AND...
THANK YOU, MINÁ-ZUKI-KUN!
I LOVE YOU FOR THIS.
YESSSS! YESSS!
AND EVERYTHING FALLS INTO PLACE AFTER THAT.
PSYCHED MINAZUKI
AAAH!
VROOM
本日発売
HUH?
WHAT? YOU'RE SO HAPPY WITH MY PRESENT, YOU'RE SQUEALING WITH PLEASURE, MARON-SAN?!
BOOK
WHISPER

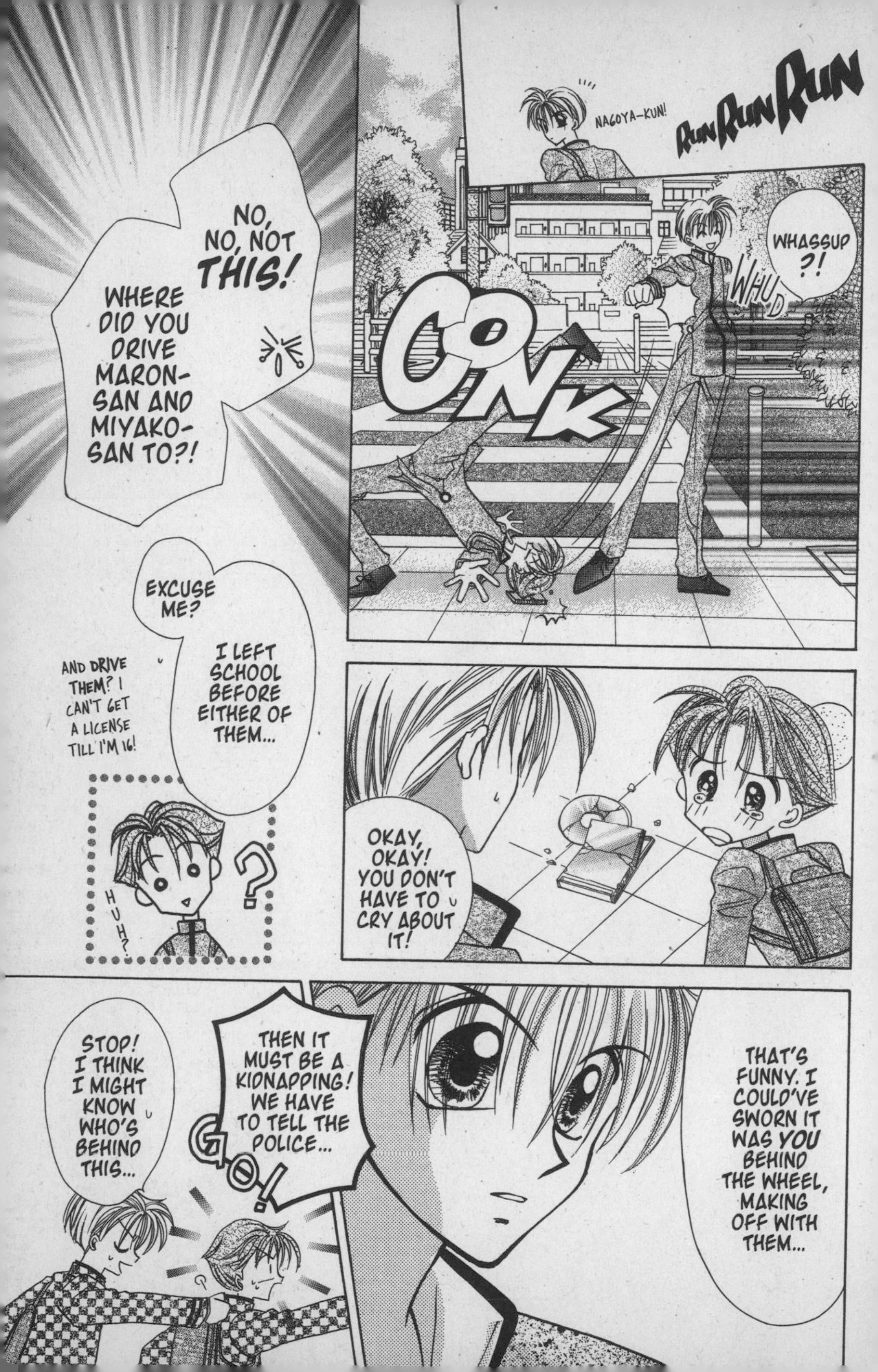
RUN RUN RUN
NAGOYA-KUN!
WHASSUP ?!
WHUD
CONK
OKAY, OKAY! YOU DON'T HAVE TO CRY ABOUT IT!
NO, NO, NOT THIS!
WHERE DID YOU DRIVE MARON-SAN AND MIYAKO-SAN TO?!
EXCUSE ME?
I LEFT SCHOOL BEFORE EITHER OF THEM...
AND DRIVE THEM? I CAN'T GET A LICENSE TILL I'M 16!
HUH?
THAT'S FUNNY. I COULD'VE SWORN IT WAS YOU BEHIND THE WHEEL, MAKING OFF WITH THEM...
THEN IT MUST BE A KIDNAPPING! WE HAVE TO TELL THE POLICE...
GO!
STOP! I THINK I MIGHT KNOW WHO'S BEHIND THIS...

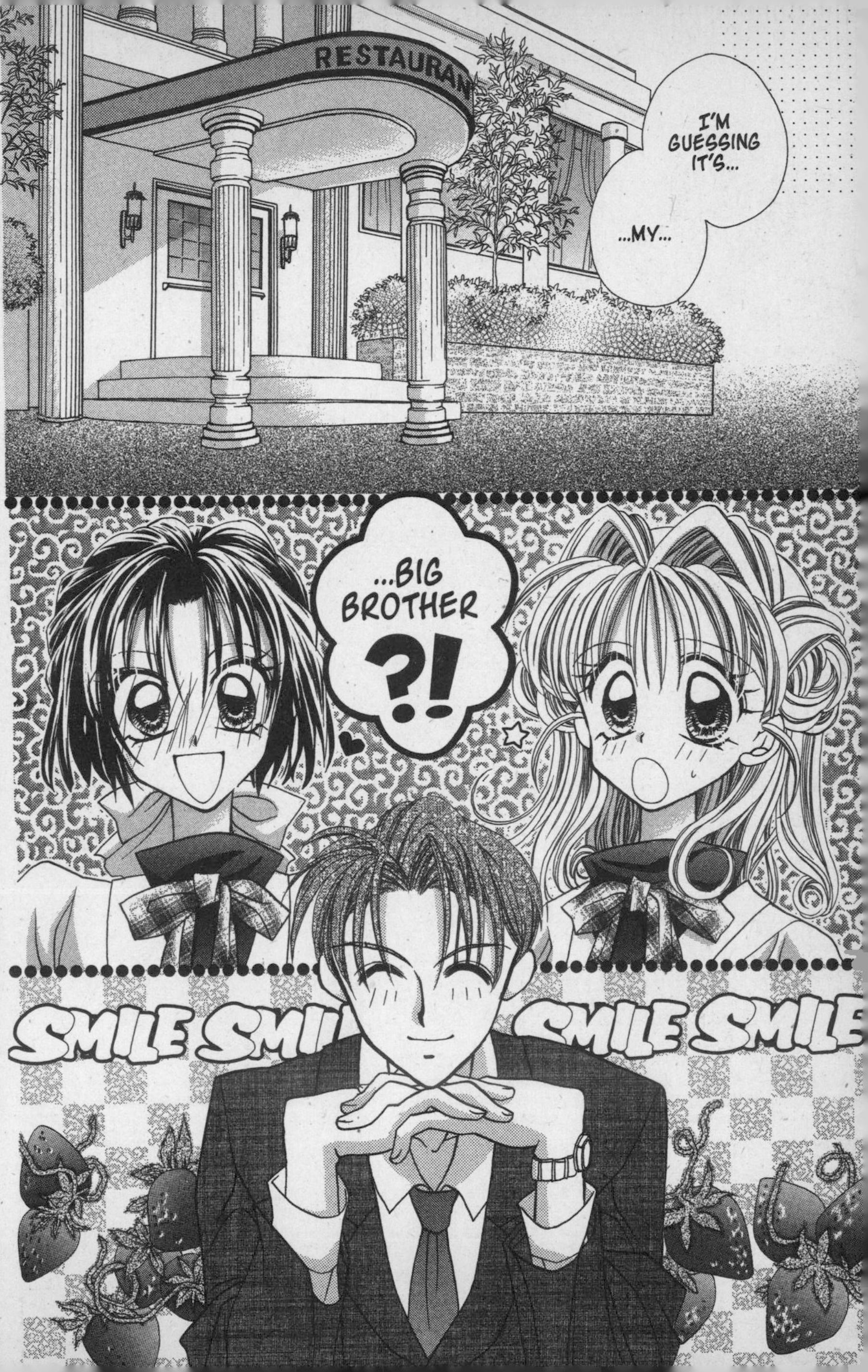
RESTAURAN
I'M GUESSING IT'S...
...MY...
...BIG BROTHER ?!
SMILE SMILE SMILE SMILE

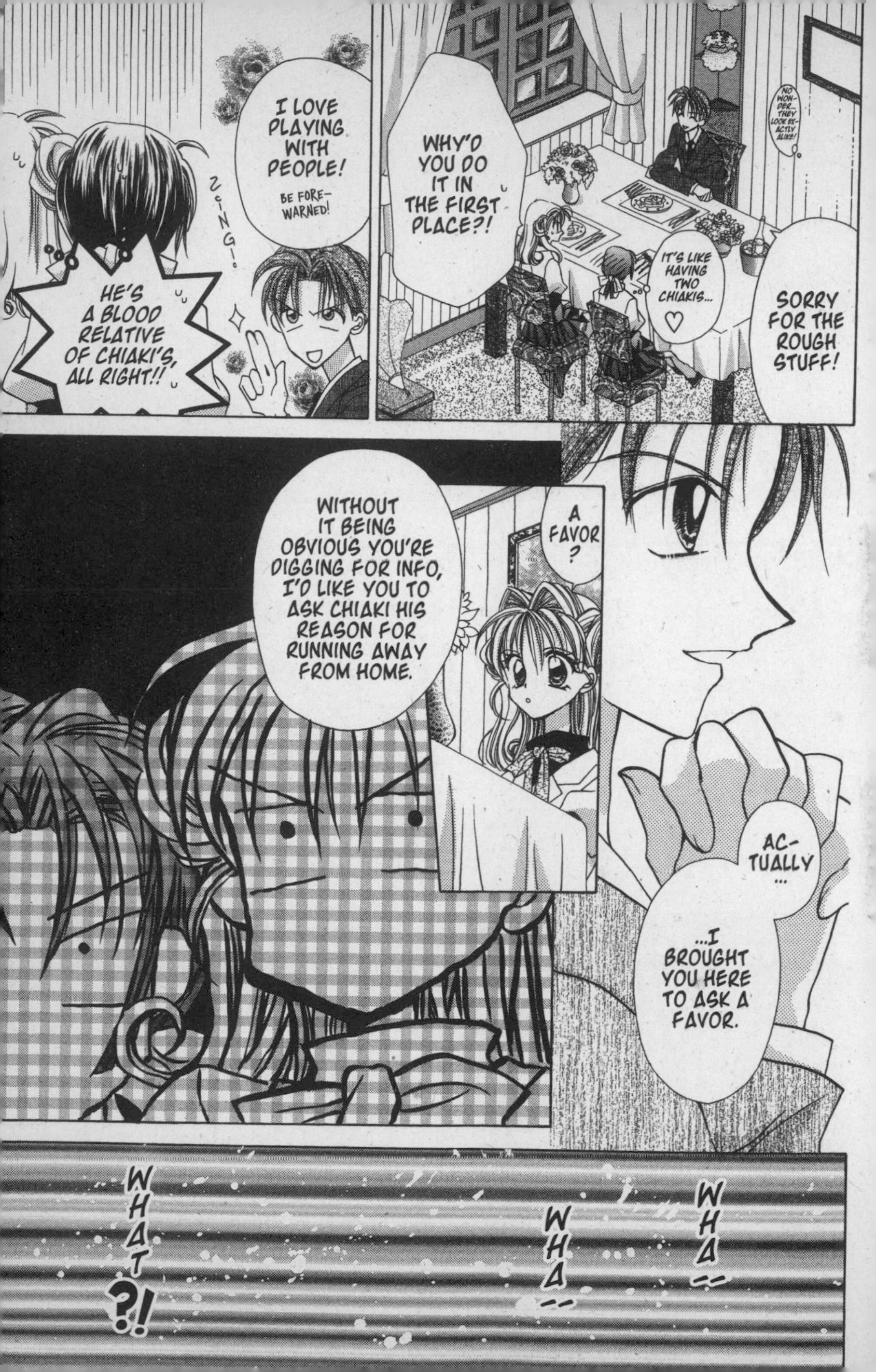
SORRY FOR THE ROUGH STUFF!
NO WONDER... THEY LOOK EXACTLY ALIKE!
IT'S LIKE HAVING TWO CHIAKIS... ♡
WHY'D YOU DO IT IN THE FIRST PLACE?!
I LOVE PLAYING WITH PEOPLE!
BE FORE-WARNED!
ZING!
HE'S A BLOOD RELATIVE OF CHIAKI'S, ALL RIGHT!!
ACTUALLY...
...I BROUGHT YOU HERE TO ASK A FAVOR.
A FAVOR?
WITHOUT IT BEING OBVIOUS YOU'RE DIGGING FOR INFO, I'D LIKE YOU TO ASK CHIAKI HIS REASON FOR RUNNING AWAY FROM HOME.
WHA--
WHA--
WHAT?!

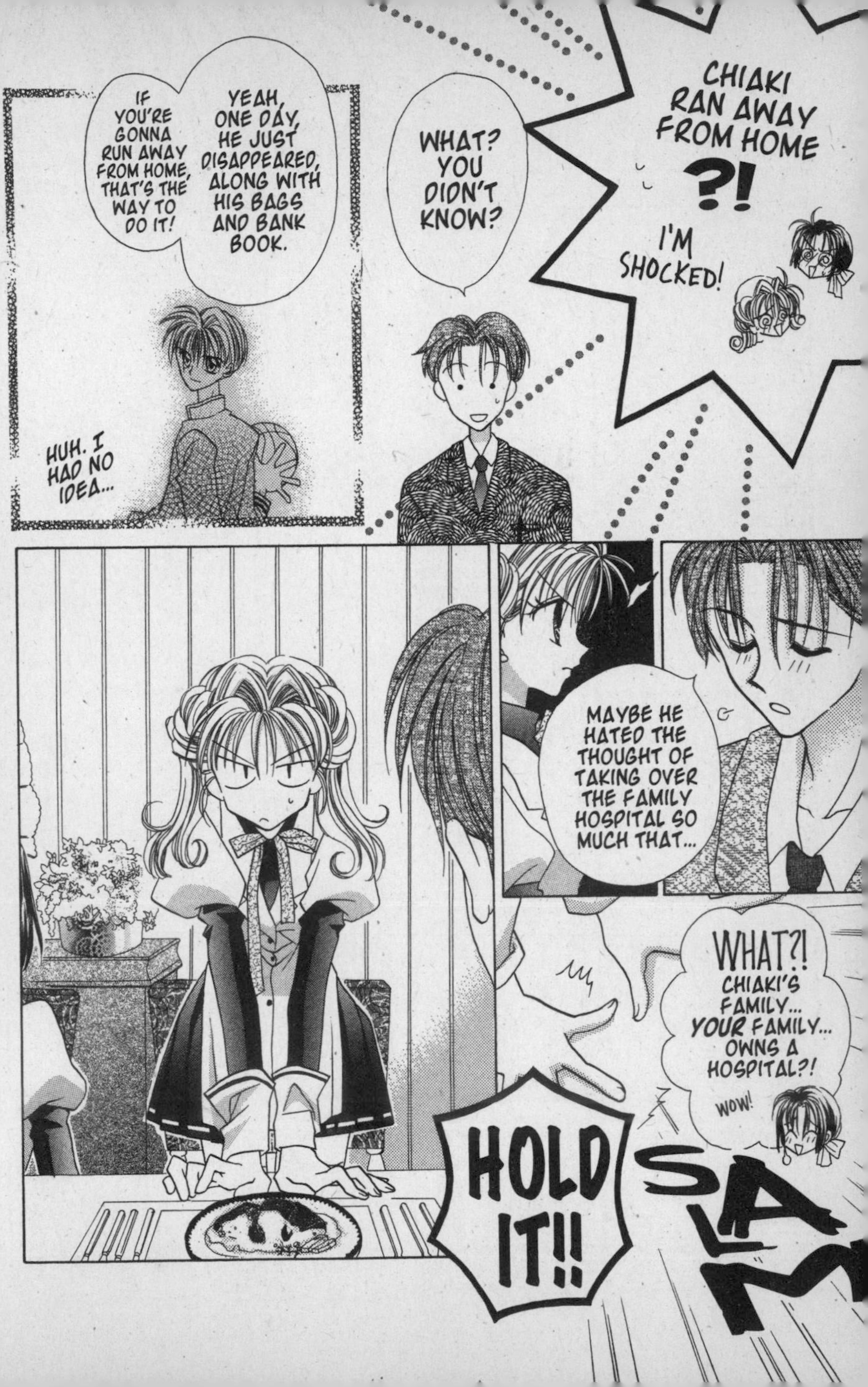
CHIAKI RAN AWAY FROM HOME ?!
I'M SHOCKED!
WHAT? YOU DIDN'T KNOW?
YEAH, ONE DAY, HE JUST DISAPPEARED, ALONG WITH HIS BAGS AND BANK BOOK.
IF YOU'RE GONNA RUN AWAY FROM HOME, THAT'S THE WAY TO DO IT!
HUH. I HAD NO IDEA...
MAYBE HE HATED THE THOUGHT OF TAKING OVER THE FAMILY HOSPITAL SO MUCH THAT...
WHAT?! CHIAKI'S FAMILY... YOUR FAMILY... OWNS A HOSPITAL?!
WOW!
HOLD IT!!
SLAM

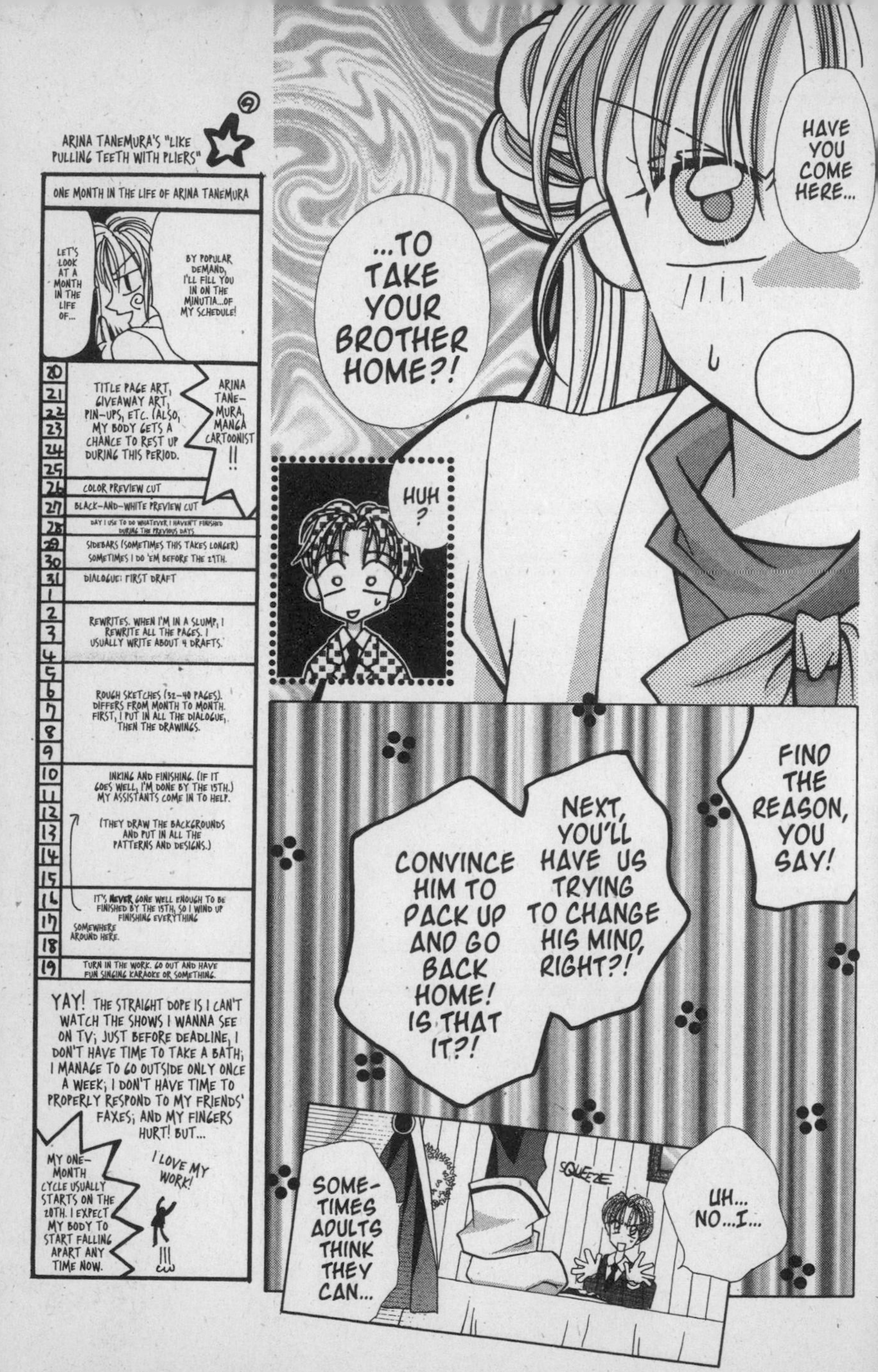
HAVE YOU COME HERE...
...TO TAKE YOUR BROTHER HOME?!
HUH?
FIND THE REASON, YOU SAY!
NEXT, YOU'LL HAVE US TRYING TO CHANGE HIS MIND, RIGHT?!
CONVINCE HIM TO PACK UP AND GO BACK HOME! IS THAT IT?!
UH... NO...I...
SQUEEZE
SOME-TIMES ADULTS THINK THEY CAN...

9

ARINA TANEMURA'S "LIKE PULLING TEETH WITH PLIERS"

ONE MONTH IN THE LIFE OF ARINA TANEMURA

LET'S LOOK AT A MONTH IN THE LIFE OF...

BY POPULAR DEMAND, I'LL FILL YOU IN ON THE MINUTIA...OF MY SCHEDULE!

ARINA TANE-MURA, MANGA CARTOONIST!!

20–25	TITLE PAGE ART, GIVEAWAY ART, PIN-UPS, ETC. (ALSO, MY BODY GETS A CHANCE TO REST UP DURING THIS PERIOD.
26	COLOR PREVIEW CUT
27	BLACK-AND-WHITE PREVIEW CUT
28	DAY I USE TO DO WHATEVER I HAVEN'T FINISHED DURING THE PREVIOUS DAYS
29–30	SIDEBARS (SOMETIMES THIS TAKES LONGER) SOMETIMES I DO 'EM BEFORE THE 29TH.
31	DIALOGUE: FIRST DRAFT
1–4	REWRITES. WHEN I'M IN A SLUMP, I REWRITE ALL THE PAGES. I USUALLY WRITE ABOUT 4 DRAFTS.
5–9	ROUGH SKETCHES (32–40 PAGES). DIFFERS FROM MONTH TO MONTH. FIRST, I PUT IN ALL THE DIALOGUE, THEN THE DRAWINGS.
10–15	INKING AND FINISHING. (IF IT GOES WELL, I'M DONE BY THE 15TH.) MY ASSISTANTS COME IN TO HELP. (THEY DRAW THE BACKGROUNDS AND PUT IN ALL THE PATTERNS AND DESIGNS.)
16–18	IT'S NEVER GONE WELL ENOUGH TO BE FINISHED BY THE 15TH, SO I WIND UP FINISHING EVERYTHING SOMEWHERE AROUND HERE.
19	TURN IN THE WORK. GO OUT AND HAVE FUN SINGING KARAOKE OR SOMETHING.

YAY! THE STRAIGHT DOPE IS I CAN'T WATCH THE SHOWS I WANNA SEE ON TV; JUST BEFORE DEADLINE, I DON'T HAVE TIME TO TAKE A BATH; I MANAGE TO GO OUTSIDE ONLY ONCE A WEEK; I DON'T HAVE TIME TO PROPERLY RESPOND TO MY FRIENDS' FAXES; AND MY FINGERS HURT! BUT...

MY ONE-MONTH CYCLE USUALLY STARTS ON THE 20TH. I EXPECT MY BODY TO START FALLING APART ANY TIME NOW.

I LOVE MY WORK!

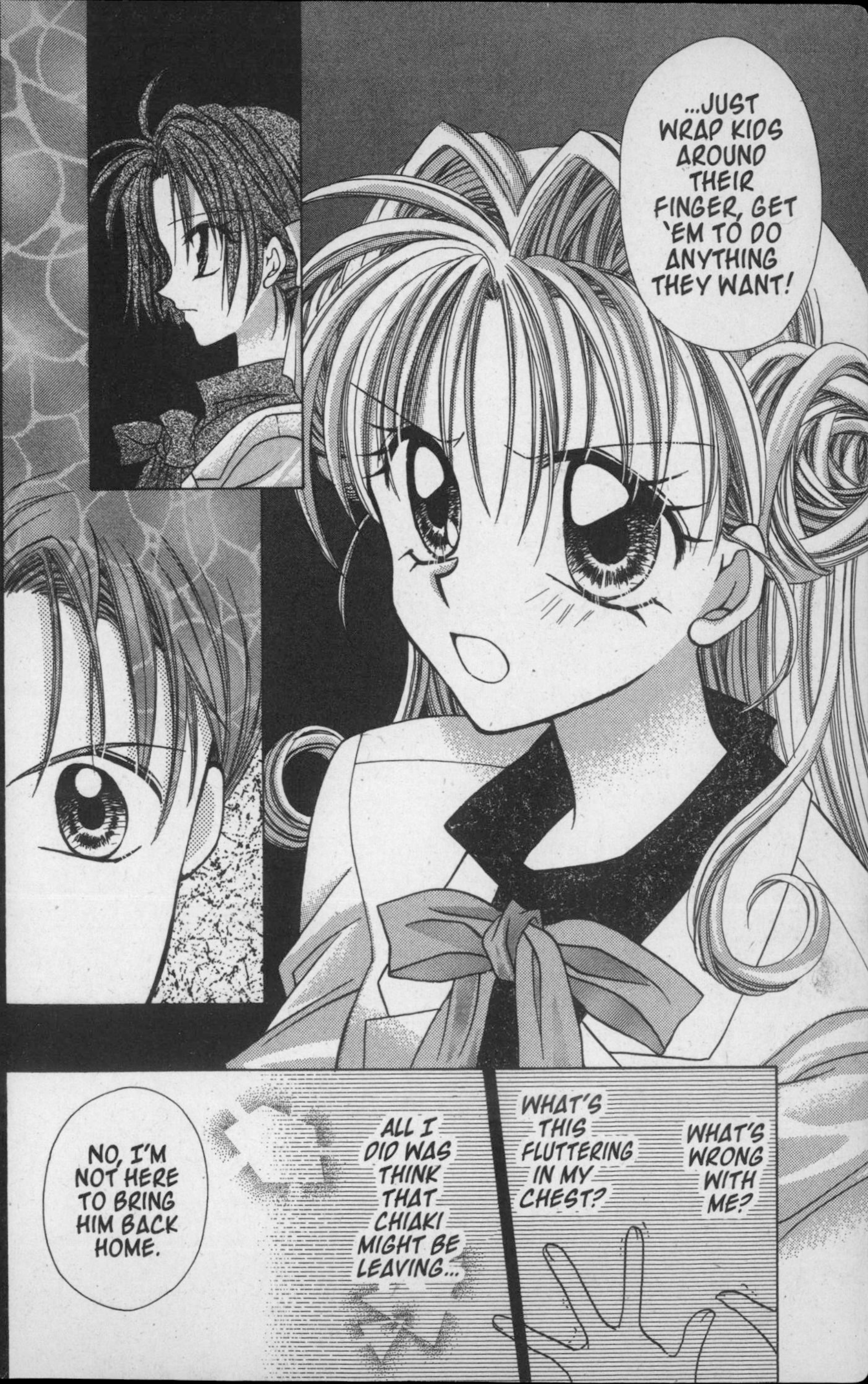
...JUST WRAP KIDS AROUND THEIR FINGER, GET 'EM TO DO ANYTHING THEY WANT!
WHAT'S WRONG WITH ME?
WHAT'S THIS FLUTTERING IN MY CHEST?
ALL I DID WAS THINK THAT CHIAKI MIGHT BE LEAVING...
NO, I'M NOT HERE TO BRING HIM BACK HOME.

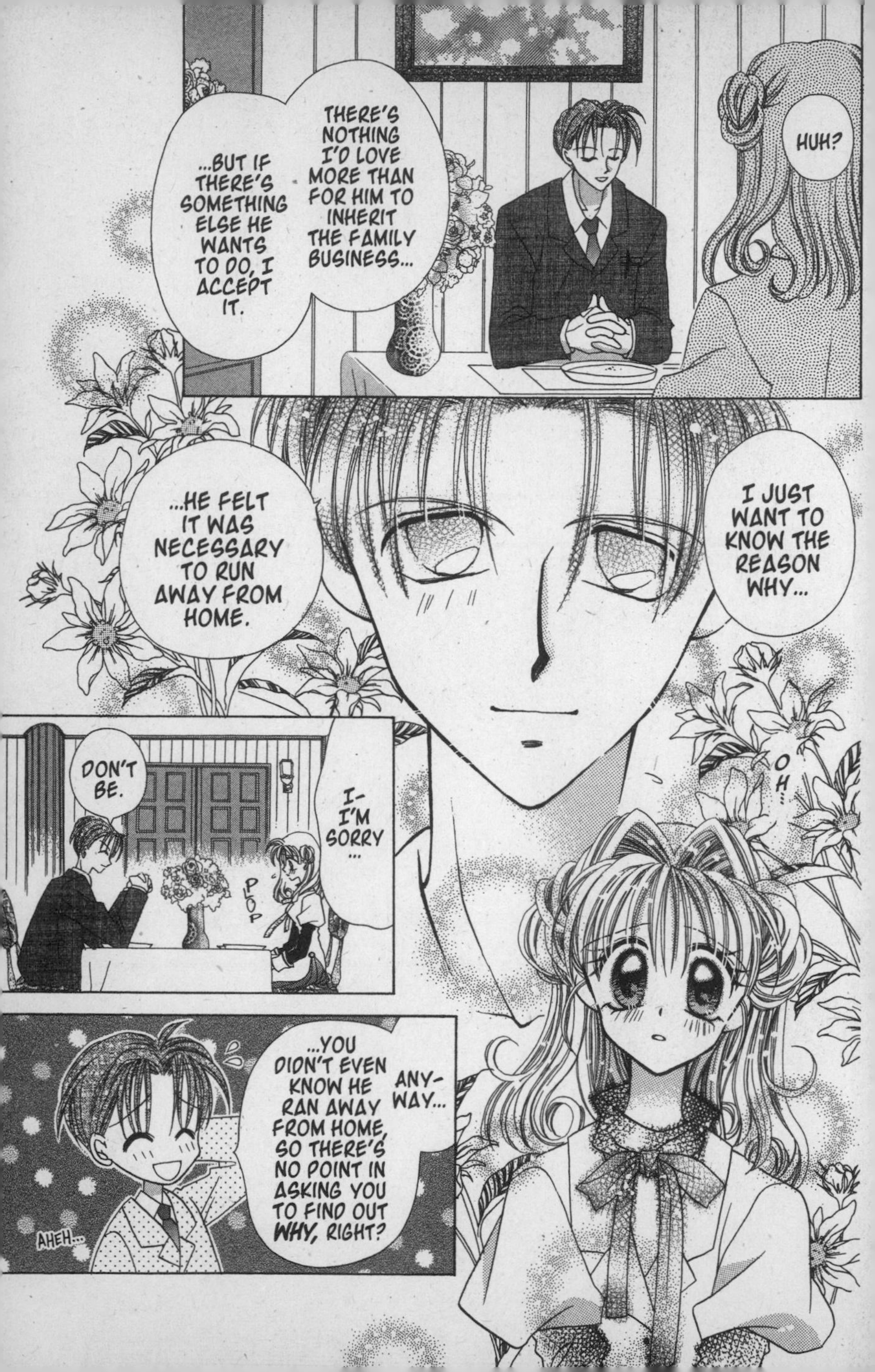
HUH?
THERE'S NOTHING I'D LOVE MORE THAN FOR HIM TO INHERIT THE FAMILY BUSINESS...
...BUT IF THERE'S SOMETHING ELSE HE WANTS TO DO, I ACCEPT IT.
I JUST WANT TO KNOW THE REASON WHY...
...HE FELT IT WAS NECESSARY TO RUN AWAY FROM HOME.
OH...
I- I'M SORRY...
PLOP
DON'T BE.
ANY-WAY...
...YOU DIDN'T EVEN KNOW HE RAN AWAY FROM HOME, SO THERE'S NO POINT IN ASKING YOU TO FIND OUT **WHY**, RIGHT?
AHEH...

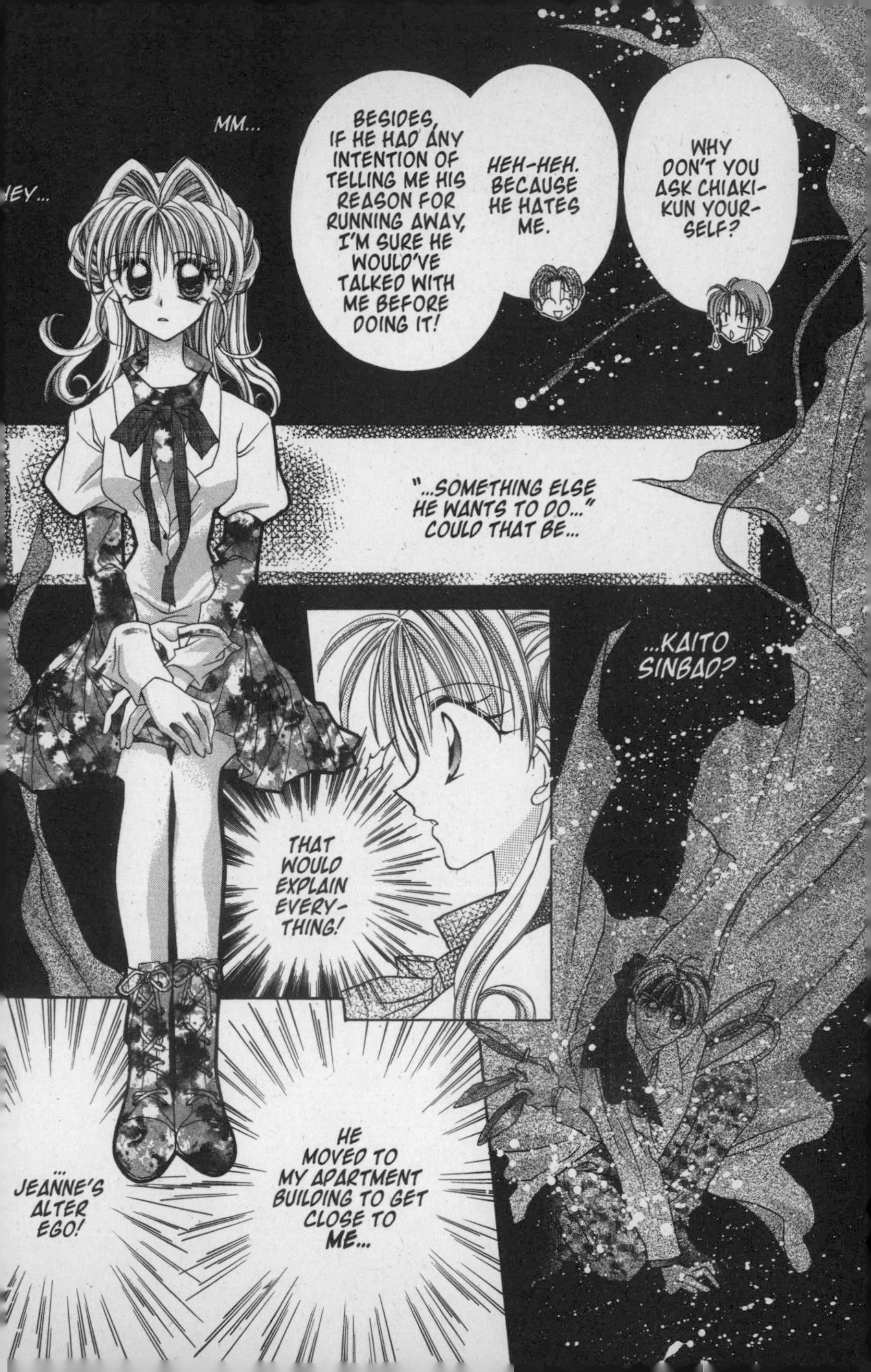
WHY DON'T YOU ASK CHIAKI-KUN YOUR-SELF?
HEH-HEH. BECAUSE HE HATES ME.
BESIDES, IF HE HAD ANY INTENTION OF TELLING ME HIS REASON FOR RUNNING AWAY, I'M SURE HE WOULD'VE TALKED WITH ME BEFORE DOING IT!
MM...
HEY...
"...SOMETHING ELSE HE WANTS TO DO..." COULD THAT BE...
...KAITO SINBAD?
THAT WOULD EXPLAIN EVERY-THING!
HE MOVED TO MY APARTMENT BUILDING TO GET CLOSE TO ME...
...JEANNE'S ALTER EGO!

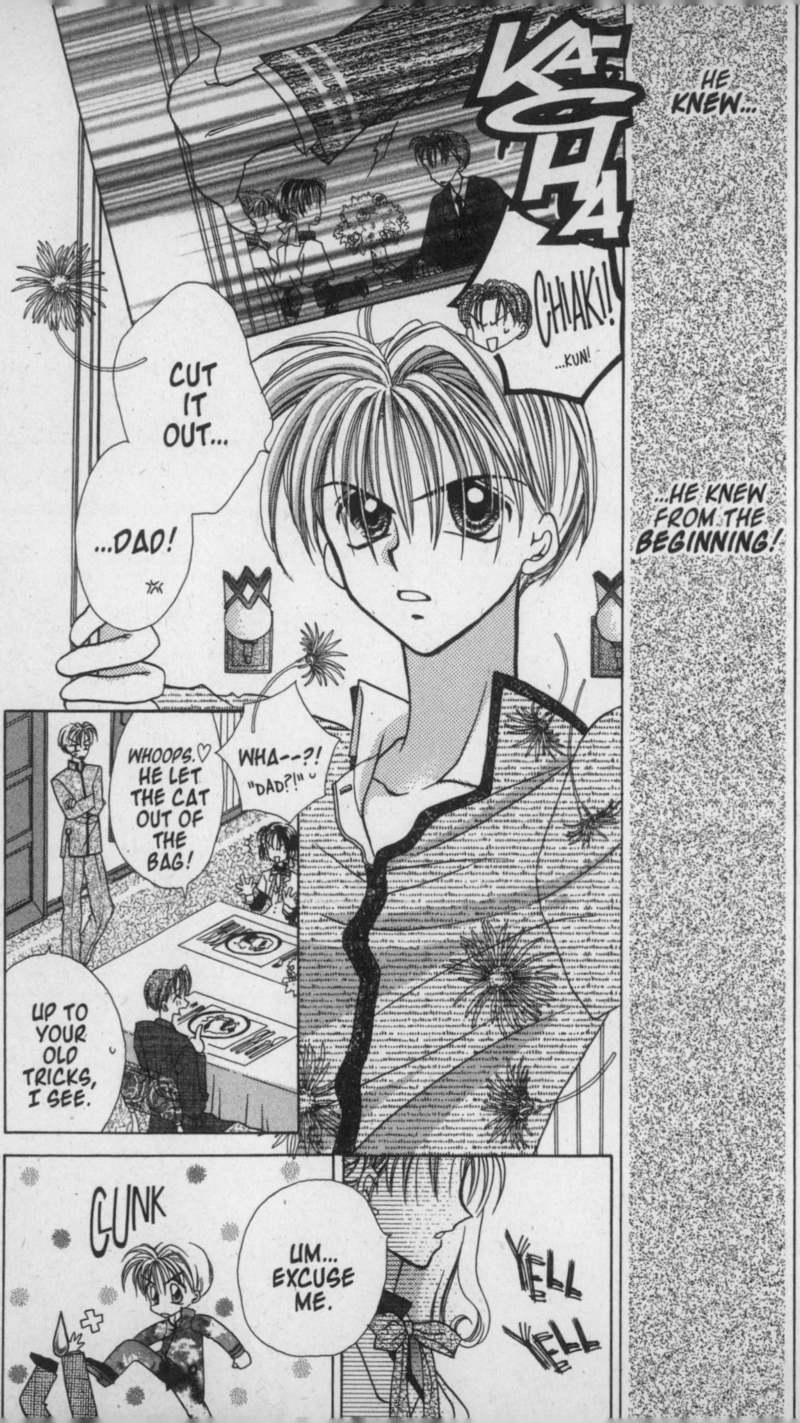
HE KNEW...
...HE KNEW FROM THE BEGINNING!
KA-CHA
CHIAKI! ...KUN!
CUT IT OUT... ...DAD!
WHA--?! "DAD?!"
WHOOPS.♡ HE LET THE CAT OUT OF THE BAG!
UP TO YOUR OLD TRICKS, I SEE.
YELL YELL
UM... EXCUSE ME.
CLUNK

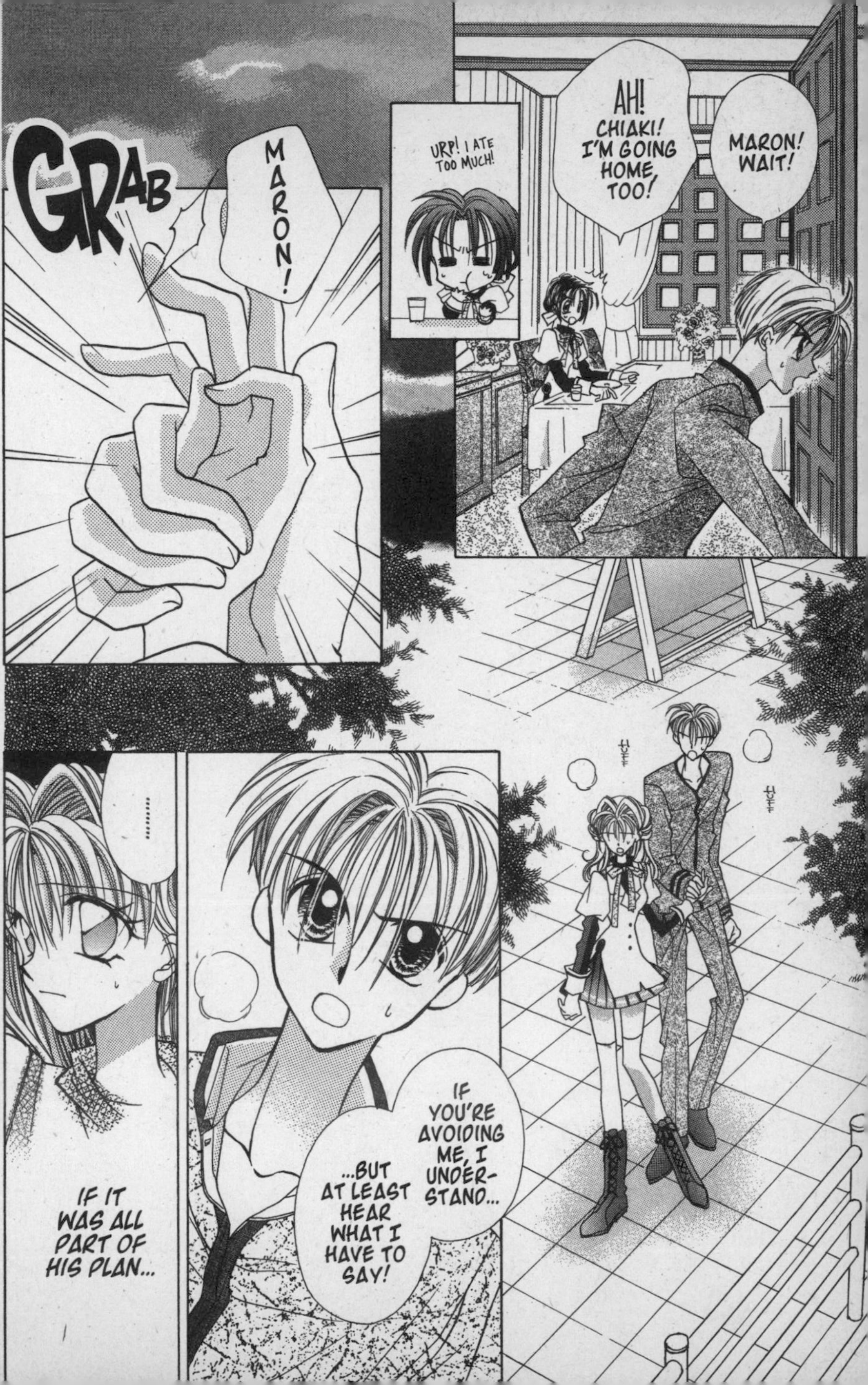
MARON! WAIT!
AH! CHIAKI! I'M GOING HOME, TOO!
URP! I ATE TOO MUCH!
MARON!
GRAB
HUFF
HUFF
IF YOU'RE AVOIDING ME, I UNDER-STAND...
...BUT AT LEAST HEAR WHAT I HAVE TO SAY!
......
IF IT WAS ALL PART OF HIS PLAN...

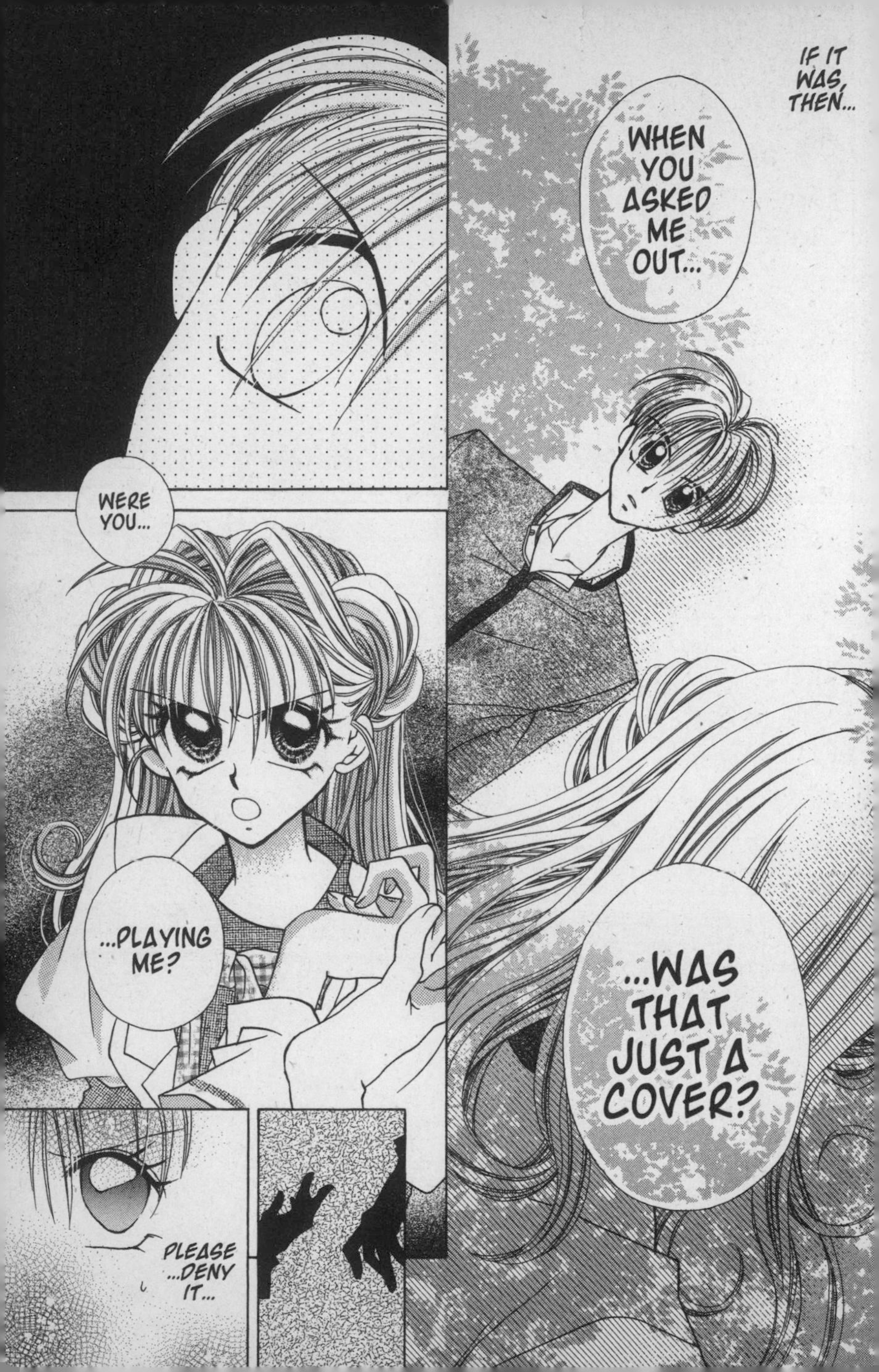
IF IT WAS, THEN...
WHEN YOU ASKED ME OUT...
...WAS THAT JUST A COVER?
WERE YOU...
...PLAYING ME?
PLEASE ...DENY IT...

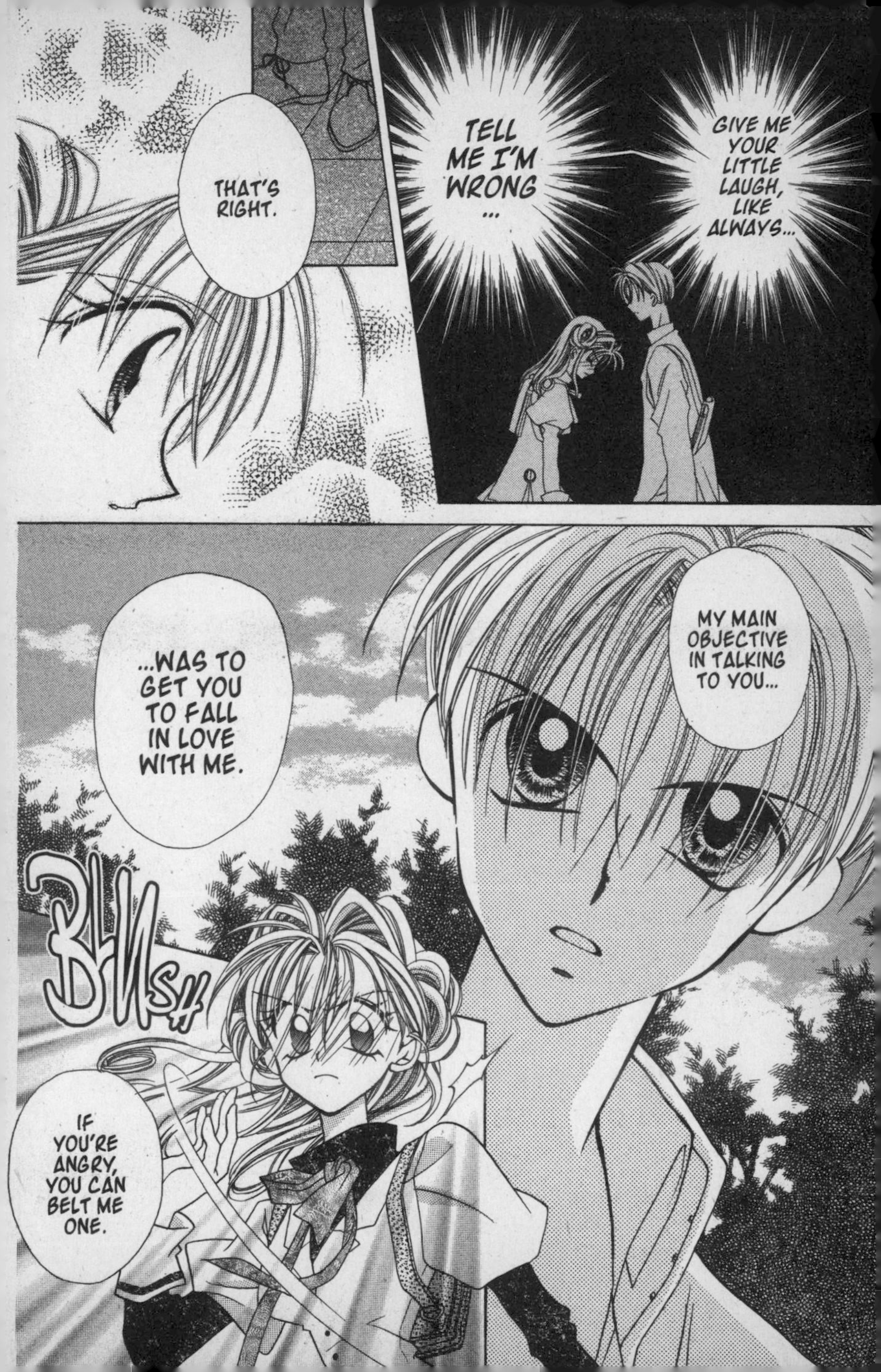
GIVE ME YOUR LITTLE LAUGH, LIKE ALWAYS...
TELL ME I'M WRONG...
THAT'S RIGHT.
MY MAIN OBJECTIVE IN TALKING TO YOU...
...WAS TO GET YOU TO FALL IN LOVE WITH ME.
BLUSH
IF YOU'RE ANGRY, YOU CAN BELT ME ONE.

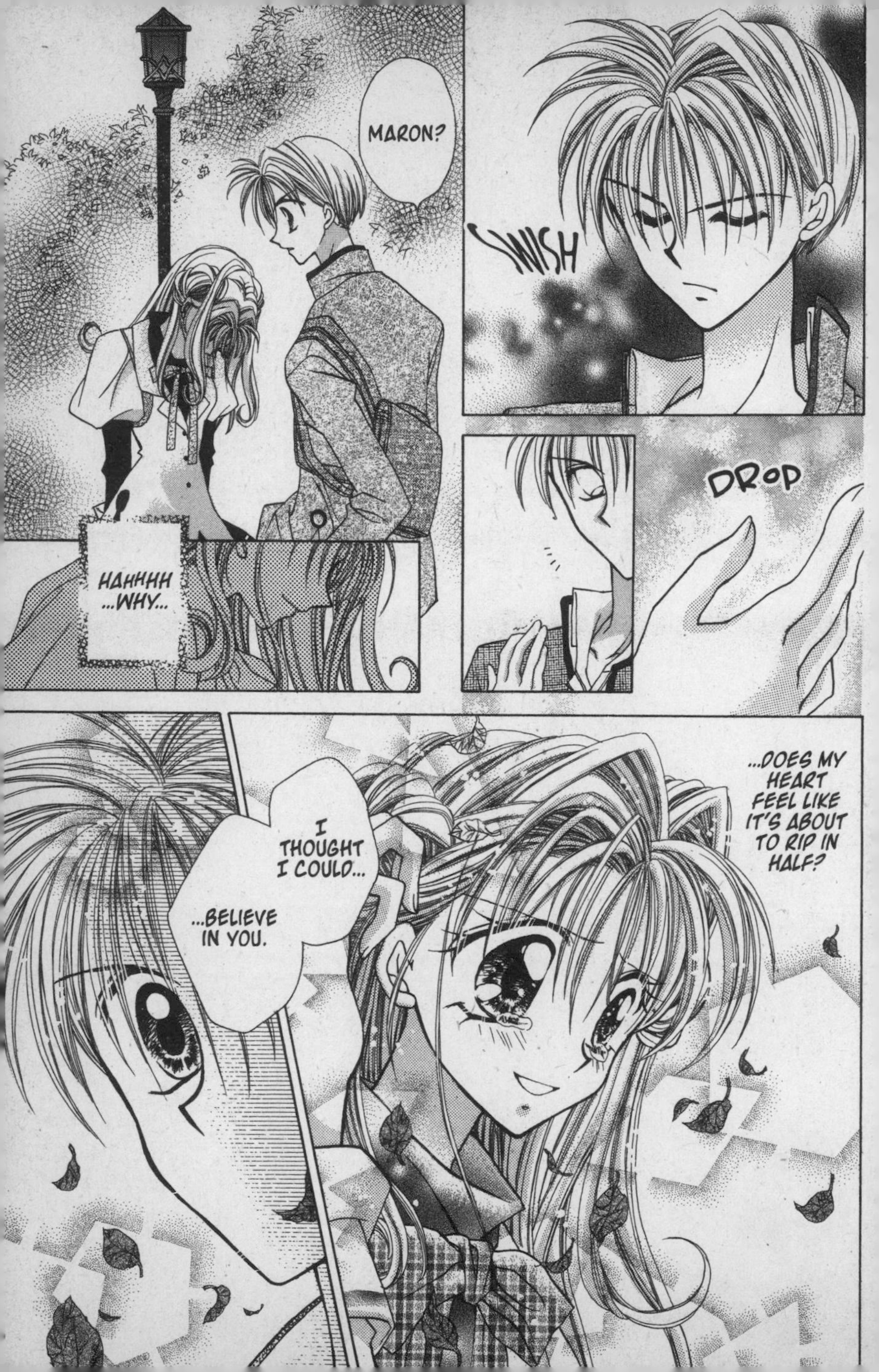
SWISH
DROP
MARON?
HAHHHH ...WHY...
...DOES MY HEART FEEL LIKE IT'S ABOUT TO RIP IN HALF?
I THOUGHT I COULD...
...BELIEVE IN YOU.

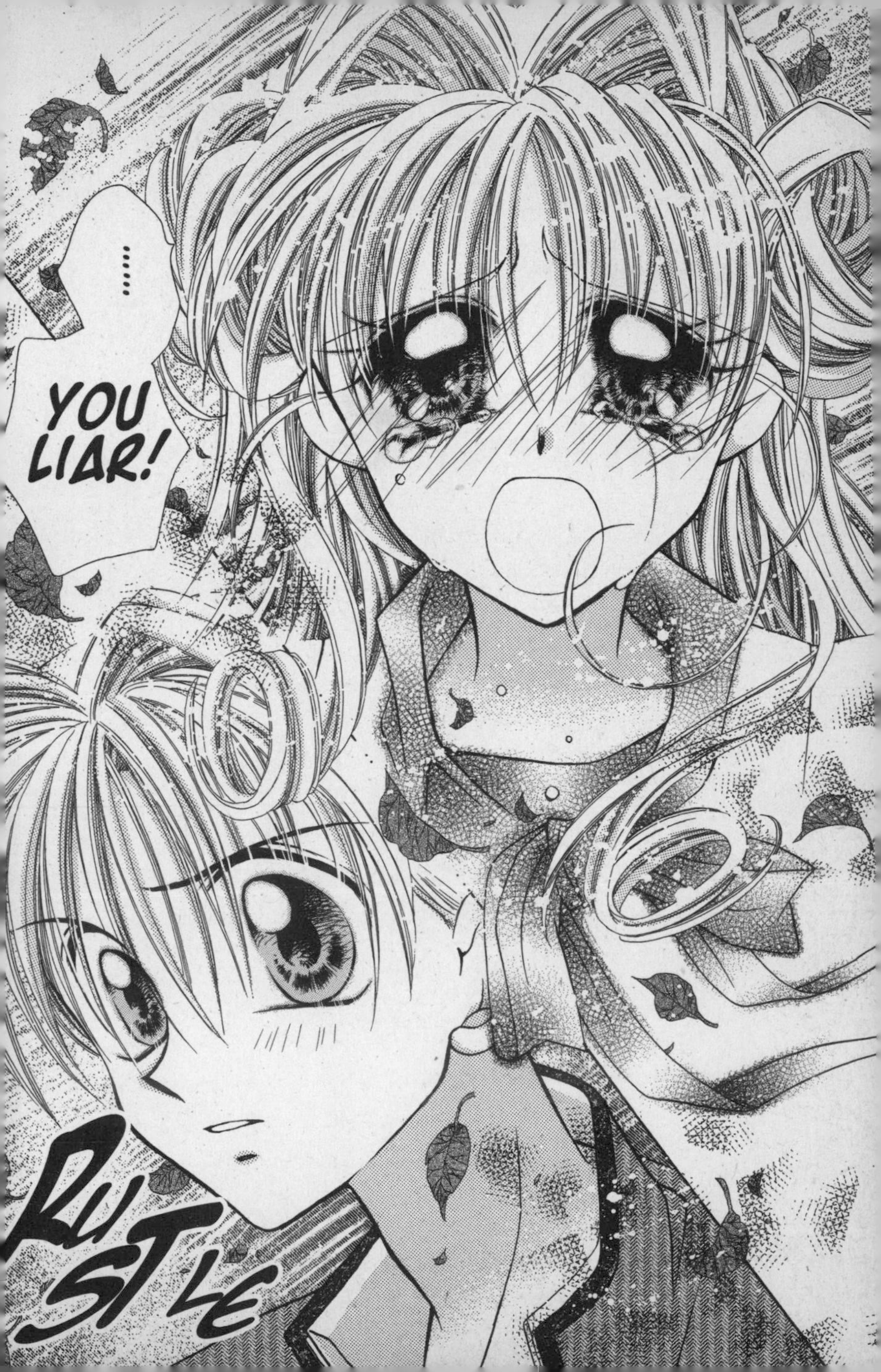
......
YOU LIAR!
RUSTLE

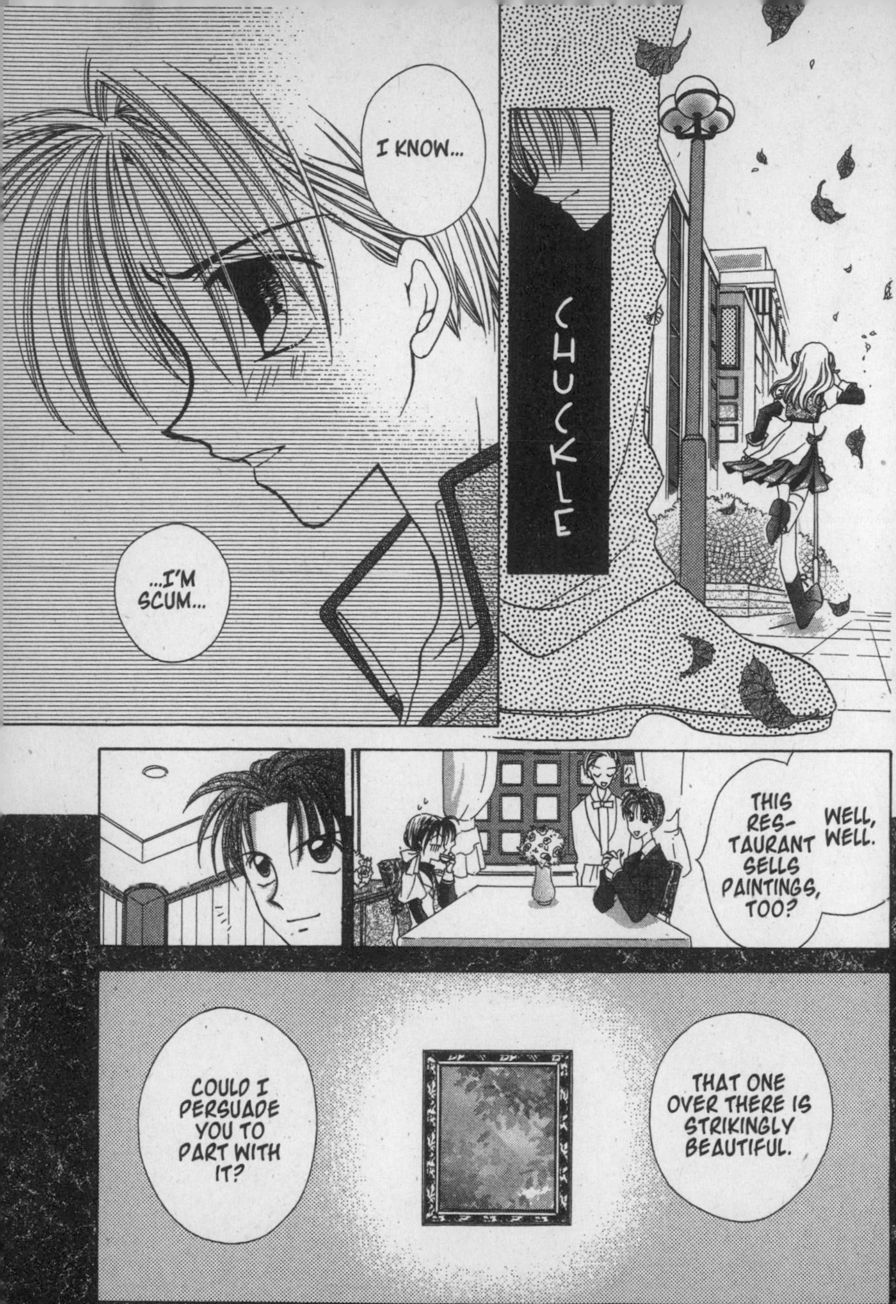
CHUCKLE
I KNOW...
...I'M SCUM...
WELL, WELL.
THIS RES-TAURANT SELLS PAINTINGS, TOO?
THAT ONE OVER THERE IS STRIKINGLY BEAUTIFUL.
COULD I PERSUADE YOU TO PART WITH IT?

Chapter 6: The End

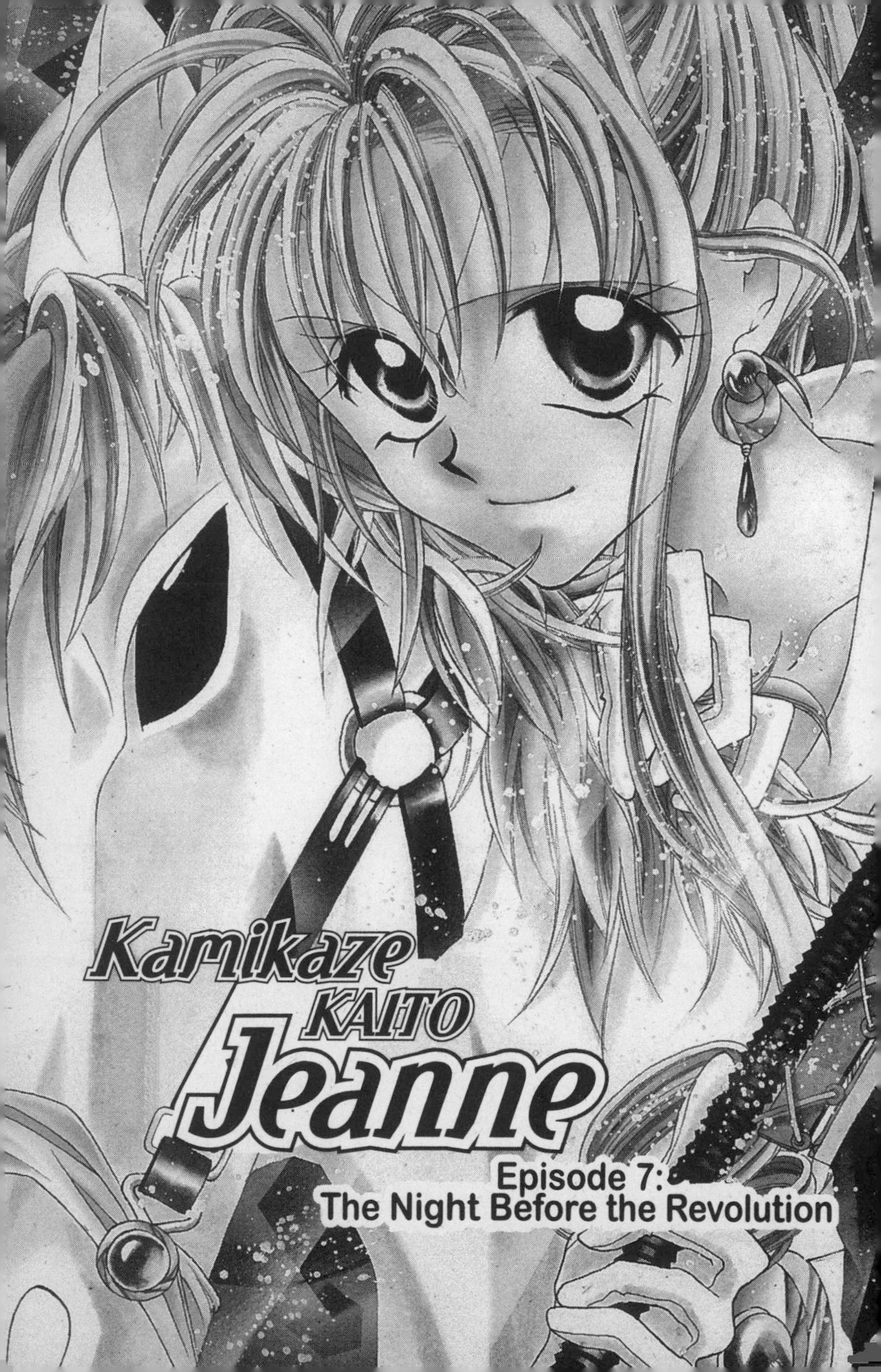
Kamikaze KAITO Jeanne
Episode 7:
The Night Before the Revolution

A Lot of Work to Do♥ Supplemental

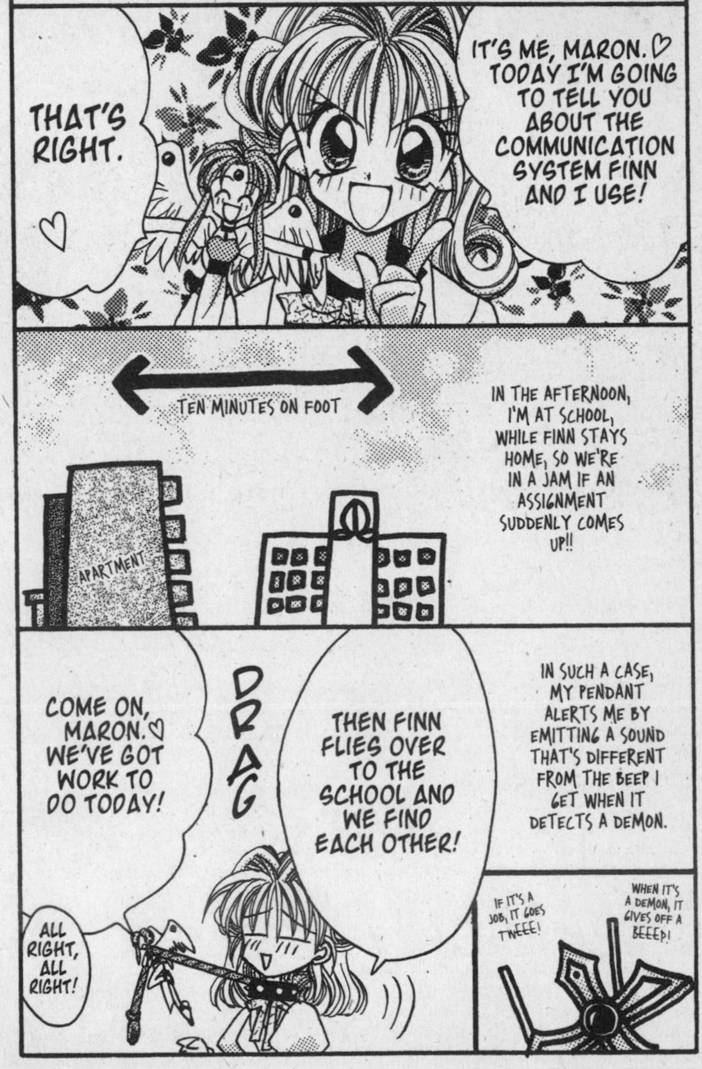
IT'S ME, MARON.♡ TODAY I'M GOING TO TELL YOU ABOUT THE COMMUNICATION SYSTEM FINN AND I USE!
THAT'S RIGHT. ♡
IN THE AFTERNOON, I'M AT SCHOOL, WHILE FINN STAYS HOME, SO WE'RE IN A JAM IF AN ASSIGNMENT SUDDENLY COMES UP!!
TEN MINUTES ON FOOT
APARTMENT
IN SUCH A CASE, MY PENDANT ALERTS ME BY EMITTING A SOUND THAT'S DIFFERENT FROM THE BEEP I GET WHEN IT DETECTS A DEMON.
WHEN IT'S A DEMON, IT GIVES OFF A BEEEP!
IF IT'S A JOB, IT GOES TWEEE!
THEN FINN FLIES OVER TO THE SCHOOL AND WE FIND EACH OTHER!
DRAG
COME ON, MARON.♡ WE'VE GOT WORK TO DO TODAY!
ALL RIGHT, ALL RIGHT!

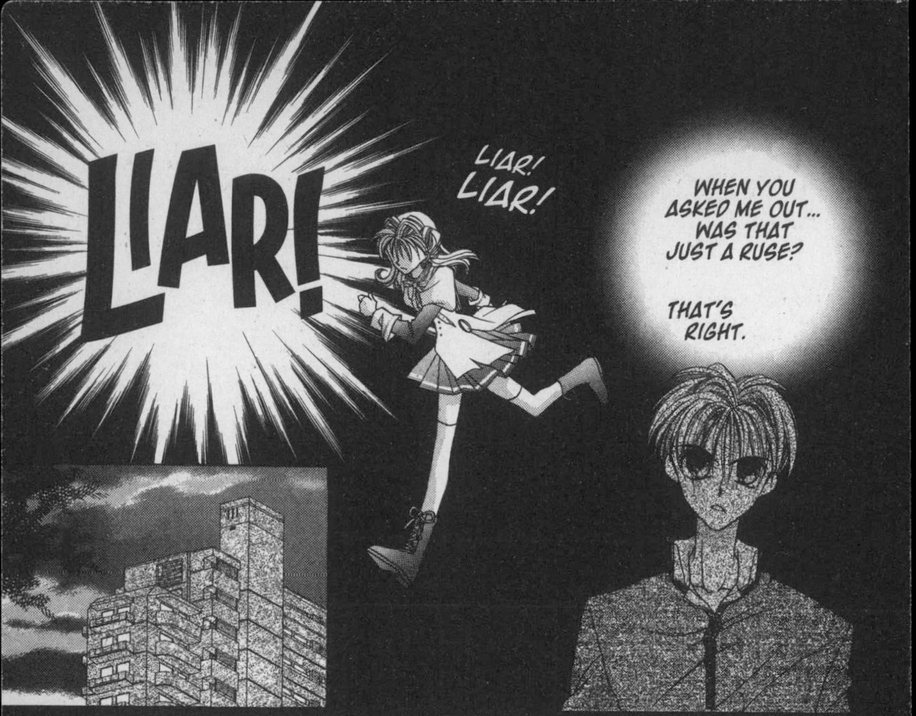
WHEN YOU ASKED ME OUT... WAS THAT JUST A RUSE?
THAT'S RIGHT.
LIAR! LIAR!
LIAR!

Episode 7: THE NIGHT BEFORE THE REVOLUTION
TAGLINE: "I WANTED TO BELIEVE..." (This time only, Kikuzo-san came up with the tagline instead of Obashi-san. Readers have told me that reading the tagline alone made them sad. Thank you.) Mmm...Maron-chan...remains unhappy...Of course, the title page has a Jeanne D'Arc motif. By the way, I depict Jeanne-chan holding red roses a lot, but inquiring readers are under the impression that the real Jeanne D'Arc actually had a thing for white lilies. The problem I have with that is Jeanne-chan's costume is white, so white flowers would be too hard to spot...hence, I go with red roses. (Plus, I'm mad about red roses anyway--and cherry blossoms!!!) In this story, Maron-chan participates in various activities at school, showing us what an outstanding student she is. However, when you think that she's probably been going all out these last several years to gain her parents' praise when they eventually return home...well, it just seems heartbreaking...SOB...SIGH...

Episode 8: REAL HEART TAGLINE: "I WANT TO FLY AWAY RIGHT NOW..." (This is a good one, editor-san!!!) The reaction to this was tremendous. The title page, popular with fans, took me half a day to finish and...I dunno...I kind of like it. I loved it while I was drawing the rough sketch, but somehow...mmm...ah, forget about it! It gives off the feeling, as the tagline goes, that she wants to fly away, across the ocean and to her parents' side...I want to reunite Maron-chan with her folks at some point. Since starting this series, I'd been waiting for my chance to draw this image, so I was happy just to be able to finally do it. I tend to draw serious, gloomy images, so I was scared of the readers' reactions to it, but I was very pleasantly surprised when the drawing proved to be a big hit with readers. Usually, the most fun I have writing is right here, in these sidebars, but this time I had a blast with the characters' dialogue! (Um...even though it was a tough situation for Maron-chan...) Oh yeah, this time around, Miyako-chan, too, became a mega-fave character for readers! It's like this story sets her up for the one that directly follows (and stars her), "Miyako-Catharsis." (Wait, did I plan it that way?!) Miyako-chan really is a good girl! Anyway, the meaning behind the title of this episode is self-evident. It's about Maron-chan's feelings, and the idea that love equals trust, and trust becomes courage. Actually, this is the theme of "Kamikaze Kaito Jeanne" as a whole. Yep. For now, episode eight represents the "first climax" of the series to me, so I'm glad I had a good grasp of the theme while doing it. Oh, that's right! A friend of mine mentioned that she was happy with this story and happy for Maron-chan because she finally got to make a wish...To be continued!

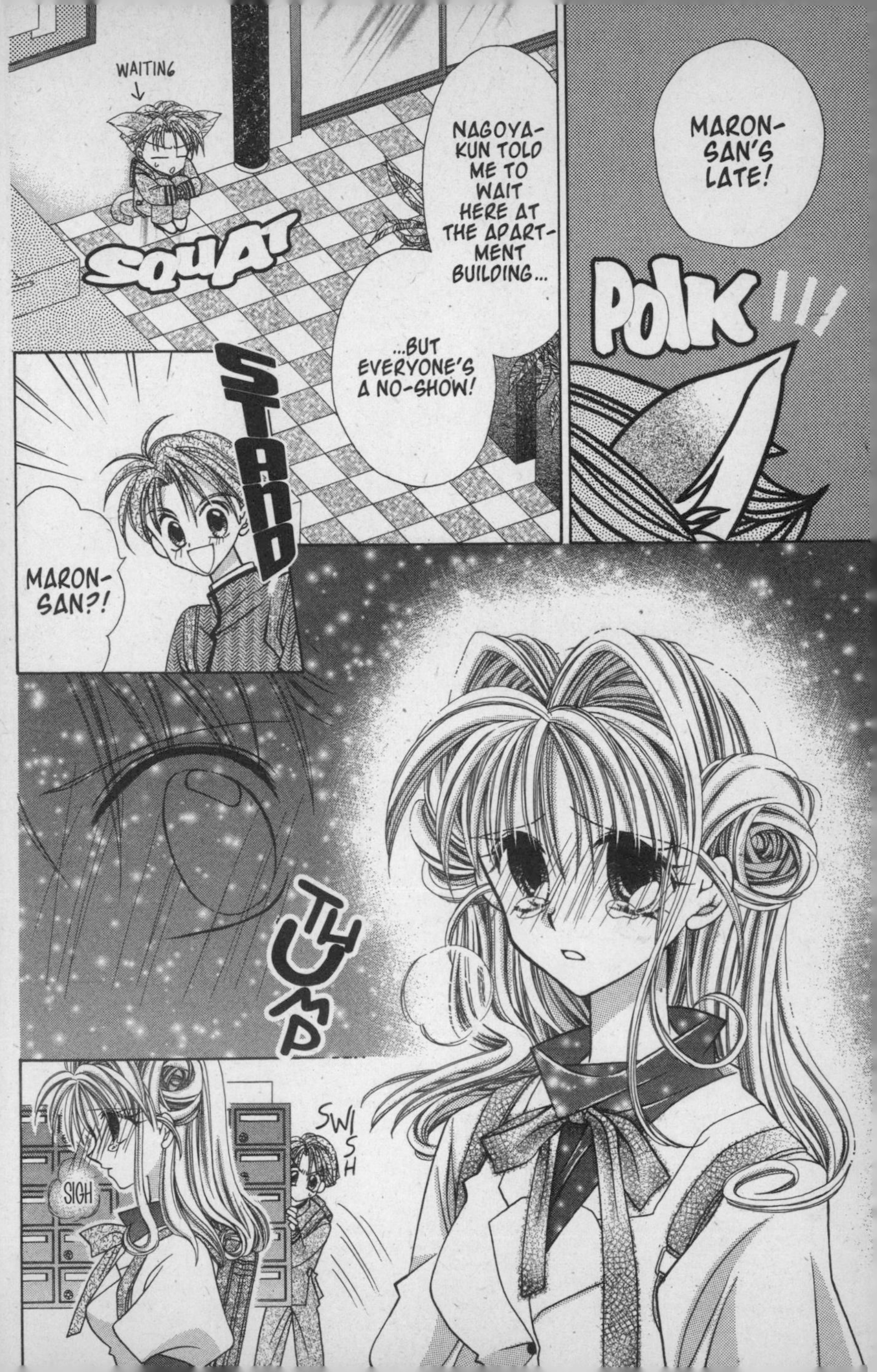
MARON-SAN'S LATE!
POIK
WAITING
SQUAT
NAGOYA-KUN TOLD ME TO WAIT HERE AT THE APARTMENT BUILDING...
...BUT EVERYONE'S A NO-SHOW!
STAND
MARON-SAN?!
THUMP
SWISH
SIGH

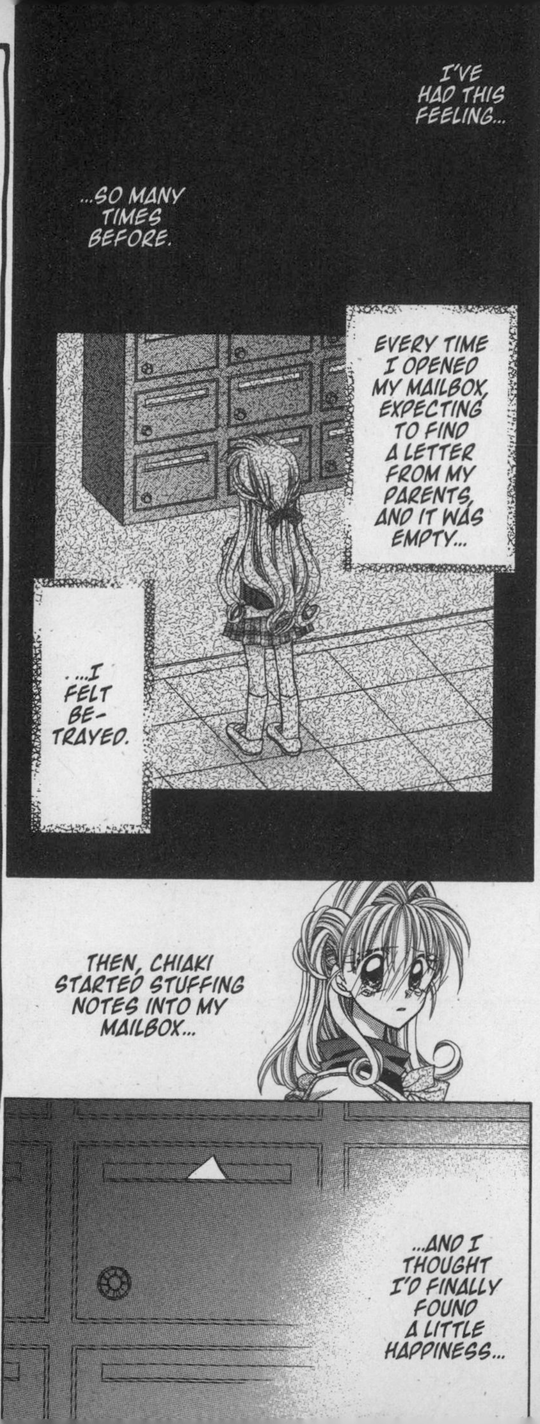
I'VE HAD THIS FEELING...
...SO MANY TIMES BEFORE.
EVERY TIME I OPENED MY MAILBOX, EXPECTING TO FIND A LETTER FROM MY PARENTS, AND IT WAS EMPTY...
...I FELT BE-TRAYED.
THEN, CHIAKI STARTED STUFFING NOTES INTO MY MAILBOX...
...AND I THOUGHT I'D FINALLY FOUND A LITTLE HAPPINESS...

4 SIGH...Anime...I can't believe it's really gonna happen...Actually, it still seems like a dream. Despite what I've said before, it appears that I'm pleased as punch about the whole thing. The sponsor is the famous Bandai, so toys will be released as well. (I wonder if they'll come out with a ribbon weapon? If they do, I'll dance with it...I could do it during my breaks here at work.) Also slated to go on sale (tentatively) are trading cards and figures! YESSS!

Ah! Oh, yeah. Also, Morinaga (the candy company) is a co-sponsor ♡ I just **love** Morinaga...Seriously. For almost forever (ever since elementary school!!!), "Ototo" has been my favorite snack in the whole wide world!

Whenever I would go to the local amusement park, I'd sometimes end up with only 1,030 yen for the way home (not including train fare). So I'd empty my purse and buy a jumbo Ototo (1,000 yen) at the park's souvenir shop, then go home! Morinaga-sama...You wouldn't be able to make "JEANNE Ototo," would you? <<<Ahhh! She's serious about it! Talk about getting carried away! Who do you think you are?!

While we're on the subject of getting carried away, I'll tell you about the dreams I had as a third-year high school student.

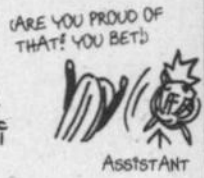
(ARE YOU PROUD OF THAT! YOU BET!)
ASSISTANT

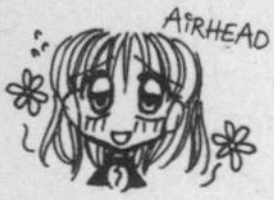
AIRHEAD

I wanted to be either a songwriter, singer, voice actress, or manga cartoonist...

Right now, I still have aspirations of being a voice actress or song-writer, one or the other (I don't have any faith in my singing ability...) Eh-heh. No? Impossible? I'm not fooling around here! I'm serious!

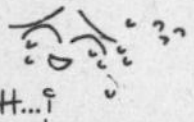

Okay...SIGHHHHH...I know! I'm an idiot! What...what was I saying?!

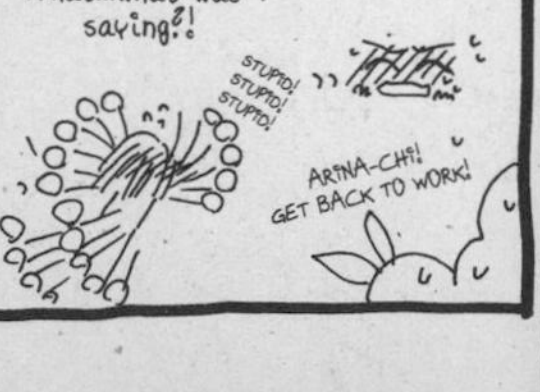
STUPID! STUPID! STUPID!
ARINA-CHI! GET BACK TO WORK!

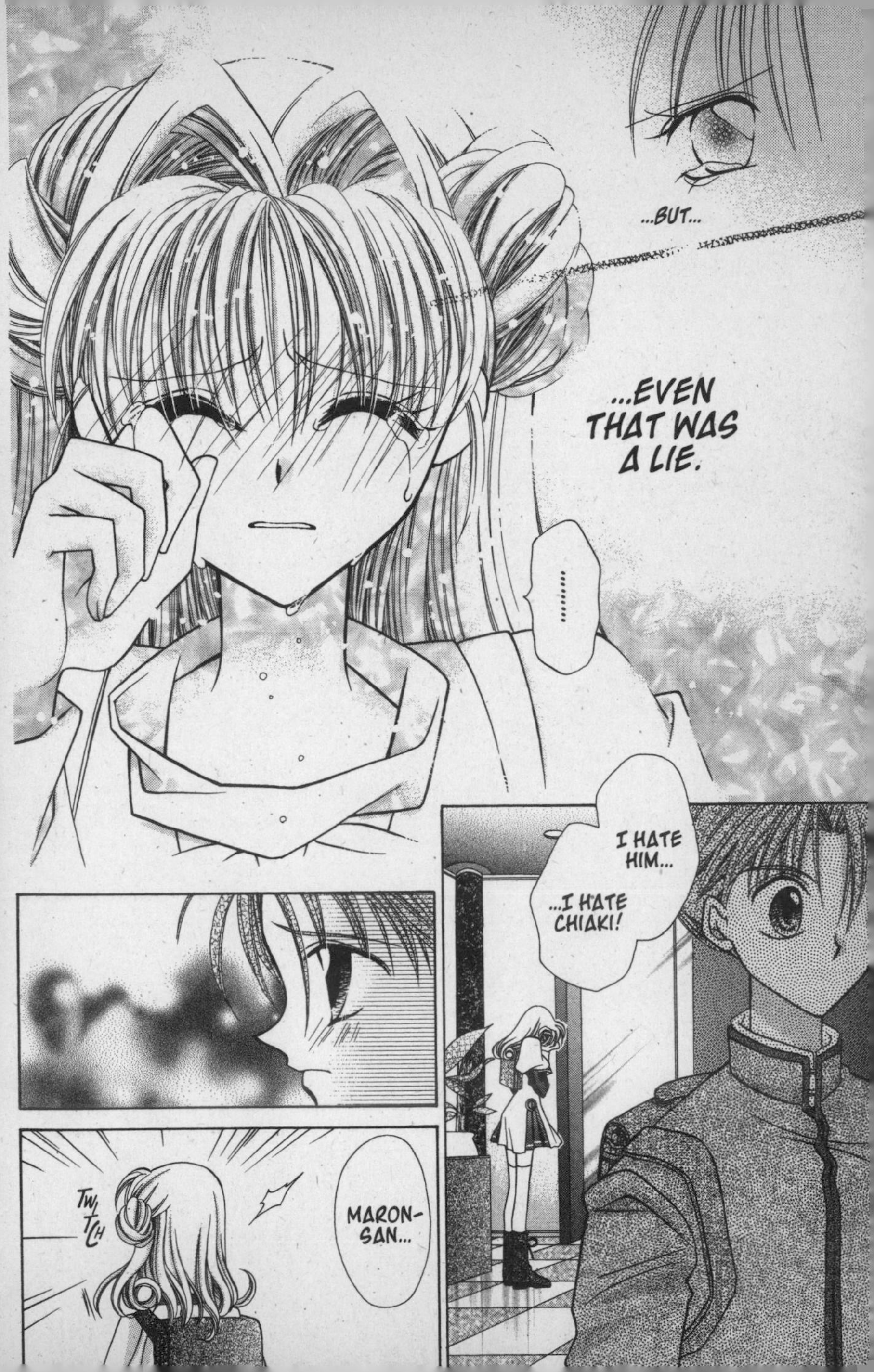
...BUT...
...EVEN THAT WAS A LIE.
......
I HATE HIM...
...I HATE CHIAKI!
TWITCH
MARON-SAN...

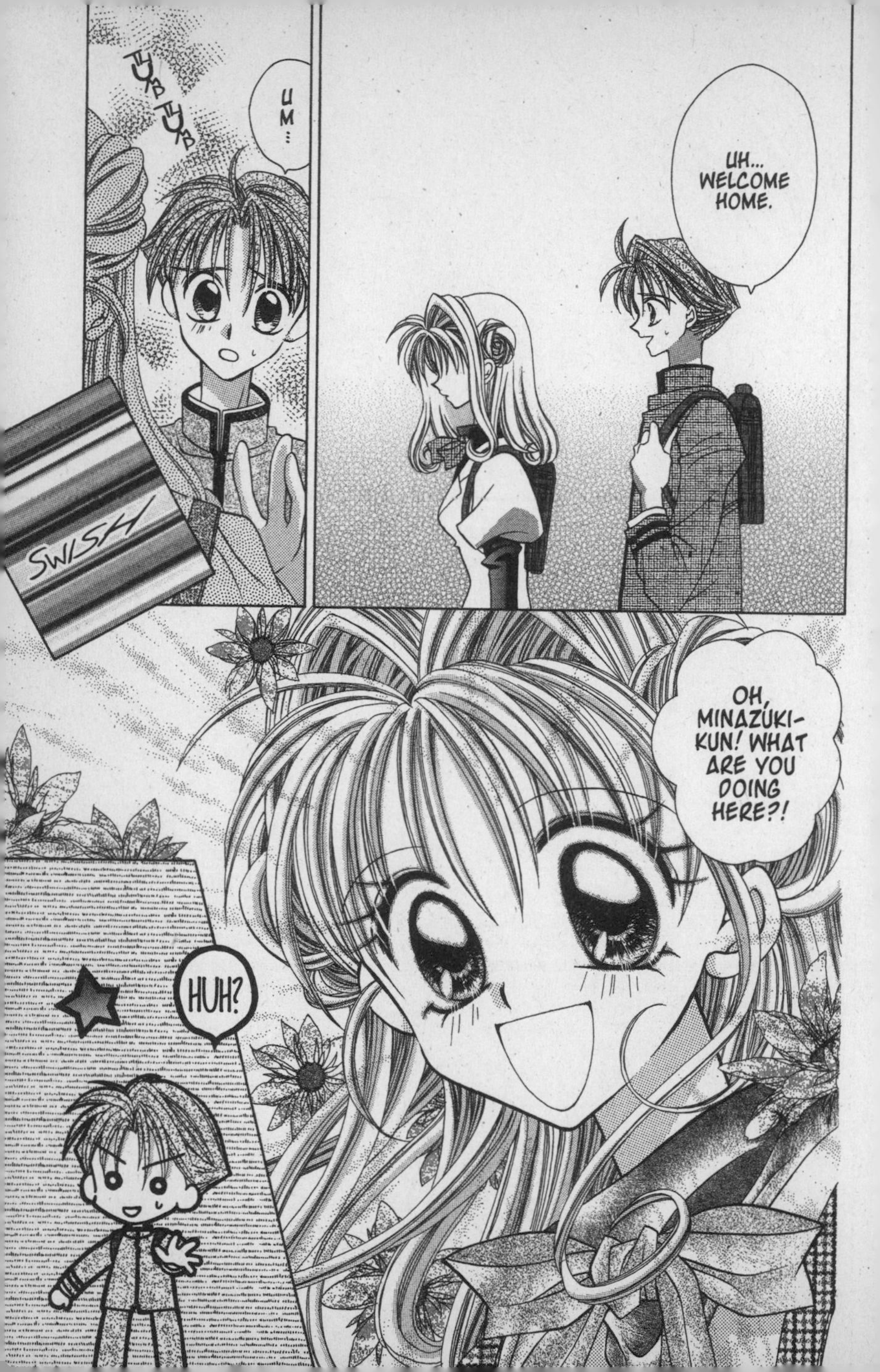
UH... WELCOME HOME.
THUMP THUMP
UM...
SWISH
OH, MINAZUKI-KUN! WHAT ARE YOU DOING HERE?!
HUH?

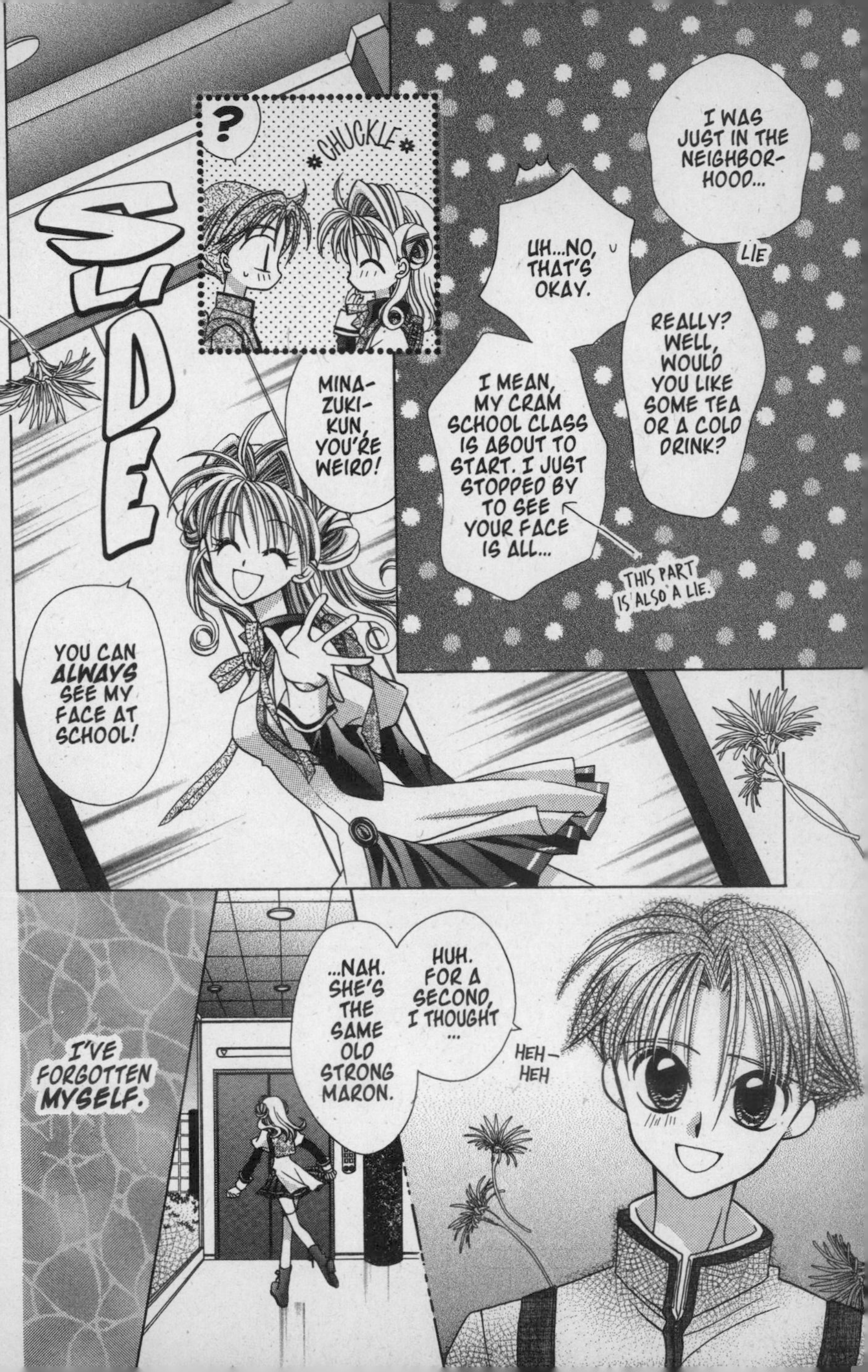
I WAS JUST IN THE NEIGHBOR-HOOD...
LIE
REALLY? WELL, WOULD YOU LIKE SOME TEA OR A COLD DRINK?
UH...NO, THAT'S OKAY.
I MEAN, MY CRAM SCHOOL CLASS IS ABOUT TO START. I JUST STOPPED BY TO SEE YOUR FACE IS ALL...
THIS PART IS ALSO A LIE.
?
CHUCKLE
SLIDE
MINA-ZUKI-KUN, YOU'RE WEIRD!
YOU CAN **ALWAYS** SEE MY FACE AT SCHOOL!
HUH. FOR A SECOND, I THOUGHT...
...NAH. SHE'S THE SAME OLD STRONG MARON.
HEH-HEH
I'VE FORGOTTEN **MYSELF**.

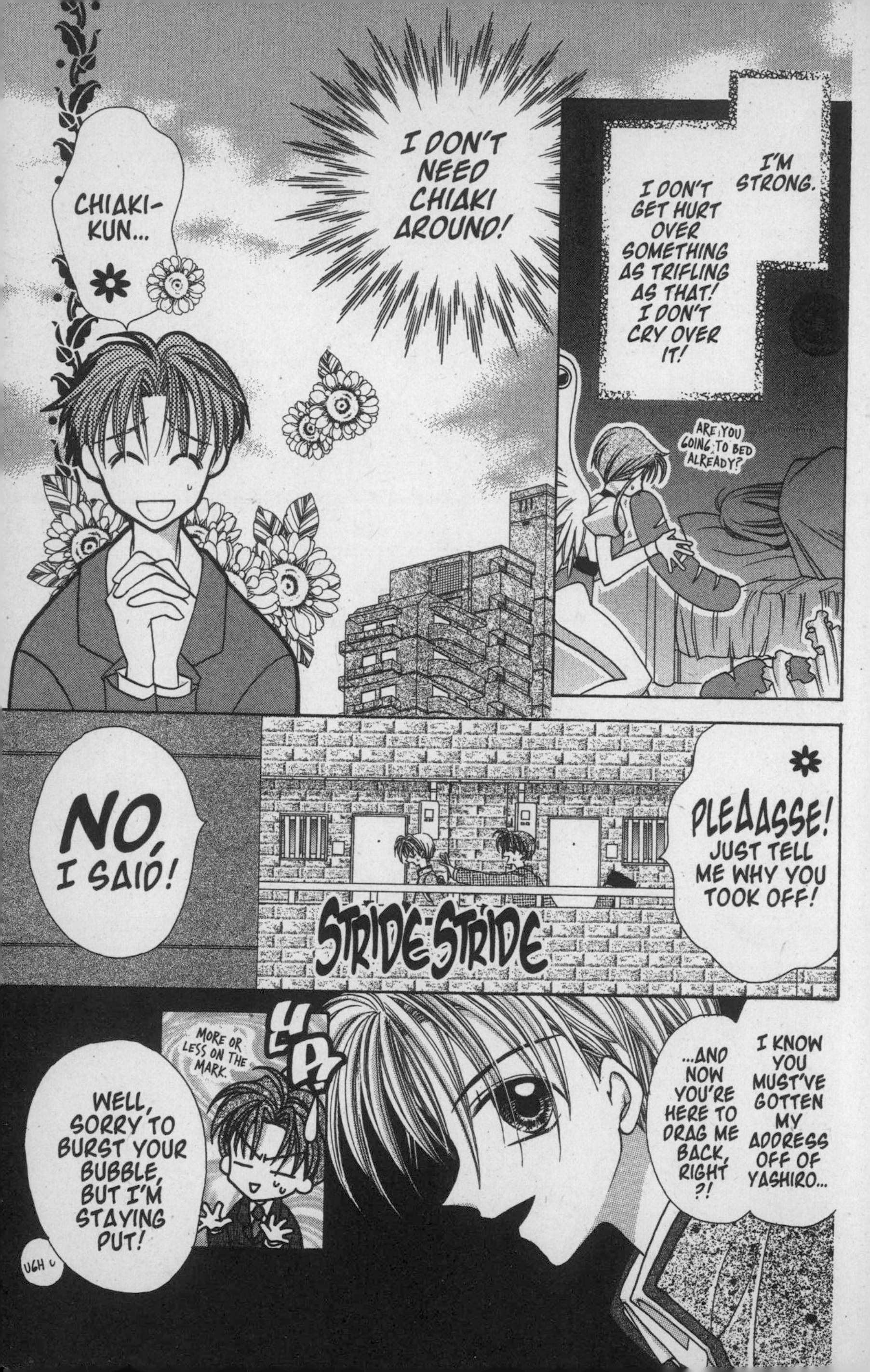
I'M STRONG.
I DON'T GET HURT OVER SOMETHING AS TRIFLING AS THAT! I DON'T CRY OVER IT!
ARE YOU GOING TO BED ALREADY?
I DON'T NEED CHIAKI AROUND!
CHIAKI-KUN...
PLEAAASSE! JUST TELL ME WHY YOU TOOK OFF!
STRIDE STRIDE
NO, I SAID!
I KNOW YOU MUST'VE GOTTEN MY ADDRESS OFF OF YASHIRO...
...AND NOW YOU'RE HERE TO DRAG ME BACK, RIGHT?!
MORE OR LESS ON THE MARK.
WELL, SORRY TO BURST YOUR BUBBLE, BUT I'M STAYING PUT!
UGH

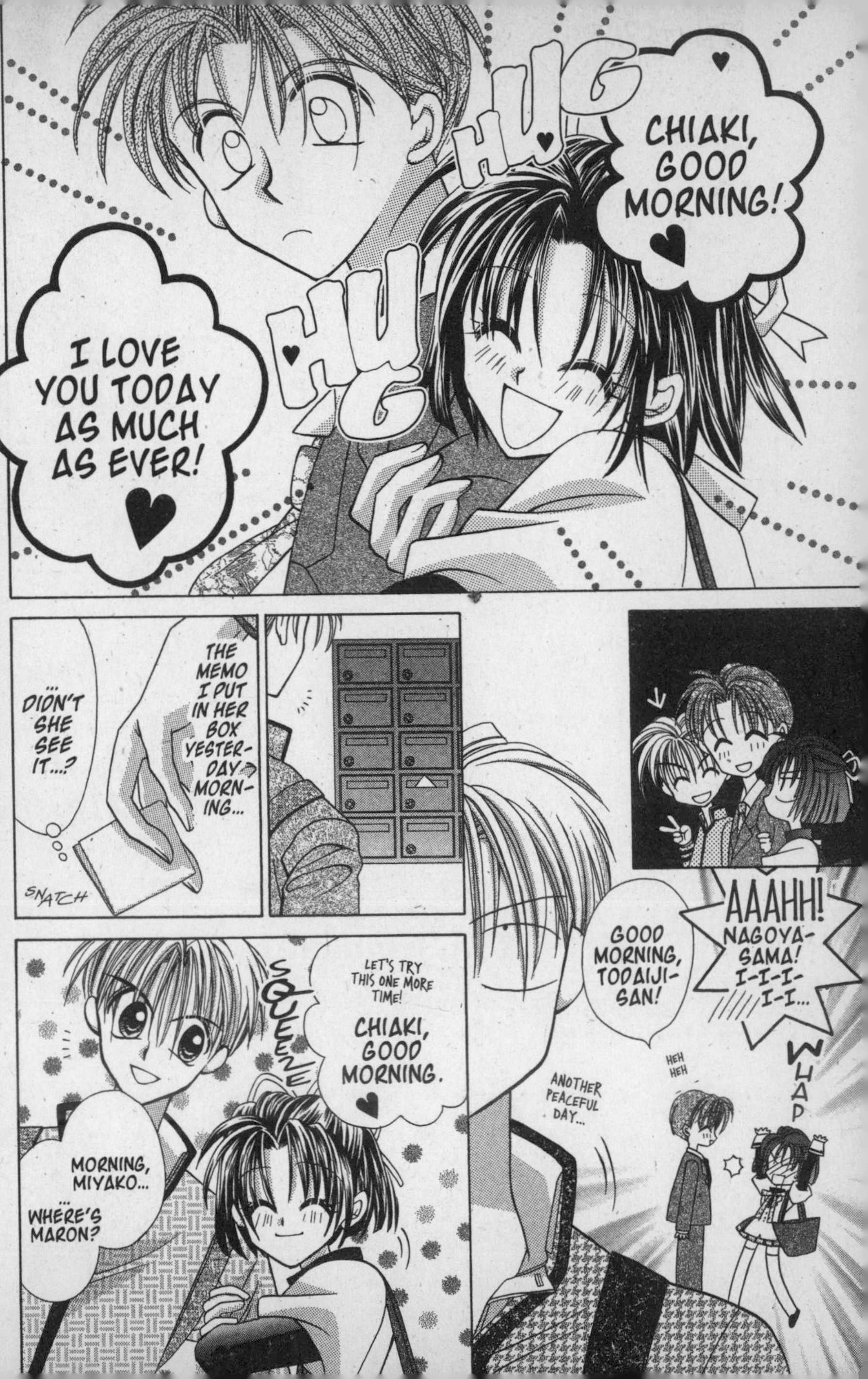
HUG
HUG
CHIAKI, GOOD MORNING!
I LOVE YOU TODAY AS MUCH AS EVER!
THE MEMO I PUT IN HER BOX YESTER-DAY MORNING...
...DIDN'T SHE SEE IT...?
SNATCH
SQUEEZE
LET'S TRY THIS ONE MORE TIME!
CHIAKI, GOOD MORNING.
MORNING, MIYAKO...
...WHERE'S MARON?
GOOD MORNING, TODAIJI-SAN!
AAAHH! NAGOYA-SAMA! I-I-I-I-I...
WHAP
HEH HEH
ANOTHER PEACEFUL DAY...

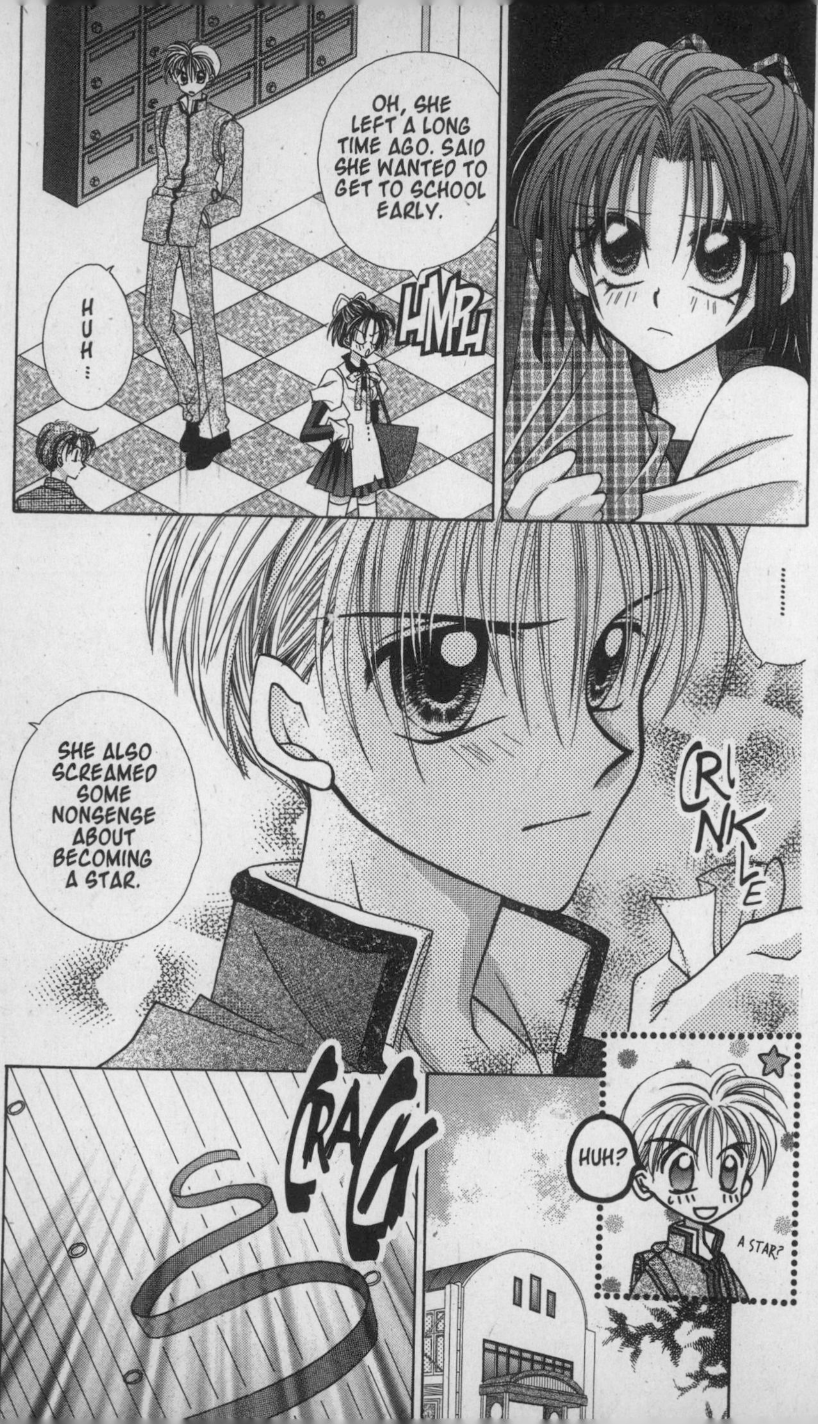
OH, SHE LEFT A LONG TIME AGO. SAID SHE WANTED TO GET TO SCHOOL EARLY.
HMPH
HUH...
......
CRINKLE
SHE ALSO SCREAMED SOME NONSENSE ABOUT BECOMING A STAR.
HUH?
A STAR?
CRACK

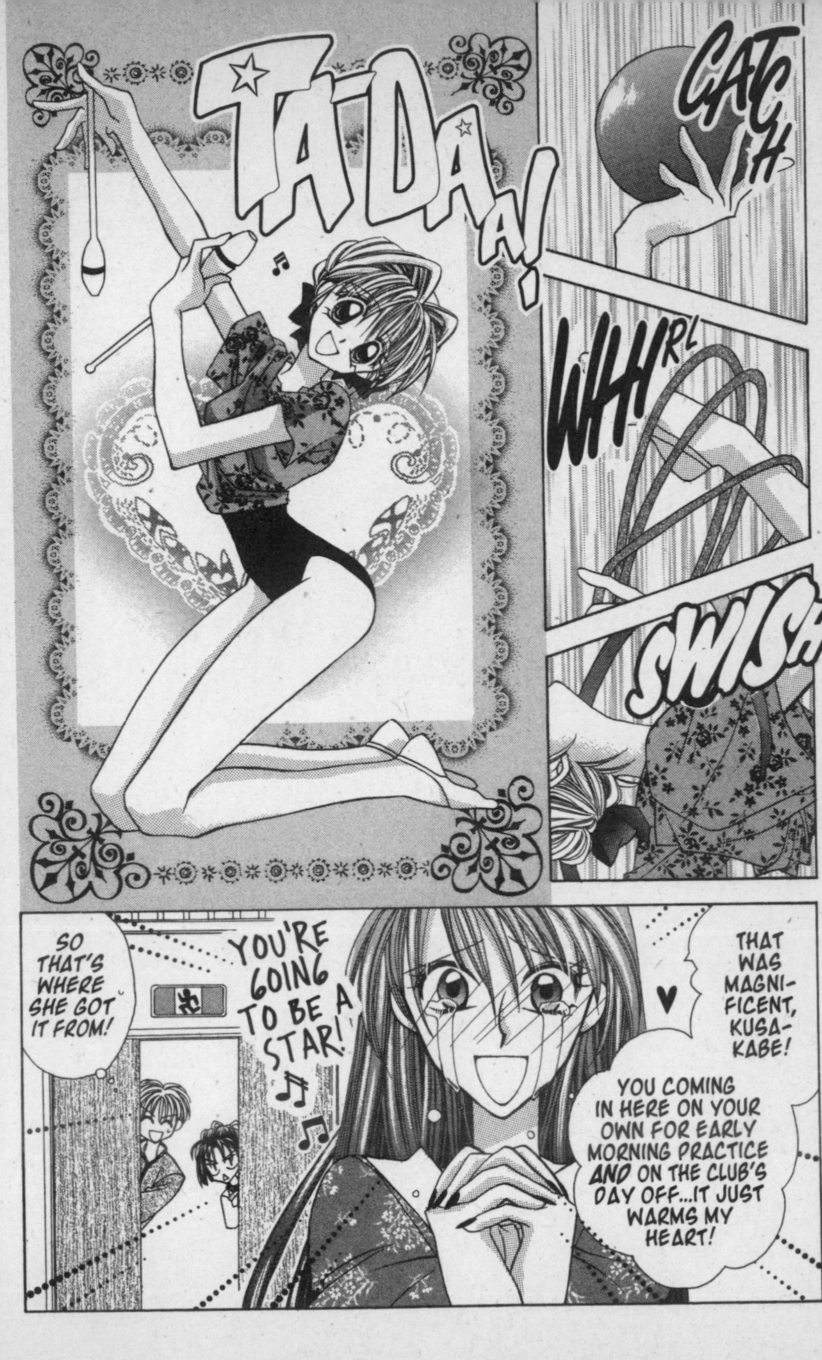
CATCH
WHIRL
SWISH
TA-DAA!
THAT WAS MAGNIFICENT, KUSAKABE!
YOU COMING IN HERE ON YOUR OWN FOR EARLY MORNING PRACTICE AND ON THE CLUB'S DAY OFF...IT JUST WARMS MY HEART!
YOU'RE GOING TO BE A STAR!
SO THAT'S WHERE SHE GOT IT FROM!

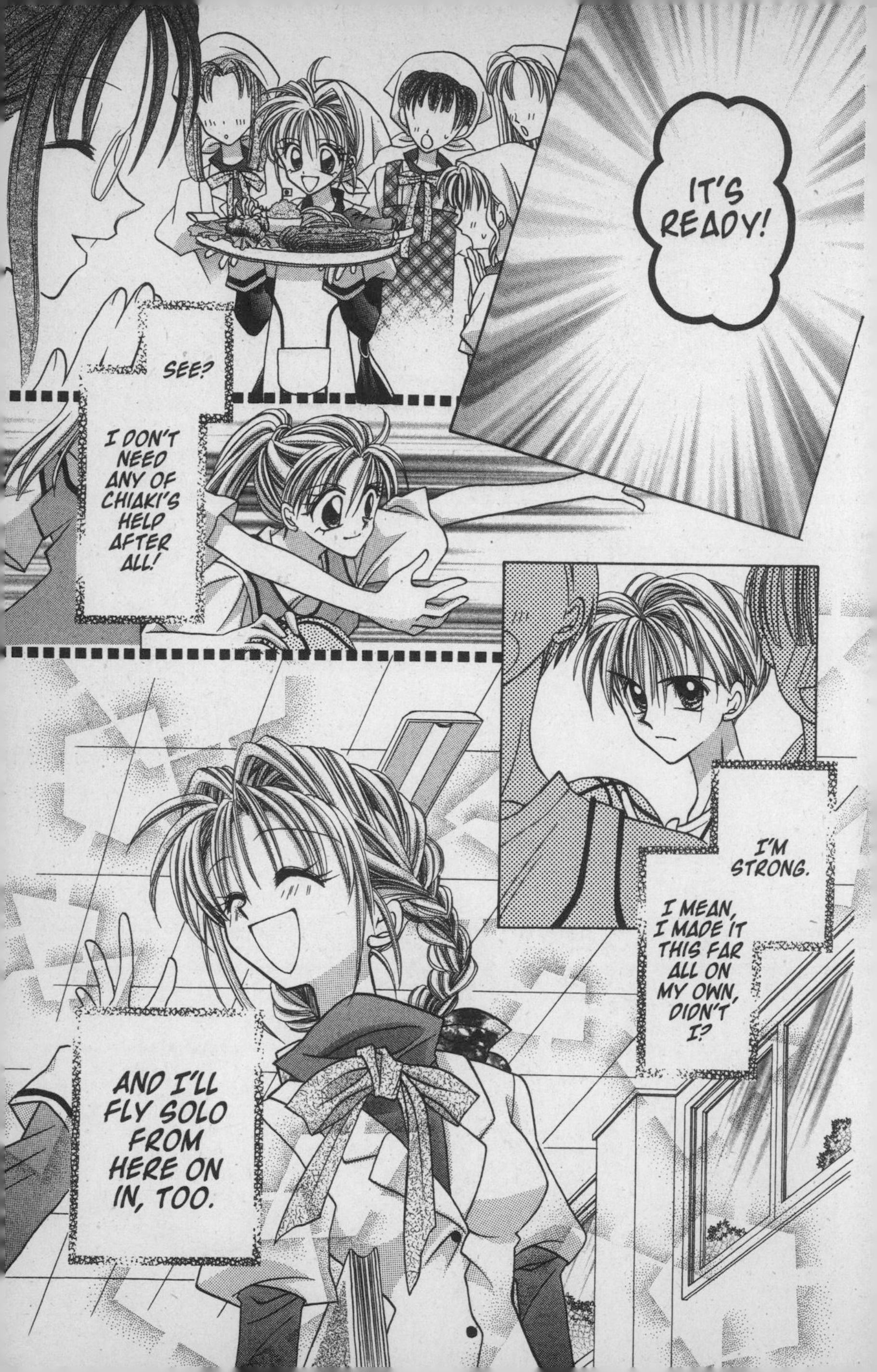
IT'S READY!
SEE?
I DON'T NEED ANY OF CHIAKI'S HELP AFTER ALL!
I'M STRONG.
I MEAN, I MADE IT THIS FAR ALL ON MY OWN, DIDN'T I?
AND I'LL FLY SOLO FROM HERE ON IN, TOO.

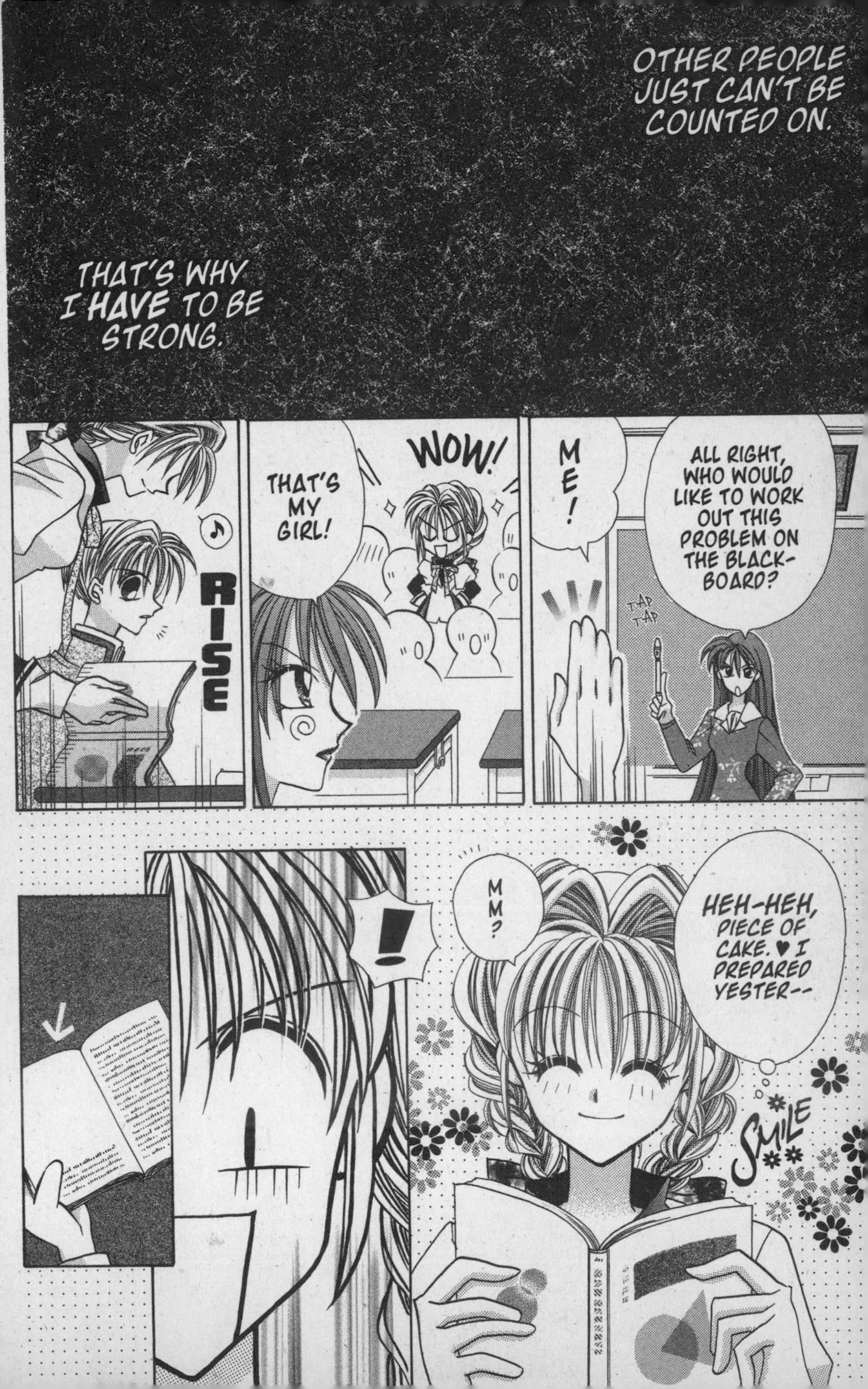
OTHER PEOPLE JUST CAN'T BE COUNTED ON.
THAT'S WHY I HAVE TO BE STRONG.
ALL RIGHT, WHO WOULD LIKE TO WORK OUT THIS PROBLEM ON THE BLACK-BOARD?
TAP TAP
ME!
WOW!
THAT'S MY GIRL!
♪
RISE
HEH-HEH, PIECE OF CAKE. ♥ I PREPARED YESTER--
MM?
SMILE
!

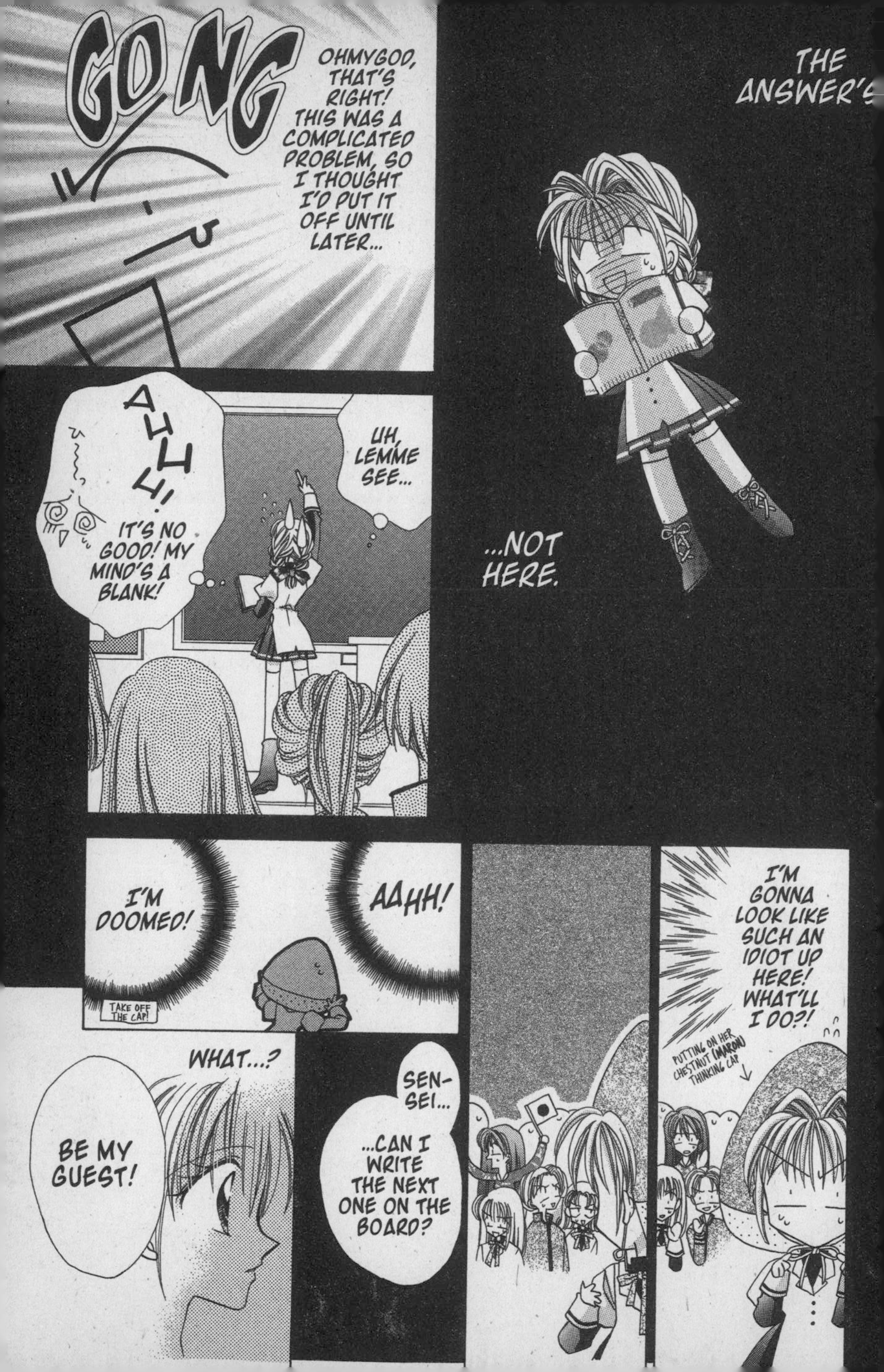
THE ANSWER'S
...NOT HERE.
GONG
OHMYGOD, THAT'S RIGHT! THIS WAS A COMPLICATED PROBLEM, SO I THOUGHT I'D PUT IT OFF UNTIL LATER...
UH, LEMME SEE...
AHHH!
IT'S NO GOOD! MY MIND'S A BLANK!
I'M GONNA LOOK LIKE SUCH AN IDIOT UP HERE! WHAT'LL I DO?!
PUTTING ON HER CHESTNUT (MARON) THINKING CAP
AAHH!
I'M DOOMED!
TAKE OFF THE CAP!
SEN-SEI...
...CAN I WRITE THE NEXT ONE ON THE BOARD?
WHAT...?
BE MY GUEST!

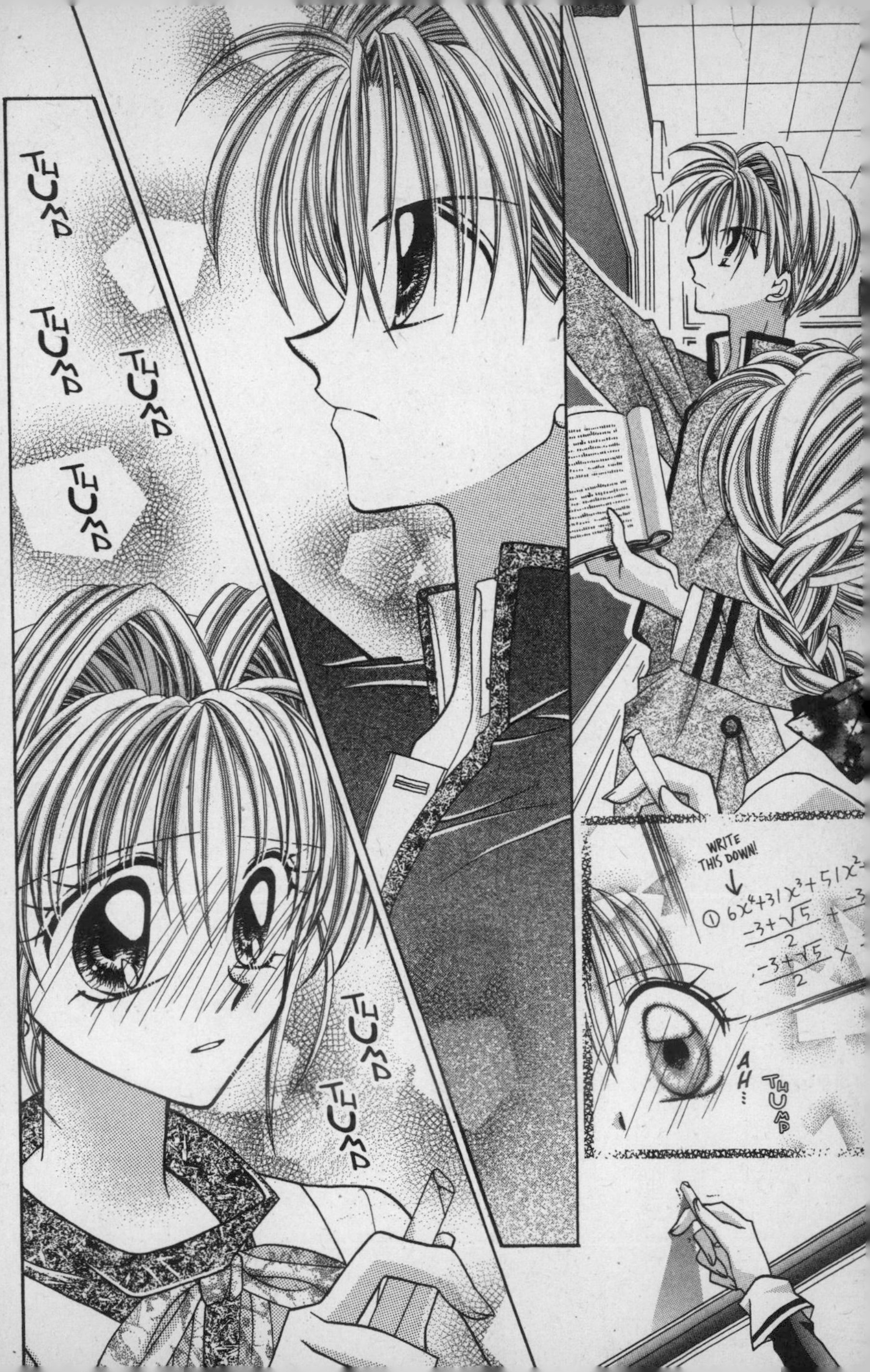
WRITE THIS DOWN!
AH...
THUMP
THUMP
THUMP
THUMP
THUMP
THUMP
THUMP

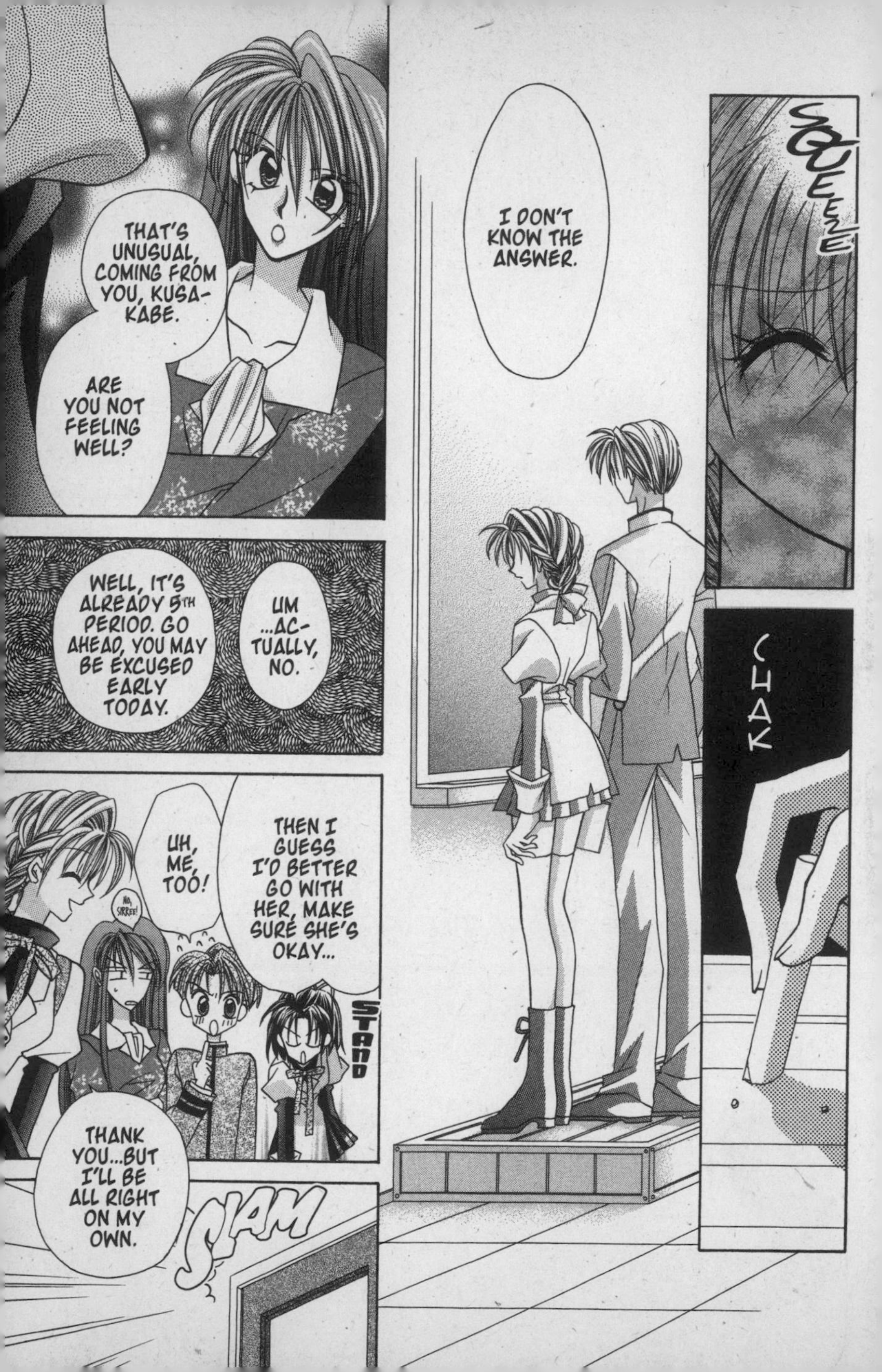
SQUEEZE
CHAK
I DON'T KNOW THE ANSWER.
THAT'S UNUSUAL, COMING FROM YOU, KUSA-KABE.
ARE YOU NOT FEELING WELL?
UM ...AC-TUALLY, NO.
WELL, IT'S ALREADY 5TH PERIOD. GO AHEAD, YOU MAY BE EXCUSED EARLY TODAY.
THEN I GUESS I'D BETTER GO WITH HER, MAKE SURE SHE'S OKAY...
UH, ME, TOO!
NO, SIRREE!
STAND
THANK YOU...BUT I'LL BE ALL RIGHT ON MY OWN.
SLAM

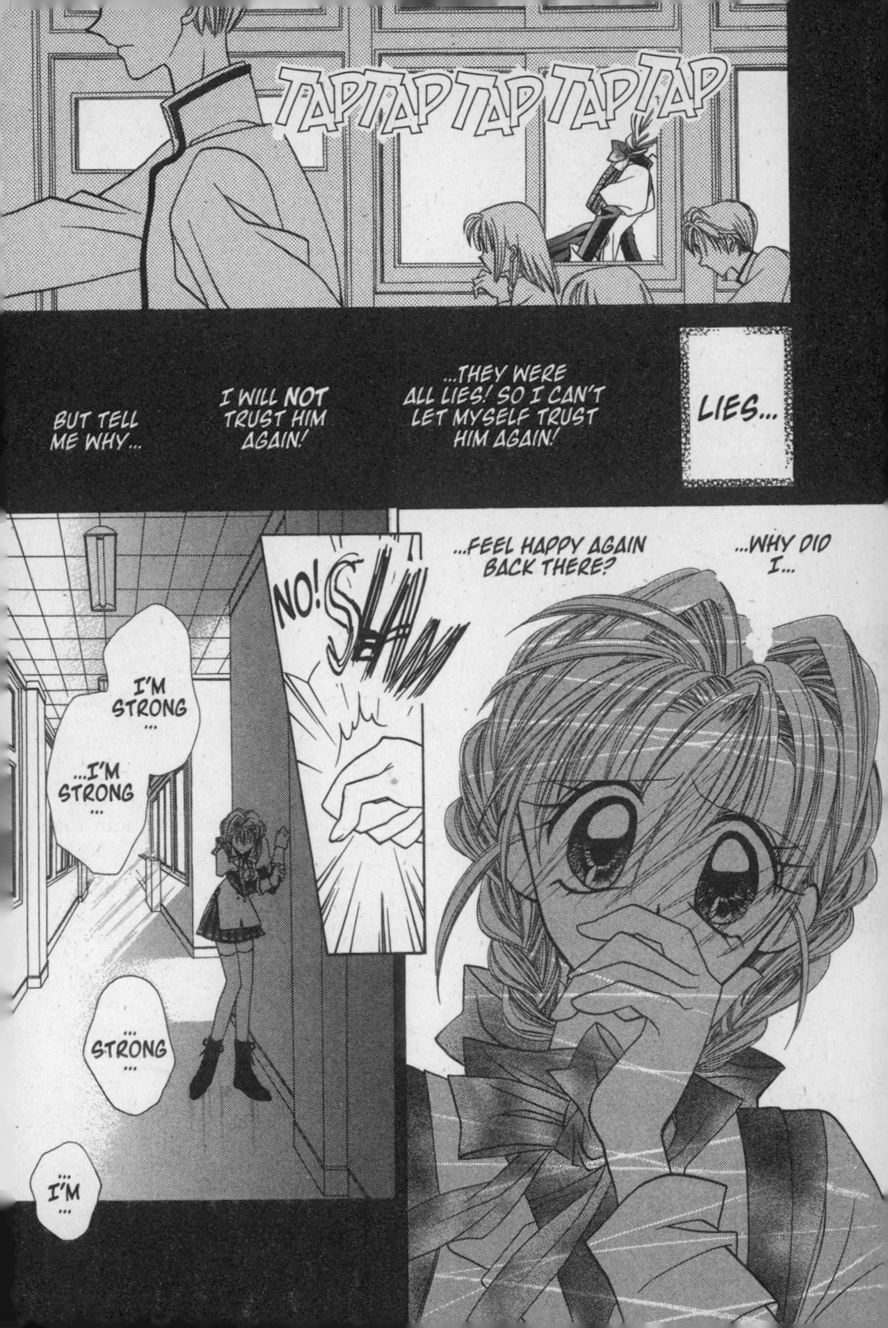
TAPTAP TAPTAP TAPTAP
LIES...
...THEY WERE ALL LIES! SO I CAN'T LET MYSELF TRUST HIM AGAIN!
I WILL NOT TRUST HIM AGAIN!
BUT TELL ME WHY...
...WHY DID I...
...FEEL HAPPY AGAIN BACK THERE?
NO!
SHAW
I'M STRONG...
...I'M STRONG...
...STRONG...
...I'M...

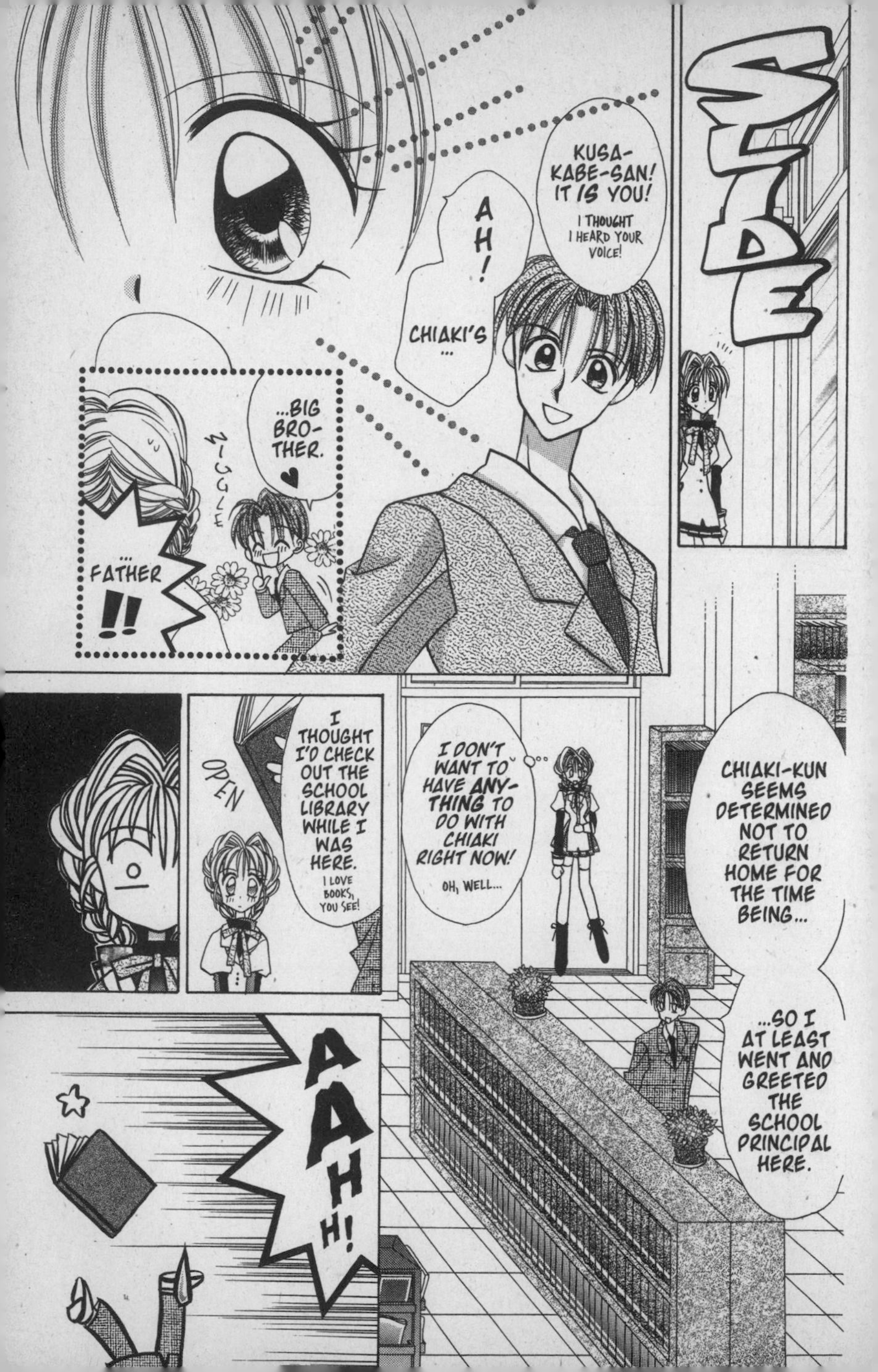
SLIDE
KUSA-KABE-SAN! IT IS YOU!
I THOUGHT I HEARD YOUR VOICE!
AH!
CHIAKI'S ...
...BIG BRO-THER. ♥
...FATHER !!
CHIAKI-KUN SEEMS DETERMINED NOT TO RETURN HOME FOR THE TIME BEING...
...SO I AT LEAST WENT AND GREETED THE SCHOOL PRINCIPAL HERE.
I DON'T WANT TO HAVE ANY-THING TO DO WITH CHIAKI RIGHT NOW!
OH, WELL...
I THOUGHT I'D CHECK OUT THE SCHOOL LIBRARY WHILE I WAS HERE.
I LOVE BOOKS, YOU SEE!
OPEN
AAHH!

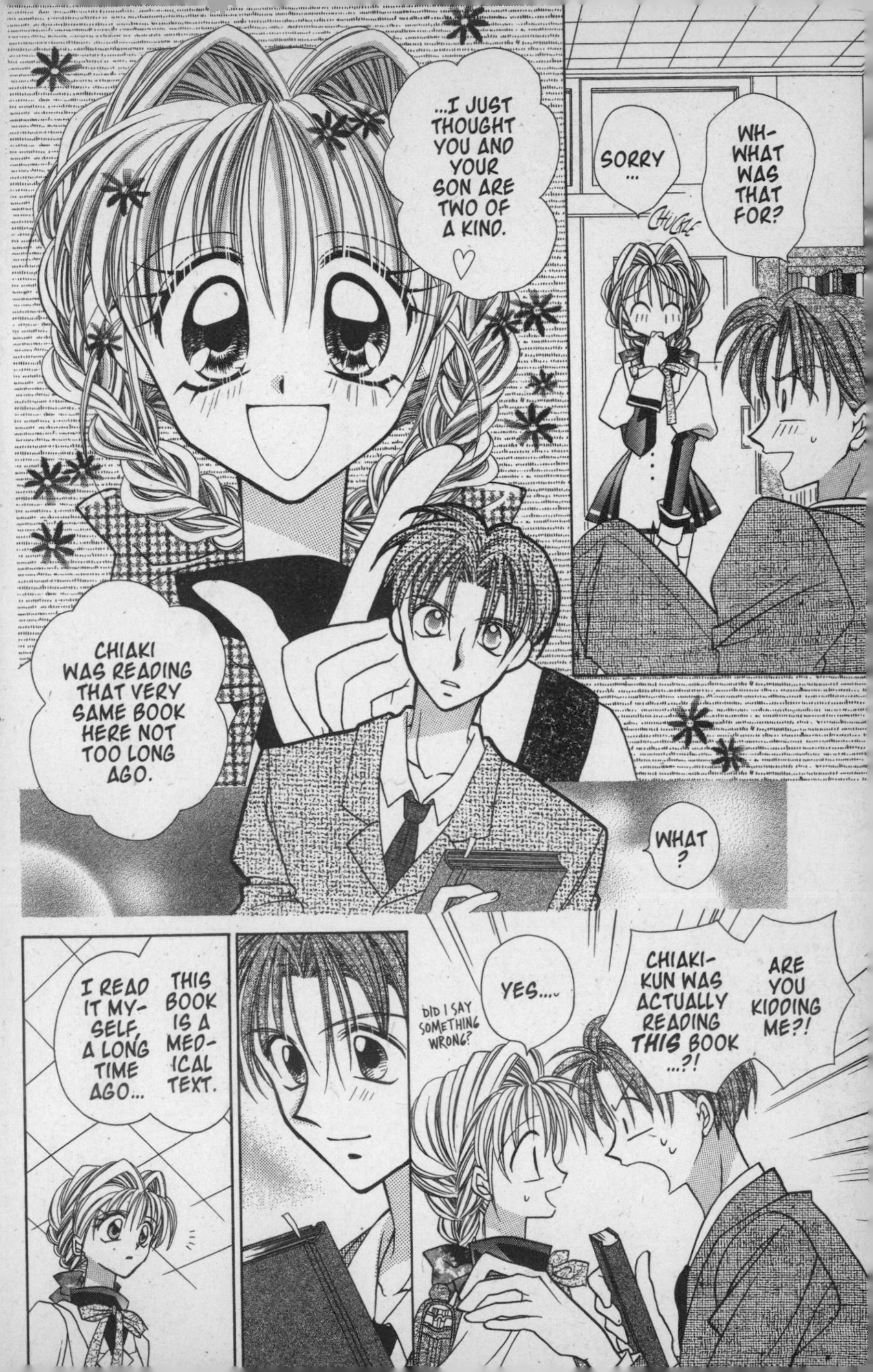
WH-WHAT WAS THAT FOR?
SORRY...
CHUCKLE
...I JUST THOUGHT YOU AND YOUR SON ARE TWO OF A KIND. ♡
CHIAKI WAS READING THAT VERY SAME BOOK HERE NOT TOO LONG AGO.
WHAT?
ARE YOU KIDDING ME?!
CHIAKI-KUN WAS ACTUALLY READING **THIS** BOOK ...?!
YES....
DID I SAY SOMETHING WRONG?
THIS BOOK IS A MEDICAL TEXT.
I READ IT MYSELF, A LONG TIME AGO...

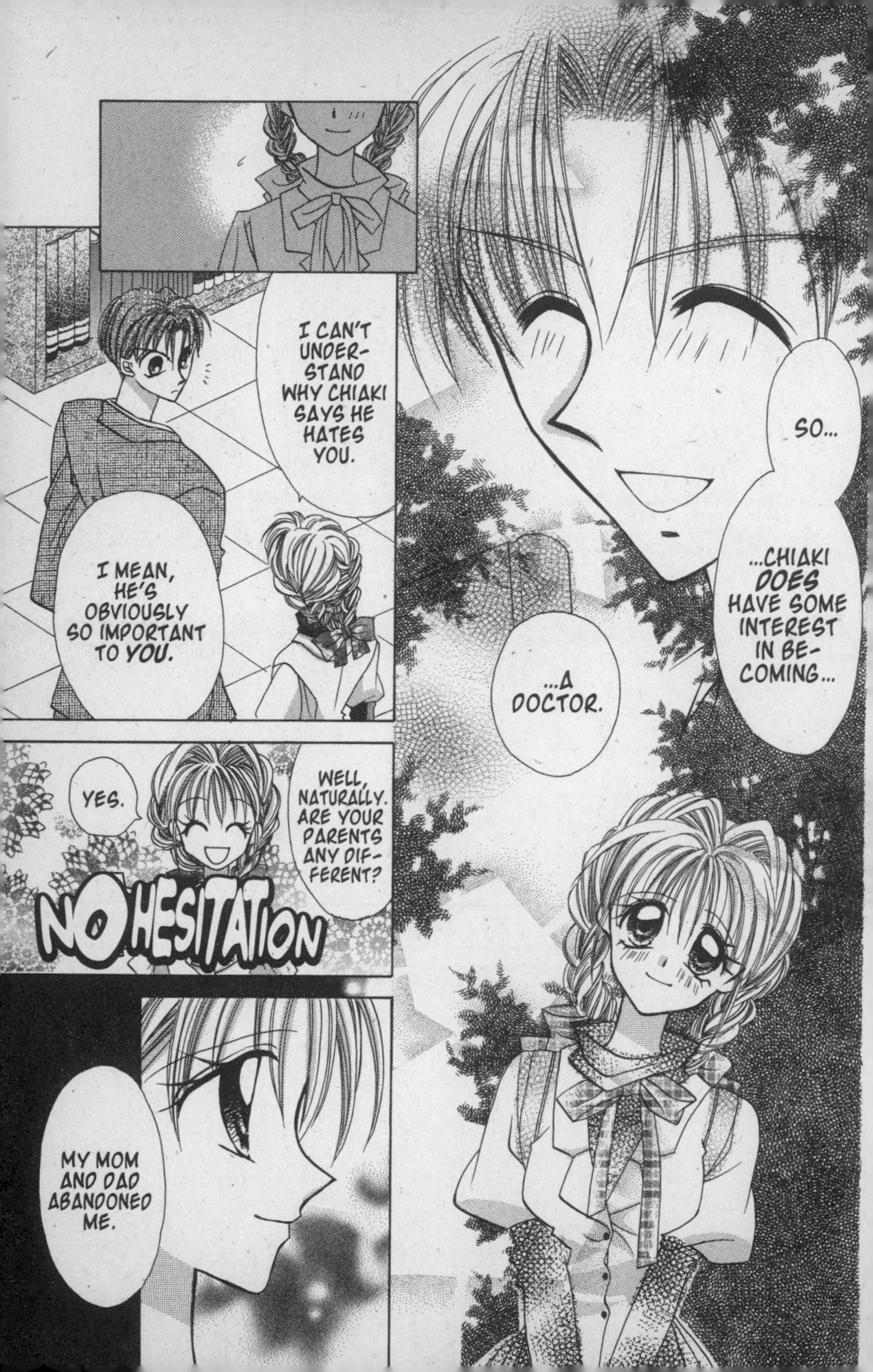
SO...
...CHIAKI DOES HAVE SOME INTEREST IN BE-COMING...
...A DOCTOR.
I CAN'T UNDER-STAND WHY CHIAKI SAYS HE HATES YOU.
I MEAN, HE'S OBVIOUSLY SO IMPORTANT TO YOU.
WELL, NATURALLY. ARE YOUR PARENTS ANY DIF-FERENT?
YES.
NO HESITATION
MY MOM AND DAD ABANDONED ME.

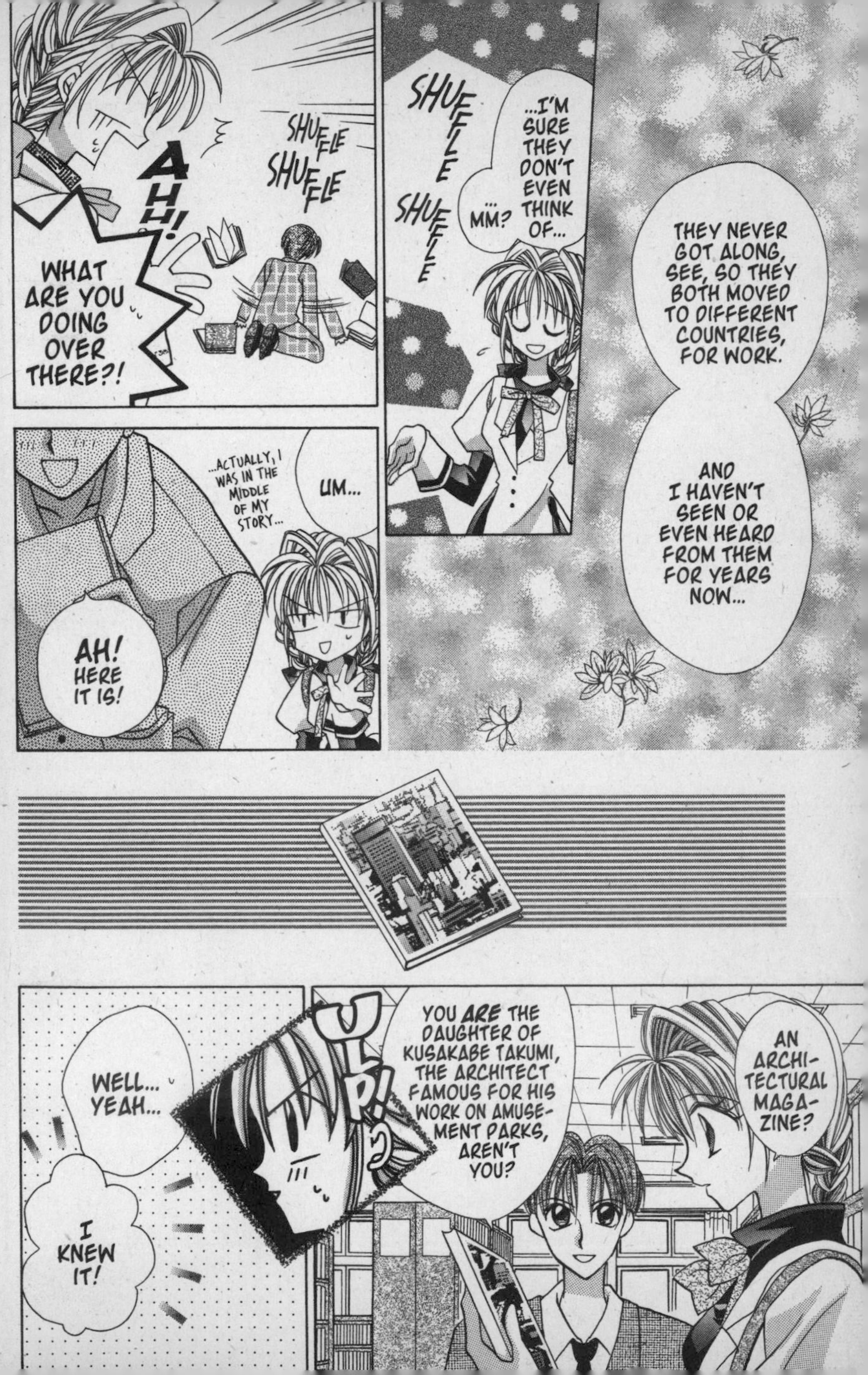
THEY NEVER GOT ALONG, SEE, SO THEY BOTH MOVED TO DIFFERENT COUNTRIES, FOR WORK.
AND I HAVEN'T SEEN OR EVEN HEARD FROM THEM FOR YEARS NOW...
...I'M SURE THEY DON'T EVEN THINK OF...
...MM?
SHUFFLE SHUFFLE
SHUFFLE SHUFFLE
AHH!
WHAT ARE YOU DOING OVER THERE?!
UM...
...ACTUALLY, I WAS IN THE MIDDLE OF MY STORY...
AH! HERE IT IS!
AN ARCHITECTURAL MAGAZINE?
YOU ARE THE DAUGHTER OF KUSAKABE TAKUMI, THE ARCHITECT FAMOUS FOR HIS WORK ON AMUSEMENT PARKS, AREN'T YOU?
ULP!
WELL... YEAH...
I KNEW IT!

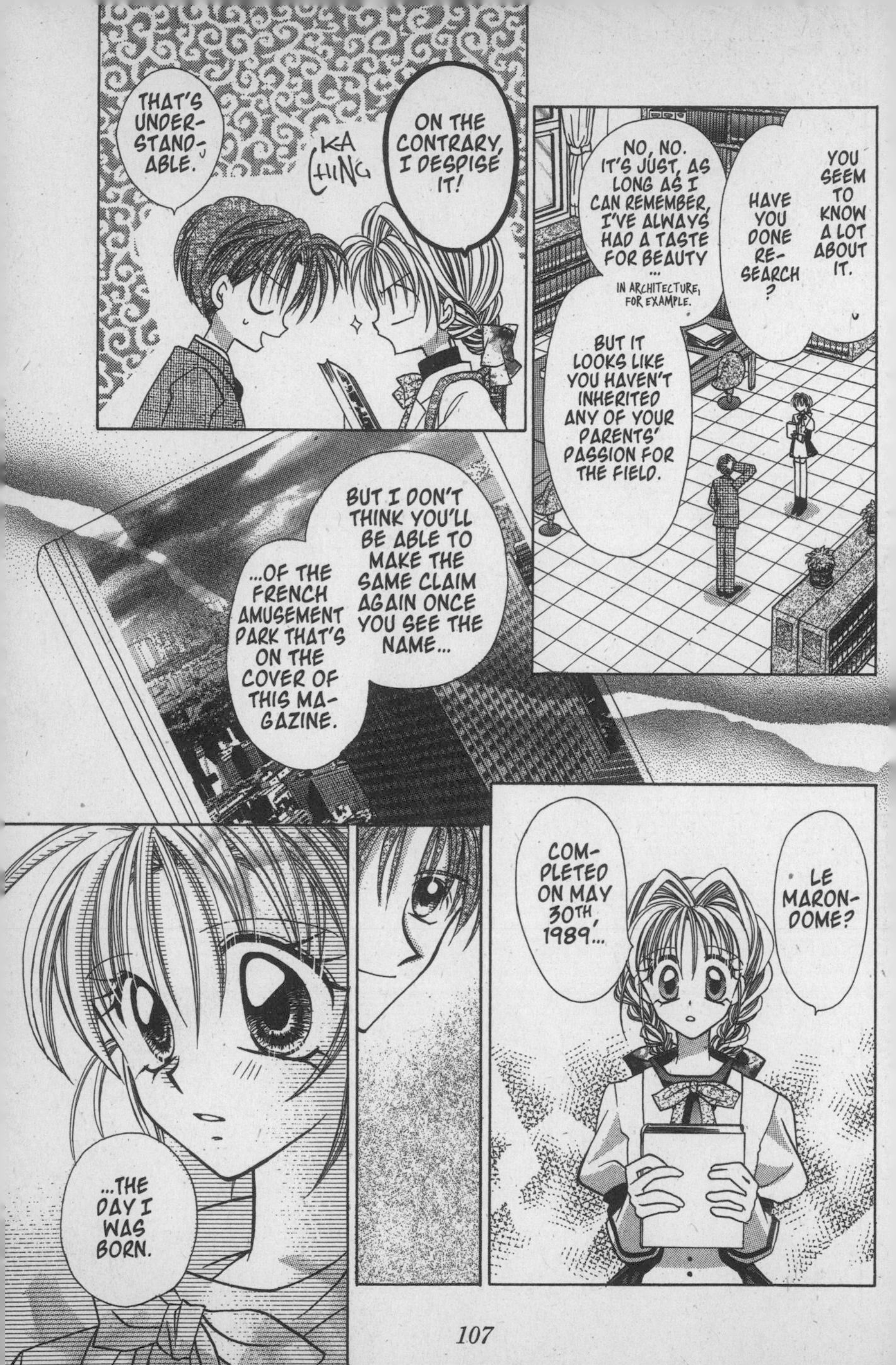
YOU SEEM TO KNOW A LOT ABOUT IT.
HAVE YOU DONE RE-SEARCH?
NO, NO. IT'S JUST, AS LONG AS I CAN REMEMBER, I'VE ALWAYS HAD A TASTE FOR BEAUTY...
IN ARCHITECTURE, FOR EXAMPLE.
BUT IT LOOKS LIKE YOU HAVEN'T INHERITED ANY OF YOUR PARENTS' PASSION FOR THE FIELD.
ON THE CONTRARY, I DESPISE IT!
KA CHING
THAT'S UNDER-STAND-ABLE.
BUT I DON'T THINK YOU'LL BE ABLE TO MAKE THE SAME CLAIM AGAIN ONCE YOU SEE THE NAME...
...OF THE FRENCH AMUSEMENT PARK THAT'S ON THE COVER OF THIS MA-GAZINE.
LE MARON-DOME?
COM-PLETED ON MAY 30TH 1989...
...THE DAY I WAS BORN.

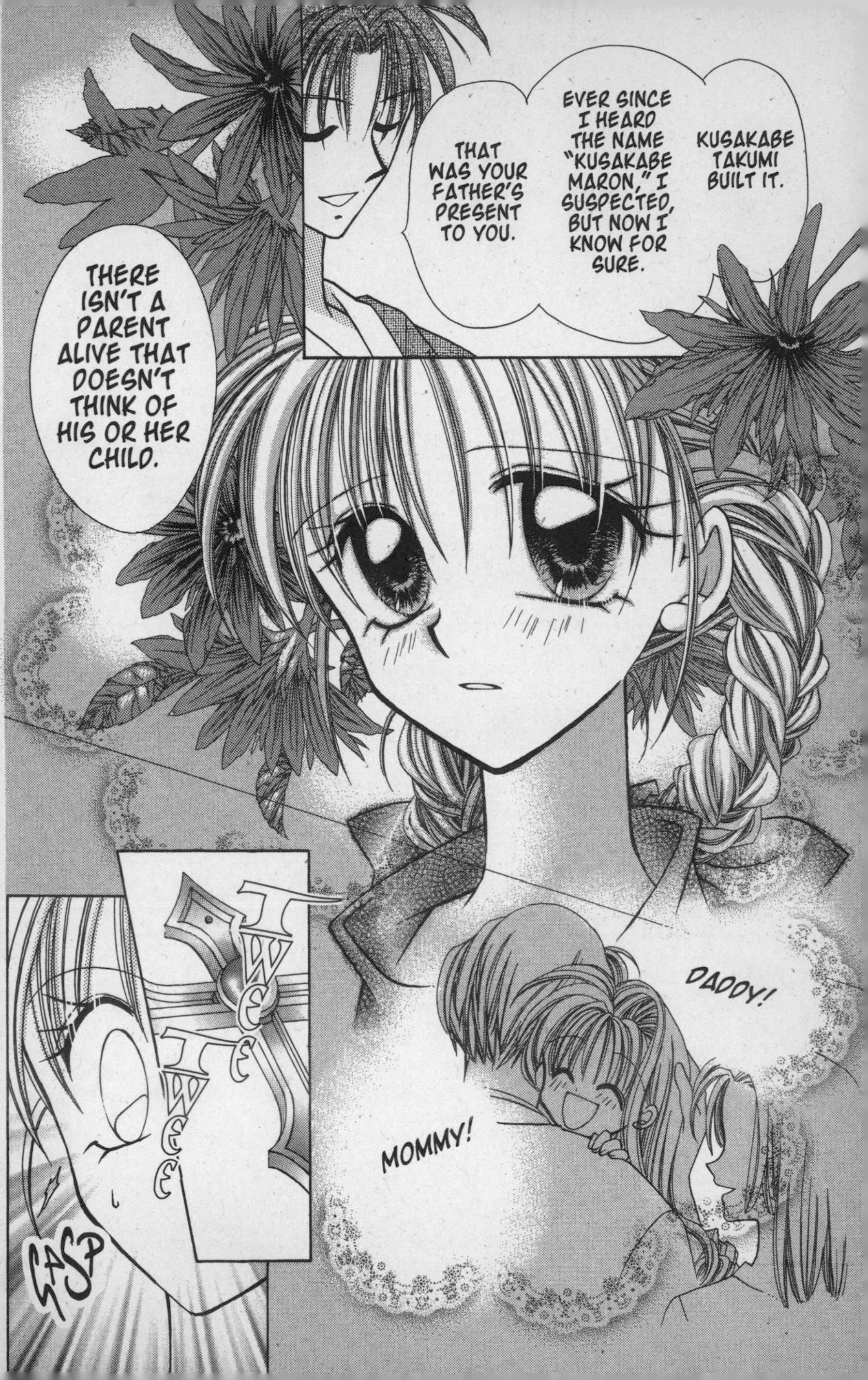
KUSAKABE TAKUMI BUILT IT.
EVER SINCE I HEARD THE NAME "KUSAKABE MARON," I SUSPECTED, BUT NOW I KNOW FOR SURE.
THAT WAS YOUR FATHER'S PRESENT TO YOU.
THERE ISN'T A PARENT ALIVE THAT DOESN'T THINK OF HIS OR HER CHILD.
DADDY!
MOMMY!
TWEE
TWEE
GASP

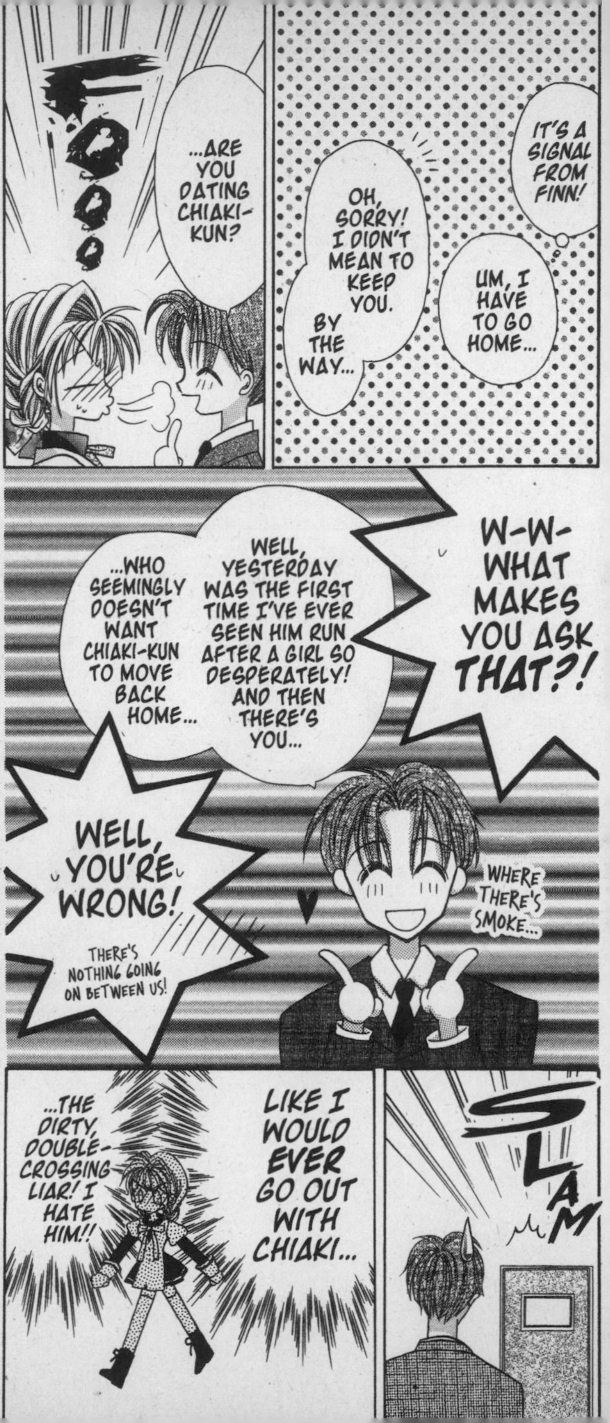
IT'S A SIGNAL FROM FINN!
UM, I HAVE TO GO HOME...
OH, SORRY! I DIDN'T MEAN TO KEEP YOU.
BY THE WAY...
...ARE YOU DATING CHIAKI-KUN?
W-W-WHAT MAKES YOU ASK THAT?!
WELL, YESTERDAY WAS THE FIRST TIME I'VE EVER SEEN HIM RUN AFTER A GIRL SO DESPERATELY! AND THEN THERE'S YOU...
...WHO SEEMINGLY DOESN'T WANT CHIAKI-KUN TO MOVE BACK HOME...
WHERE THERE'S SMOKE...
WELL, YOU'RE WRONG!
THERE'S NOTHING GOING ON BETWEEN US!
SLAM
LIKE I WOULD EVER GO OUT WITH CHIAKI...
...THE DIRTY, DOUBLE-CROSSING LIAR! I HATE HIM!!

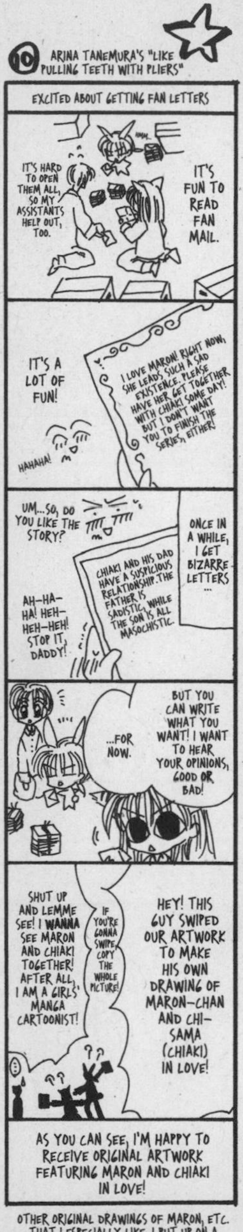
10 ARINA TANEMURA'S "LIKE PULLING TEETH WITH PLIERS"
EXCITED ABOUT GETTING FAN LETTERS
IT'S FUN TO READ FAN MAIL.
IT'S HARD TO OPEN THEM ALL, SO MY ASSISTANTS HELP OUT, TOO.
I LOVE MARON! RIGHT NOW, SHE LEADS SUCH A SAD EXISTENCE. PLEASE HAVE HER GET TOGETHER WITH CHIAKI SOME DAY! BUT I DON'T WANT YOU TO FINISH THE SERIES, EITHER!
IT'S A LOT OF FUN!
HAHAHA!
ONCE IN A WHILE, I GET BIZARRE LETTERS...
UM...SO, DO YOU LIKE THE STORY?
CHIAKI AND HIS DAD HAVE A SUSPICIOUS RELATIONSHIP. THE FATHER IS SADISTIC, WHILE THE SON IS ALL MASOCHISTIC.
AH-HA-HA! HEH-HEH-HEH! STOP IT, DADDY!
BUT YOU CAN WRITE WHAT YOU WANT! I WANT TO HEAR YOUR OPINIONS, GOOD OR BAD!
...FOR NOW.
HEY! THIS GUY SWIPED OUR ARTWORK TO MAKE HIS OWN DRAWING OF MARON-CHAN AND CHI-SAMA (CHIAKI) IN LOVE!
IF YOU'RE GONNA SWIPE, COPY THE WHOLE PICTURE!
SHUT UP AND LEMME SEE! I WANNA SEE MARON AND CHIAKI TOGETHER! AFTER ALL, I AM A GIRLS' MANGA CARTOONIST!
AS YOU CAN SEE, I'M HAPPY TO RECEIVE ORIGINAL ARTWORK FEATURING MARON AND CHIAKI IN LOVE!
OTHER ORIGINAL DRAWINGS OF MARON, ETC. THAT I ESPECIALLY LIKE, I PUT UP ON A CORKBOARD HERE. ♥ I LOVES 'EM!!

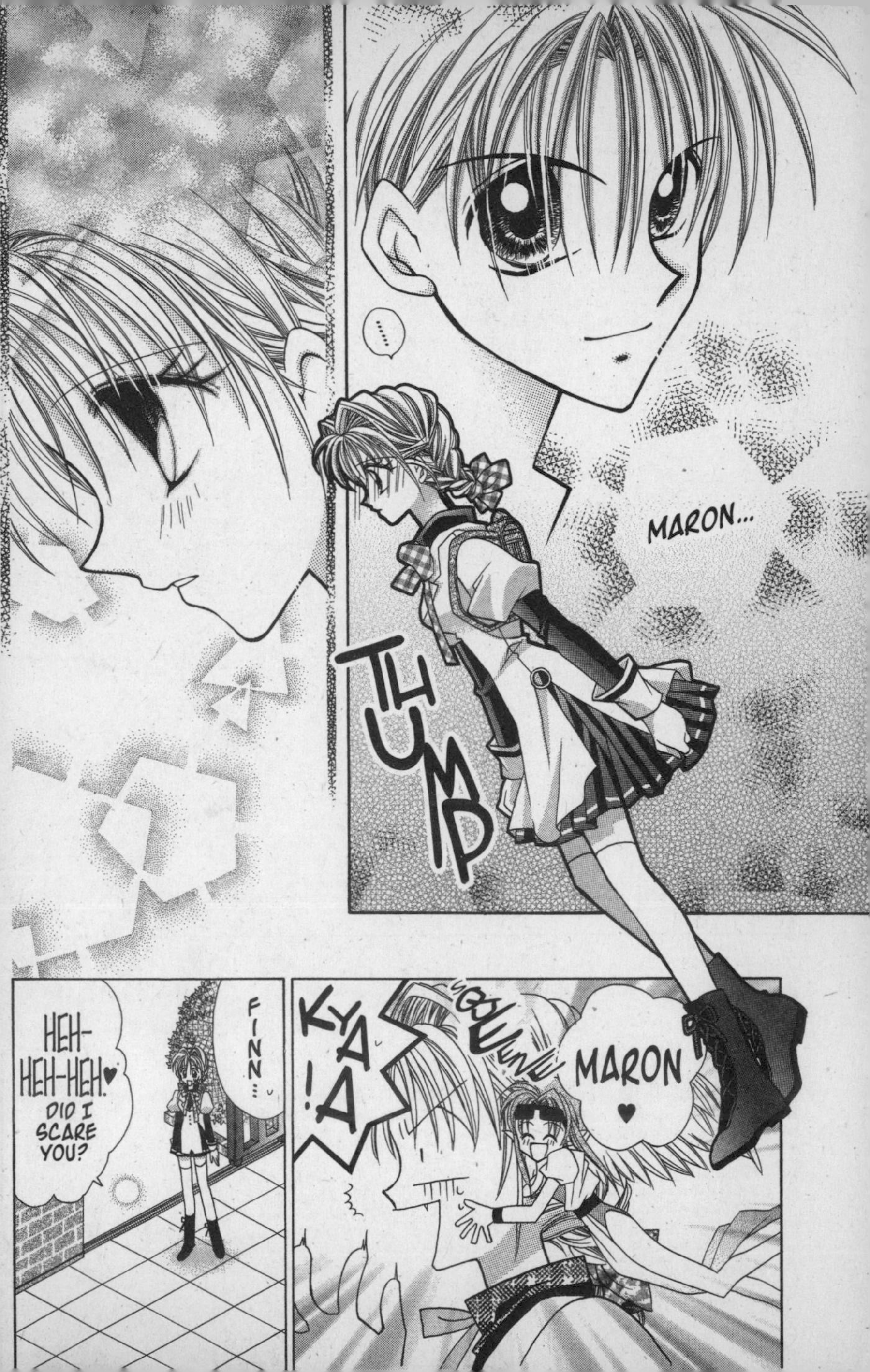

MARON...
......
THUMP
MARON ♥
SQUEEZE
KYAA!
FINN...
HEH-HEH-HEH.♥ DID I SCARE YOU?

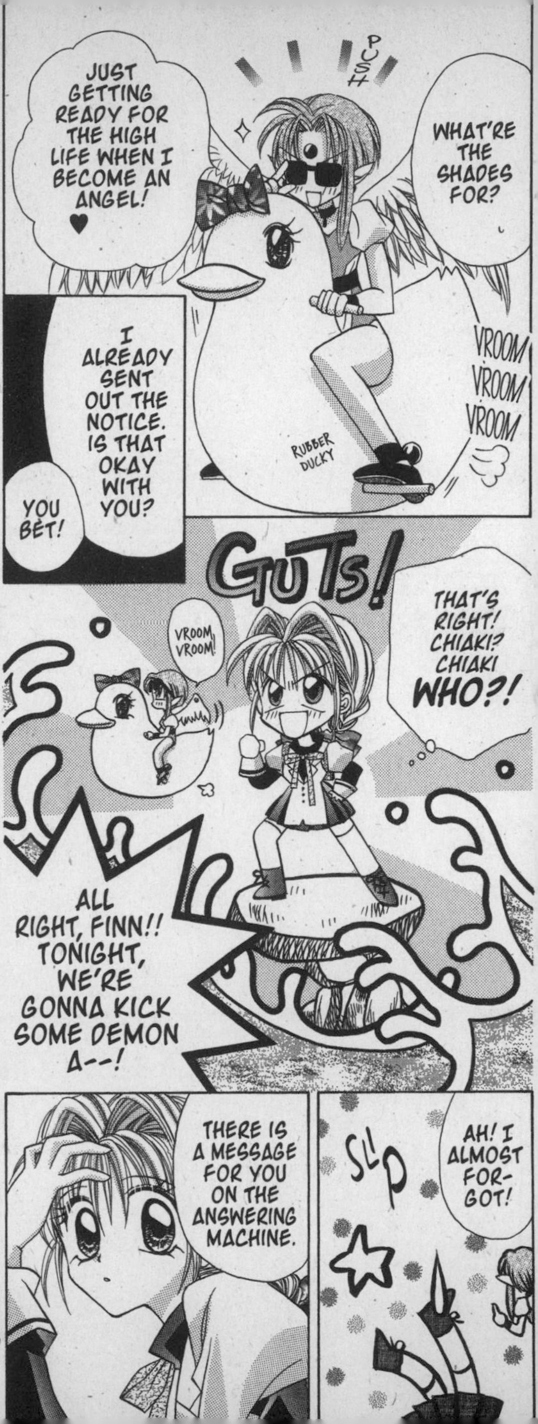
WHAT'RE THE SHADES FOR?
JUST GETTING READY FOR THE HIGH LIFE WHEN I BECOME AN ANGEL! ♥
PUSH
VROOM VROOM VROOM
RUBBER DUCKY
I ALREADY SENT OUT THE NOTICE. IS THAT OKAY WITH YOU?
YOU BET!
THAT'S RIGHT! CHIAKI? CHIAKI WHO?!
GUTS!
VROOM, VROOM!
ALL RIGHT, FINN!! TONIGHT, WE'RE GONNA KICK SOME DEMON A--!
AH! I ALMOST FOR-GOT!
SLIP
THERE IS A MESSAGE FOR YOU ON THE ANSWERING MACHINE.

5

Okay, here's my official announcement of the schedule.

STARTING ON FEBRUARY 13TH (SATURDAY), 1999, ON TV ASAHI!

For the people who bought this volume a long time after it first came out, check out the anime, every Saturday evening at 6:30 ♥ In volume one, the section featuring my angelic assistants was extremely popular, so here they are again, expounding on the animification of JEANNE!

BIRD

Congratulations! ♥ I knew you could do it, Arina-sensei!!! Really, it's sooo wonderful!! I'm really looking forward to seeing JEANNE actually **move**--(not to mention Chiaki! ♥) There is a certain sadness as well, knowing that the Jeanne us Ribon Kids know and love will become **everyone's** JEANNE...but my happiness outweighs that small misgiving. ♥ I'm a little worried that Arina-sensei will become even busier and therefore more susceptible to colds and such, but I want to be right alongside her, doing my best. ♥ Ah! Thanks to the readers who sent me mail about my 4-panel comic in the back of JEANNE vol. 1! It makes me appreciate being an assistant even more. ♥ (LOL) By the way, I'm not a manga cartoonist myself (LOL) See ya! ♥

RUKA KAZUKI

Heartfelt congratulations to Arina-sensei for the Jeanne anime!!! Wowie! This kinda thing is just amazing! I mean, now it's a cartoon! On TV!! Moving!! Arina-sensei, you're amazing! I hope to be like Arina-sensei one day. (Of course, I know there's no way!) And so, from here on in as well, Arina-sensei, take care of your health and keep on keeping on with manga and mimicry. ♥ Recently, your imitation of a certain person has become dead on. It's so funny! HAHAHA!

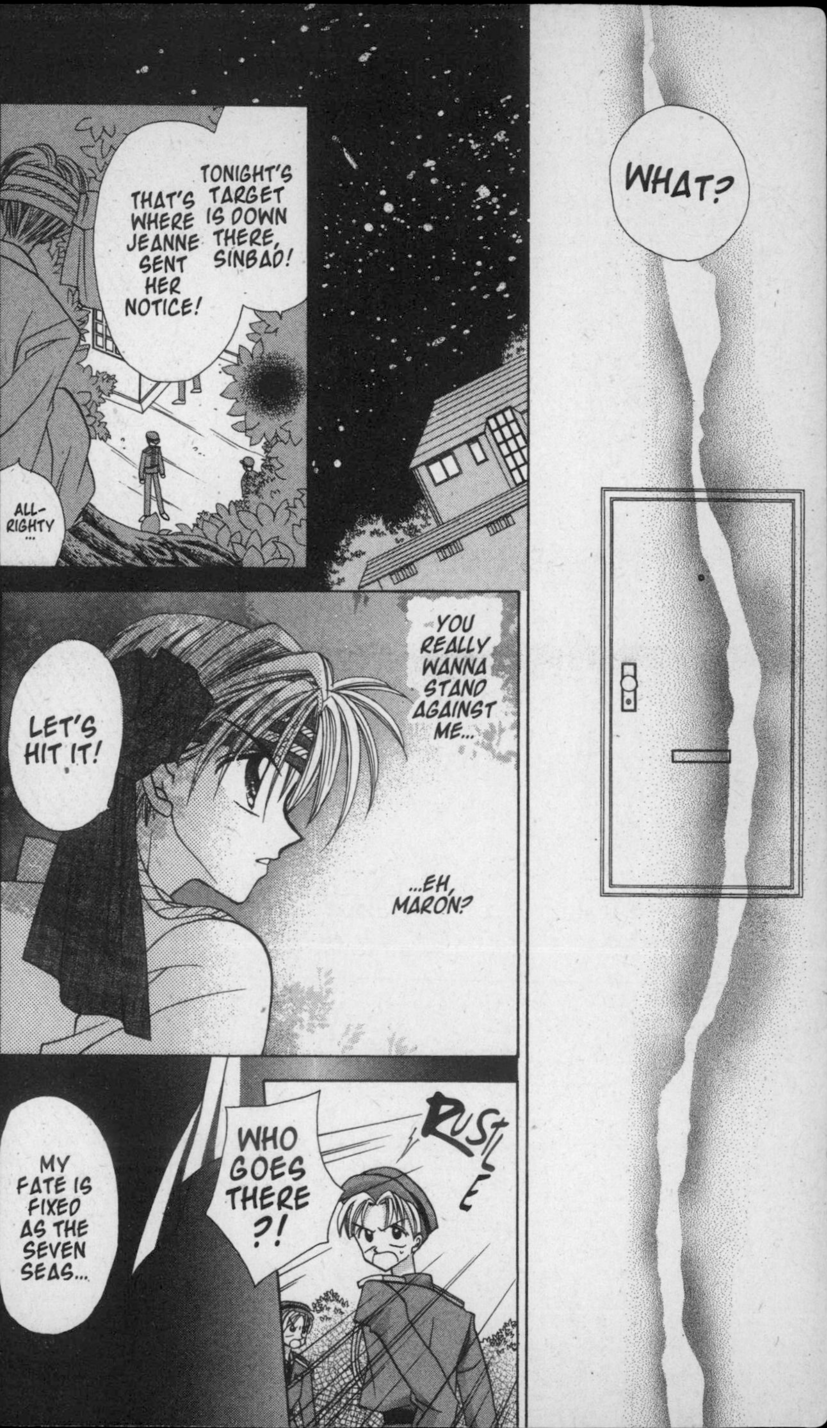
WHAT?
TONIGHT'S TARGET IS DOWN THERE, SINBAD!
THAT'S WHERE JEANNE SENT HER NOTICE!
ALL-RIGHTY...
YOU REALLY WANNA STAND AGAINST ME...
...EH, MARON?
LET'S HIT IT!
RUSTLE
WHO GOES THERE?!
MY FATE IS FIXED AS THE SEVEN SEAS...

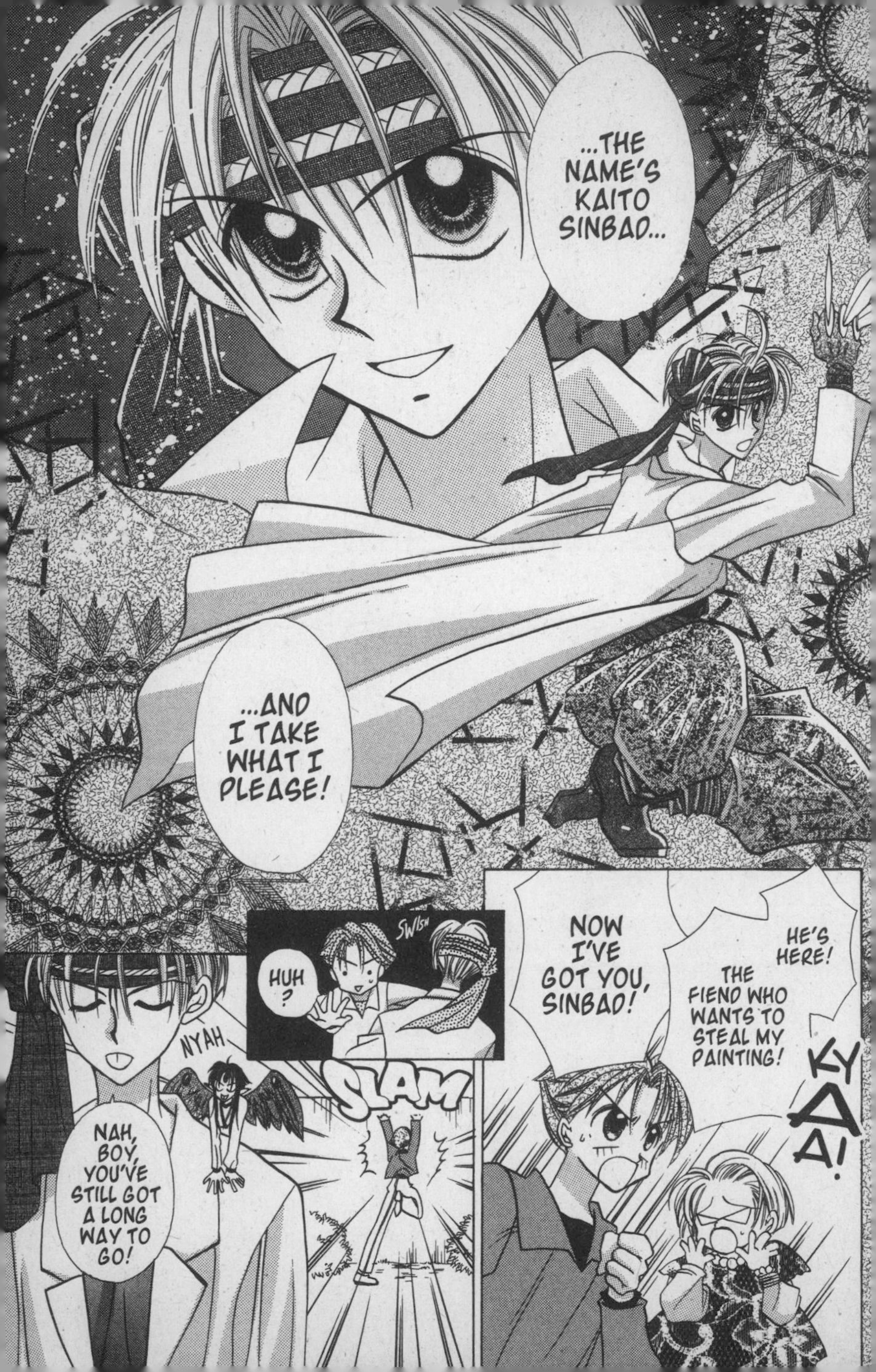
...THE NAME'S KAITO SINBAD...
...AND I TAKE WHAT I PLEASE!
HE'S HERE!
THE FIEND WHO WANTS TO STEAL MY PAINTING!
NOW I'VE GOT YOU, SINBAD!
KYAA!
SWISH
HUH?
SLAM
NYAH
NAH, BOY, YOU'VE STILL GOT A LONG WAY TO GO!

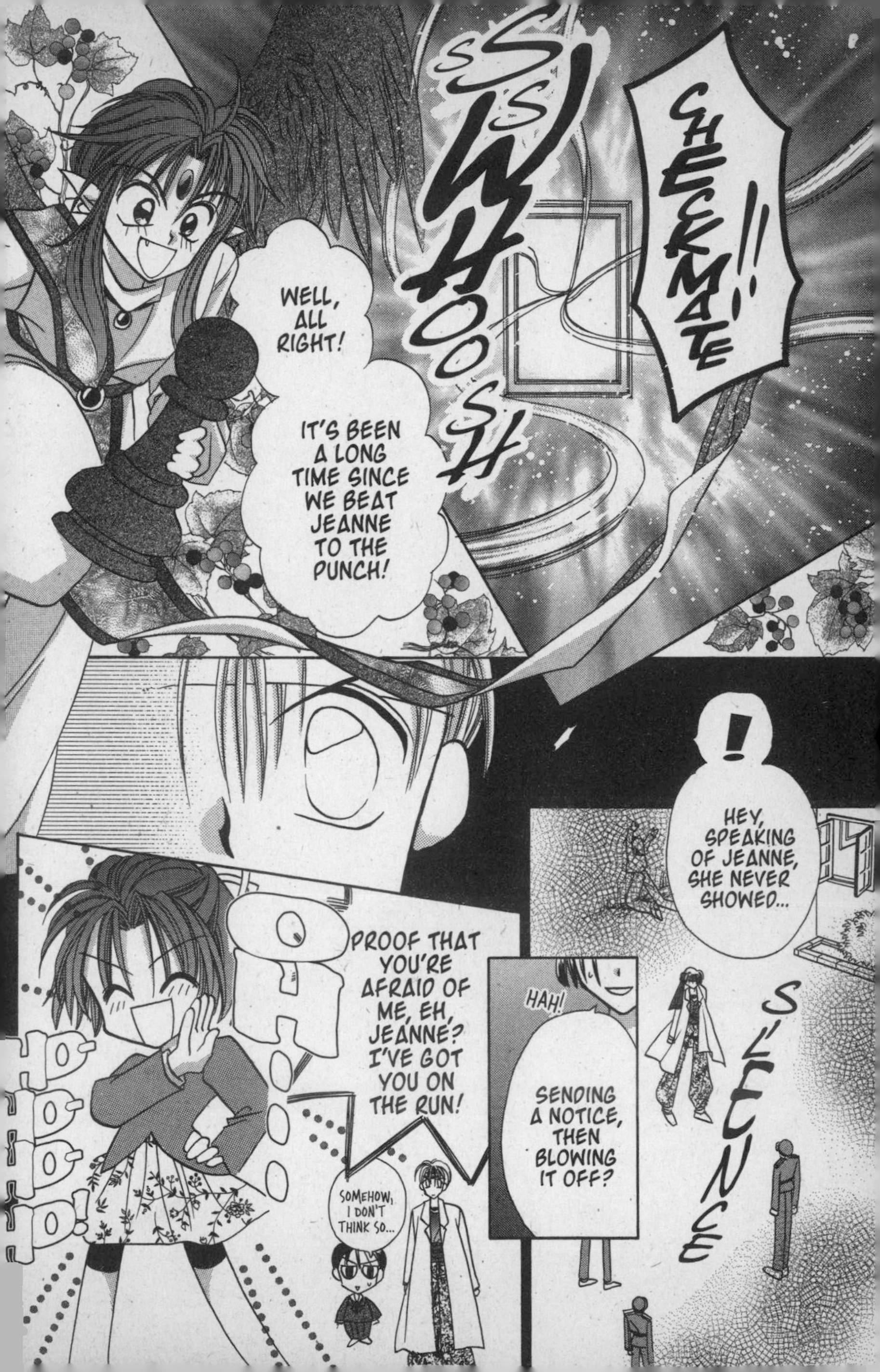
CHECKMATE!!
SSSWHOOSH
WELL, ALL RIGHT!
IT'S BEEN A LONG TIME SINCE WE BEAT JEANNE TO THE PUNCH!
!
HEY, SPEAKING OF JEANNE, SHE NEVER SHOWED...
SILENCE
HAH!
SENDING A NOTICE, THEN BLOWING IT OFF?
PROOF THAT YOU'RE AFRAID OF ME, EH, JEANNE? I'VE GOT YOU ON THE RUN!
HO-HO-HO-HO!
SOMEHOW, I DON'T THINK SO...

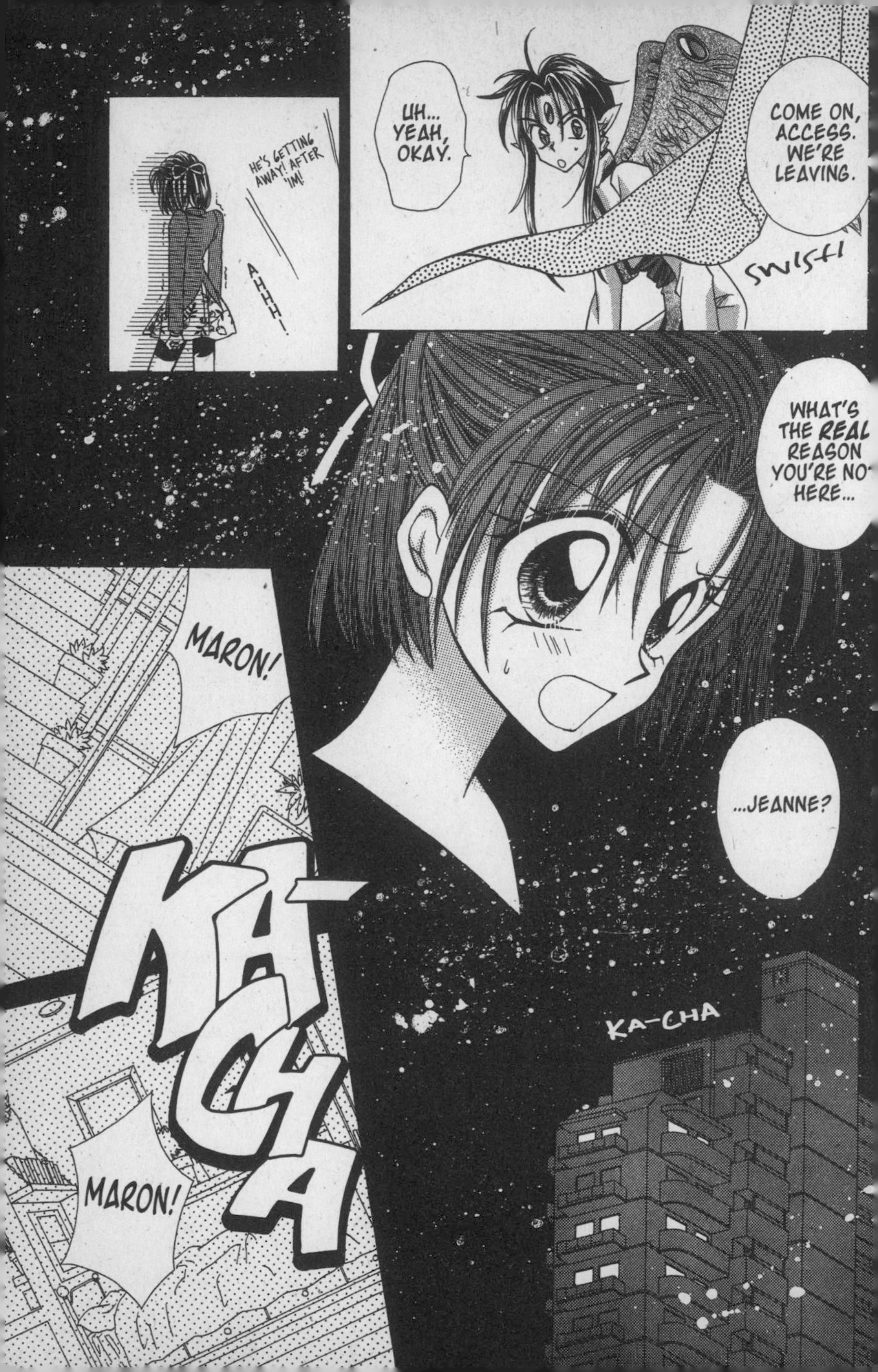
COME ON, ACCESS. WE'RE LEAVING.
SWISH
UH... YEAH, OKAY.
HE'S GETTING AWAY! AFTER 'IM!
AHHH!
WHAT'S THE REAL REASON YOU'RE NO HERE...
...JEANNE?
MARON!
KA-CHA
MARON!
KA-CHA

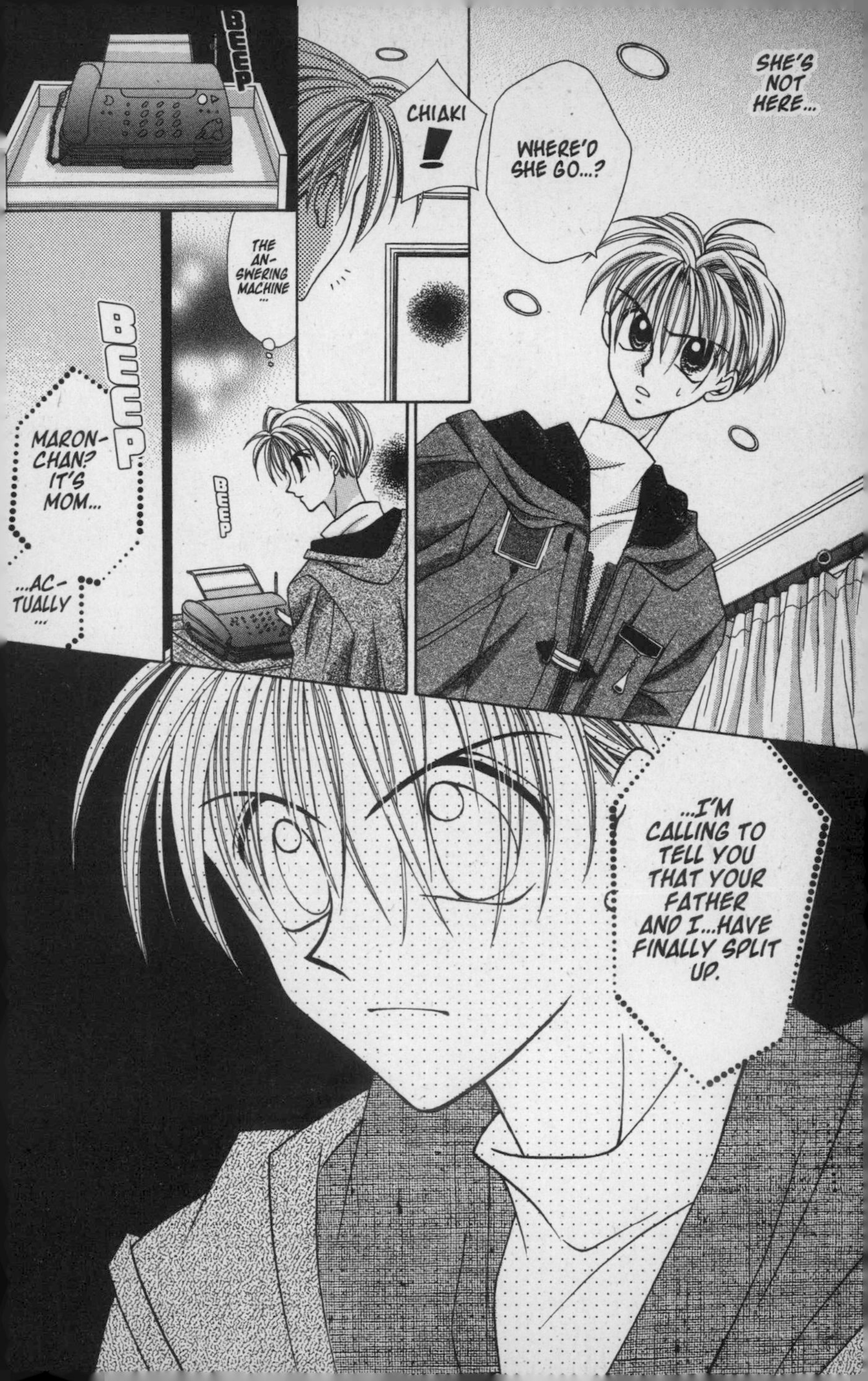
SHE'S NOT HERE...
WHERE'D SHE GO...?
CHIAKI !
BEEP
THE AN-SWERING MACHINE ...
BEEP
BEEP
MARON-CHAN? IT'S MOM...
...AC-TUALLY ...
...I'M CALLING TO TELL YOU THAT YOUR FATHER AND I...HAVE FINALLY SPLIT UP.

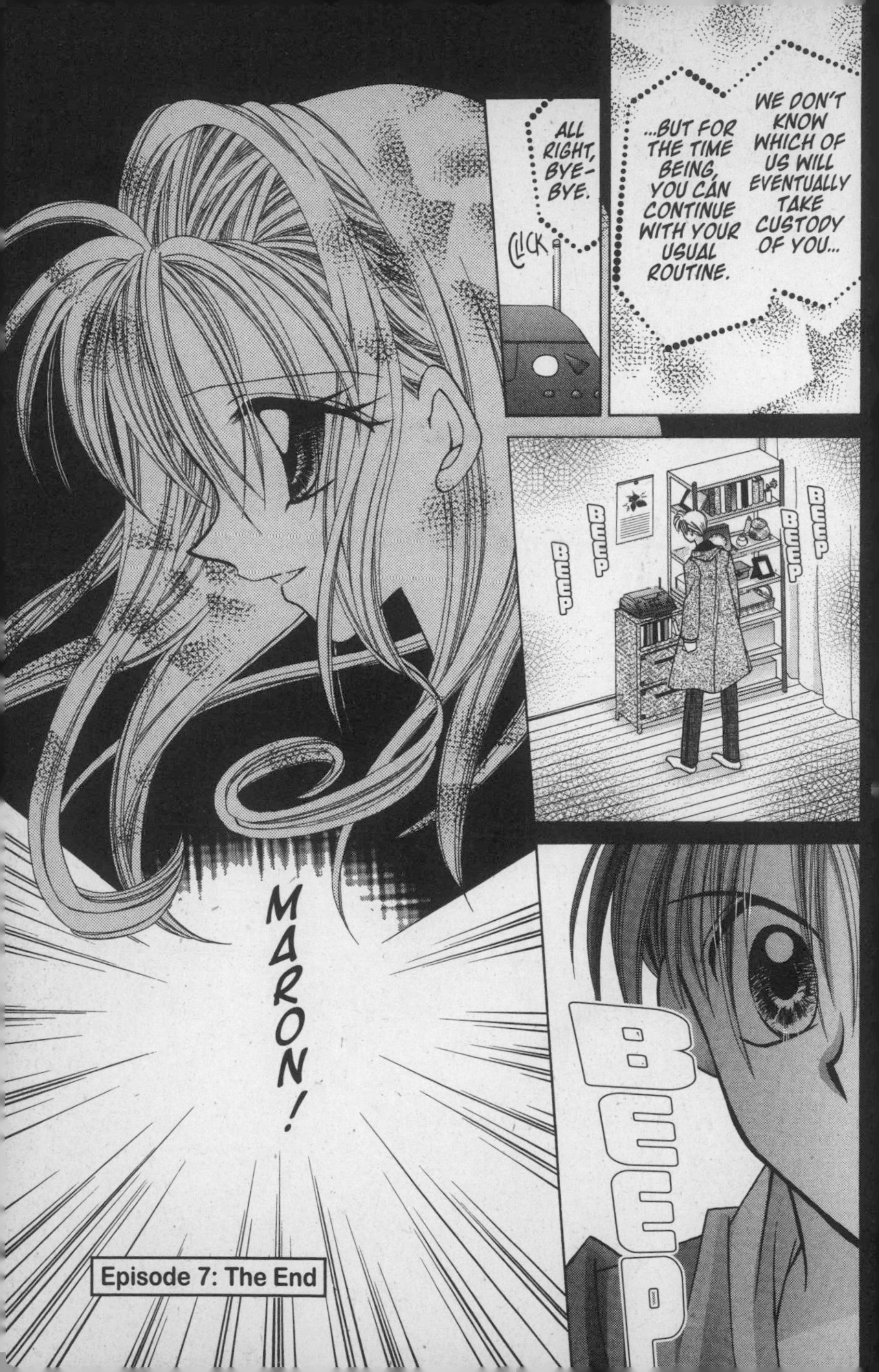
WE DON'T KNOW WHICH OF US WILL EVENTUALLY TAKE CUSTODY OF YOU...
...BUT FOR THE TIME BEING, YOU CAN CONTINUE WITH YOUR USUAL ROUTINE.
ALL RIGHT, BYE-BYE.
CLICK
BEEP
BEEP
BEEP
BEEP
BEEP
MARON!
Episode 7: The End

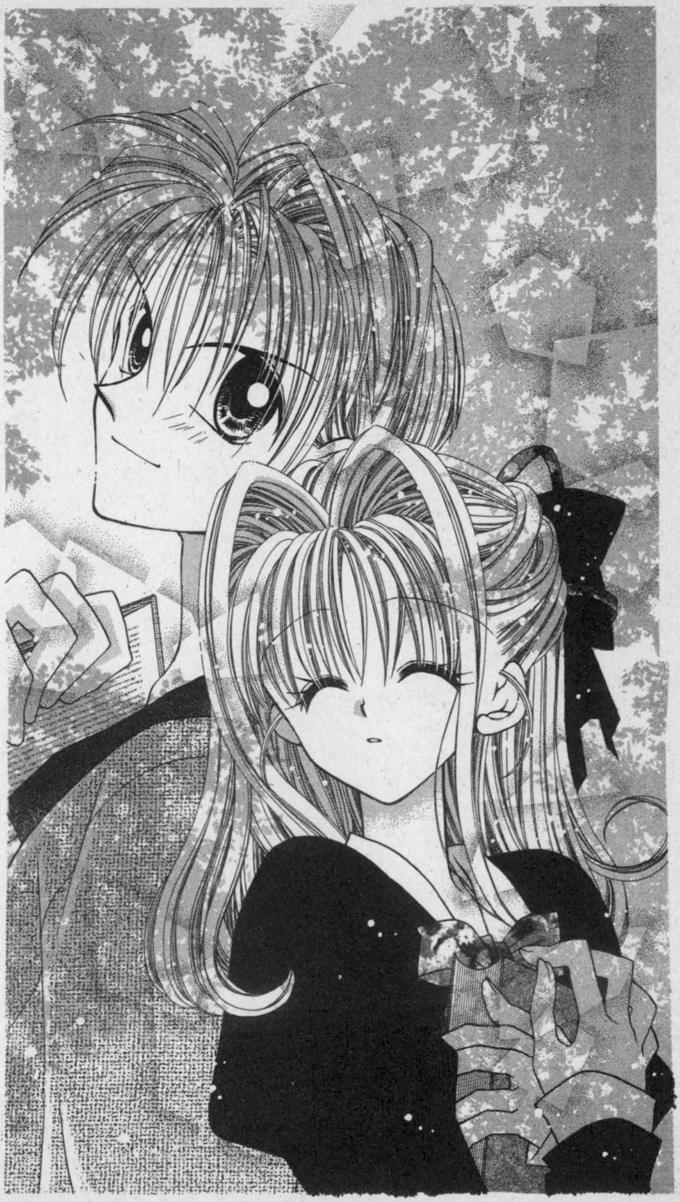

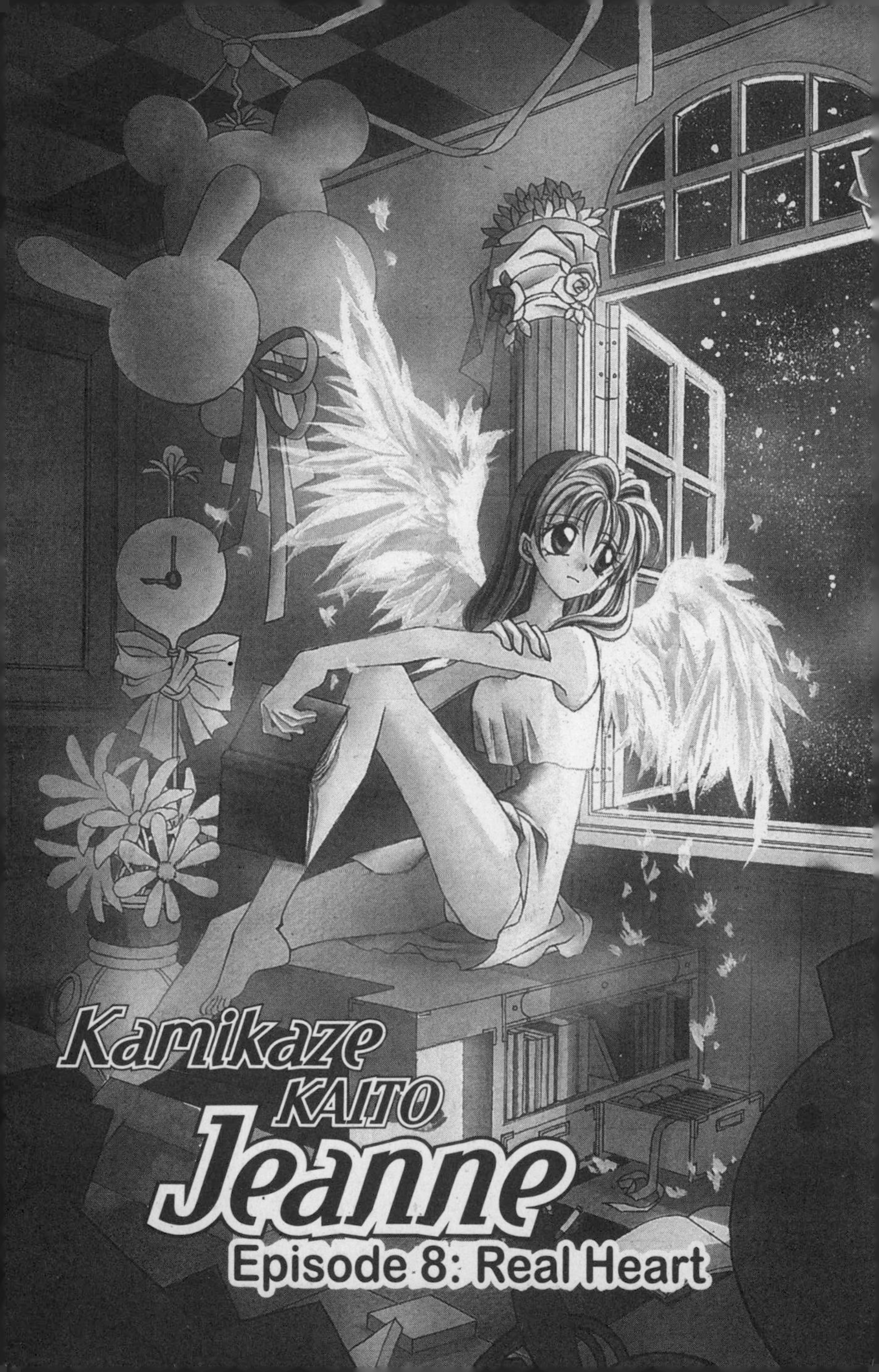
Kamikaze
KAITO
Jeanne
Episode 8: Real Heart

Maron's parents: Where are they now?

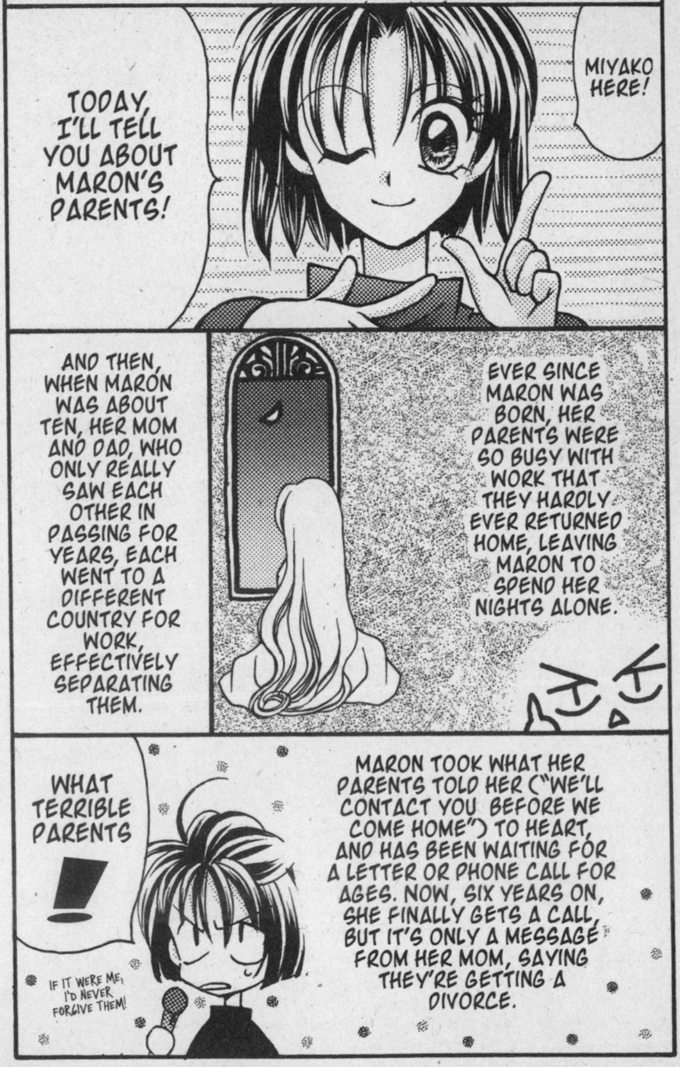
MIYAKO HERE!
TODAY, I'LL TELL YOU ABOUT MARON'S PARENTS!
EVER SINCE MARON WAS BORN, HER PARENTS WERE SO BUSY WITH WORK THAT THEY HARDLY EVER RETURNED HOME, LEAVING MARON TO SPEND HER NIGHTS ALONE.
AND THEN, WHEN MARON WAS ABOUT TEN, HER MOM AND DAD, WHO ONLY REALLY SAW EACH OTHER IN PASSING FOR YEARS, EACH WENT TO A DIFFERENT COUNTRY FOR WORK, EFFECTIVELY SEPARATING THEM.
MARON TOOK WHAT HER PARENTS TOLD HER ("WE'LL CONTACT YOU BEFORE WE COME HOME") TO HEART, AND HAS BEEN WAITING FOR A LETTER OR PHONE CALL FOR AGES. NOW, SIX YEARS ON, SHE FINALLY GETS A CALL, BUT IT'S ONLY A MESSAGE FROM HER MOM, SAYING THEY'RE GETTING A DIVORCE.
WHAT TERRIBLE PARENTS!
IF IT WERE ME, I'D NEVER FORGIVE THEM!

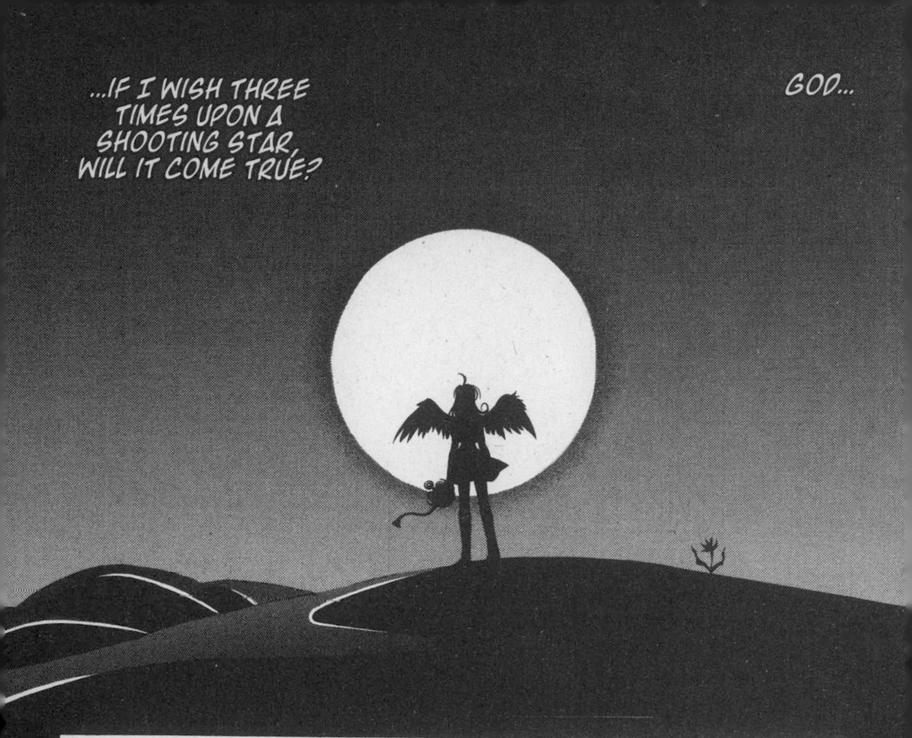
GOD...
...IF I WISH THREE TIMES UPON A SHOOTING STAR, WILL IT COME TRUE?

Episode 8 COMMENTS CONTINUED>>>

"What?! That's how she really is?!" I was bowled over when I heard that. "But really, I've always wanted courage." Yep, just what she says. I hope everyone "got" it!

There are so many songs that go well with this episode that I nearly wore out my 5-CD-holding boom box playing 'em over and over again while creating the E.P. So here are my musical suggestions for episode 8 and as an added bonus, suggestions from readers about other songs that fit JEANNE to a tee.♥

SONGS THAT I THINK ARE PERFECT FOR THIS EPISODE	SONGS READERS TOLD ME ABOUT
KOMM, SUSSER TOD Arianne (I love it! My karaoke specialty) WHITE LOVE Speed (The lyrics are a perfect match) GLORIA (I want to deliver to you) Hayashibara Megumi (gooood stuff) HOLY EYES (YOUR DREAM IS MY DREAM) Komori Manami (from Chiaki to Maron♥) LIKE ME Kuwajima Noriko (Maron's voice actress's song♥) LIVING DAYLIGHTS TWO-MIX (Maron's secret theme song) BELIEVE MY BRAVE HEART TWO-MIX (I wanna listen to this song even till the last episode.) ETERNAL WIND (THE SMILE AT THE CENTER OF THE GLOWING WIND) Moriguchi Hiroko-san♥	JUST ONE WISH Komatsu Miho (I bought the CD! Great song!!) LIKE STANDING ON ICE Komatsu Miho (Her songs are **really** good!) JUST AS YOU ARE IS OKAY Sakamoto Maaya (I like this one. It really fits...Yep.) WORLD OF CHANCE ENCOUNTERS My Little Lover (I like My Little Lover, too.) THERE WILL BE LOVER THERE The Brilliant Green (also goes well with vol. 1. Good one!) Mmm...There were some more, but I forget at the moment...Sorry...

So listen to these songs while reading episode 8, okay?♥ To the fans who sent their ideas in to me, sorry for printing them here without permission! Please don't be angry!

MIYAKO CATHARSIS

A bonus story. It's only 15 pages and I'm really happy I did it, but it was a toughie! I had a really tight schedule at the time, with a lot of other Ribon work that had to get done, specifically color cuts! I love coloring, but hate inking in color because I'm bad at it! (I like inking in black-and-white 'cause it's relatively easy.♥) In this story, featuring Maron-chan and Miyako-chan (or, as I call her, "Miyan-chan"), I wanted to define their connection...Bless the readers, who went over each scene with a fine-tooth comb to glean all they could from it. (Contented SIGH.) I want to write another story along these lines, maybe about Chiaki's childhood days or the past of Finn and Access, etc.

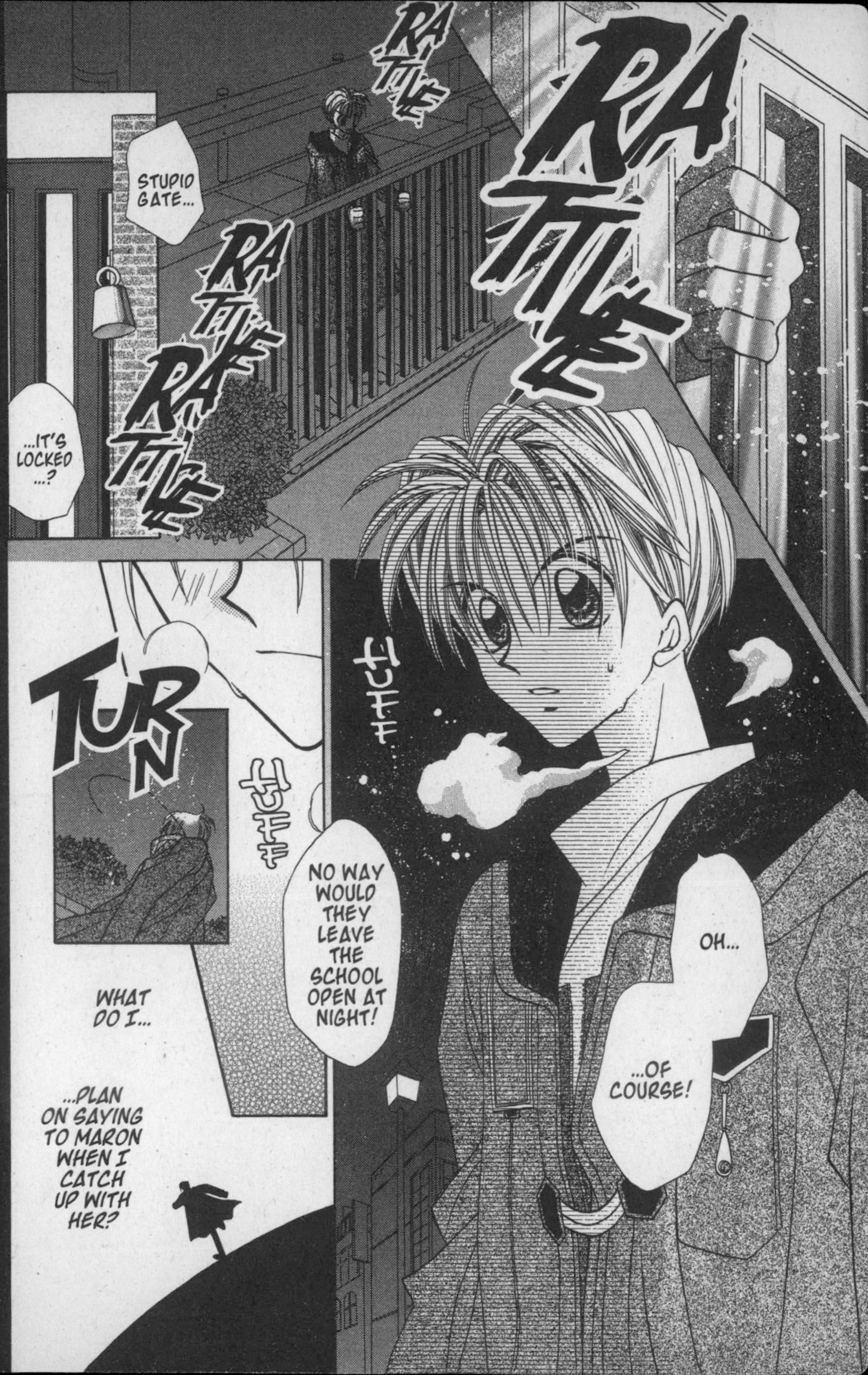
RATTLE
RATTLE
RATTLE
RATTLE
STUPID GATE...
...IT'S LOCKED ...?
HUFF
HUFF
OH...
...OF COURSE!
NO WAY WOULD THEY LEAVE THE SCHOOL OPEN AT NIGHT!
TURN
WHAT DO I...
...PLAN ON SAYING TO MARON WHEN I CATCH UP WITH HER?

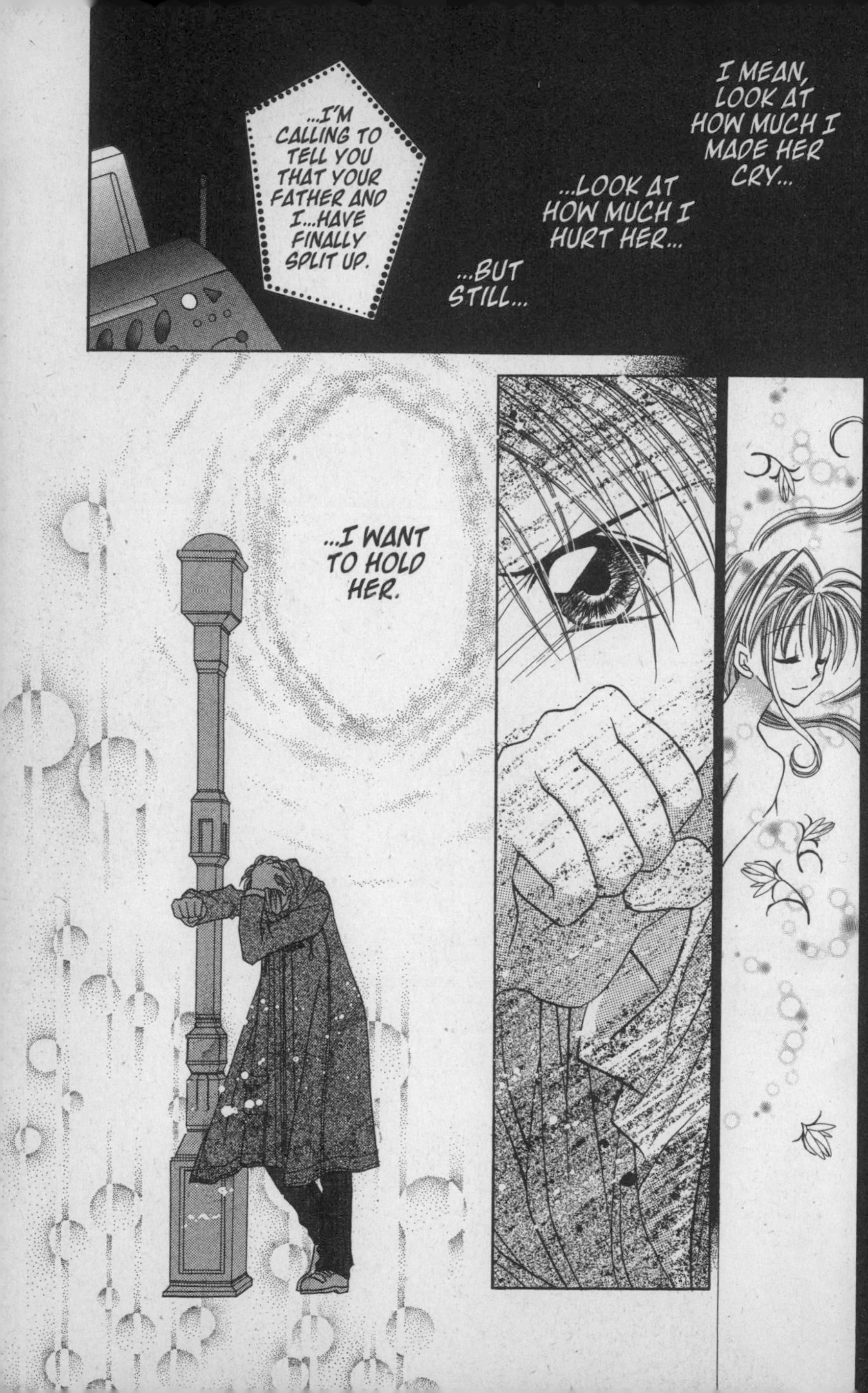
I MEAN, LOOK AT HOW MUCH I MADE HER CRY...
...LOOK AT HOW MUCH I HURT HER...
...BUT STILL...
...I'M CALLING TO TELL YOU THAT YOUR FATHER AND I...HAVE FINALLY SPLIT UP.
...I WANT TO HOLD HER.

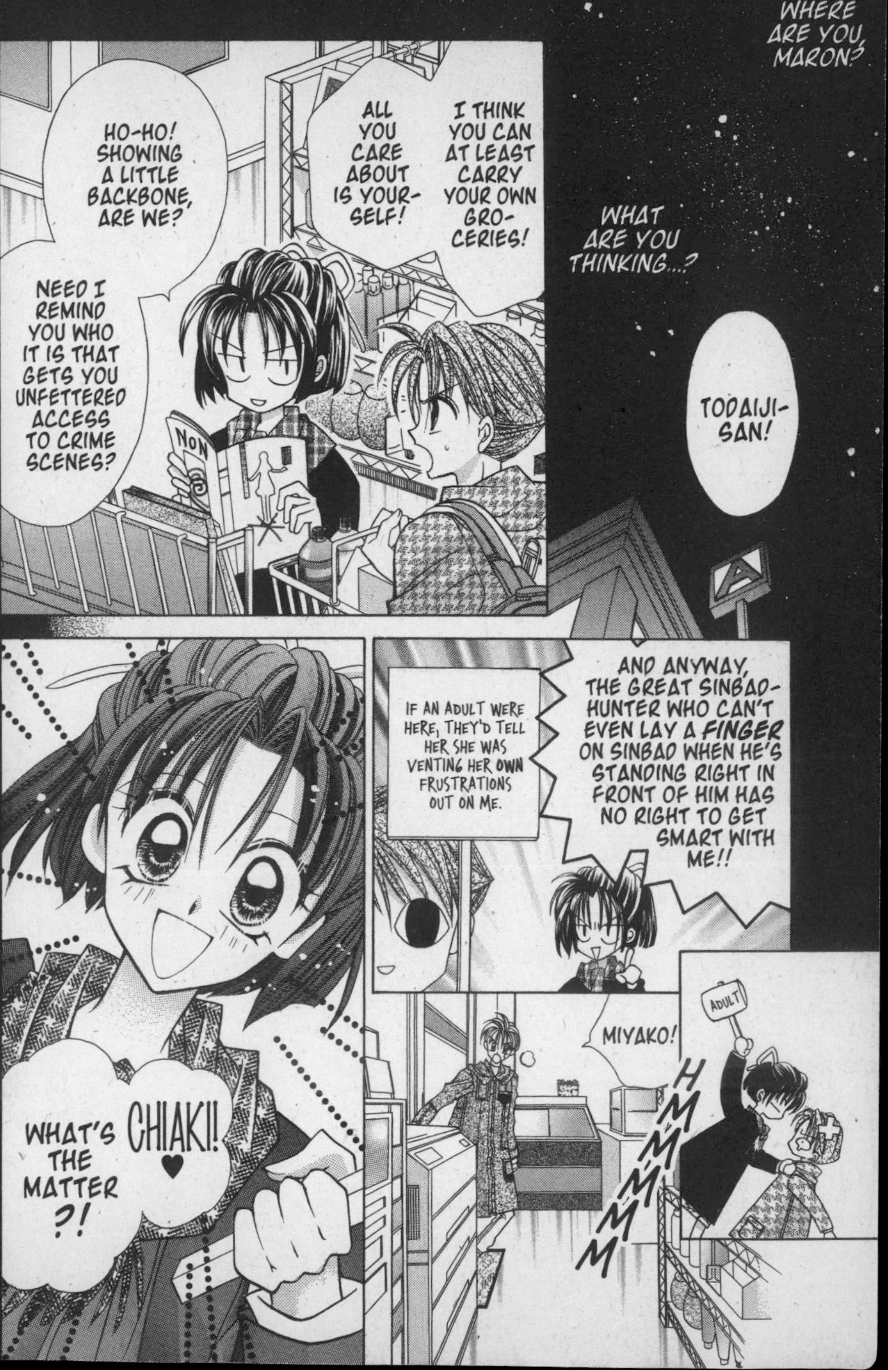
WHERE ARE YOU, MARON?
WHAT ARE YOU THINKING...?
TODAIJI-SAN!
I THINK YOU CAN AT LEAST CARRY YOUR OWN GRO-CERIES!
ALL YOU CARE ABOUT IS YOUR-SELF!
HO-HO! SHOWING A LITTLE BACKBONE, ARE WE?
NEED I REMIND YOU WHO IT IS THAT GETS YOU UNFETTERED ACCESS TO CRIME SCENES?
NON
AND ANYWAY, THE GREAT SINBAD-HUNTER WHO CAN'T EVEN LAY A FINGER ON SINBAD WHEN HE'S STANDING RIGHT IN FRONT OF HIM HAS NO RIGHT TO GET SMART WITH ME!!
IF AN ADULT WERE HERE, THEY'D TELL HER SHE WAS VENTING HER OWN FRUSTRATIONS OUT ON ME.
ADULT
MIYAKO!
HMMMMMMM
CHIAKI! ♥
WHAT'S THE MATTER ?!

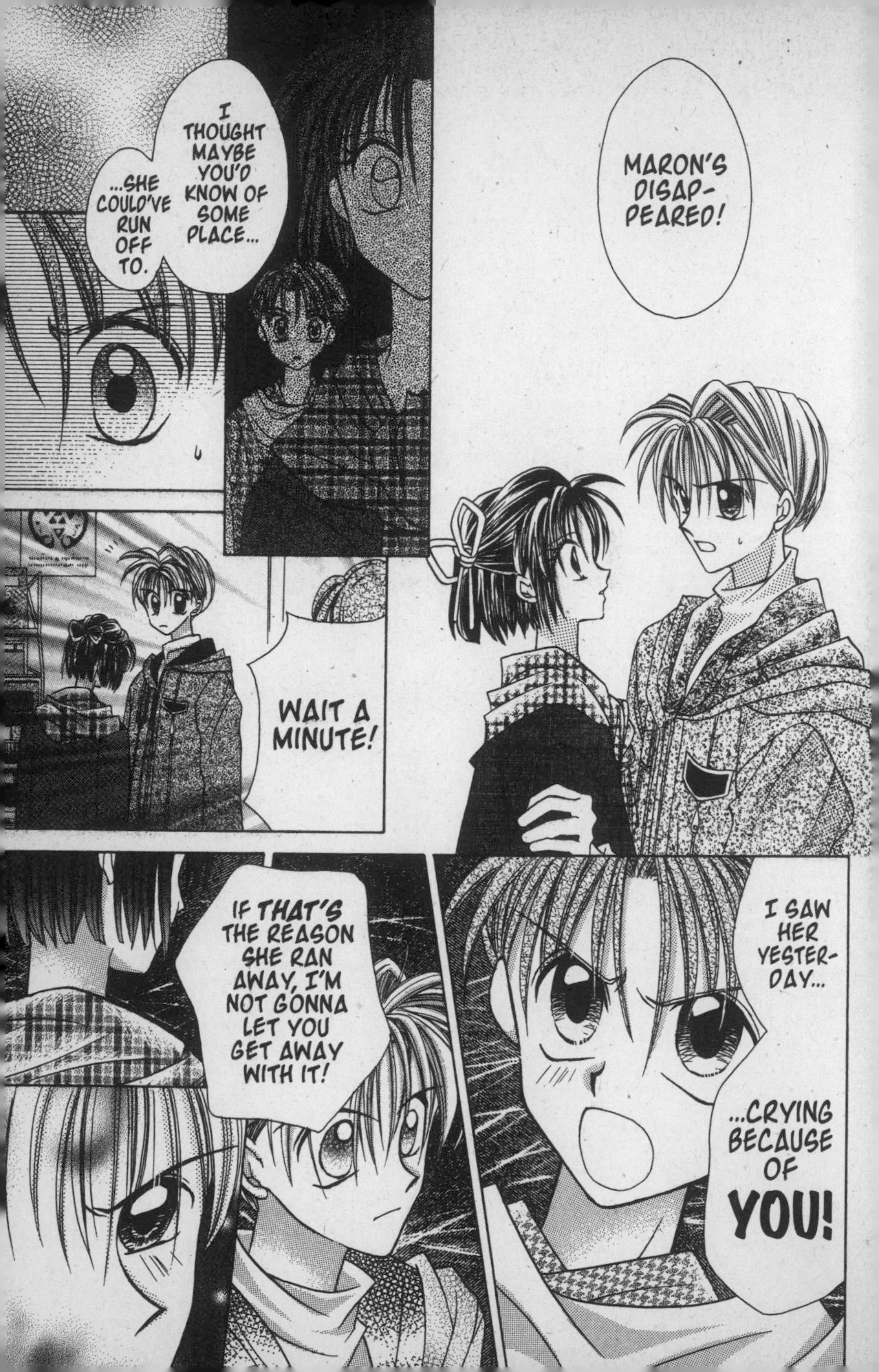
MARON'S DISAP-PEARED!
I THOUGHT MAYBE YOU'D KNOW OF SOME PLACE...
...SHE COULD'VE RUN OFF TO.
WAIT A MINUTE!
I SAW HER YESTER-DAY...
...CRYING BECAUSE OF YOU!
IF THAT'S THE REASON SHE RAN AWAY, I'M NOT GONNA LET YOU GET AWAY WITH IT!

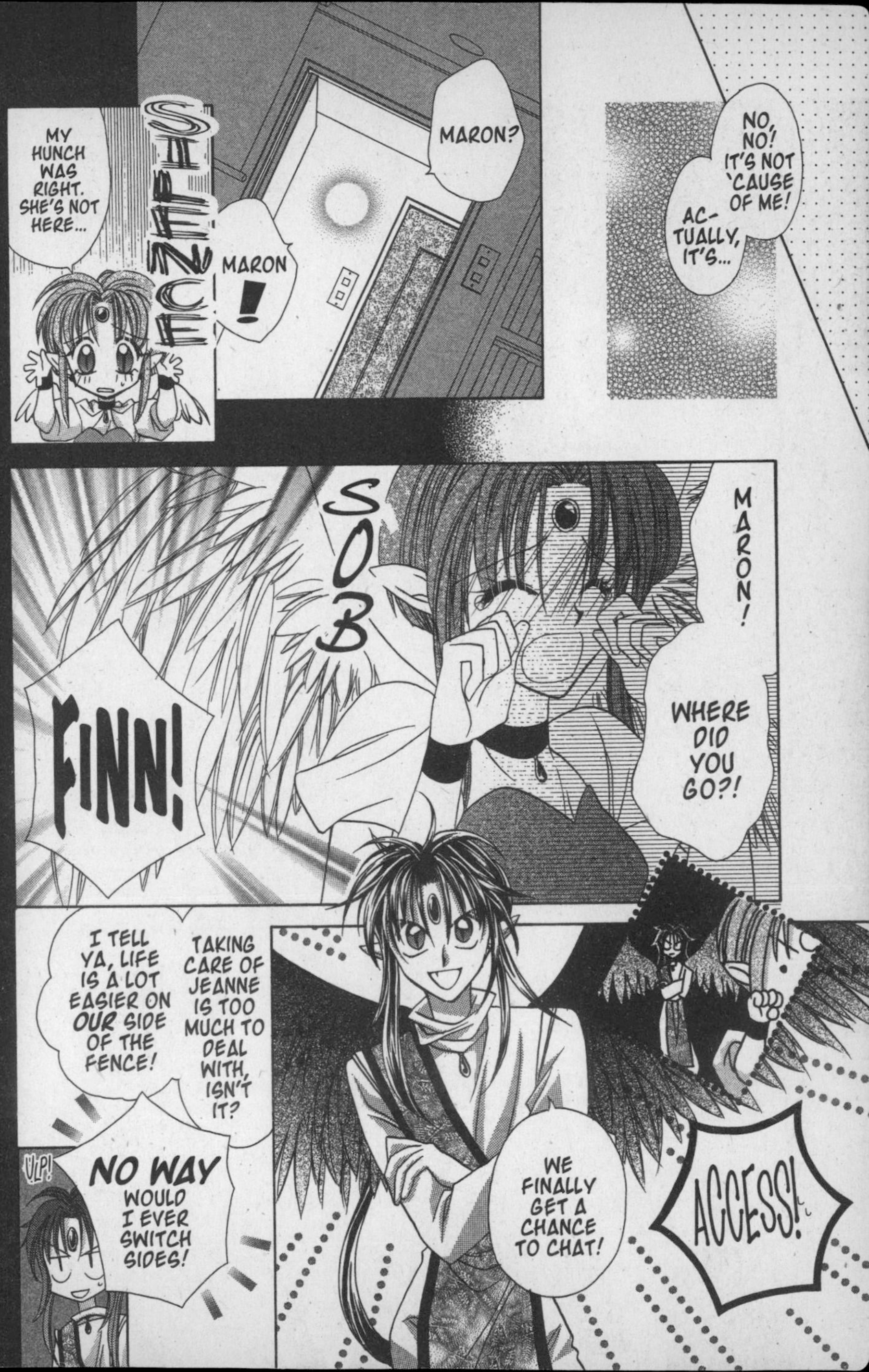
NO, NO! IT'S NOT 'CAUSE OF ME! ACTUALLY, IT'S...
MARON?
MARON!
SILENCE
MY HUNCH WAS RIGHT. SHE'S NOT HERE...
MARON! WHERE DID YOU GO?!
SOB
FINN!
ACCESS!
WE FINALLY GET A CHANCE TO CHAT!
TAKING CARE OF JEANNE IS TOO MUCH TO DEAL WITH, ISN'T IT?
I TELL YA, LIFE IS A LOT EASIER ON OUR SIDE OF THE FENCE!
ULP!
NO WAY WOULD I EVER SWITCH SIDES!

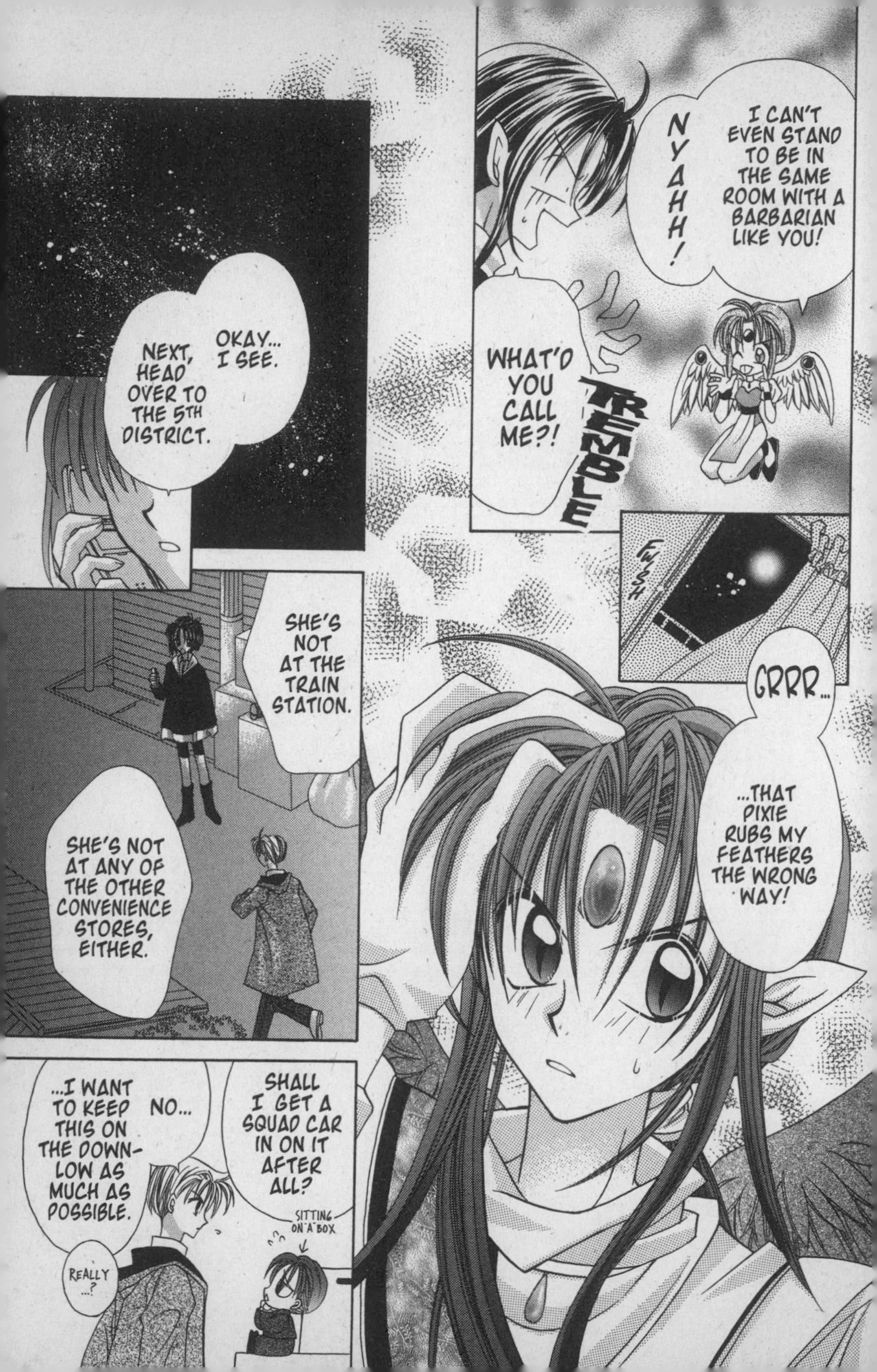
NYAHH!
I CAN'T EVEN STAND TO BE IN THE SAME ROOM WITH A BARBARIAN LIKE YOU!
WHAT'D YOU CALL ME?!
TREMBLE
FWISH
GRRR...
...THAT PIXIE RUBS MY FEATHERS THE WRONG WAY!
OKAY... I SEE.
NEXT, HEAD OVER TO THE 5TH DISTRICT.
SHE'S NOT AT THE TRAIN STATION.
SHE'S NOT AT ANY OF THE OTHER CONVENIENCE STORES, EITHER.
SHALL I GET A SQUAD CAR IN ON IT AFTER ALL?
NO...
...I WANT TO KEEP THIS ON THE DOWN-LOW AS MUCH AS POSSIBLE.
SITTING ON A BOX
REALLY ...?

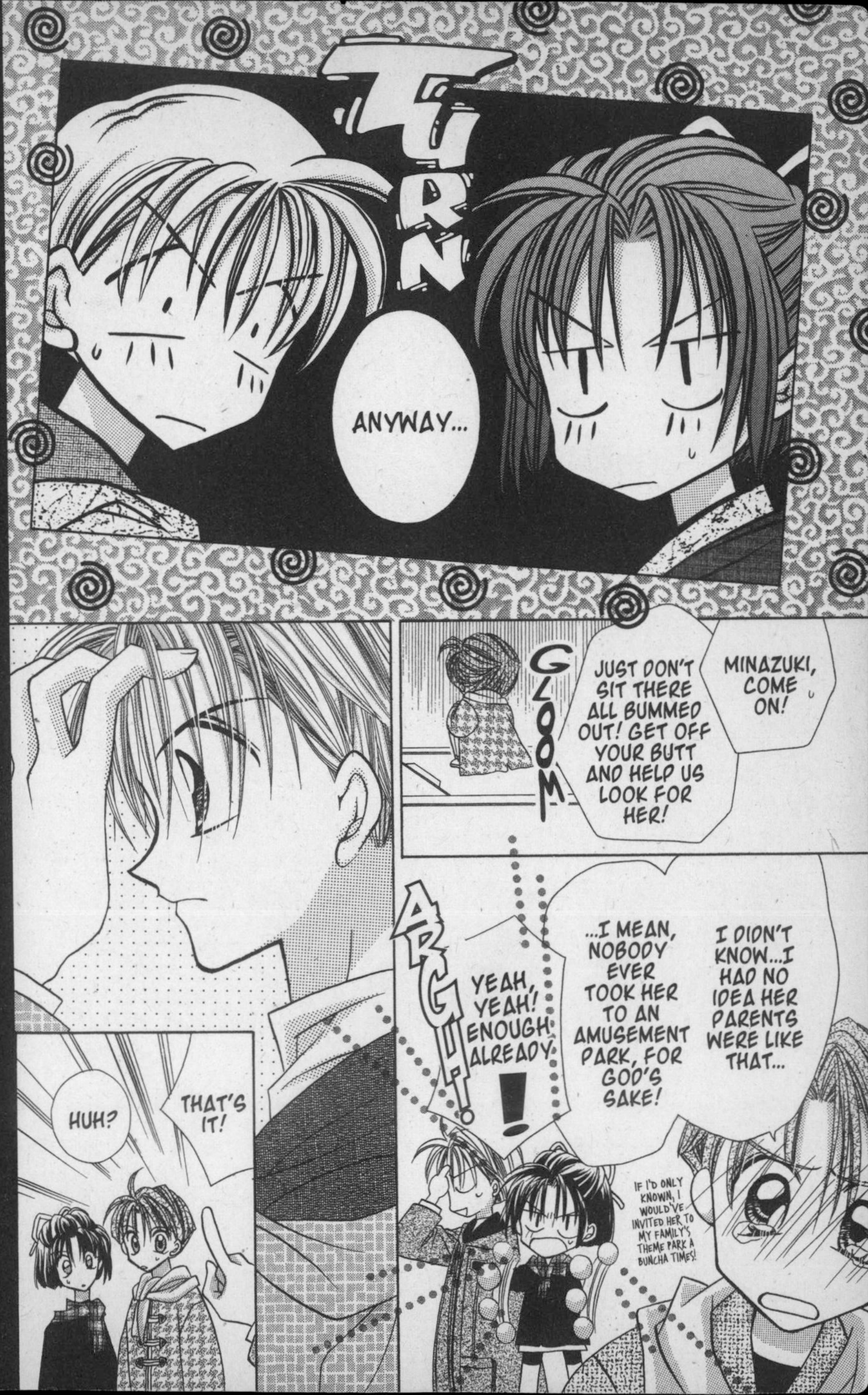

TURN
ANYWAY...
MINAZUKI, COME ON!
JUST DON'T SIT THERE ALL BUMMED OUT! GET OFF YOUR BUTT AND HELP US LOOK FOR HER!
GLOOM
I DIDN'T KNOW...I HAD NO IDEA HER PARENTS WERE LIKE THAT...
...I MEAN, NOBODY EVER TOOK HER TO AN AMUSEMENT PARK, FOR GOD'S SAKE!
YEAH, YEAH! ENOUGH ALREADY!
ARGH!
!
IF I'D ONLY KNOWN, I WOULD'VE INVITED HER TO MY FAMILY'S THEME PARK A BUNCHA TIMES!
THAT'S IT!
HUH?

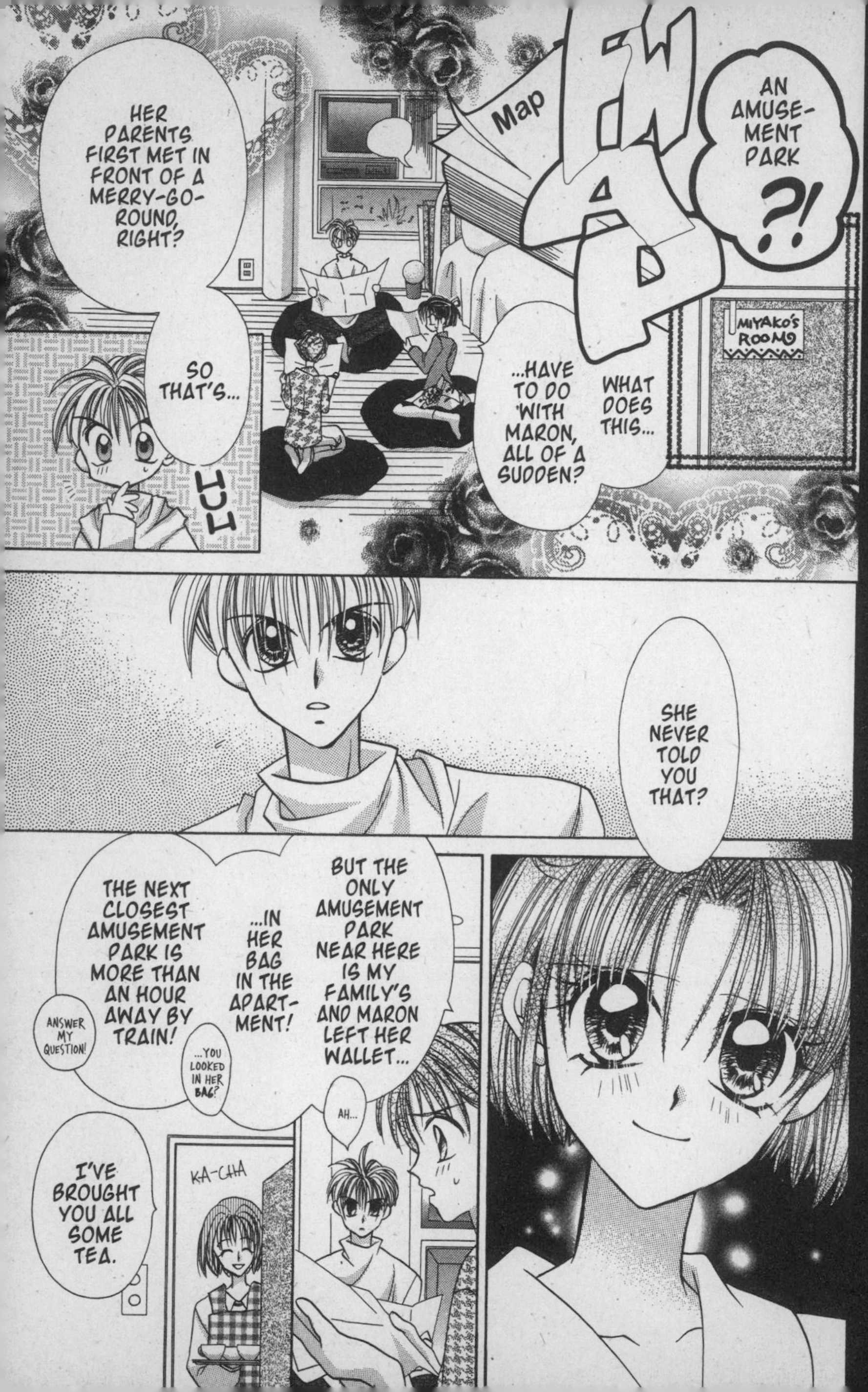
AN AMUSEMENT PARK ?!
FWAP
Map
MIYAKO'S ROOM
WHAT DOES THIS...
...HAVE TO DO WITH MARON, ALL OF A SUDDEN?
HER PARENTS FIRST MET IN FRONT OF A MERRY-GO-ROUND, RIGHT?
SO THAT'S...
HUH
SHE NEVER TOLD YOU THAT?
BUT THE ONLY AMUSEMENT PARK NEAR HERE IS MY FAMILY'S AND MARON LEFT HER WALLET...
...IN HER BAG IN THE APARTMENT!
THE NEXT CLOSEST AMUSEMENT PARK IS MORE THAN AN HOUR AWAY BY TRAIN!
...YOU LOOKED IN HER BAG?
ANSWER MY QUESTION!
AH...
KA-CHA
I'VE BROUGHT YOU ALL SOME TEA.

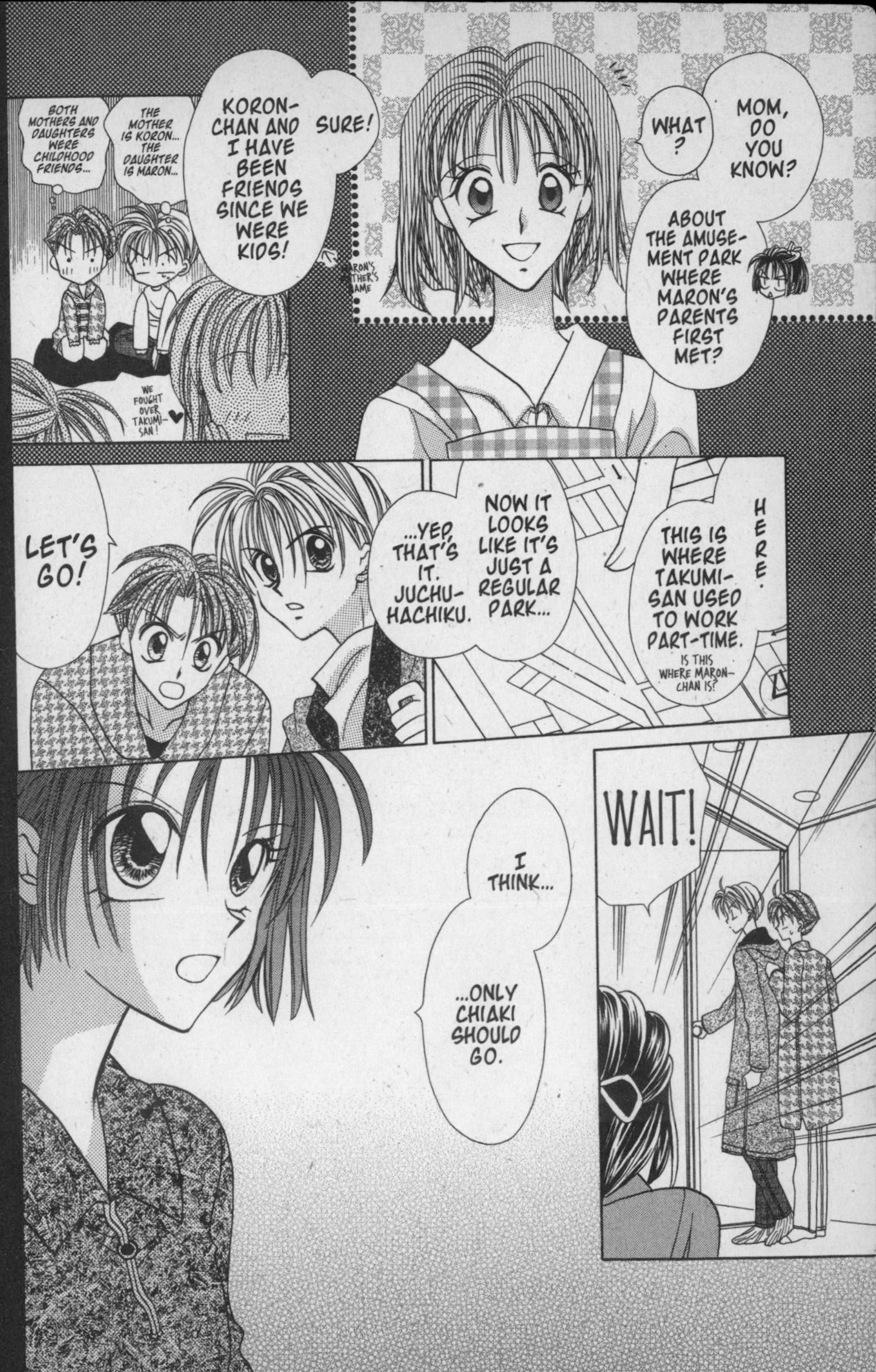
MOM, DO YOU KNOW?
WHAT?
ABOUT THE AMUSEMENT PARK WHERE MARON'S PARENTS FIRST MET?
SURE!
KORON-CHAN AND I HAVE BEEN FRIENDS SINCE WE WERE KIDS!
THE MOTHER IS KORON... THE DAUGHTER IS MARON...
BOTH MOTHERS AND DAUGHTERS WERE CHILDHOOD FRIENDS...
WE FOUGHT OVER TAKUMI-SAN!
HERE.
THIS IS WHERE TAKUMI-SAN USED TO WORK PART-TIME.
IS THIS WHERE MARON-CHAN IS?
NOW IT LOOKS LIKE IT'S JUST A REGULAR PARK...
...YEP, THAT'S IT. JUCHU-HACHIKU.
LET'S GO!
WAIT!
I THINK...
...ONLY CHIAKI SHOULD GO.

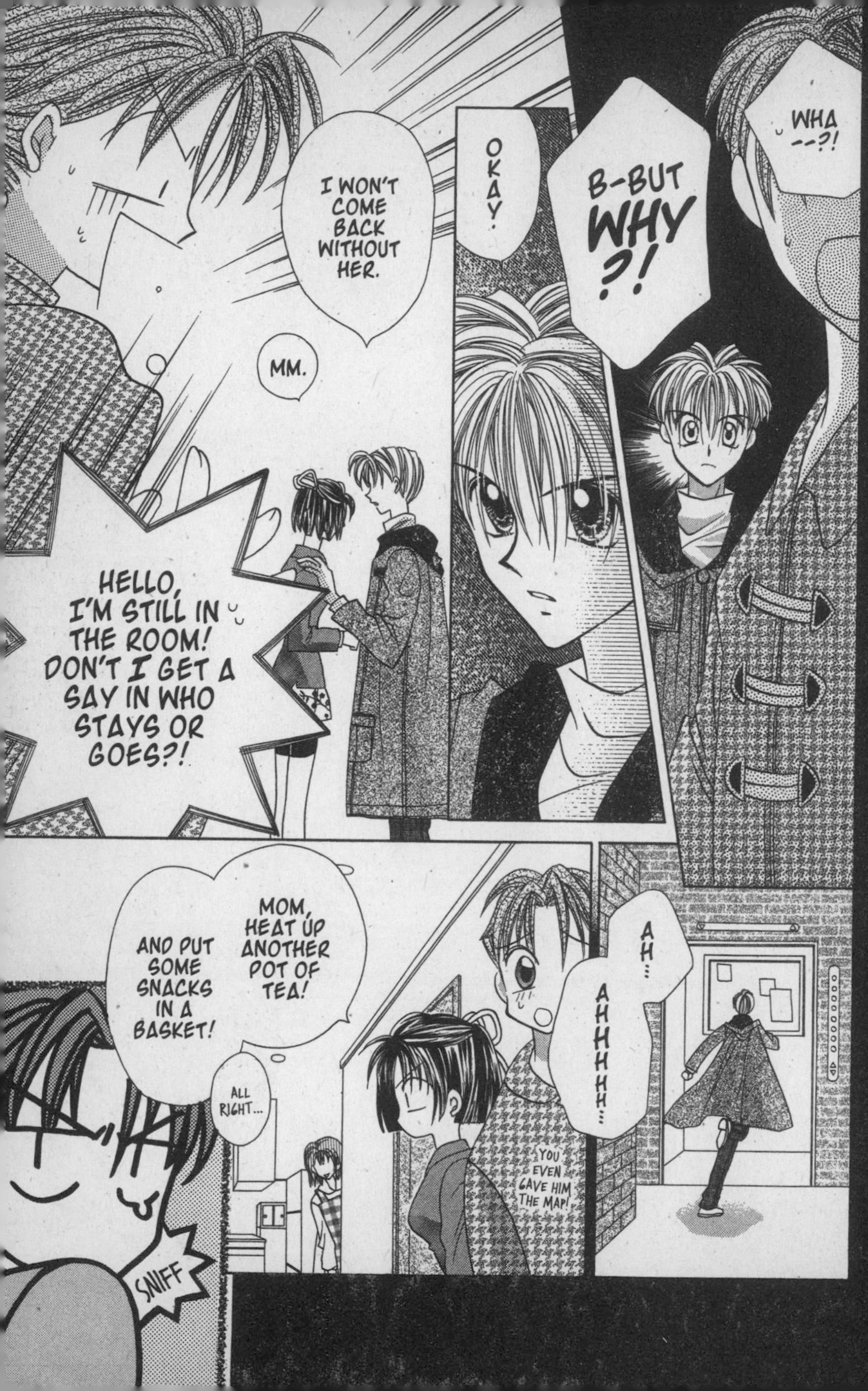
WHA --?!
B-BUT WHY?!
OKAY.
I WON'T COME BACK WITHOUT HER.
MM.
HELLO, I'M STILL IN THE ROOM! DON'T I GET A SAY IN WHO STAYS OR GOES?!
AH... AHHHHH...
YOU EVEN GAVE HIM THE MAP!
MOM, HEAT UP ANOTHER POT OF TEA!
AND PUT SOME SNACKS IN A BASKET!
ALL RIGHT...
SNIFF

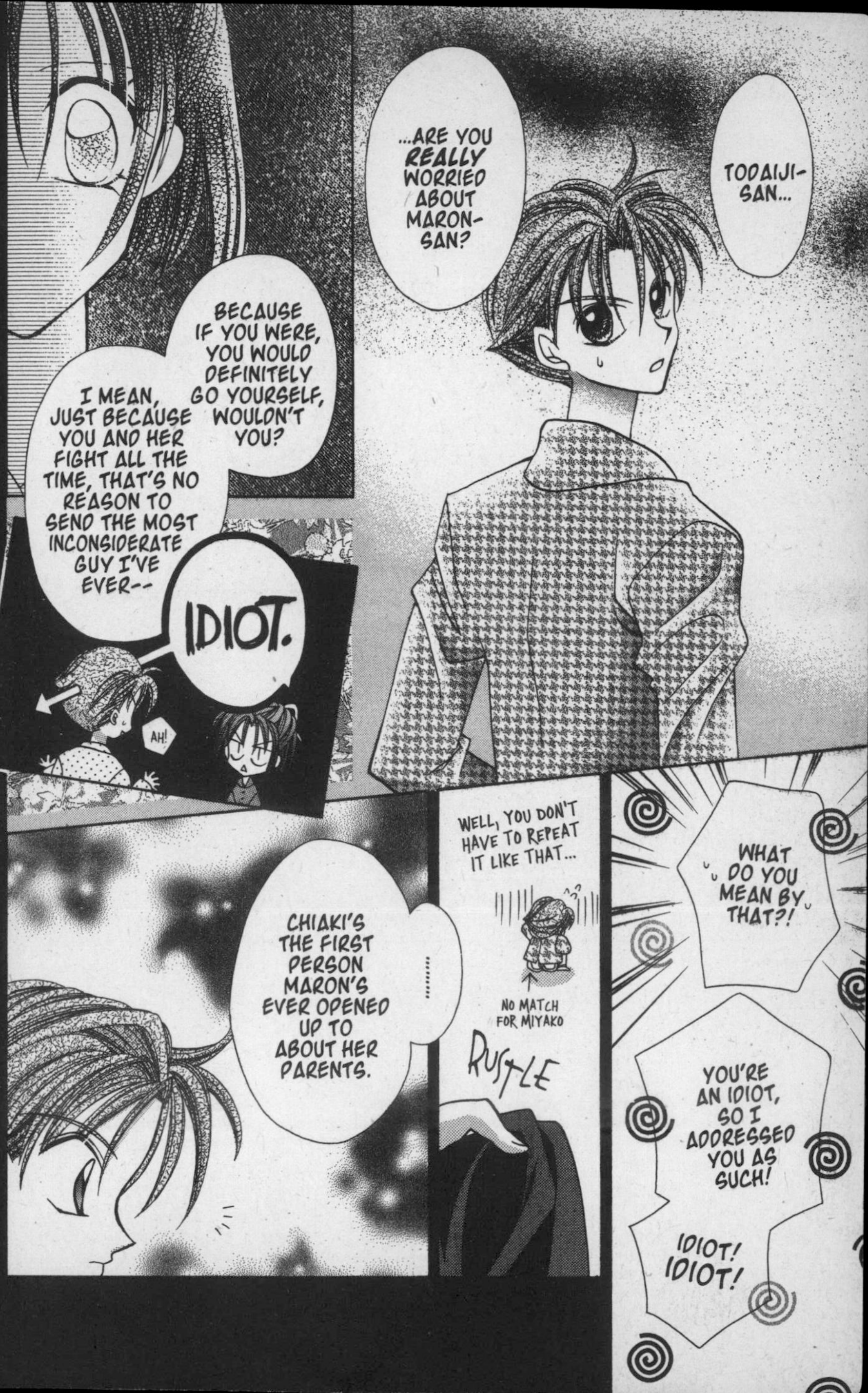
TODAIJI-SAN...
...ARE YOU REALLY WORRIED ABOUT MARON-SAN?
BECAUSE IF YOU WERE, YOU WOULD DEFINITELY GO YOURSELF, WOULDN'T YOU?
I MEAN, JUST BECAUSE YOU AND HER FIGHT ALL THE TIME, THAT'S NO REASON TO SEND THE MOST INCONSIDERATE GUY I'VE EVER--
IDIOT.
AH!
WHAT DO YOU MEAN BY THAT?!
YOU'RE AN IDIOT, SO I ADDRESSED YOU AS SUCH!
IDIOT! IDIOT!
WELL, YOU DON'T HAVE TO REPEAT IT LIKE THAT...
NO MATCH FOR MIYAKO
RUSTLE
......
CHIAKI'S THE FIRST PERSON MARON'S EVER OPENED UP TO ABOUT HER PARENTS.

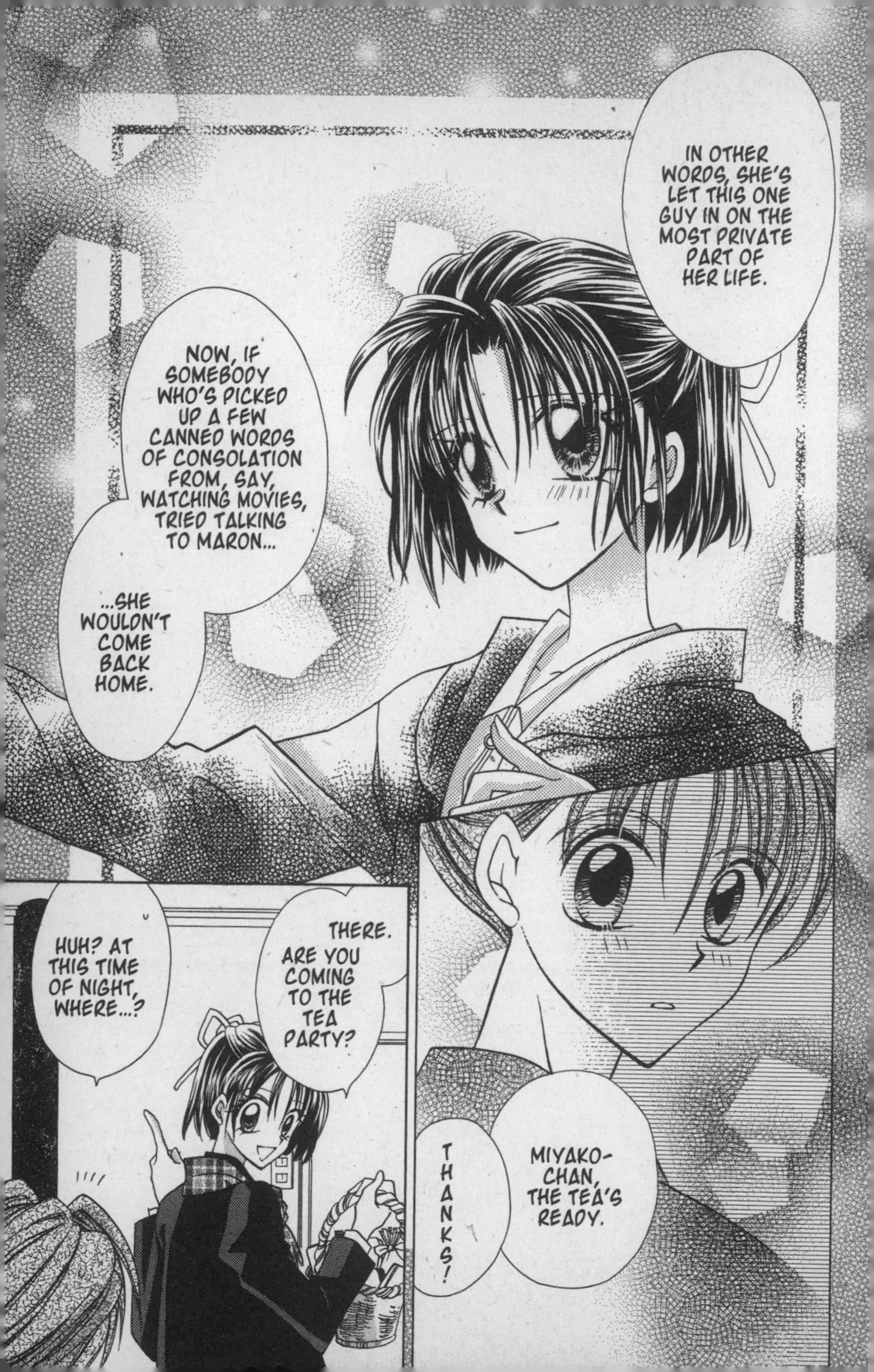
IN OTHER WORDS, SHE'S LET THIS ONE GUY IN ON THE MOST PRIVATE PART OF HER LIFE.
NOW, IF SOMEBODY WHO'S PICKED UP A FEW CANNED WORDS OF CONSOLATION FROM, SAY, WATCHING MOVIES, TRIED TALKING TO MARON...
...SHE WOULDN'T COME BACK HOME.
MIYAKO-CHAN, THE TEA'S READY.
THANKS!
THERE. ARE YOU COMING TO THE TEA PARTY?
HUH? AT THIS TIME OF NIGHT, WHERE...?

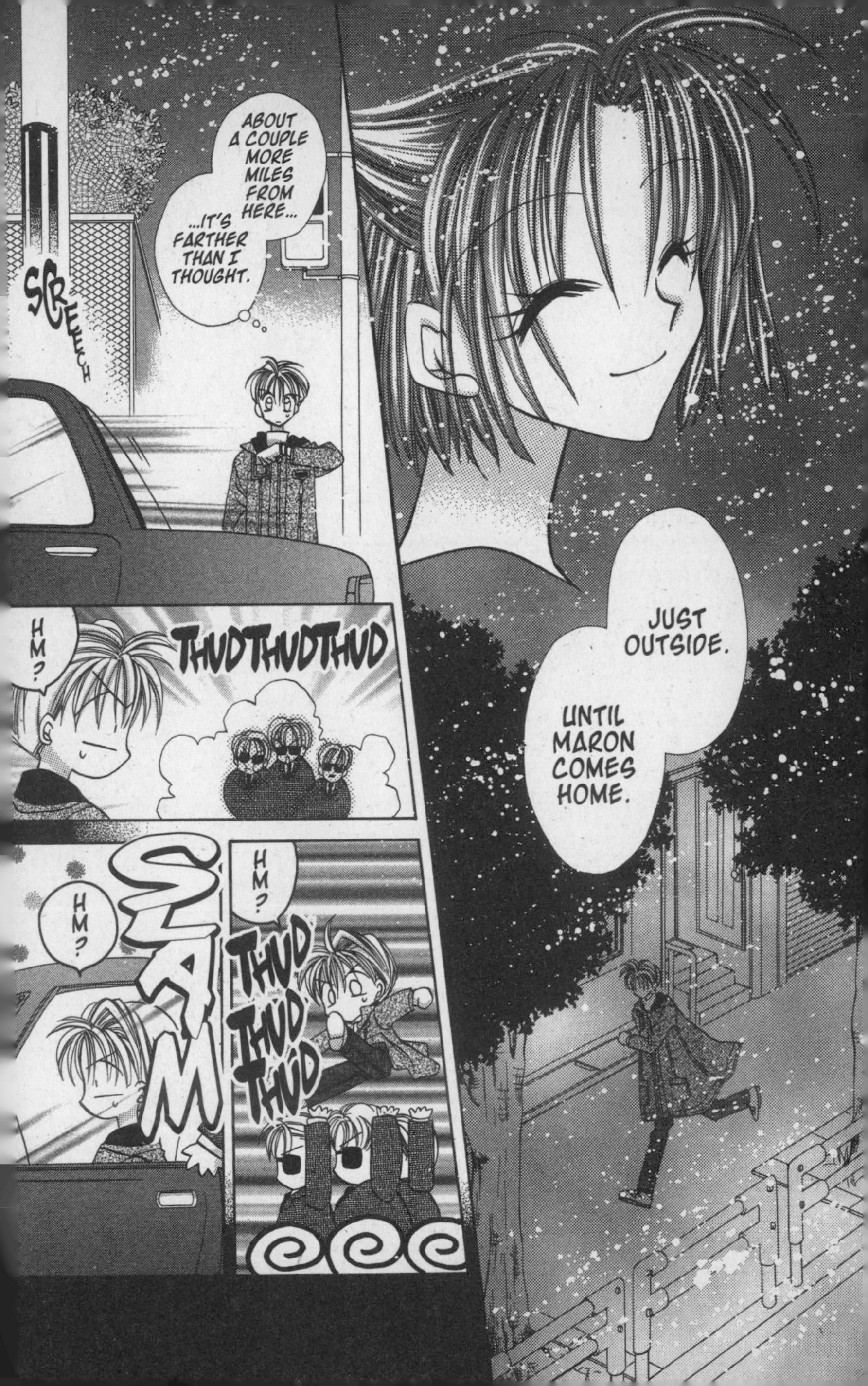
JUST OUTSIDE.
UNTIL MARON COMES HOME.
ABOUT A COUPLE MORE MILES FROM HERE...
...IT'S FARTHER THAN I THOUGHT.
SCREEECH
HM?
THUDTHUDTHUD
HM?
THUD THUD THUD
HM?
SLAM

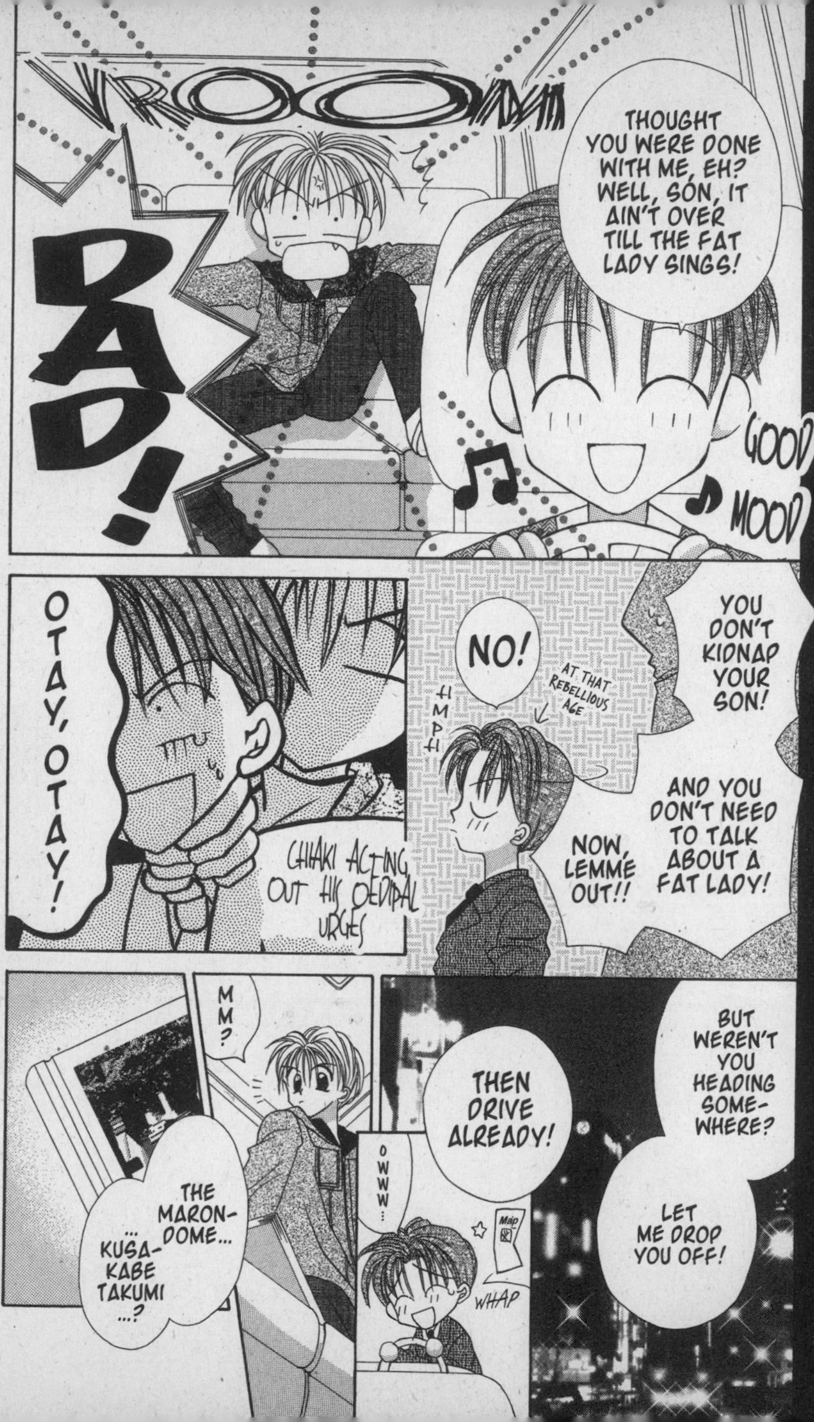
THOUGHT YOU WERE DONE WITH ME, EH? WELL, SON, IT AIN'T OVER TILL THE FAT LADY SINGS!
GOOD MOOD
VROOOOM
DAD!
YOU DON'T KIDNAP YOUR SON!
NO!
AT THAT REBELLIOUS AGE
HMPH
AND YOU DON'T NEED TO TALK ABOUT A FAT LADY!
NOW, LEMME OUT!!
OTAY, OTAY!
CHIAKI ACTING OUT HIS OEDIPAL URGES
BUT WEREN'T YOU HEADING SOME-WHERE?
LET ME DROP YOU OFF!
THEN DRIVE ALREADY!
OWWW...
Map
WHAP
MM?
THE MARON-DOME...
...KUSA-KABE TAKUMI ...?

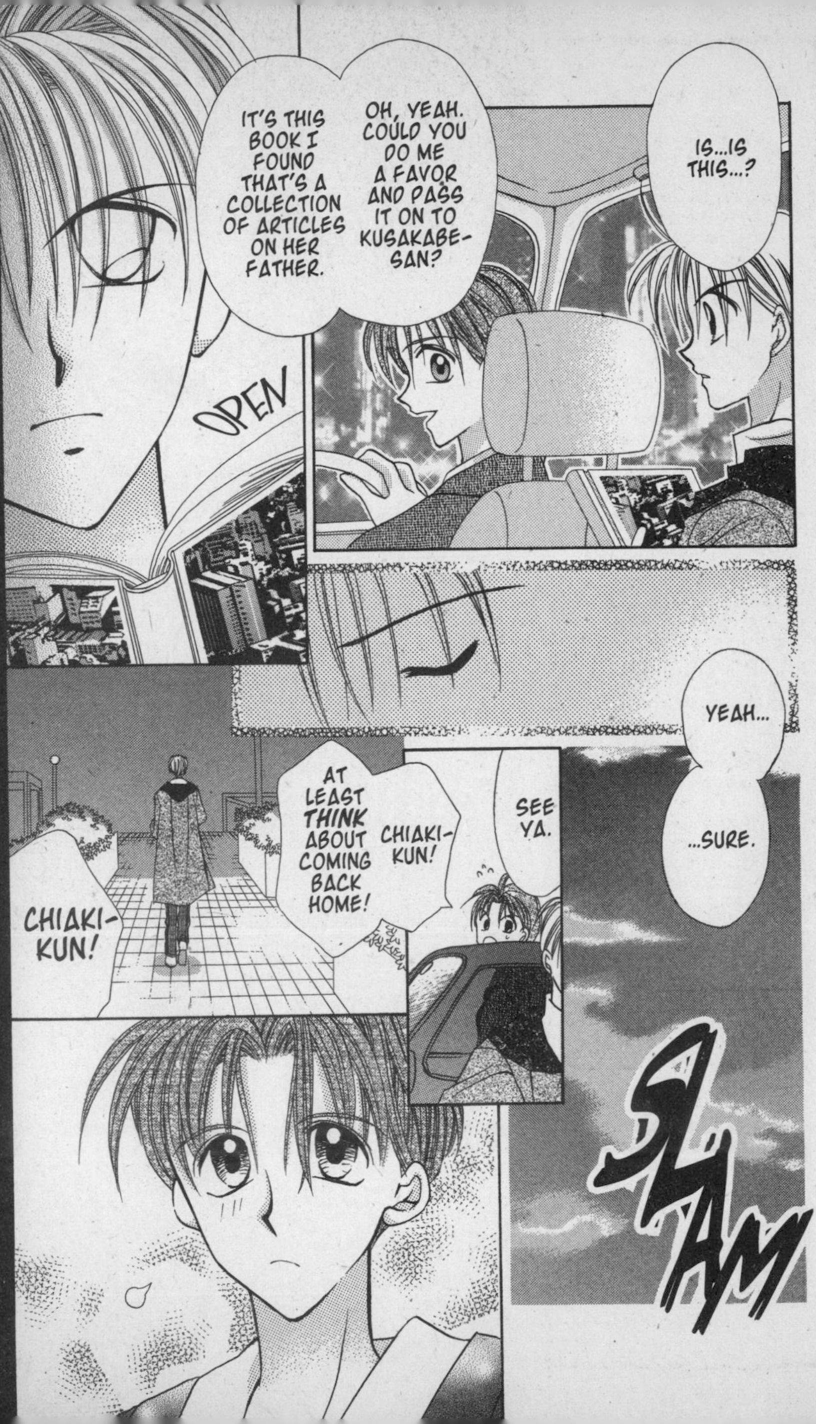

IS...IS THIS...?
OH, YEAH. COULD YOU DO ME A FAVOR AND PASS IT ON TO KUSAKABE-SAN?
IT'S THIS BOOK I FOUND THAT'S A COLLECTION OF ARTICLES ON HER FATHER.
OPEN
YEAH...
...SURE.
SLAM
SEE YA.
CHIAKI-KUN!
AT LEAST THINK ABOUT COMING BACK HOME!
CHIAKI-KUN!

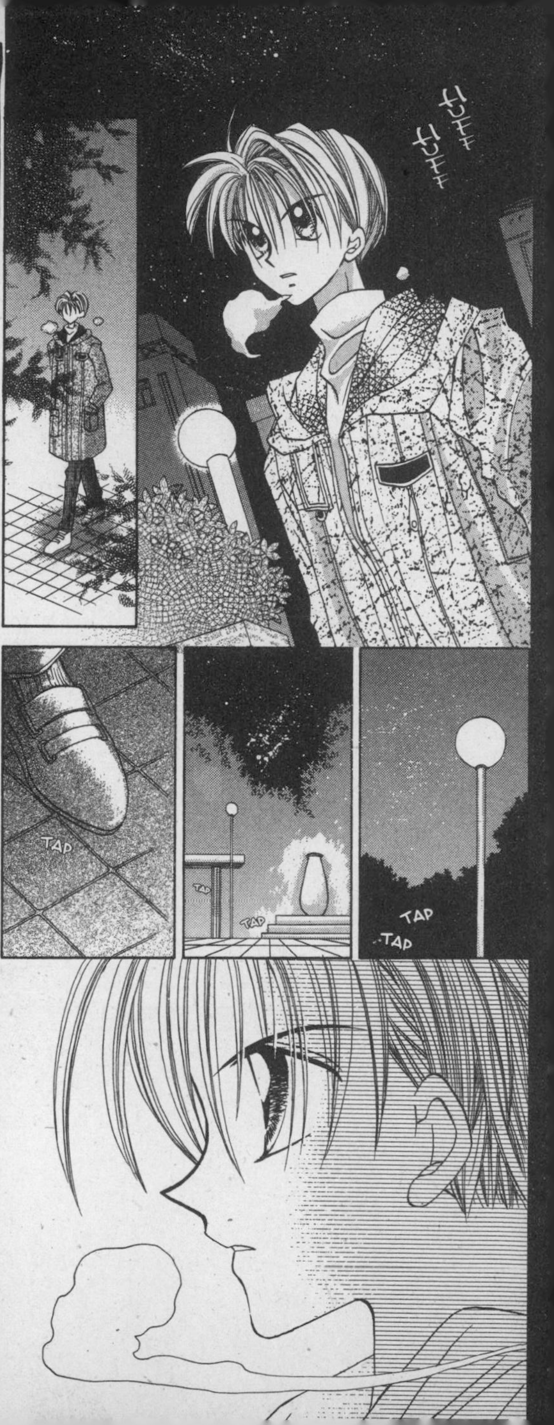
HUFF
HUFF
TAP
TAP
TAP
TAP
TAP

A REALLY HAPPY STORY

I think my fans already know this, but I'm a **huge** fan of Komori Manami-san. While working on a story, for example, I always listen to her on the radio 'cause it keeps me in a cheerful mood. When she says things like, "These are the words that'll make your dreams come true!" my energy level always gets fired up. Komori-san even called me "Arina-chi" before!

Anyway, one of my fans sent a postcard to her radio show, "Radical Communication," telling her about my infatuation with her work, as I got to write about in Ribon's newspaper, etc. I'm so glad I became a manga cartoonist! After that, I got a lot of fan letters about Komori-san talking about me on the air, but at the time, I was in the midst of a deadline crunch, so just that one time I forgot to tune in! (So if anyone out there taped the show, by chance, please send me a copy!)

However, the other day, she congratulated me on the air for the anime version of JEANNE♡ (She mentioned that week's lion's share of postcards were JEANNE-related...Everyone, thank you!!!...) Komori-san is so cute! She also said, "I wanna be Finn! I wanna be Finn! I wanna be Finn!" Unfortunately, the voice of Finn has pretty much already been cast...I'm sorry! (For various reasons, the role was given, with some lobbying on my part, to Nishihara Kumiko-san♡) However, I **do** want to hear Komori-san doing a "voice..." I heard through the grapevine that she actually is doing some voice work for a radio drama on another station, but (GROAN) I can't pick up that station from where I live...But anyway, Komori-san, you made my day! I promise to keep listening!

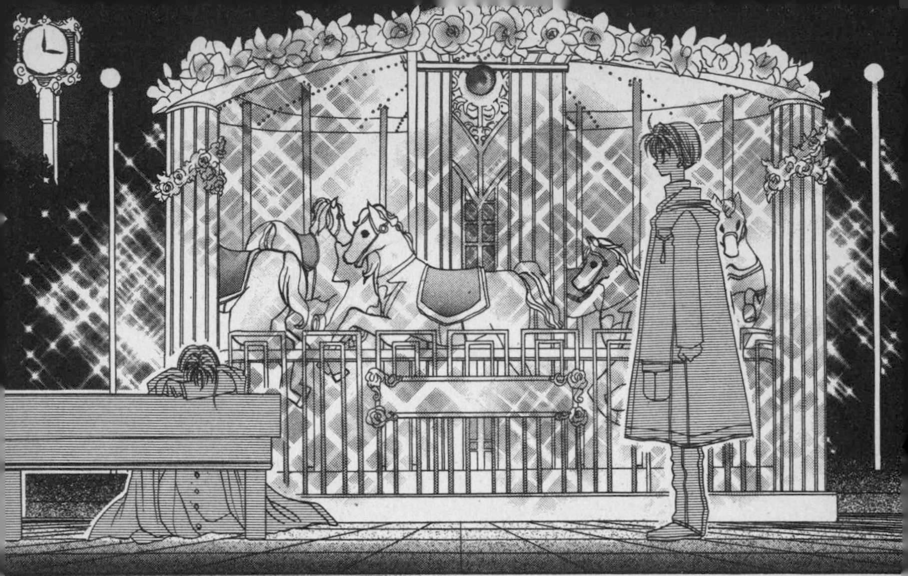
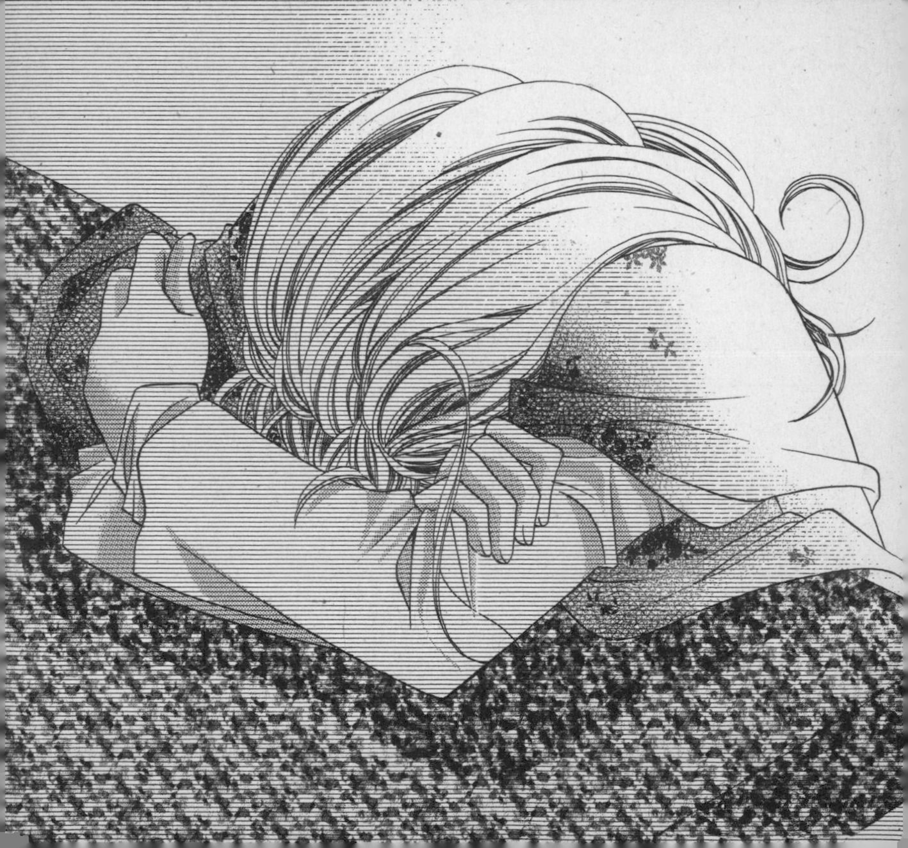

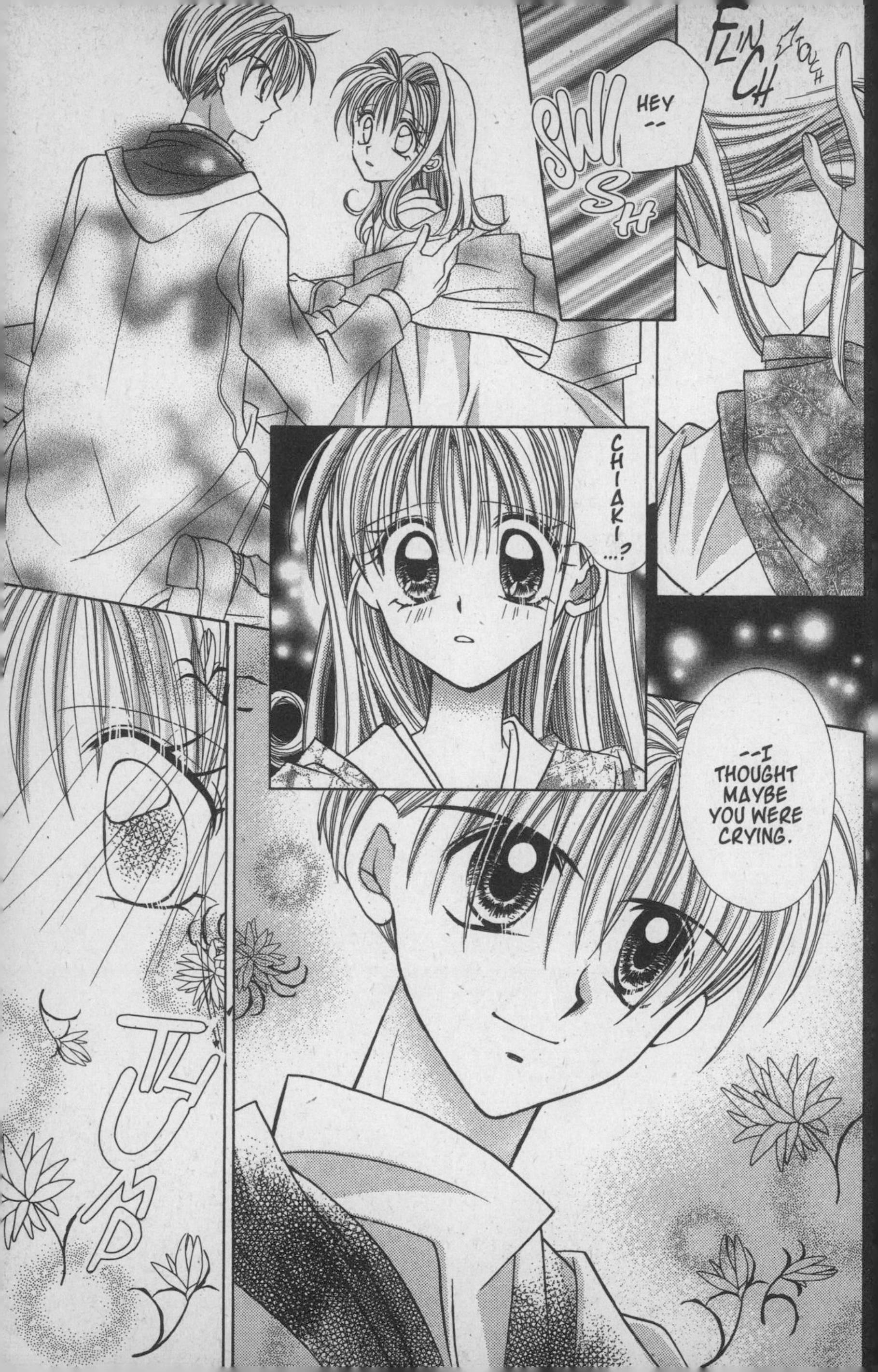
FLINCH
TOUCH
SWISH
HEY --
CHIAKI...?
--I THOUGHT MAYBE YOU WERE CRYING.
THUMP

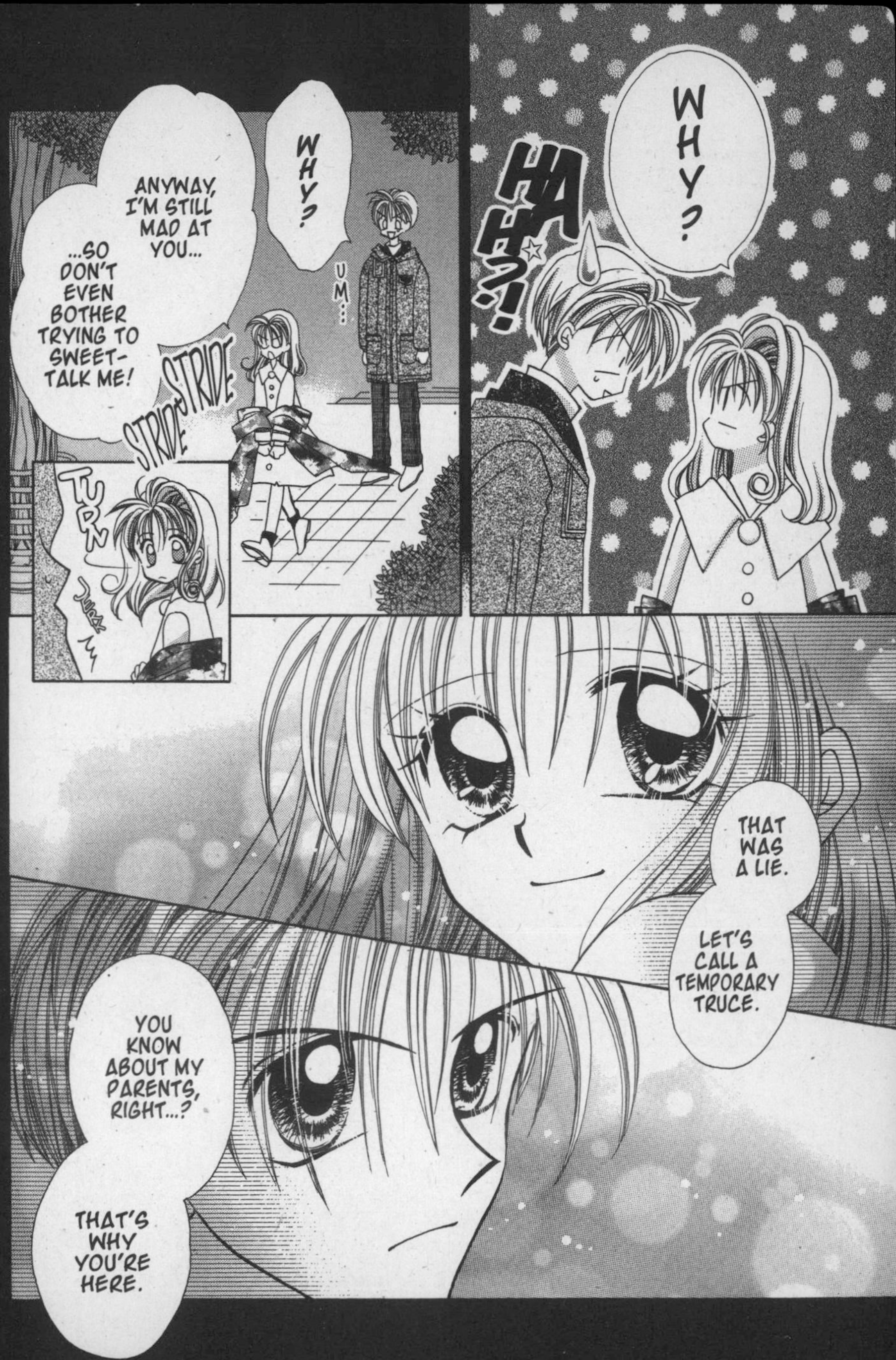
WHY?
HAH?!
WHY?
UM...
ANYWAY, I'M STILL MAD AT YOU...
...SO DON'T EVEN BOTHER TRYING TO SWEET-TALK ME!
STRIDE STRIDE
TURN
THAT WAS A LIE.
LET'S CALL A TEMPORARY TRUCE.
YOU KNOW ABOUT MY PARENTS, RIGHT...?
THAT'S WHY YOU'RE HERE.

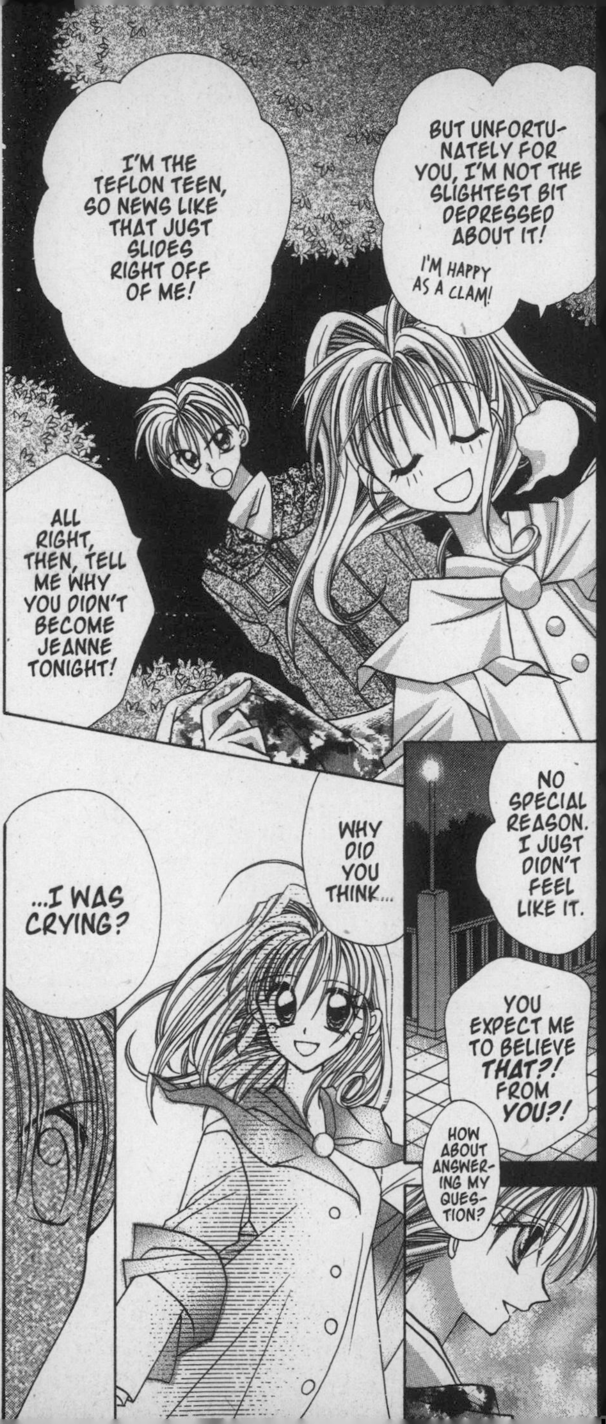
BUT UNFORTUNATELY FOR YOU, I'M NOT THE SLIGHTEST BIT DEPRESSED ABOUT IT!
I'M HAPPY AS A CLAM!
I'M THE TEFLON TEEN, SO NEWS LIKE THAT JUST SLIDES RIGHT OFF OF ME!
ALL RIGHT, THEN, TELL ME WHY YOU DIDN'T BECOME JEANNE TONIGHT!
NO SPECIAL REASON. I JUST DIDN'T FEEL LIKE IT.
YOU EXPECT ME TO BELIEVE THAT?! FROM YOU?!
HOW ABOUT ANSWERING MY QUESTION?
WHY DID YOU THINK...
...I WAS CRYING?

11 ARINA TANEMURA'S "LIKE PULLING TEETH WITH PLIERS"

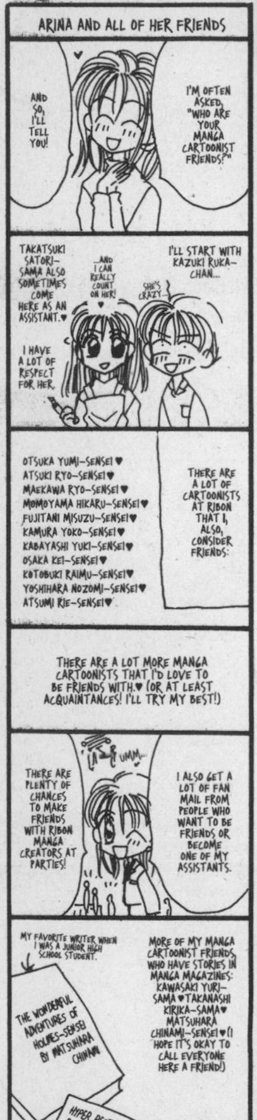
ARINA AND ALL OF HER FRIENDS
I'M OFTEN ASKED, "WHO ARE YOUR MANGA CARTOONIST FRIENDS?"
AND SO, I'LL TELL YOU!
I'LL START WITH KAZUKI RUKA-CHAN...
SHE'S CRAZY
...AND I CAN REALLY COUNT ON HER!
TAKATSUKI SATORI-SAMA ALSO SOMETIMES COME HERE AS AN ASSISTANT.♥
I HAVE A LOT OF RESPECT FOR HER.
THERE ARE A LOT OF CARTOONISTS AT RIBON THAT I, ALSO, CONSIDER FRIENDS:
OTSUKA YUMI-SENSEI♥
ATSUKI RYO-SENSEI♥
MAEKAWA RYO-SENSEI♥
MOMOYAMA HIKARU-SENSEI♥
FUJITANI MISUZU-SENSEI♥
KAMURA YOKO-SENSEI♥
KABAYASHI YUKI-SENSEI♥
OSAKA KEI-SENSEI♥
KOTOBUKI RAIMU-SENSEI♥
YOSHIHARA NOZOMI-SENSEI♥
ATSUMI RIE-SENSEI♥
THERE ARE A LOT MORE MANGA CARTOONISTS THAT I'D LOVE TO BE FRIENDS WITH.♥ (OR AT LEAST ACQUAINTANCES! I'LL TRY MY BEST!)
I ALSO GET A LOT OF FAN MAIL FROM PEOPLE WHO WANT TO BE FRIENDS OR BECOME ONE OF MY ASSISTANTS.
UMM...
THERE ARE PLENTY OF CHANCES TO MAKE FRIENDS WITH RIBON MANGA CREATORS AT PARTIES!
MORE OF MY MANGA CARTOONIST FRIENDS, WHO HAVE STORIES IN MANGA MAGAZINES: KAWASAKI YURI-SAMA♥TAKANASHI KIRIKA-SAMA♥ MATSUHARA CHINAMI-SENSEI♥ (I HOPE IT'S OKAY TO CALL EVERYONE HERE A FRIEND!)
MY FAVORITE WRITER WHEN I WAS A JUNIOR HIGH SCHOOL STUDENT.
THE WONDERFUL ADVENTURES OF HOLMES-SENSEI BY MATSUHARA CHINAMI
HYPER RESTAURANT BY TAKANASHI KIRIKA VOL 1 AND 2 NOW ON SALE! CHINAMI
← FAN♥

TO BE HONEST, I THINK I MIGHT BE GIVING EVERYONE HERE SOME TROUBLE BY OUTING THEM AS MY FRIENDS! EVERYONE HERE, PLEASE DON'T BREAK OFF OUR RELATIONSHIP BECAUSE OF THIS!

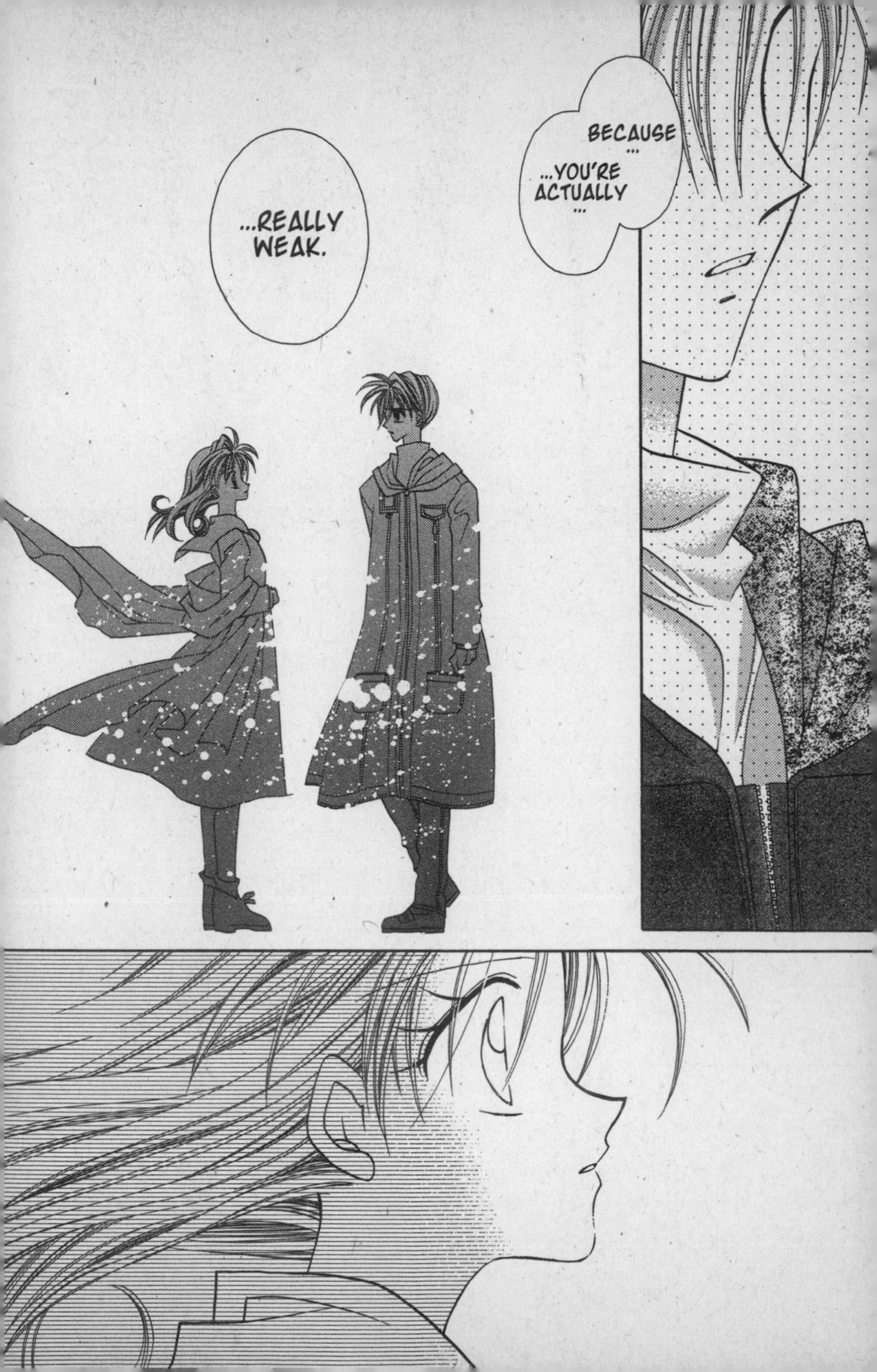
BECAUSE ... ...YOU'RE ACTUALLY ...
...REALLY WEAK.

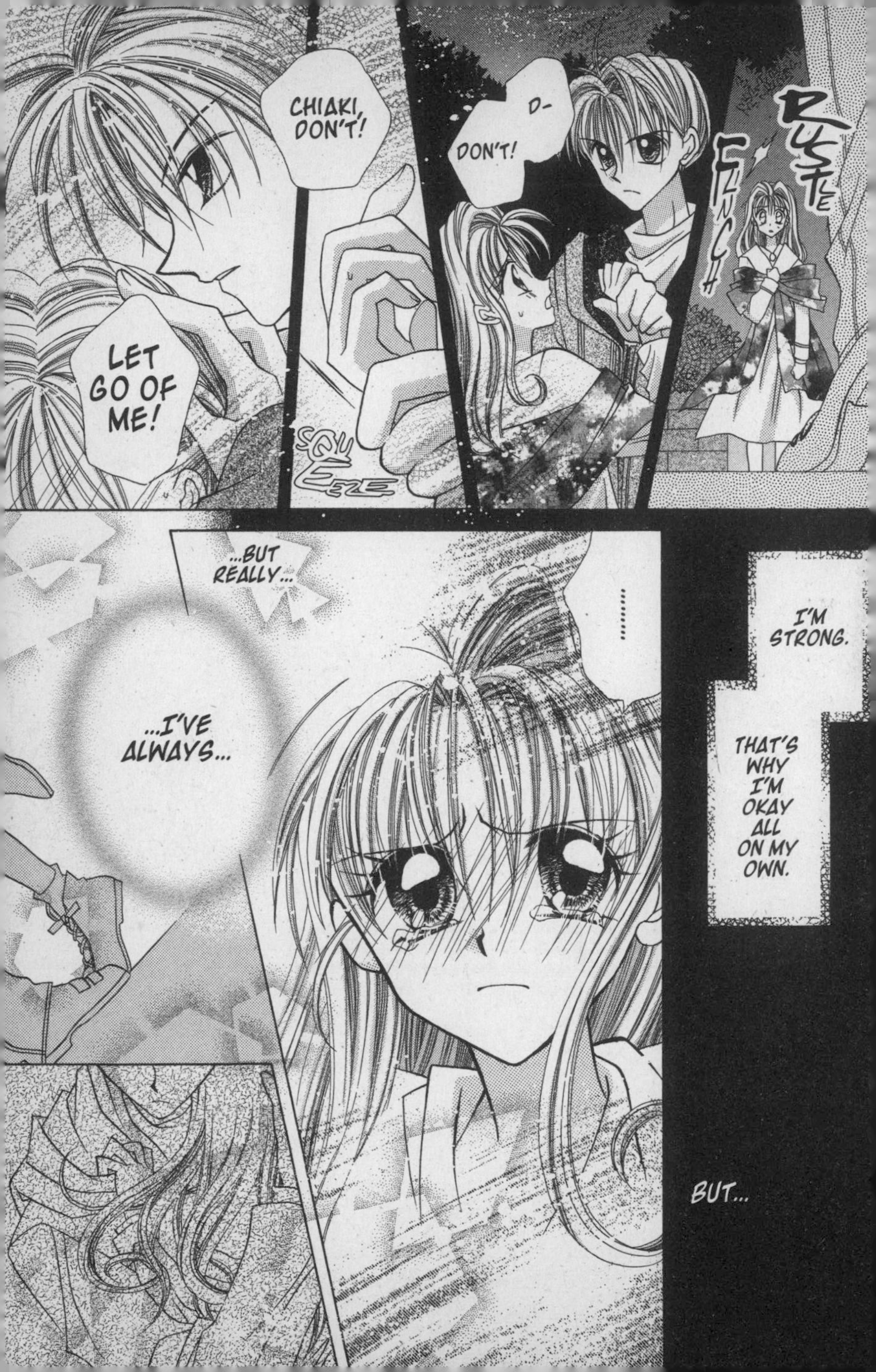
RUSTLE
FLINCH
D-
DON'T!
CHIAKI, DON'T!
SQUEEZE
LET GO OF ME!
I'M STRONG.
THAT'S WHY I'M OKAY ALL ON MY OWN.
BUT...
......
...BUT REALLY...
...I'VE ALWAYS...

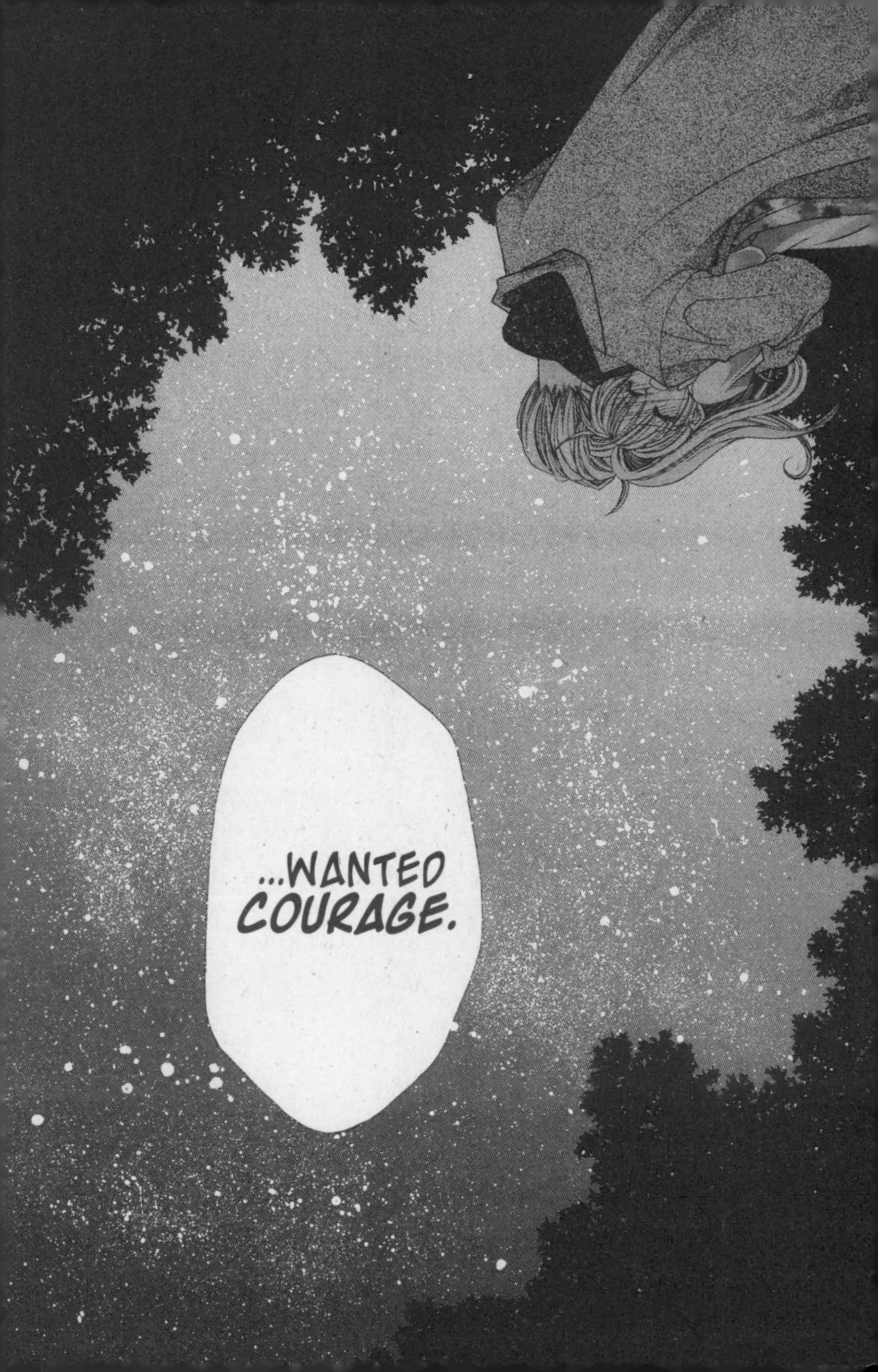
...WANTED COURAGE.

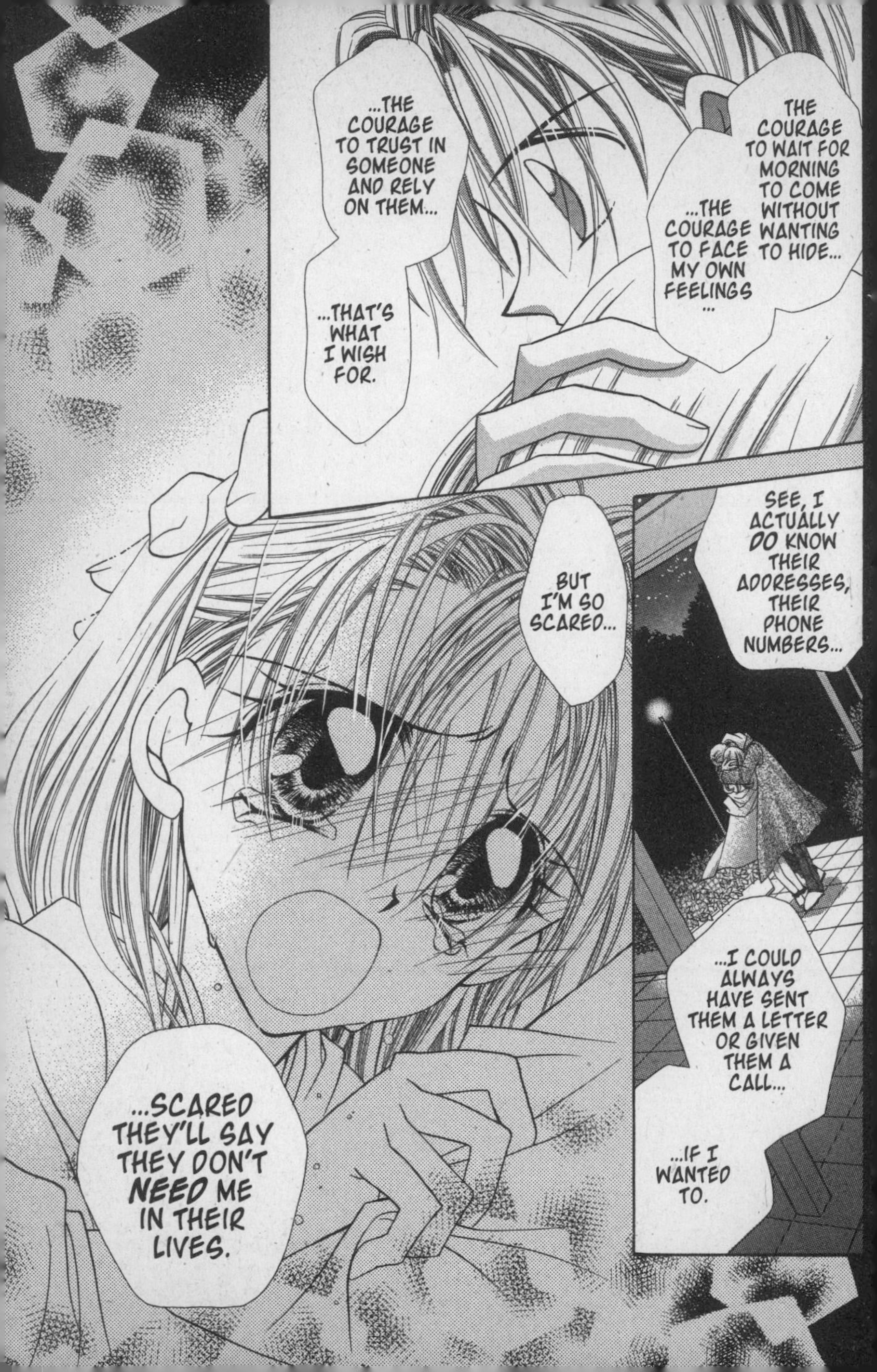
THE COURAGE TO WAIT FOR MORNING TO COME WITHOUT WANTING TO HIDE...
...THE COURAGE TO FACE MY OWN FEELINGS...
...THE COURAGE TO TRUST IN SOMEONE AND RELY ON THEM...
...THAT'S WHAT I WISH FOR.
SEE, I ACTUALLY *DO* KNOW THEIR ADDRESSES, THEIR PHONE NUMBERS...
...I COULD ALWAYS HAVE SENT THEM A LETTER OR GIVEN THEM A CALL...
...IF I WANTED TO.
BUT I'M SO SCARED...
...SCARED THEY'LL SAY THEY DON'T *NEED* ME IN THEIR LIVES.

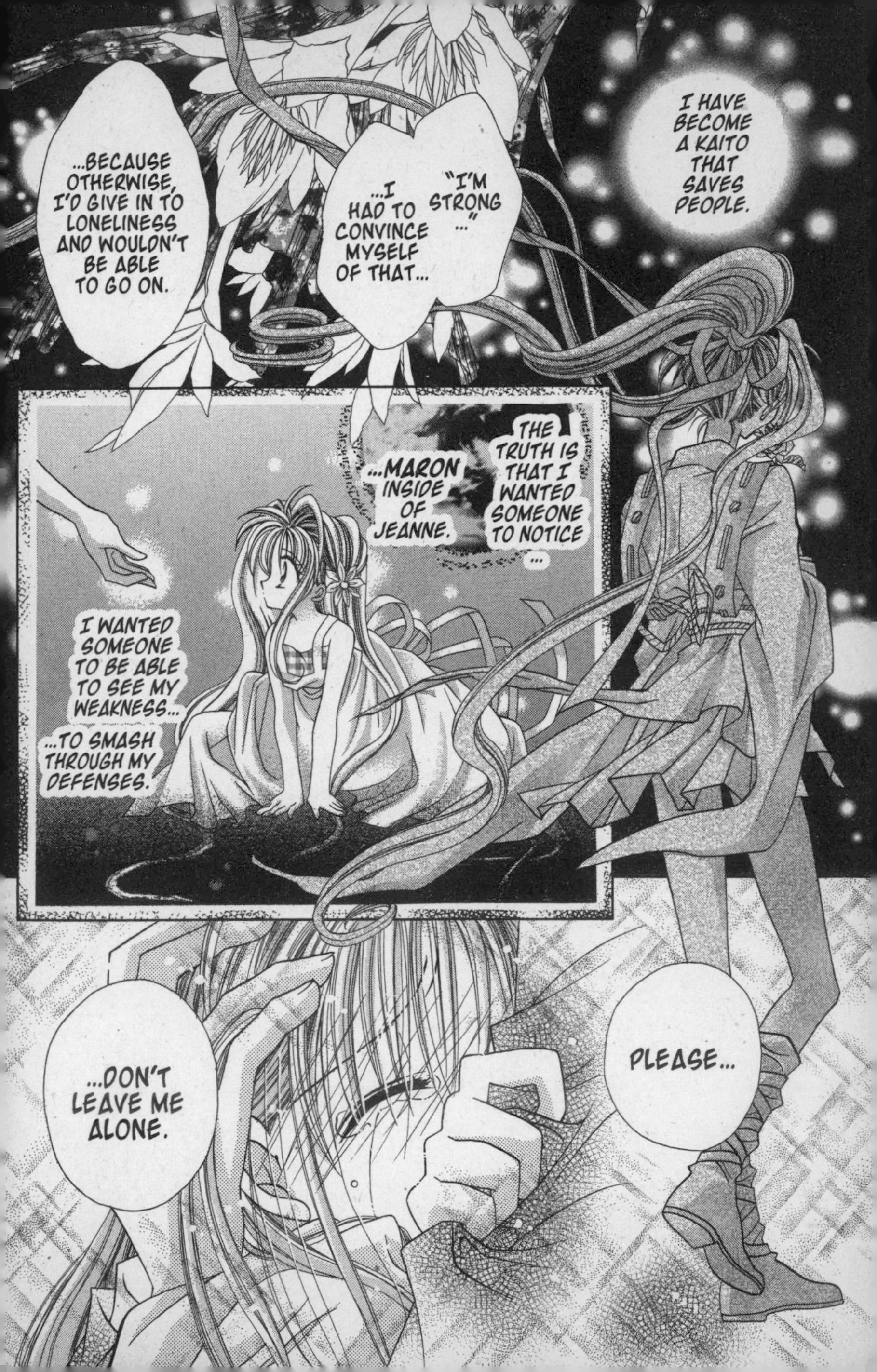
I HAVE BECOME A KAITO THAT SAVES PEOPLE.
"I'M STRONG..."
...I HAD TO CONVINCE MYSELF OF THAT...
...BECAUSE OTHERWISE, I'D GIVE IN TO LONELINESS AND WOULDN'T BE ABLE TO GO ON.
THE TRUTH IS THAT I WANTED SOMEONE TO NOTICE...
...MARON INSIDE OF JEANNE.
I WANTED SOMEONE TO BE ABLE TO SEE MY WEAKNESS...
...TO SMASH THROUGH MY DEFENSES.
PLEASE...
...DON'T LEAVE ME ALONE.

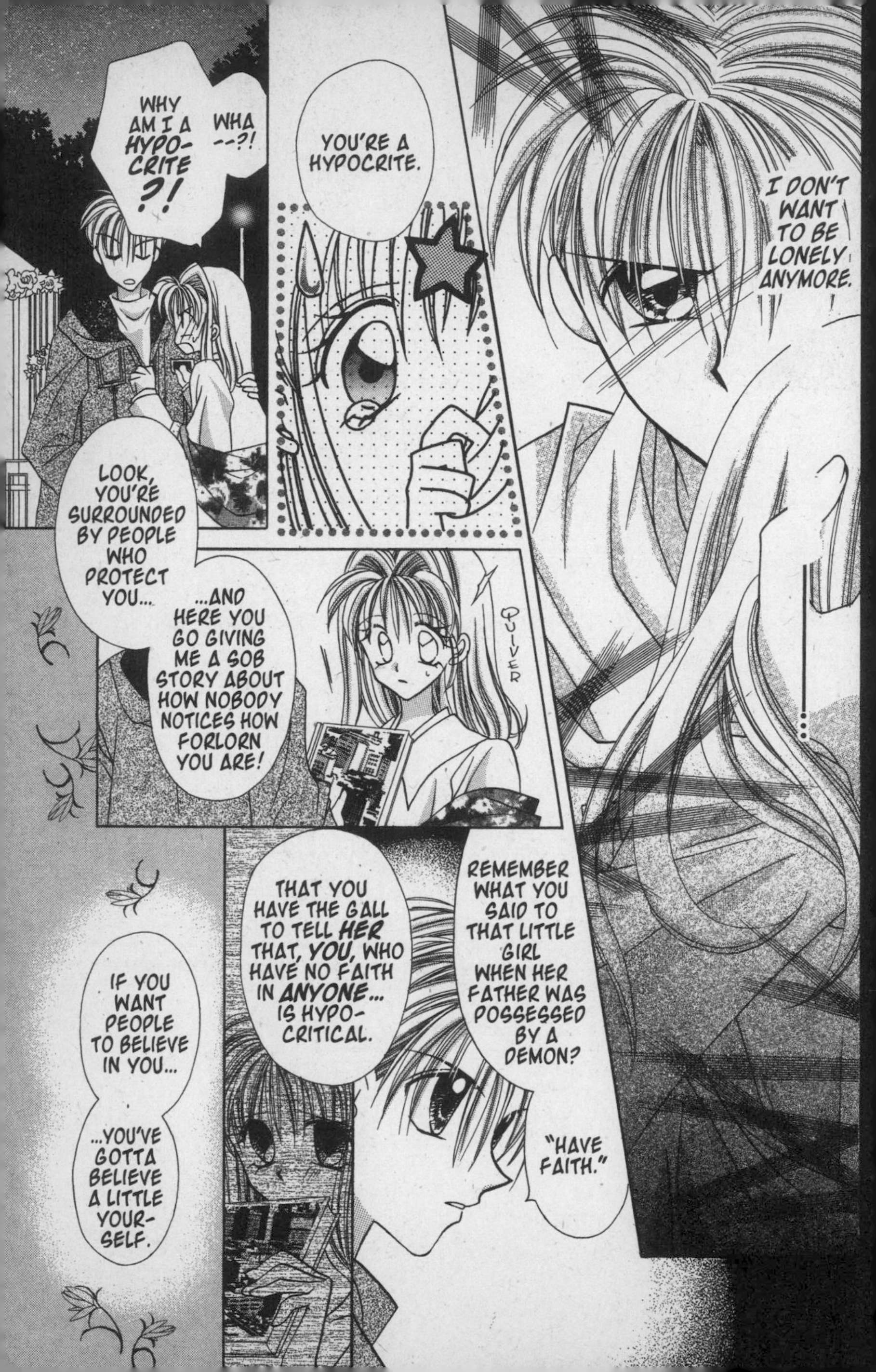
I DON'T WANT TO BE LONELY ANYMORE.
...
YOU'RE A HYPOCRITE.
WHA--?!
WHY AM I A HYPOCRITE?!
QUIVER
...AND HERE YOU GO GIVING ME A SOB STORY ABOUT HOW NOBODY NOTICES HOW FORLORN YOU ARE!
LOOK, YOU'RE SURROUNDED BY PEOPLE WHO PROTECT YOU...
REMEMBER WHAT YOU SAID TO THAT LITTLE GIRL WHEN HER FATHER WAS POSSESSED BY A DEMON?
"HAVE FAITH."
THAT YOU HAVE THE GALL TO TELL HER THAT, YOU, WHO HAVE NO FAITH IN ANYONE... IS HYPOCRITICAL.
IF YOU WANT PEOPLE TO BELIEVE IN YOU...
...YOU'VE GOTTA BELIEVE A LITTLE YOURSELF.

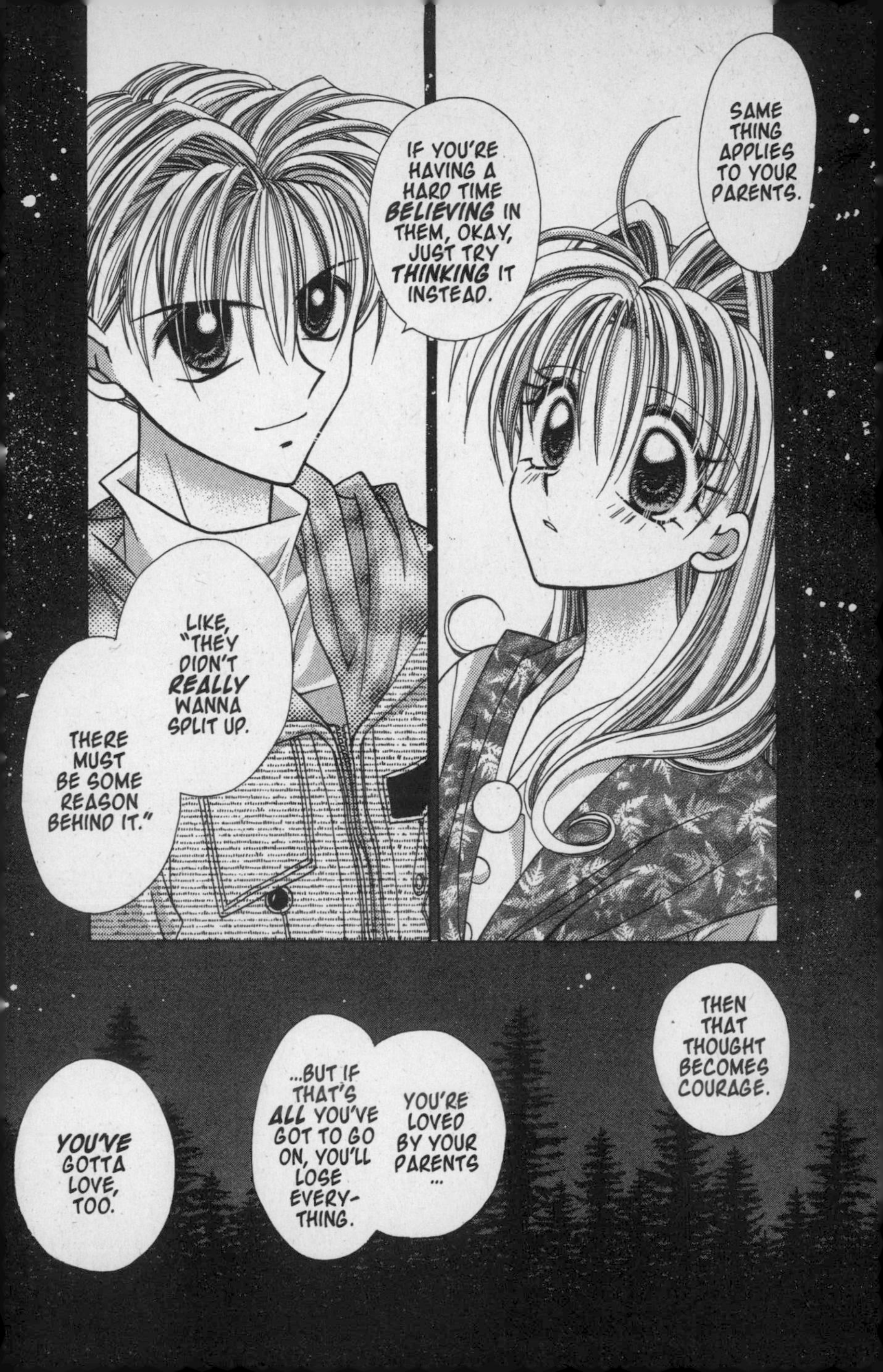
SAME THING APPLIES TO YOUR PARENTS.
IF YOU'RE HAVING A HARD TIME BELIEVING IN THEM, OKAY, JUST TRY THINKING IT INSTEAD.
LIKE, "THEY DIDN'T REALLY WANNA SPLIT UP.
THERE MUST BE SOME REASON BEHIND IT."
THEN THAT THOUGHT BECOMES COURAGE.
YOU'RE LOVED BY YOUR PARENTS...
...BUT IF THAT'S ALL YOU'VE GOT TO GO ON, YOU'LL LOSE EVERY-THING.
YOU'VE GOTTA LOVE, TOO.

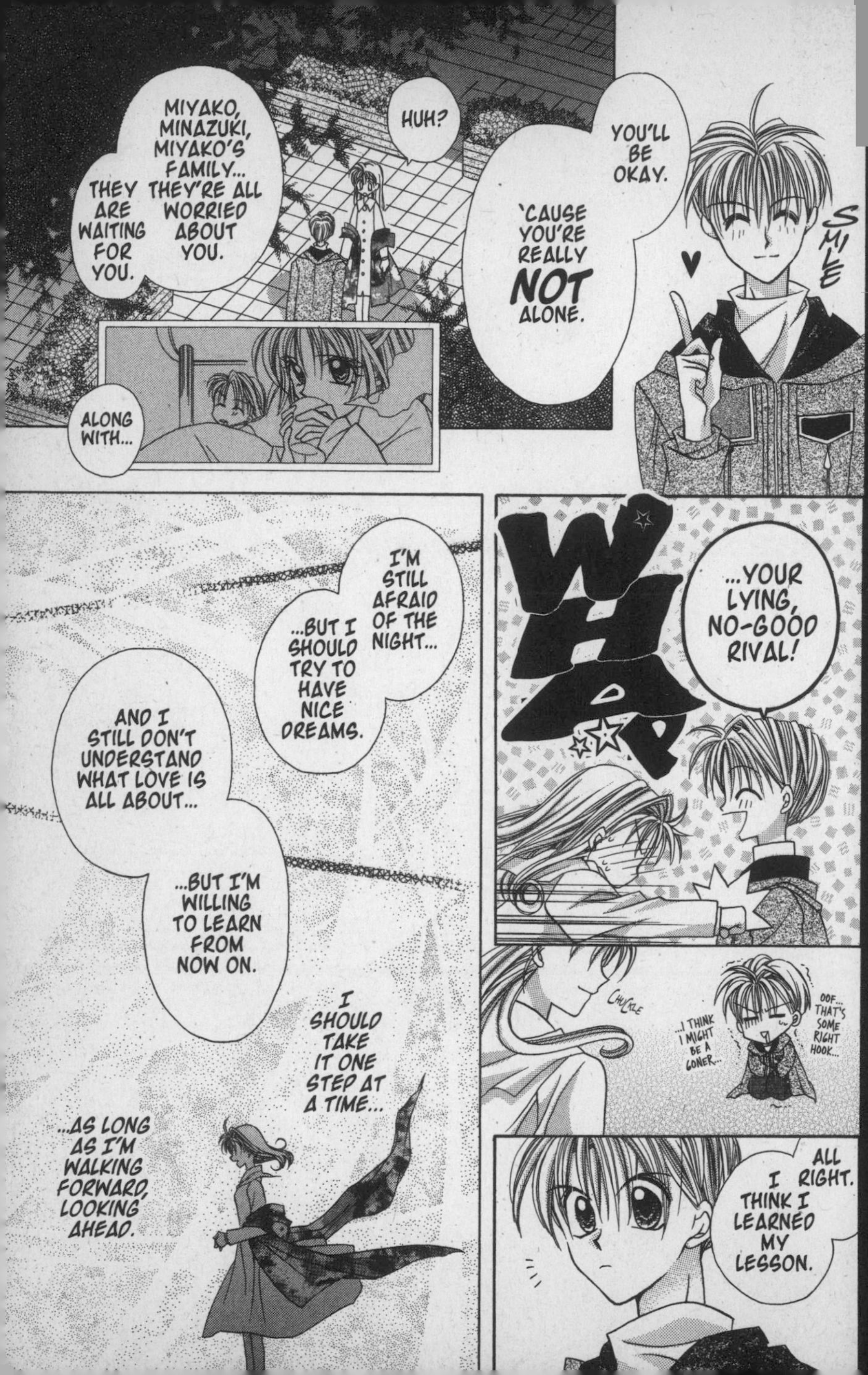
YOU'LL BE OKAY.
'CAUSE YOU'RE REALLY NOT ALONE.
SMILE
HUH?
MIYAKO, MINAZUKI, MIYAKO'S FAMILY... THEY'RE ALL WORRIED ABOUT YOU.
THEY ARE WAITING FOR YOU.
ALONG WITH...
WHAP
...YOUR LYING, NO-GOOD RIVAL!
CHUCKLE
OOF... THAT'S SOME RIGHT HOOK...
...I THINK I MIGHT BE A GONER...
ALL RIGHT.
I THINK I LEARNED MY LESSON.
I'M STILL AFRAID OF THE NIGHT...
...BUT I SHOULD TRY TO HAVE NICE DREAMS.
AND I STILL DON'T UNDERSTAND WHAT LOVE IS ALL ABOUT...
...BUT I'M WILLING TO LEARN FROM NOW ON.
I SHOULD TAKE IT ONE STEP AT A TIME...
...AS LONG AS I'M WALKING FORWARD, LOOKING AHEAD.

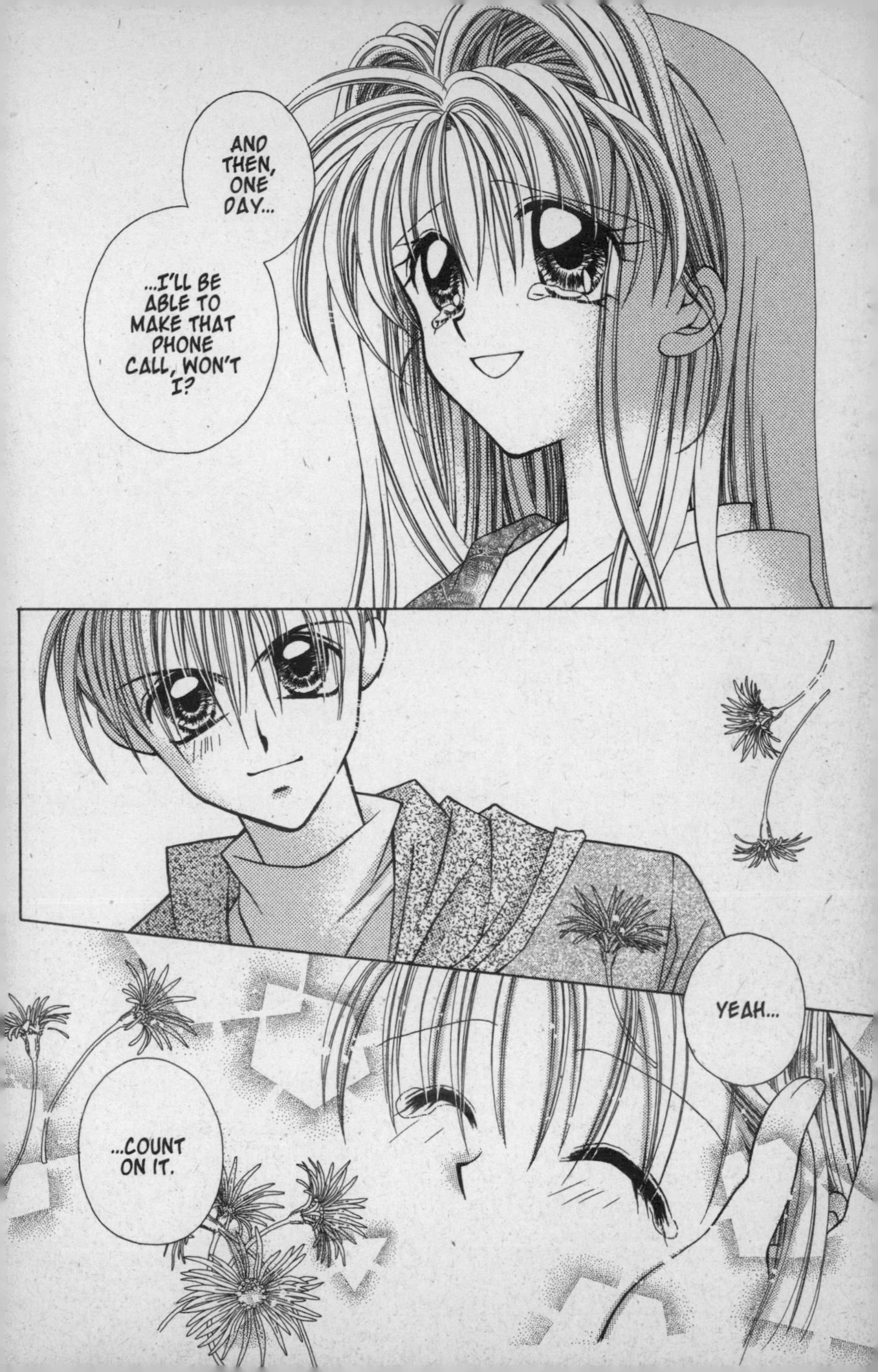
AND THEN, ONE DAY...
...I'LL BE ABLE TO MAKE THAT PHONE CALL, WON'T I?
YEAH...
...COUNT ON IT.

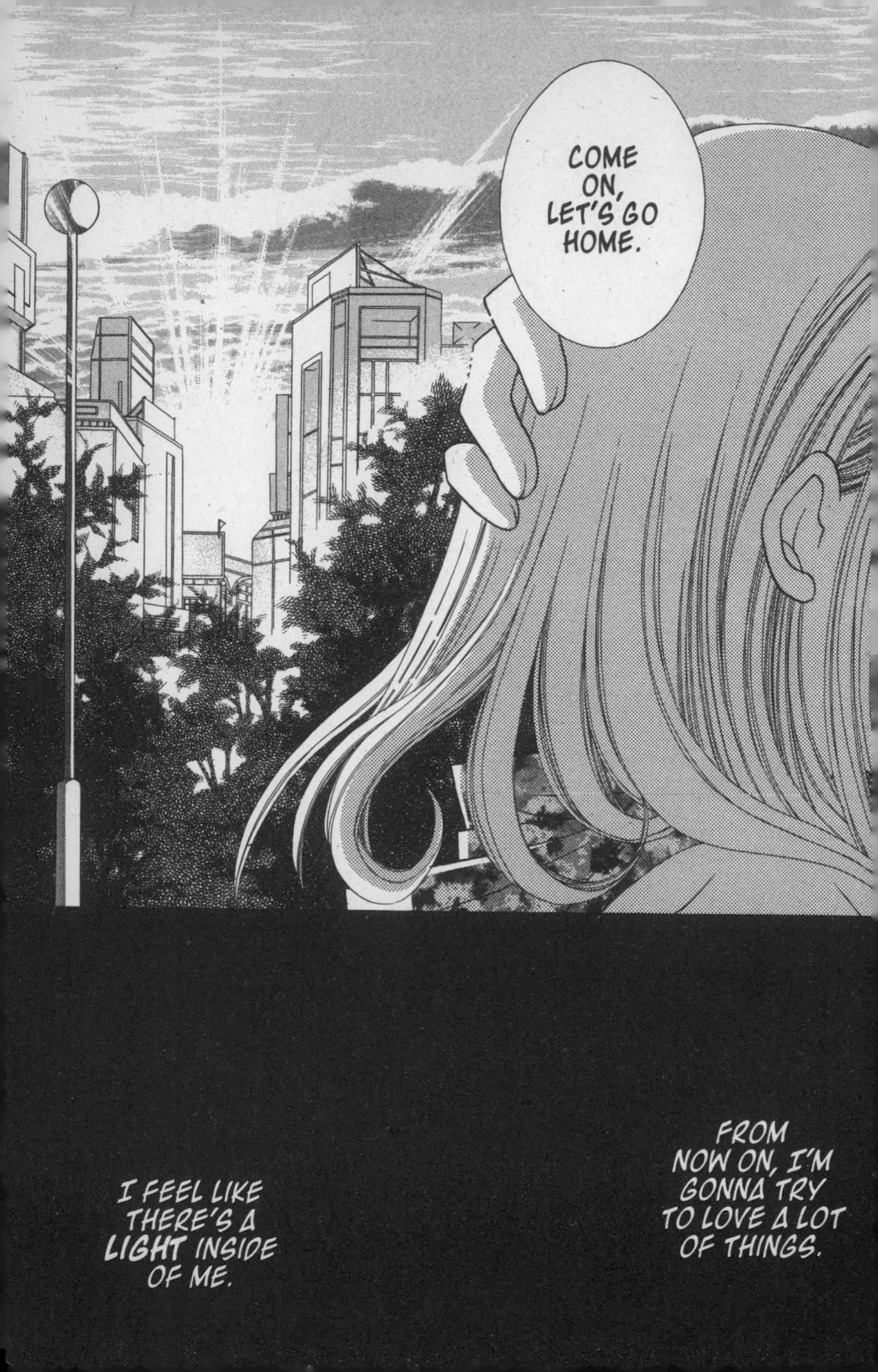
COME ON, LET'S GO HOME.
FROM NOW ON, I'M GONNA TRY TO LOVE A LOT OF THINGS.
I FEEL LIKE THERE'S A **LIGHT** INSIDE OF ME.

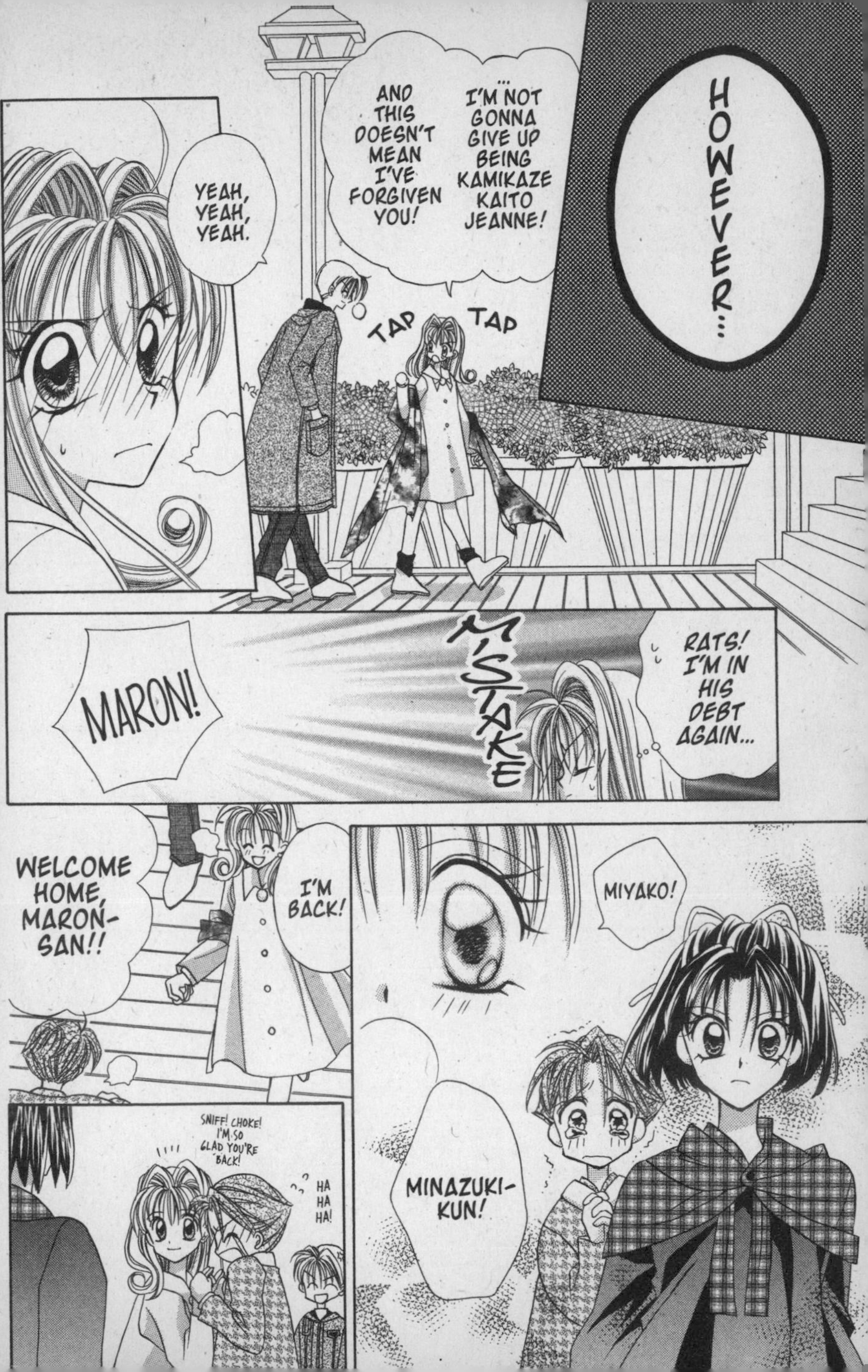
HOWEVER...
...I'M NOT GONNA GIVE UP BEING KAMIKAZE KAITO JEANNE!
AND THIS DOESN'T MEAN I'VE FORGIVEN YOU!
TAP TAP
YEAH, YEAH, YEAH.
RATS! I'M IN HIS DEBT AGAIN...
MISTAKE
MARON!
MIYAKO!
MINAZUKI-KUN!
I'M BACK!
WELCOME HOME, MARON-SAN!!
SNIFF! CHOKE! I'M SO GLAD YOU'RE BACK!
HA HA HA!

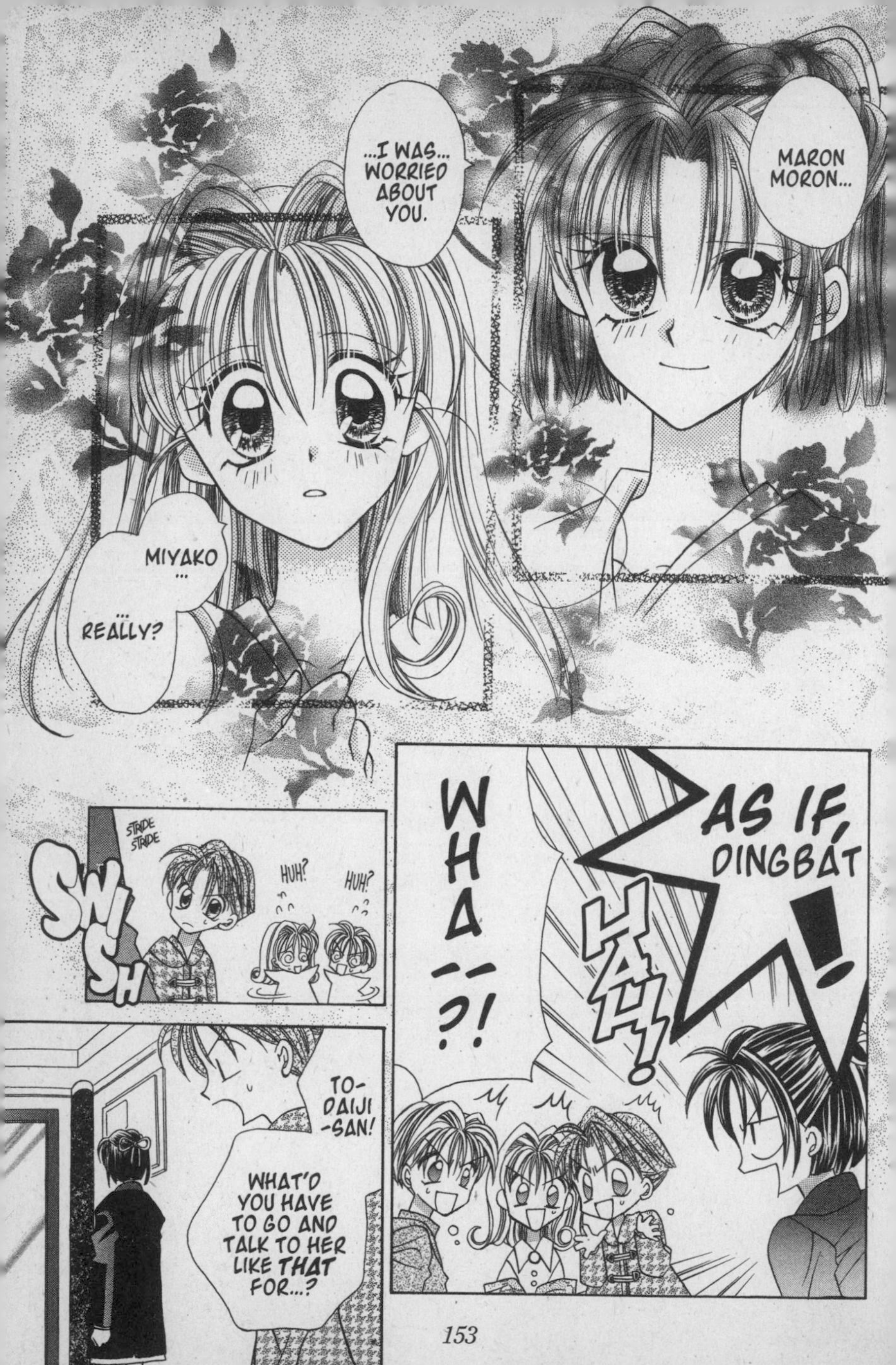
MARON MORON...
...I WAS... WORRIED ABOUT YOU.
MIYAKO ... ... REALLY?
AS IF, DINGBAT!
HAH!
WHA--?!
STRIDE STRIDE
HUH?
HUH?
SWISH
TO-DAIJI-SAN!
WHAT'D YOU HAVE TO GO AND TALK TO HER LIKE *THAT* FOR...?

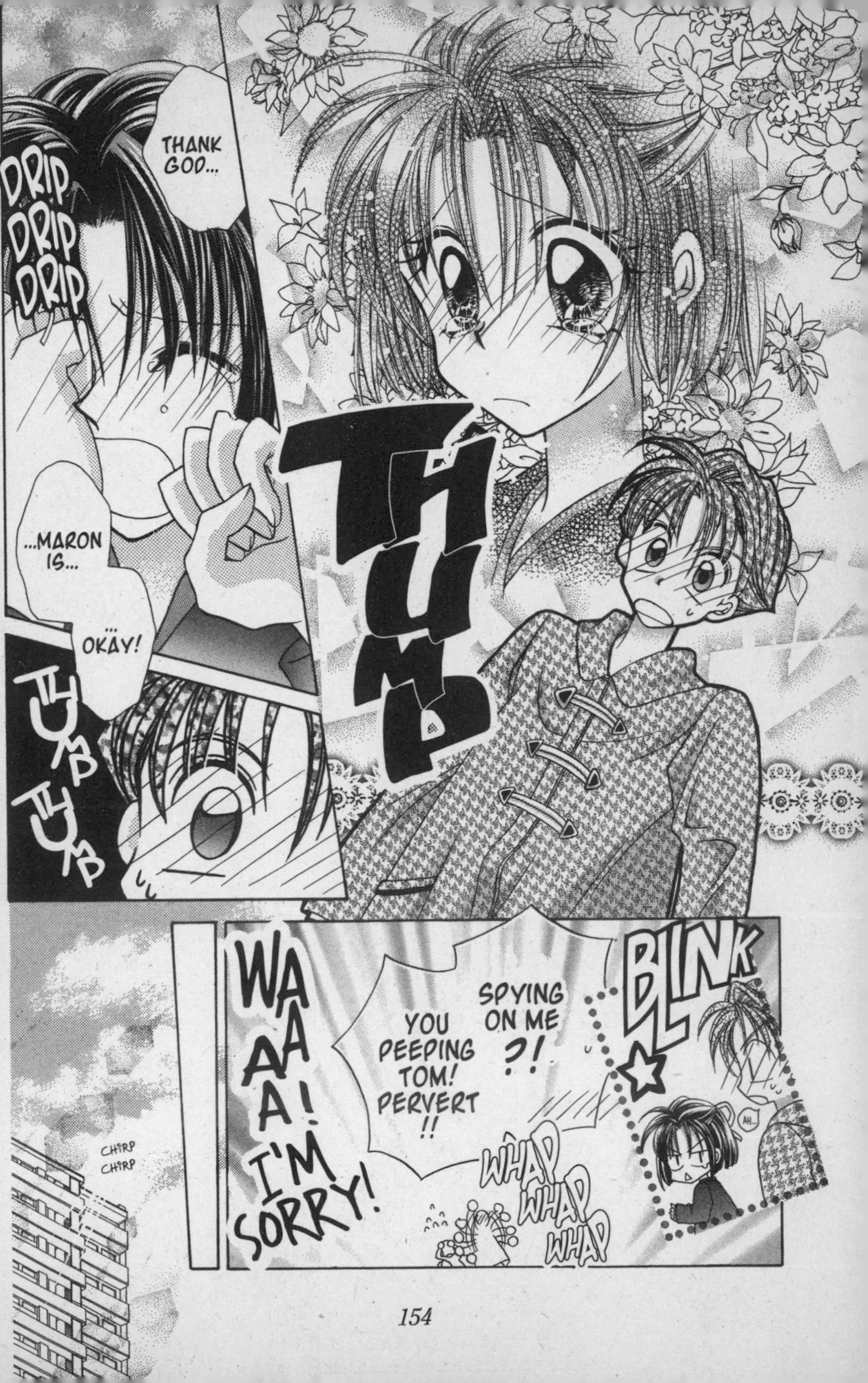
THUMP
THANK GOD...
DRIP DRIP DRIP
...MARON IS...
...OKAY!
THUMP THUMP
BLINK
AH...
SPYING ON ME ?!
YOU PEEPING TOM! PERVERT !!
WAAAAA! I'M SORRY!
WHAP WHAP WHAP
CHIRP CHIRP

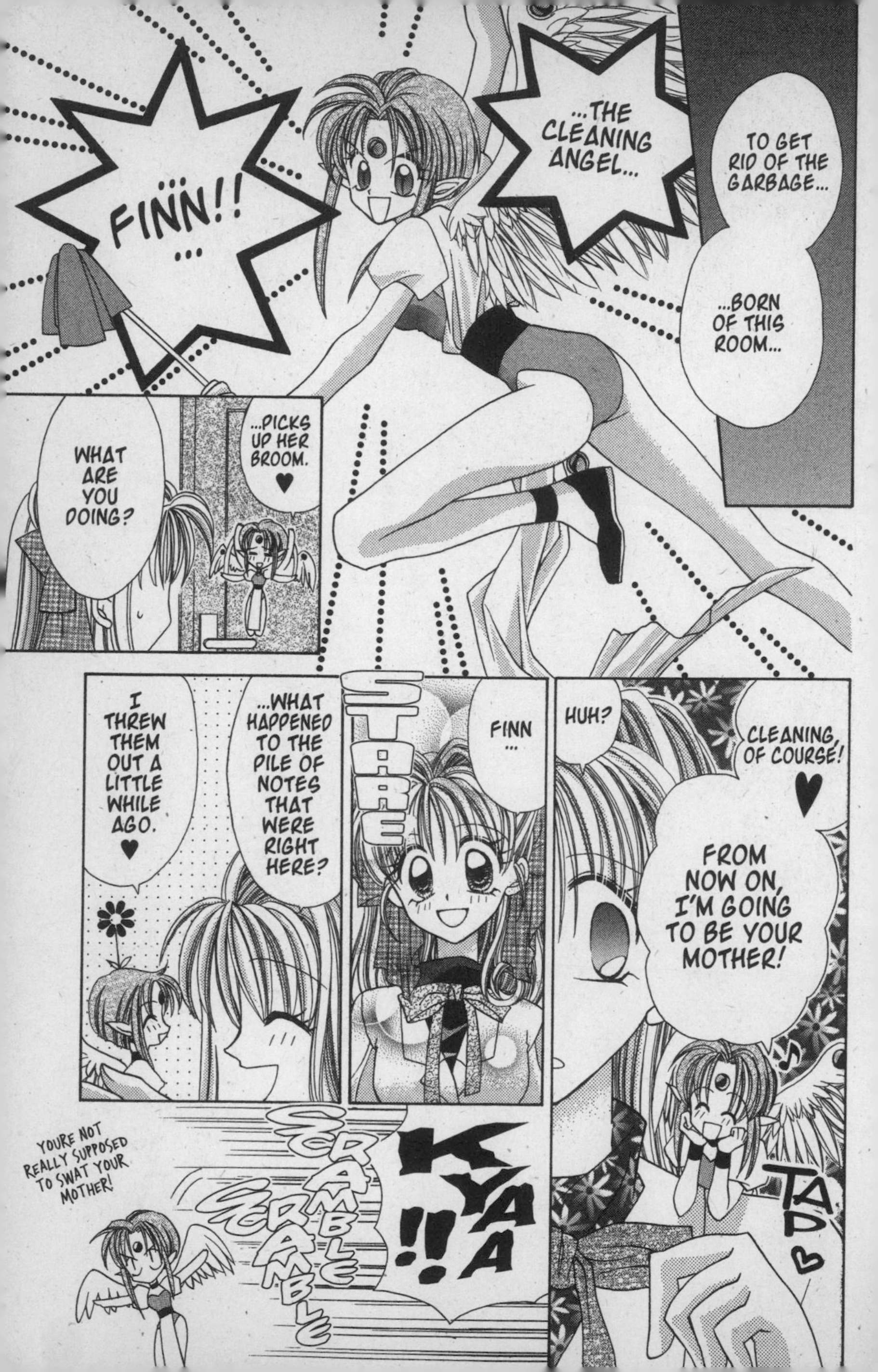
TO GET RID OF THE GARBAGE...
...BORN OF THIS ROOM...
...THE CLEANING ANGEL...
...FINN!!...
...PICKS UP HER BROOM. ♥
WHAT ARE YOU DOING?
HUH?
CLEANING, OF COURSE! ♥
FROM NOW ON, I'M GOING TO BE YOUR MOTHER!
TAP ♥
FINN...
STARE
...WHAT HAPPENED TO THE PILE OF NOTES THAT WERE RIGHT HERE?
I THREW THEM OUT A LITTLE WHILE AGO. ♥
KYAA!!
SCRAMBLE SCRAMBLE
YOURE NOT REALLY SUPPOSED TO SWAT YOUR MOTHER!

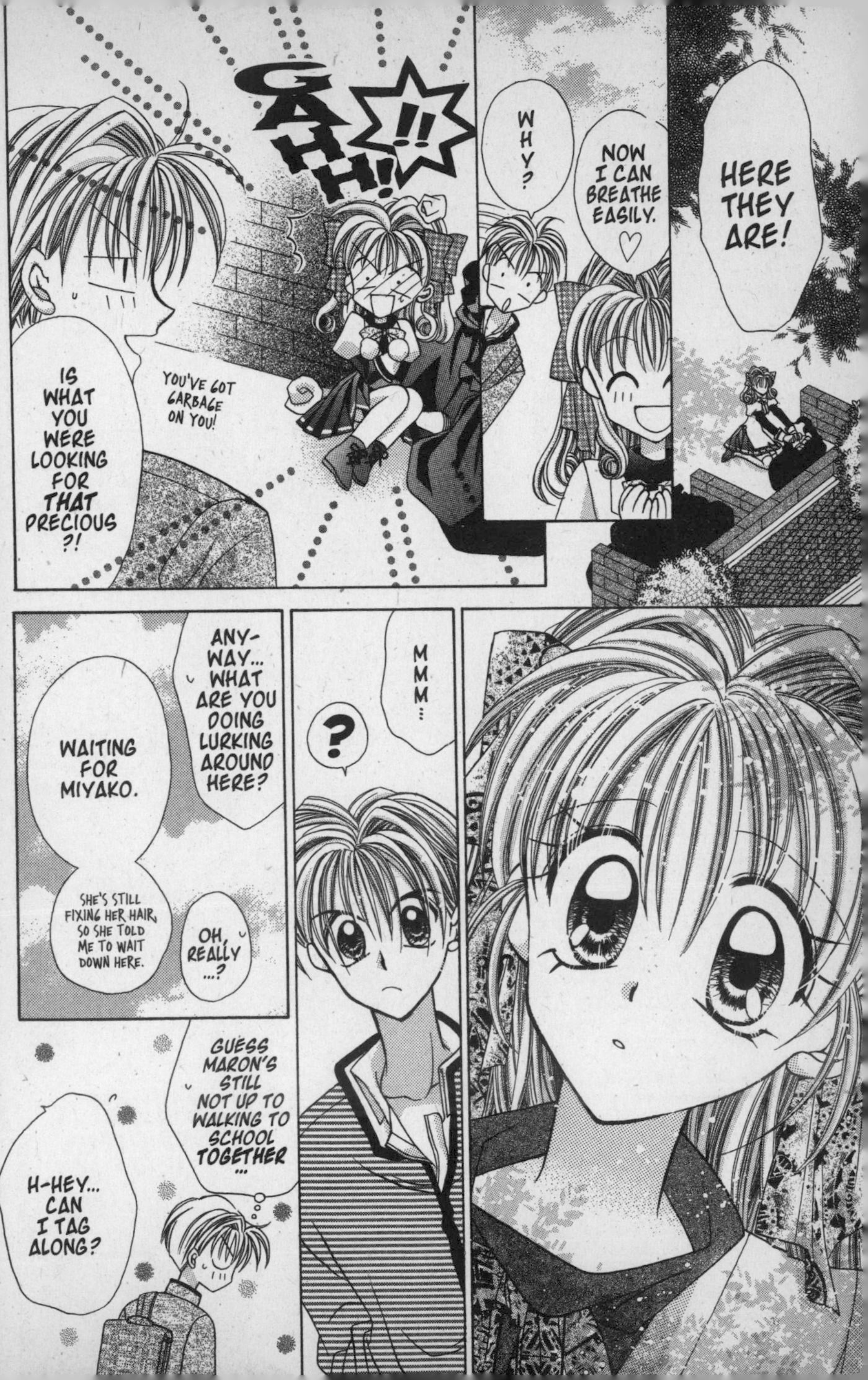
HERE THEY ARE!
NOW I CAN BREATHE EASILY. ♡
WHY?
GAHH!!!
YOU'VE GOT GARBAGE ON YOU!
IS WHAT YOU WERE LOOKING FOR THAT PRECIOUS?!
MMM...
?
ANY-WAY... WHAT ARE YOU DOING LURKING AROUND HERE?
WAITING FOR MIYAKO.
SHE'S STILL FIXING HER HAIR, SO SHE TOLD ME TO WAIT DOWN HERE.
OH, REALLY ...?
GUESS MARON'S STILL NOT UP TO WALKING TO SCHOOL TOGETHER ...
H-HEY... CAN I TAG ALONG?

SEE YOU NEXT TIME.

That's right, folks, we're down to the last column of the book. (Ahhh! I still have a script to write! I don't have time!) So, I want to thank everybody for their fan letters. ♥ Honestly, I love reading them; they make me so happy. ♥♥♥

But one thing I can't do is send you my comics or artwork. Sorry, no dice! I can't play favorites with anyone...and I don't have the time...or the money...so forget it! And another thing, I'd rather not have letters, presents, etc. sent to my home. I'm overjoyed when I receive such items, but I'd like to maintain my privacy. Sorry...To the reader who sent me a congratulatory note on the animification of JEANNE, along with flowers, to my place, I was really happy when they came. ♥ But I don't want you readers spending that much money on me when the best way for you to communicate your feelings is just by sending me a letter. So from now on, please, no more presents sent to my house. (The presents I have received till now, though, I am using ♥ and are decorating my place.)

By the way, if you send me a letter, I'll get it within a week (sometimes 4 days, which is fast). During busy times, I've received two boxes full of letters and once, I even got 5 boxes of letters, which just floored me!

I never throw your letters away, though; I keep 'em all, so:

Please send me your thoughts, feelings, etc. on this volume to:

CMX
888 Prospect Street
Suite 240
La Jolla, CA 92037

Postcards are fine, too. ♥ Oh yeah, and make sure you put your return address on the envelope!

SPECIAL THANKS

Mizuse Ai-niyomin, Kazuki Ruka-chi, Asano Kyakya-rin, Takatsuki Satorin, and Nakamura Chiho-chan. You've all been a great help!

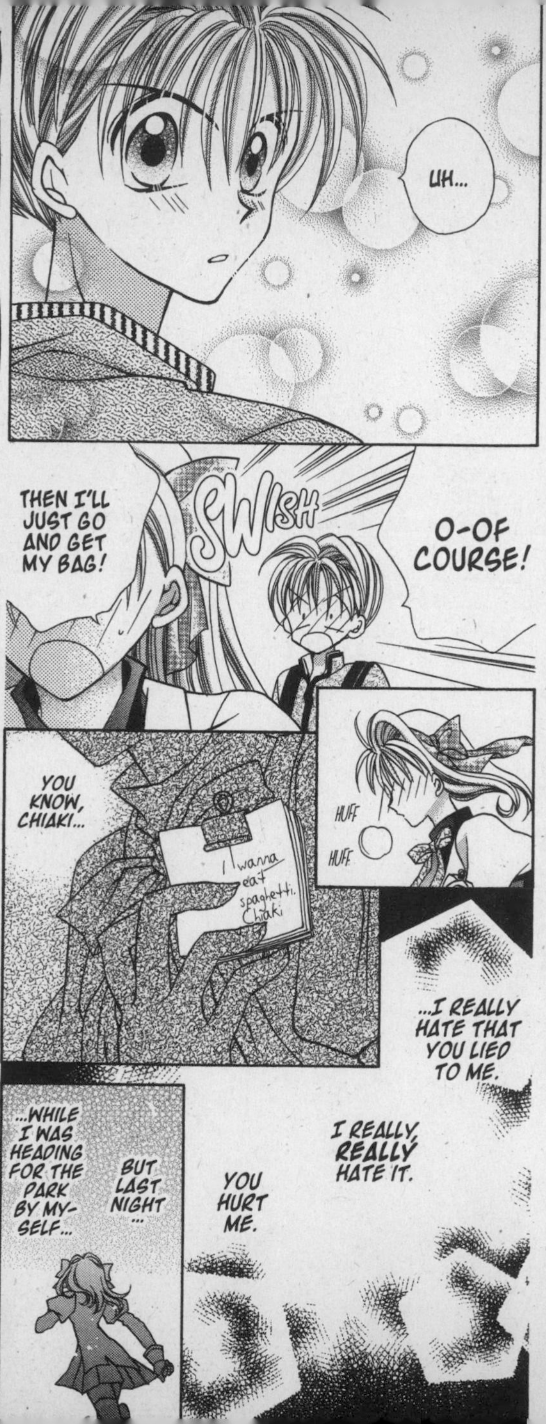
UH...
O-OF COURSE!
SWISH
THEN I'LL JUST GO AND GET MY BAG!
HUFF
HUFF
YOU KNOW, CHIAKI...
I wanna eat spaghetti. Chiaki
...I REALLY HATE THAT YOU LIED TO ME.
I REALLY, REALLY HATE IT.
YOU HURT ME.
BUT LAST NIGHT...
...WHILE I WAS HEADING FOR THE PARK BY MY-SELF...

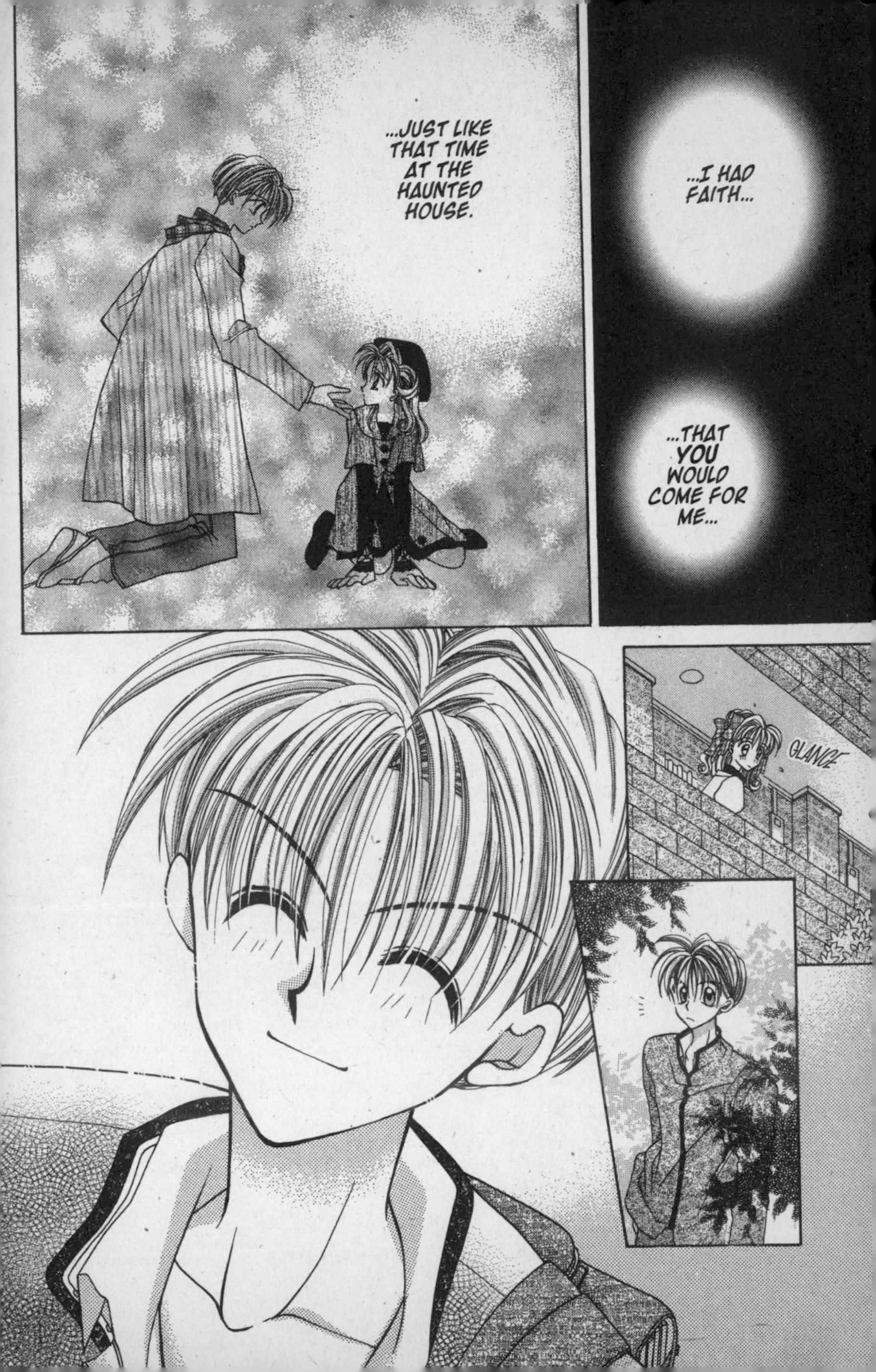
...I HAD FAITH...
...THAT YOU WOULD COME FOR ME...
...JUST LIKE THAT TIME AT THE HAUNTED HOUSE.
GLANCE

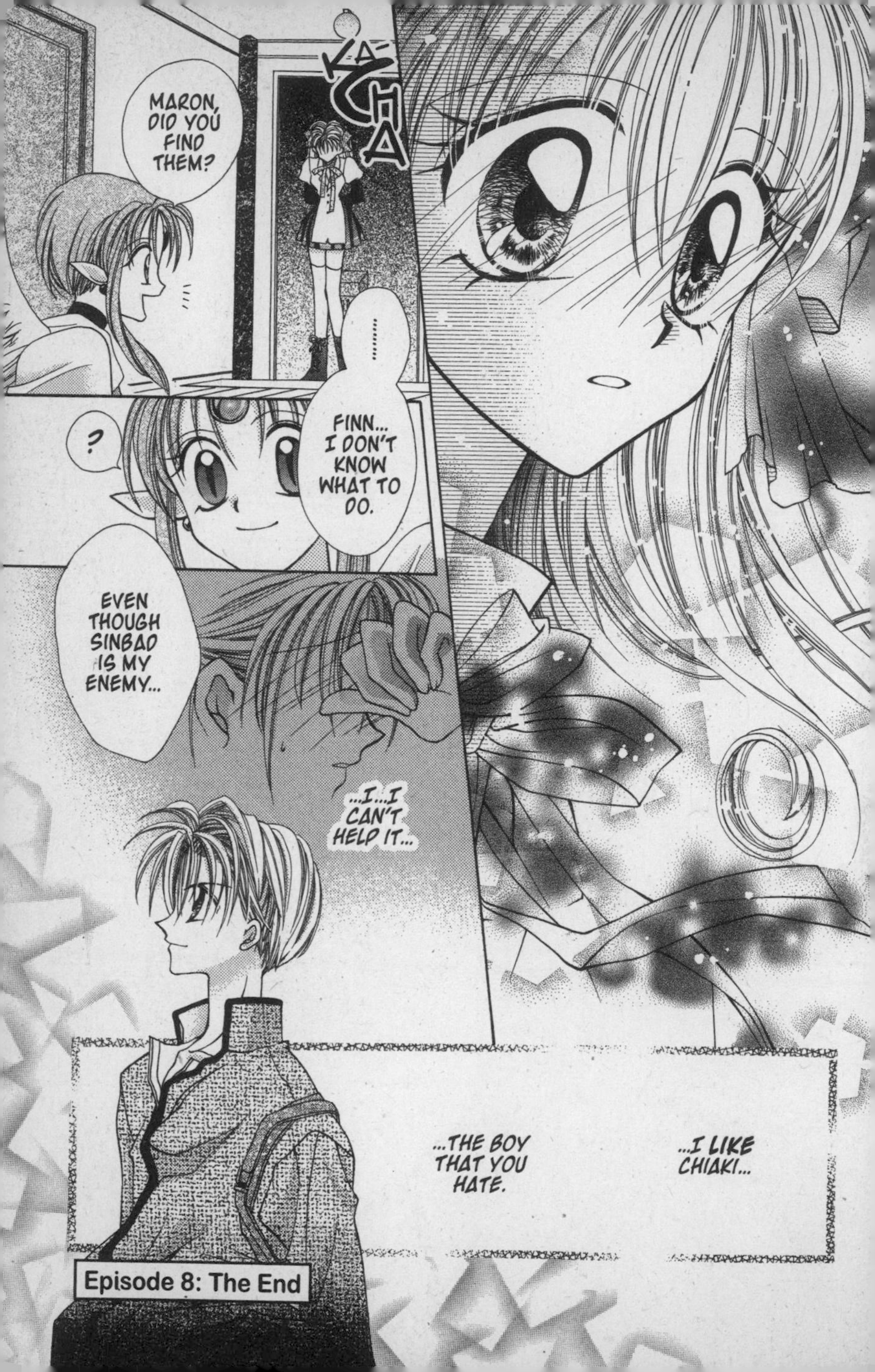
KA-CHA
MARON, DID YOU FIND THEM?
......
FINN... I DON'T KNOW WHAT TO DO.
?
EVEN THOUGH SINBAD IS MY ENEMY...
...I...I CAN'T HELP IT...
...I LIKE CHIAKI...
...THE BOY THAT YOU HATE.
Episode 8: The End

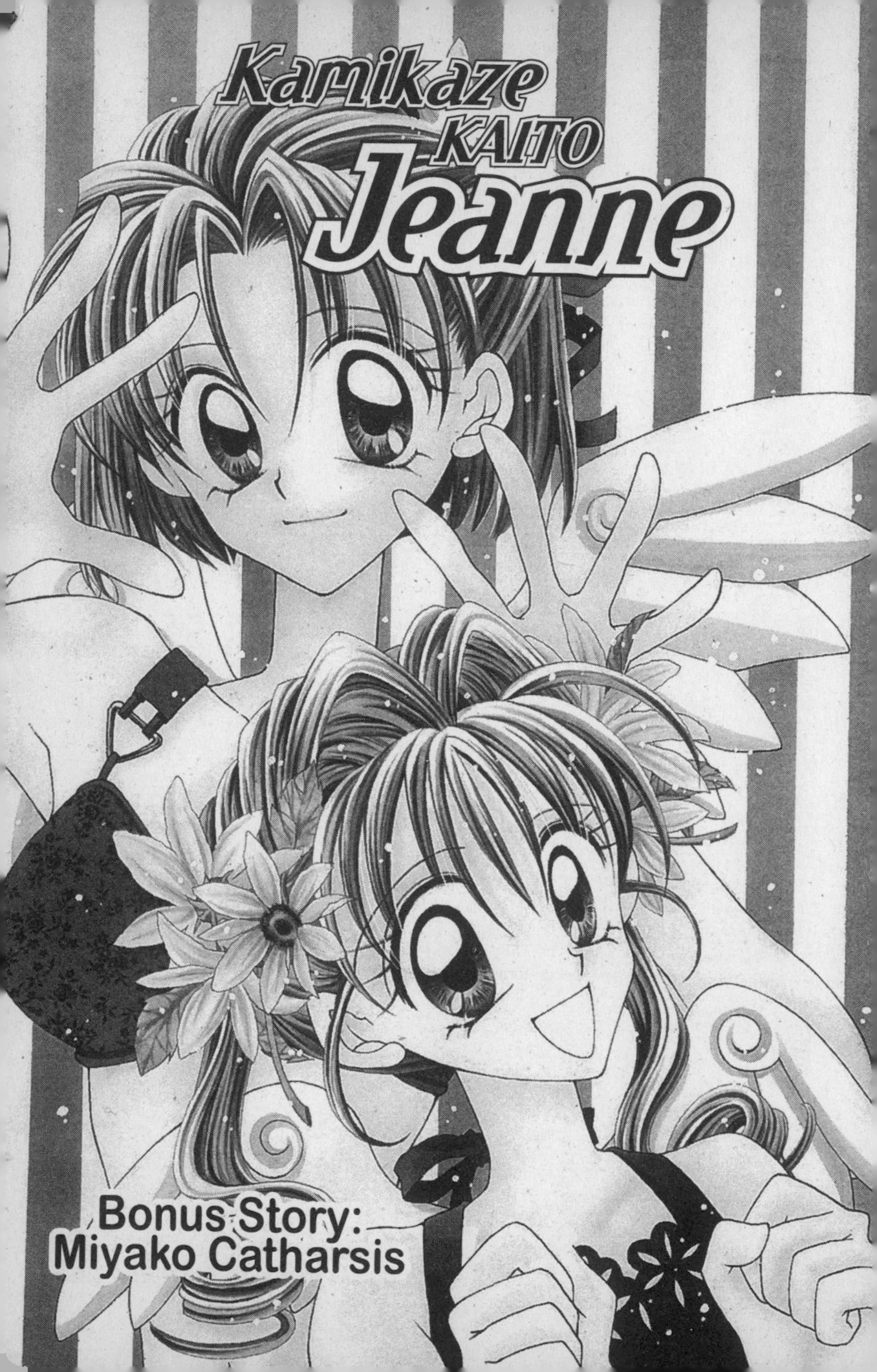
Kamikaze
KAITO
Jeanne
Bonus Story:
Miyako Catharsis

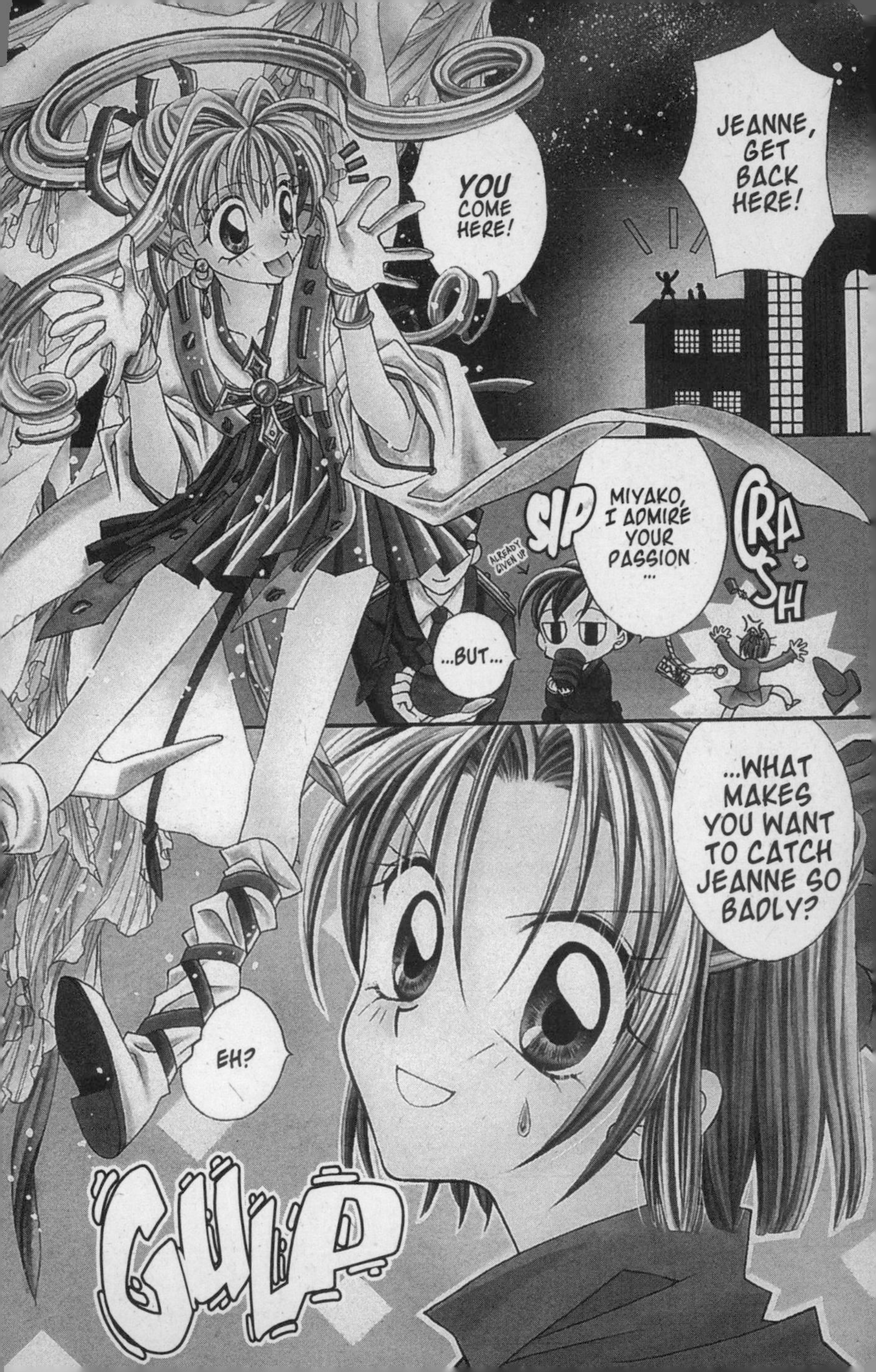
JEANNE, GET BACK HERE!
YOU COME HERE!
CRASH
MIYAKO, I ADMIRE YOUR PASSION ...
SIP
ALREADY GIVEN UP
...BUT...
...WHAT MAKES YOU WANT TO CATCH JEANNE SO BADLY?
EH?
GULP

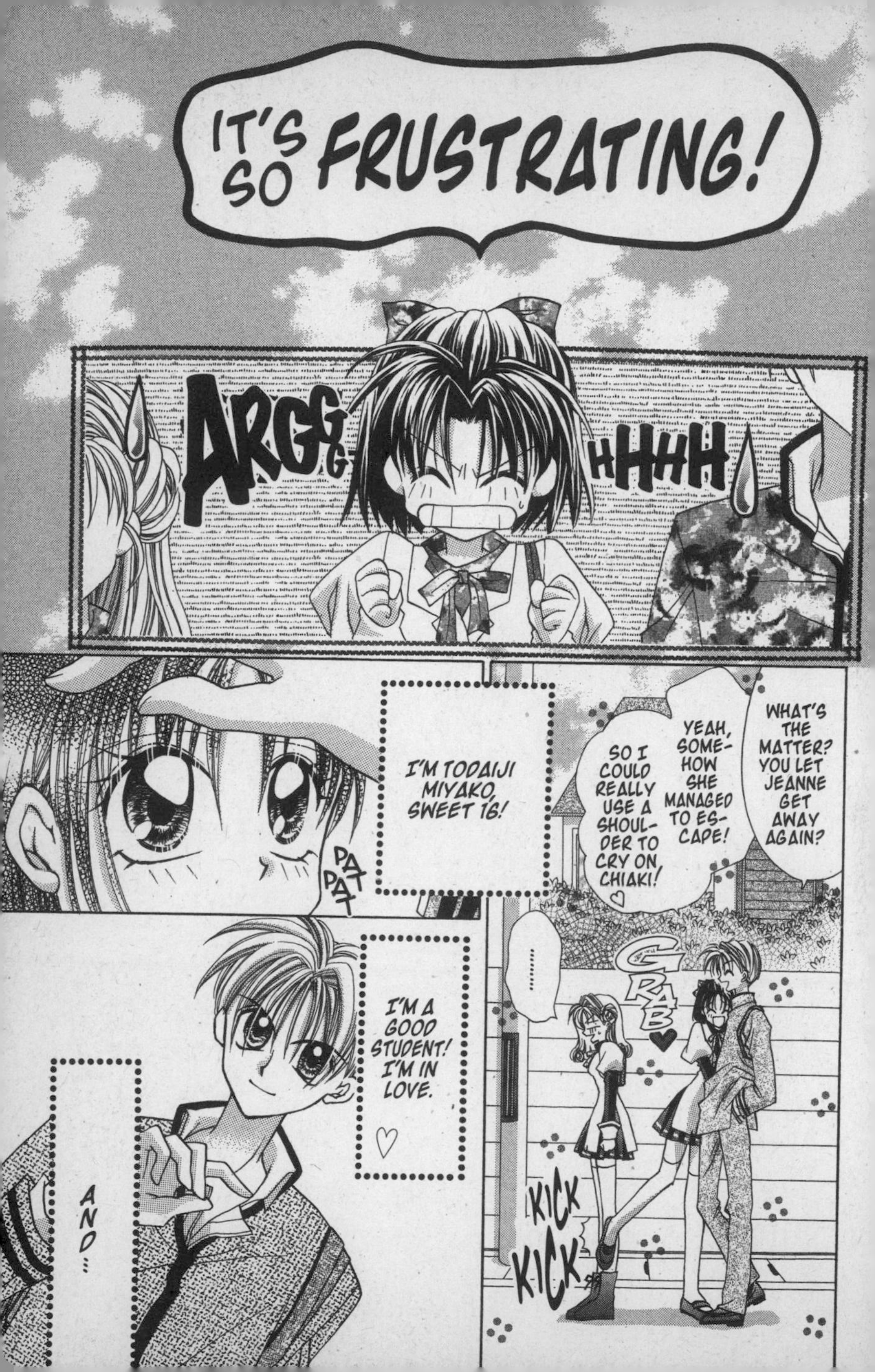
IT'S SO FRUSTRATING!
ARGGG-HHHH
WHAT'S THE MATTER? YOU LET JEANNE GET AWAY AGAIN?
YEAH, SOME-HOW SHE MANAGED TO ES-CAPE!
SO I COULD REALLY USE A SHOUL-DER TO CRY ON, CHIAKI! ♡
I'M TODAIJI MIYAKO, SWEET 16!
PAT PAT
......
GRAB ♥
KICK KICK
I'M A GOOD STUDENT! I'M IN LOVE. ♡
AND...

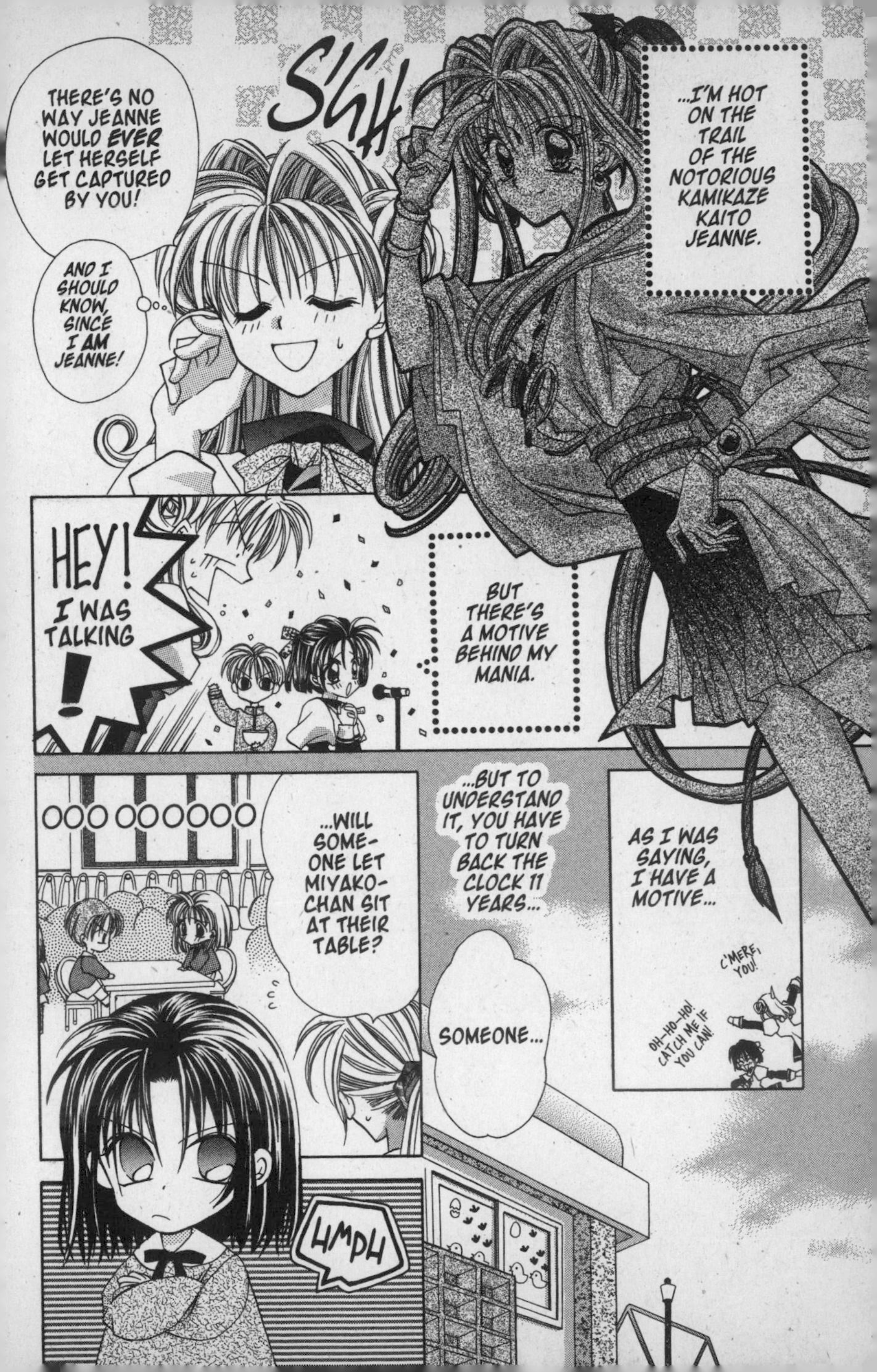
...I'M HOT ON THE TRAIL OF THE NOTORIOUS KAMIKAZE KAITO JEANNE.
SIGH
THERE'S NO WAY JEANNE WOULD EVER LET HERSELF GET CAPTURED BY YOU!
AND I SHOULD KNOW, SINCE I AM JEANNE!
BUT THERE'S A MOTIVE BEHIND MY MANIA.
HEY! I WAS TALKING!
AS I WAS SAYING, I HAVE A MOTIVE...
C'MERE, YOU!
OH-HO-HO! CATCH ME IF YOU CAN!
...BUT TO UNDERSTAND IT, YOU HAVE TO TURN BACK THE CLOCK 11 YEARS...
OOO OOOOOO
...WILL SOME-ONE LET MIYAKO-CHAN SIT AT THEIR TABLE?
SOMEONE...
HMPH

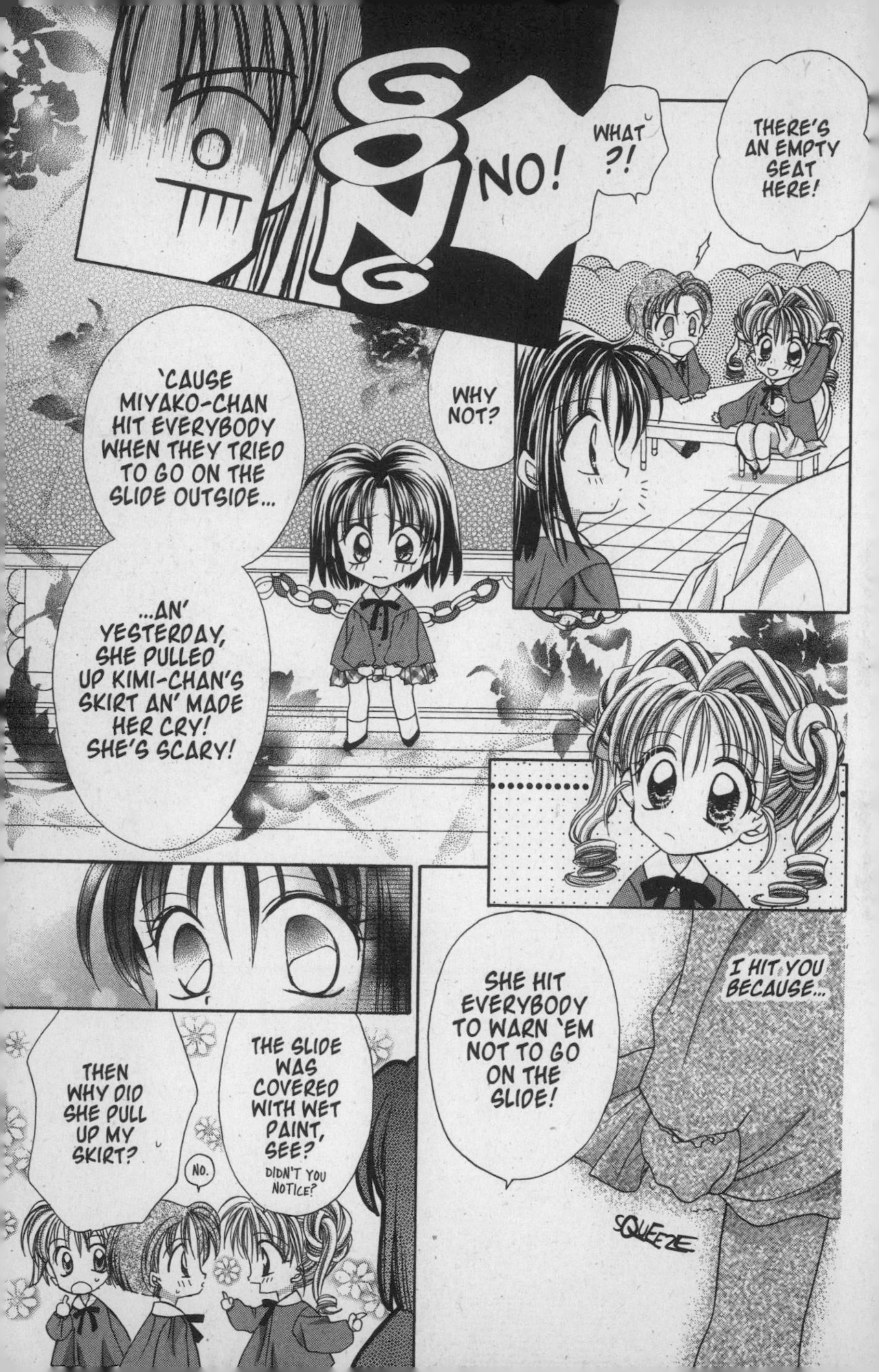
THERE'S AN EMPTY SEAT HERE!
WHAT ?!
NO!
GONG
WHY NOT?
'CAUSE MIYAKO-CHAN HIT EVERYBODY WHEN THEY TRIED TO GO ON THE SLIDE OUTSIDE...
...AN' YESTERDAY, SHE PULLED UP KIMI-CHAN'S SKIRT AN' MADE HER CRY! SHE'S SCARY!
......
I HIT YOU BECAUSE...
SHE HIT EVERYBODY TO WARN 'EM NOT TO GO ON THE SLIDE!
SQUEEZE
THE SLIDE WAS COVERED WITH WET PAINT, SEE?
DIDN'T YOU NOTICE?
NO.
THEN WHY DID SHE PULL UP MY SKIRT?

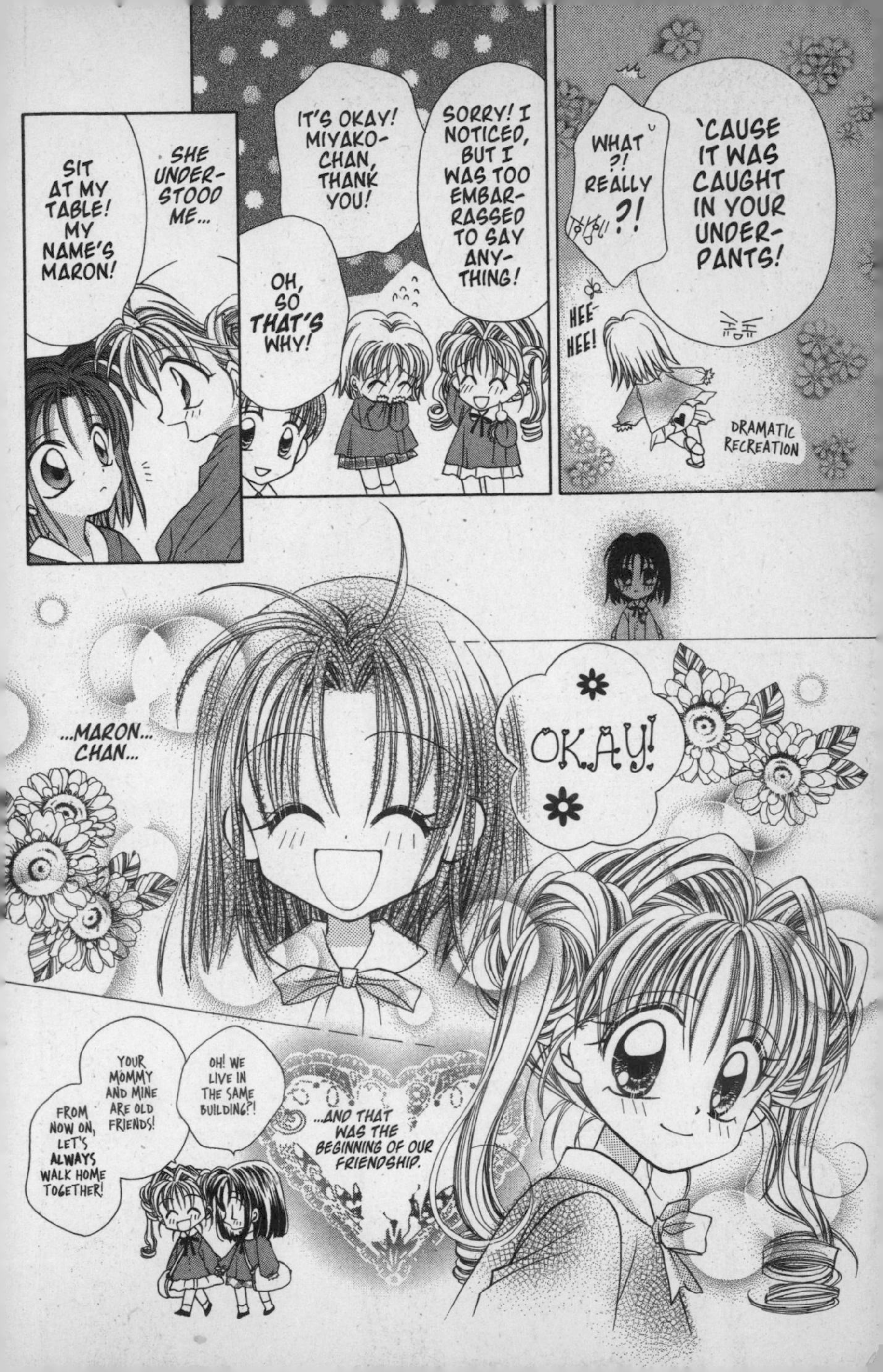
'CAUSE IT WAS CAUGHT IN YOUR UNDERPANTS!
WHAT?! REALLY?!
HEE-HEE!
DRAMATIC RECREATION
SORRY! I NOTICED, BUT I WAS TOO EMBARRASSED TO SAY ANYTHING!
IT'S OKAY! MIYAKO-CHAN, THANK YOU!
OH, SO THAT'S WHY!
SHE UNDERSTOOD ME...
SIT AT MY TABLE! MY NAME'S MARON!
OKAY!
...MARON... CHAN...
...AND THAT WAS THE BEGINNING OF OUR FRIENDSHIP.
OH! WE LIVE IN THE SAME BUILDING?!
YOUR MOMMY AND MINE ARE OLD FRIENDS!
FROM NOW ON, LET'S ALWAYS WALK HOME TOGETHER!

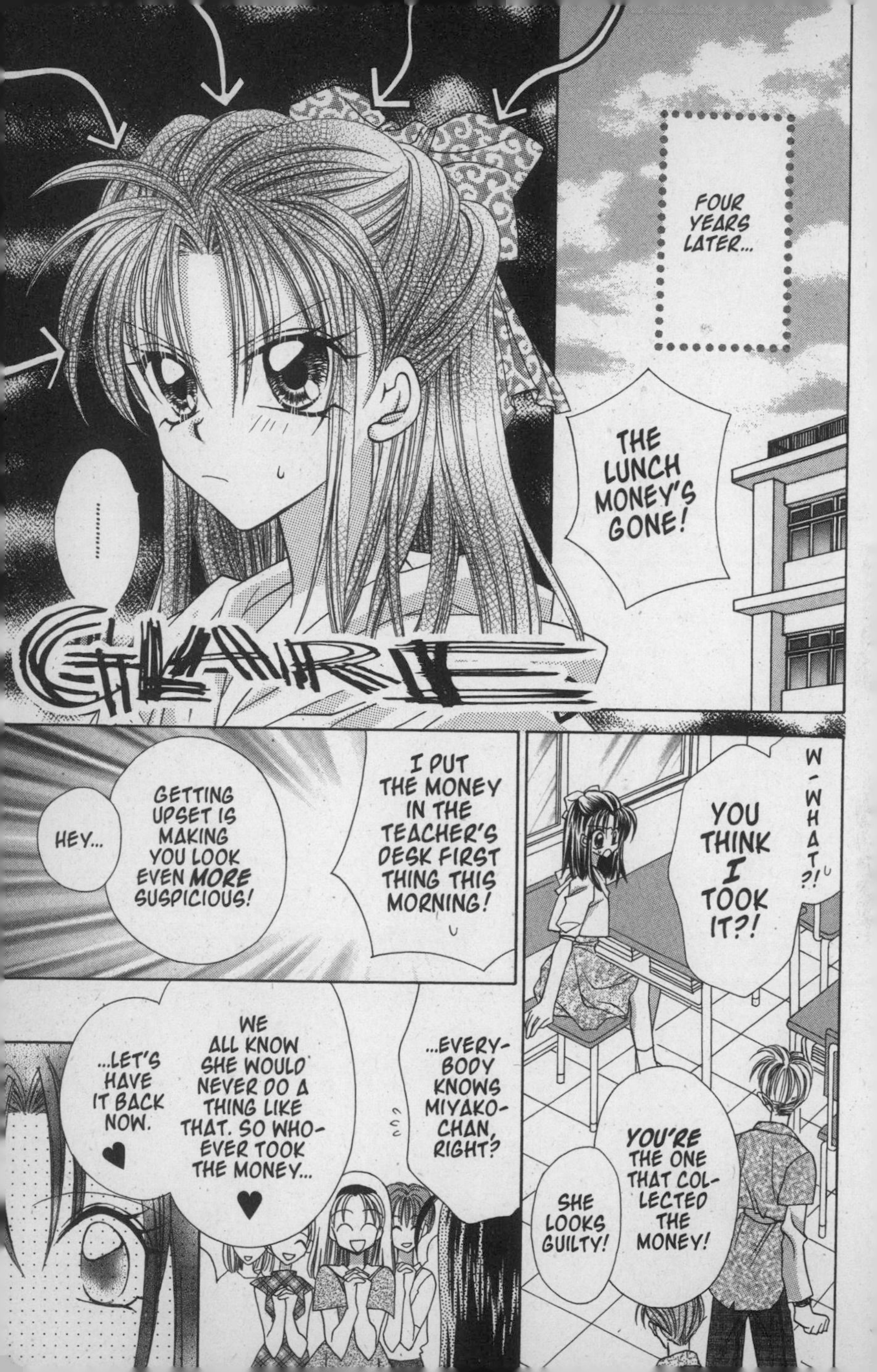
FOUR YEARS LATER...
THE LUNCH MONEY'S GONE!
......
W-WHAT?!
YOU THINK I TOOK IT?!
YOU'RE THE ONE THAT COLLECTED THE MONEY!
SHE LOOKS GUILTY!
I PUT THE MONEY IN THE TEACHER'S DESK FIRST THING THIS MORNING!
GETTING UPSET IS MAKING YOU LOOK EVEN MORE SUSPICIOUS!
HEY...
...EVERYBODY KNOWS MIYAKO-CHAN, RIGHT?
WE ALL KNOW SHE WOULD NEVER DO A THING LIKE THAT. SO WHOEVER TOOK THE MONEY...
...LET'S HAVE IT BACK NOW.

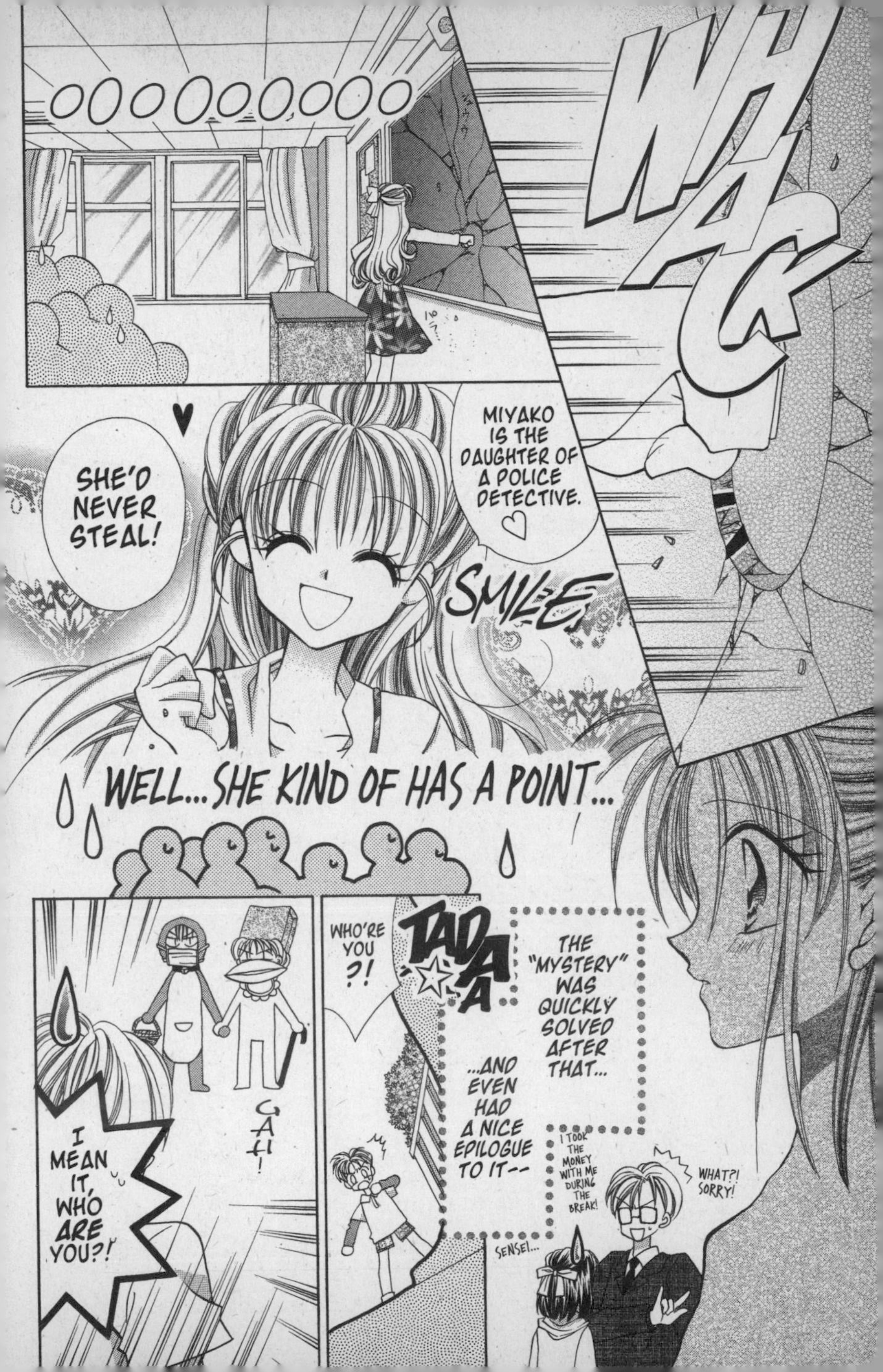
WHAG
OOOOOOOOOO
MIYAKO IS THE DAUGHTER OF A POLICE DETECTIVE. ♡
SHE'D NEVER STEAL!
SMILE
WELL...SHE KIND OF HAS A POINT...
THE "MYSTERY" WAS QUICKLY SOLVED AFTER THAT...
...AND EVEN HAD A NICE EPILOGUE TO IT--
I TOOK THE MONEY WITH ME DURING THE BREAK!
WHAT?! SORRY!
SENSEI...
TADAA
WHO'RE YOU ?!
GAH!
I MEAN IT, WHO ARE YOU?!

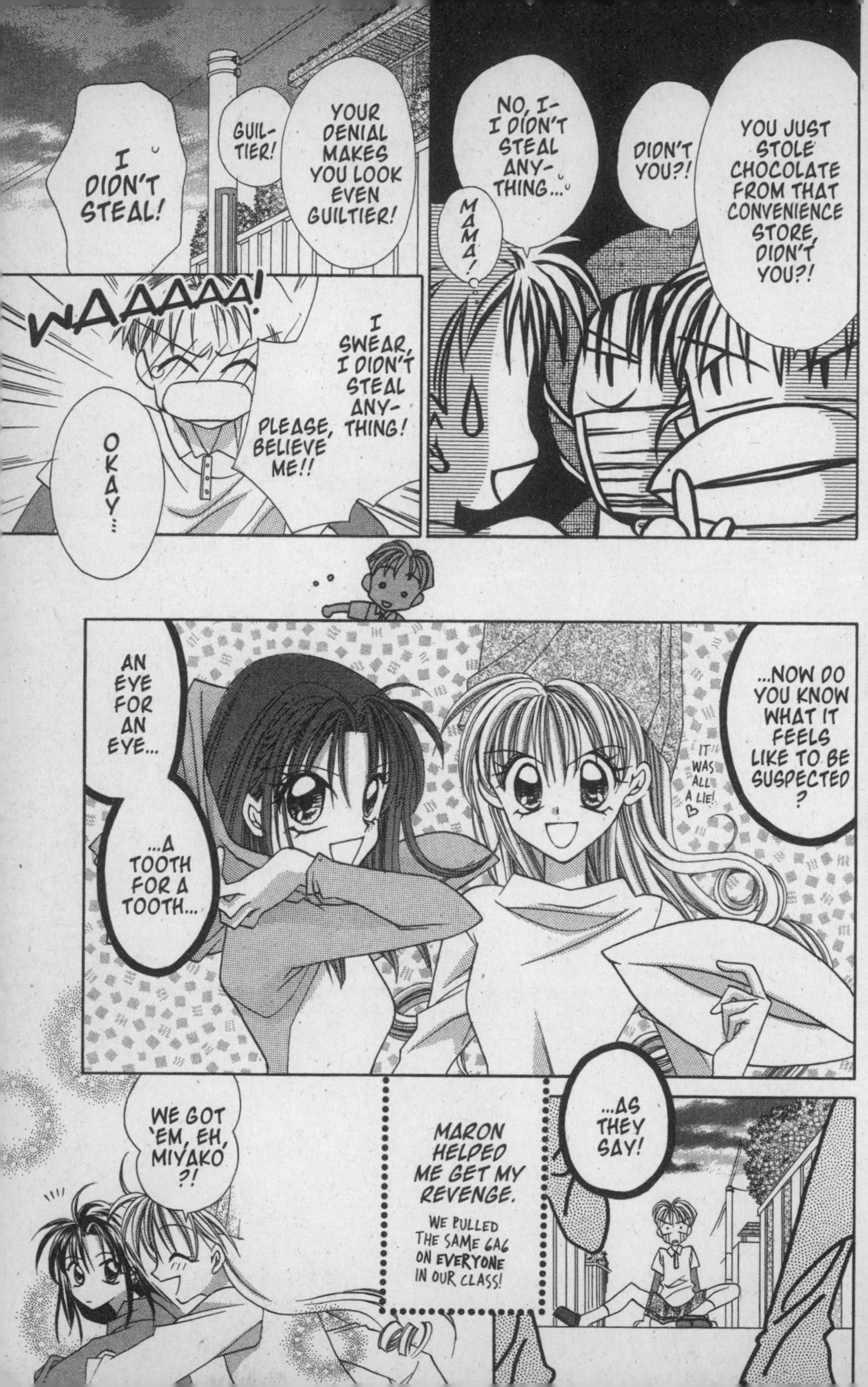
YOU JUST STOLE CHOCOLATE FROM THAT CONVENIENCE STORE, DIDN'T YOU?!
DIDN'T YOU?!
NO, I- I DIDN'T STEAL ANY-THING...
MAMA!
YOUR DENIAL MAKES YOU LOOK EVEN GUILTIER!
GUIL-TIER!
I DIDN'T STEAL!
WAAAAA!
I SWEAR, I DIDN'T STEAL ANY-THING!
PLEASE, BELIEVE ME!!
OKAY...
...NOW DO YOU KNOW WHAT IT FEELS LIKE TO BE SUSPECTED?
IT WAS ALL A LIE!
AN EYE FOR AN EYE...
...A TOOTH FOR A TOOTH...
...AS THEY SAY!
MARON HELPED ME GET MY REVENGE.
WE PULLED THE SAME GAG ON EVERYONE IN OUR CLASS!
WE GOT 'EM, EH, MIYAKO?!

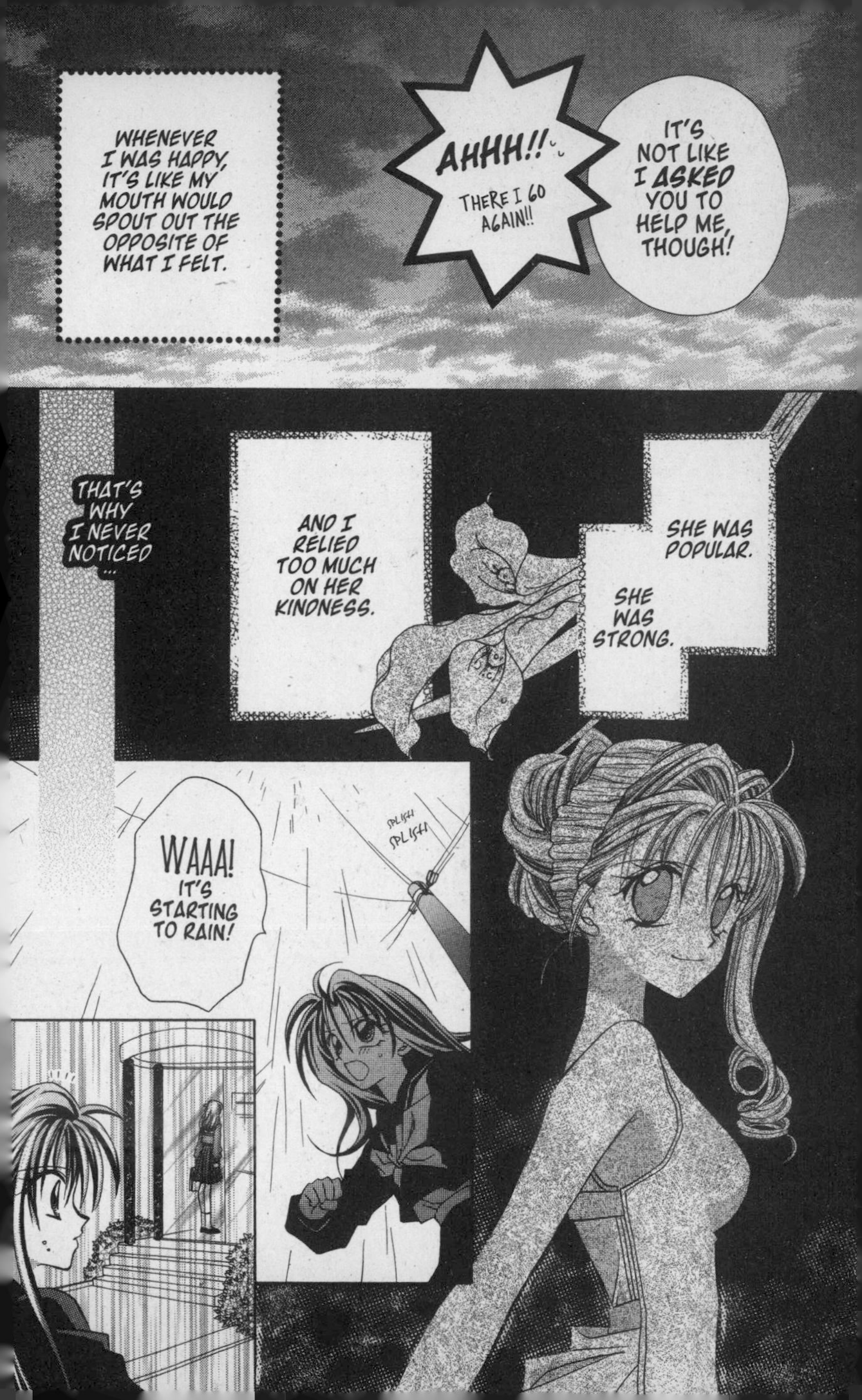
IT'S NOT LIKE I ASKED YOU TO HELP ME, THOUGH!
AHHH!!
THERE I GO AGAIN!!
WHENEVER I WAS HAPPY, IT'S LIKE MY MOUTH WOULD SPOUT OUT THE OPPOSITE OF WHAT I FELT.
SHE WAS POPULAR.
SHE WAS STRONG.
AND I RELIED TOO MUCH ON HER KINDNESS.
THAT'S WHY I NEVER NOTICED...
SPLISH SPLISH
WAAA! IT'S STARTING TO RAIN!

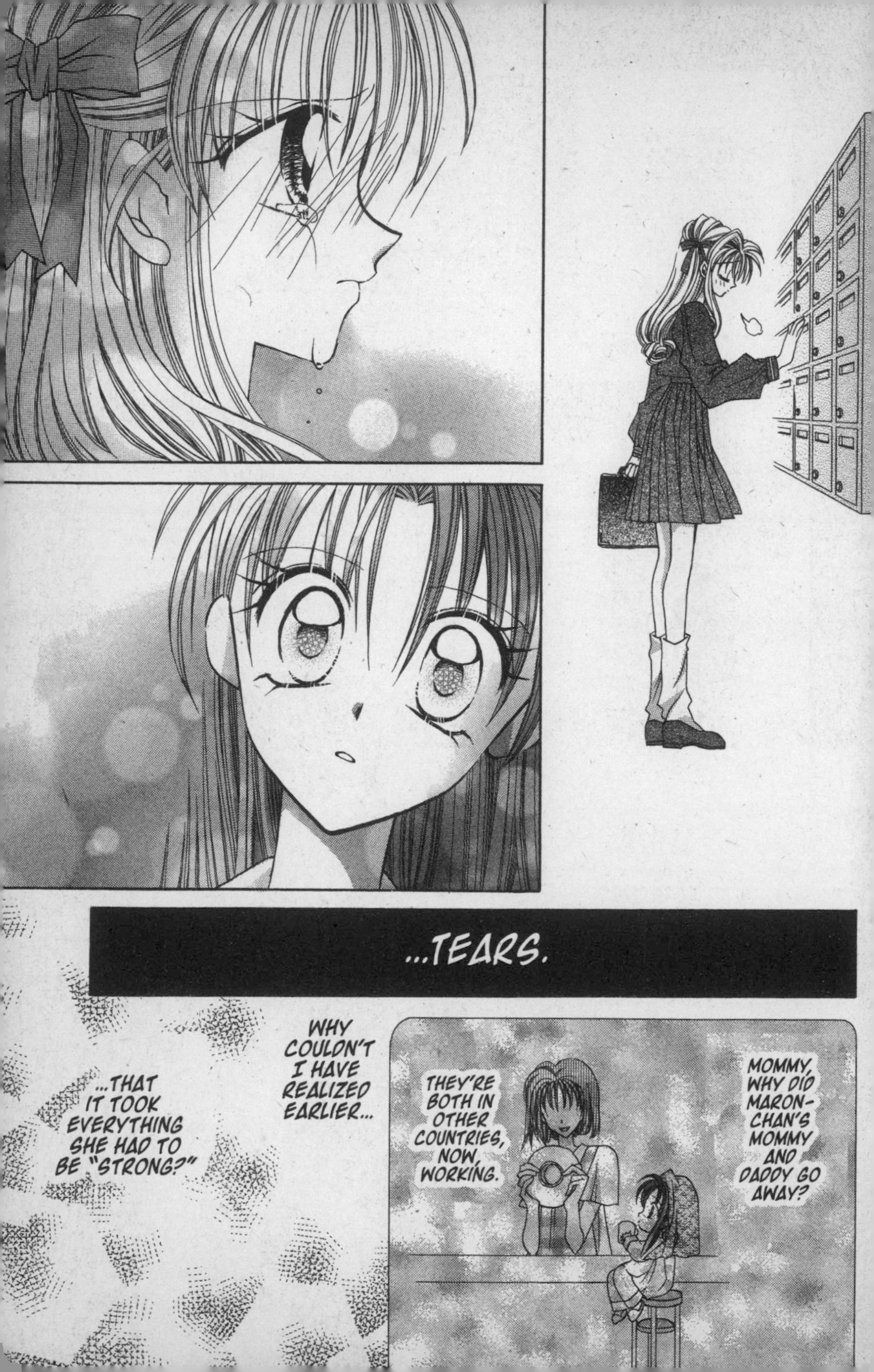
...TEARS.
MOMMY, WHY DID MARON-CHAN'S MOMMY AND DADDY GO AWAY?
THEY'RE BOTH IN OTHER COUNTRIES, NOW, WORKING.
WHY COULDN'T I HAVE REALIZED EARLIER...
...THAT IT TOOK EVERYTHING SHE HAD TO BE "STRONG?"

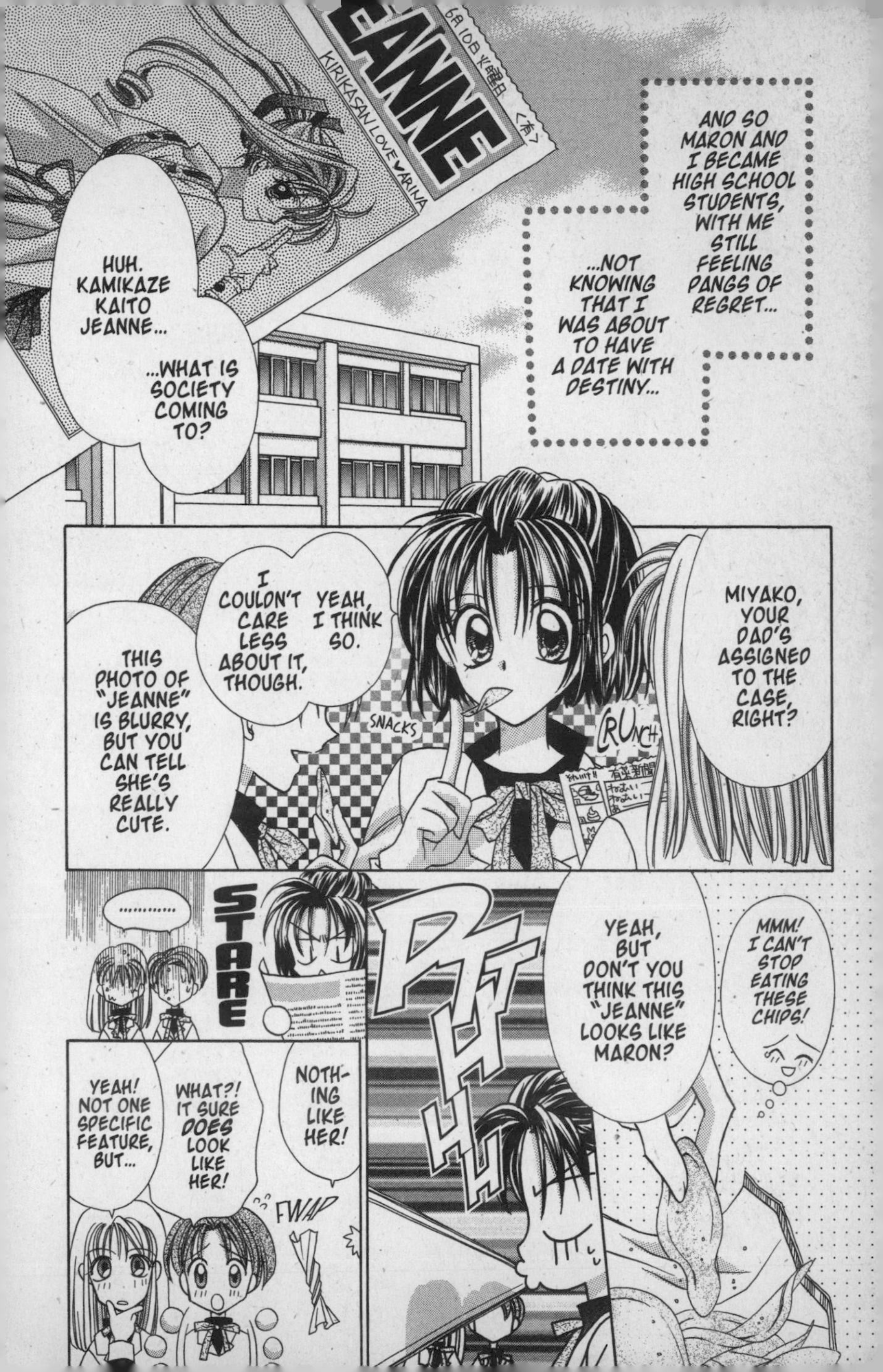
JEANNE
KIRIKASAN LOVE♥ARINA
AND SO MARON AND I BECAME HIGH SCHOOL STUDENTS, WITH ME STILL FEELING PANGS OF REGRET...
...NOT KNOWING THAT I WAS ABOUT TO HAVE A DATE WITH DESTINY...
HUH. KAMIKAZE KAITO JEANNE...
...WHAT IS SOCIETY COMING TO?
MIYAKO, YOUR DAD'S ASSIGNED TO THE CASE, RIGHT?
CRUNCH
YEAH, I THINK SO.
I COULDN'T CARE LESS ABOUT IT, THOUGH.
SNACKS
THIS PHOTO OF "JEANNE" IS BLURRY, BUT YOU CAN TELL SHE'S REALLY CUTE.
MMM! I CAN'T STOP EATING THESE CHIPS!
YEAH, BUT DON'T YOU THINK THIS "JEANNE" LOOKS LIKE MARON?
STARE
....
NOTHING LIKE HER!
WHAT?! IT SURE DOES LOOK LIKE HER!
YEAH! NOT ONE SPECIFIC FEATURE, BUT...
FWAP

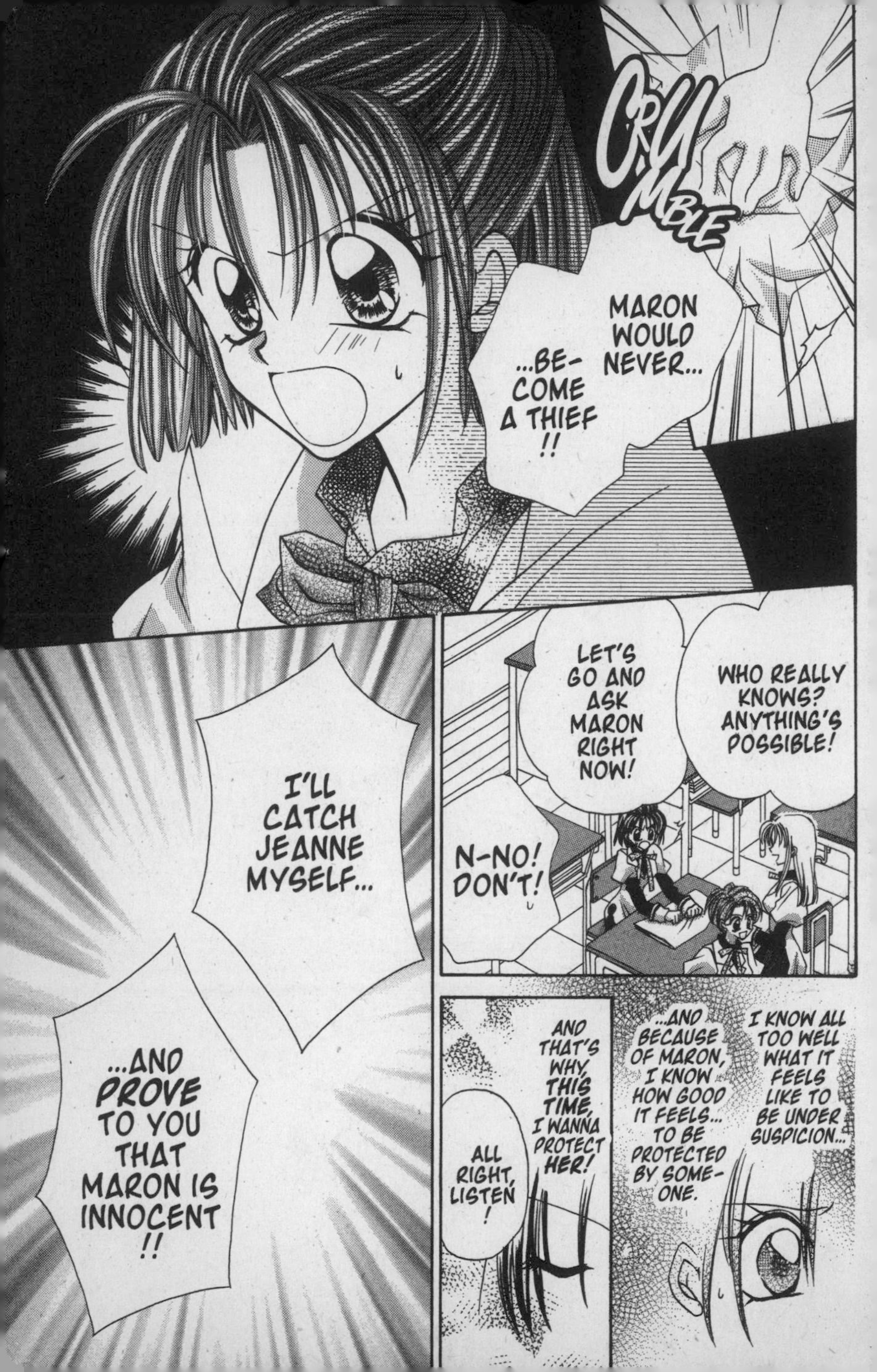
CRUMBLE
MARON WOULD NEVER...
...BECOME A THIEF!!
WHO REALLY KNOWS? ANYTHING'S POSSIBLE!
LET'S GO AND ASK MARON RIGHT NOW!
N-NO! DON'T!
I KNOW ALL TOO WELL WHAT IT FEELS LIKE TO BE UNDER SUSPICION...
...AND BECAUSE OF MARON, I KNOW HOW GOOD IT FEELS... TO BE PROTECTED BY SOMEONE.
AND THAT'S WHY, THIS TIME, I WANNA PROTECT HER!
ALL RIGHT, LISTEN!
I'LL CATCH JEANNE MYSELF...
...AND PROVE TO YOU THAT MARON IS INNOCENT!!

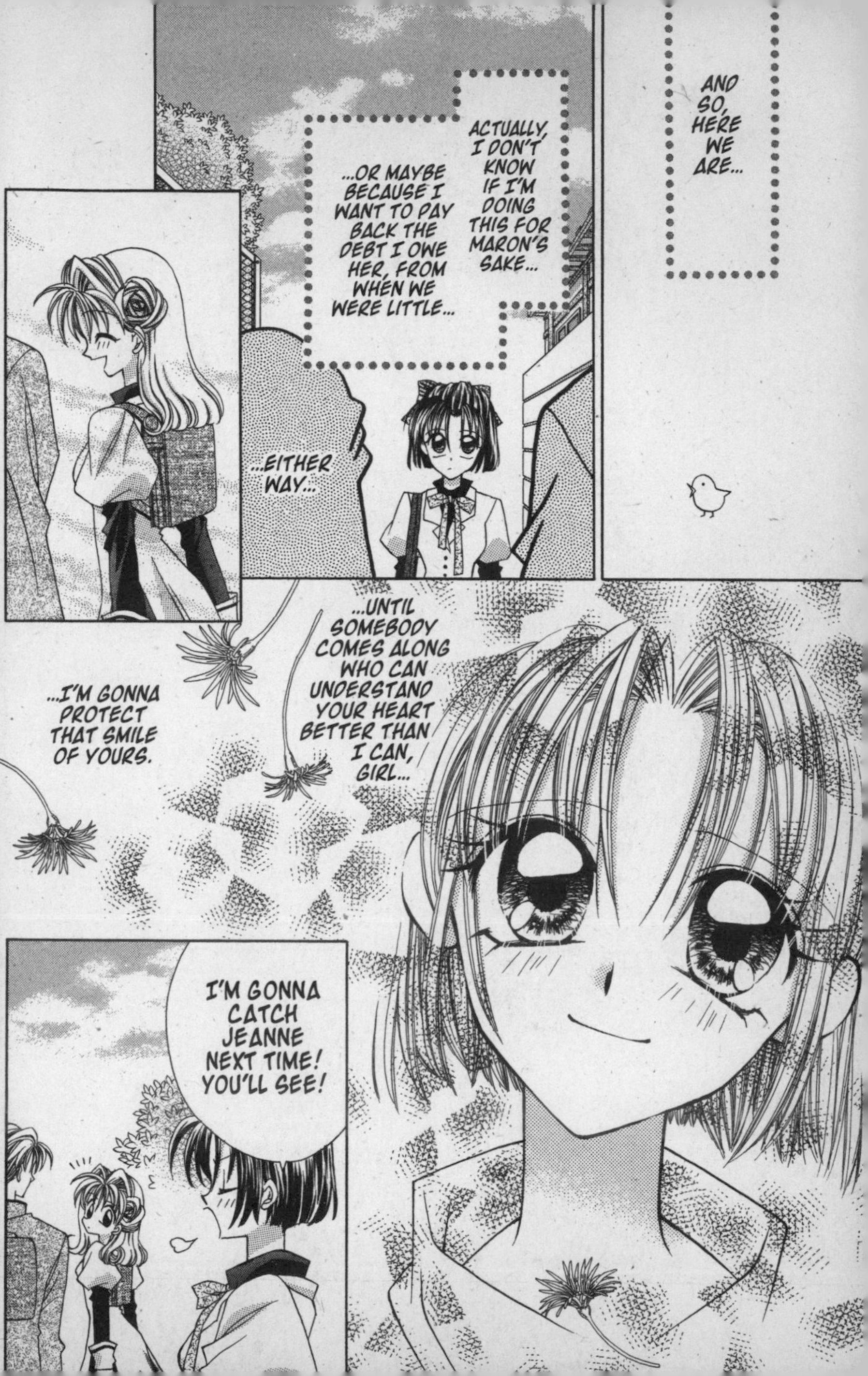
AND SO, HERE WE ARE...
ACTUALLY, I DON'T KNOW IF I'M DOING THIS FOR MARON'S SAKE...
...OR MAYBE BECAUSE I WANT TO PAY BACK THE DEBT I OWE HER, FROM WHEN WE WERE LITTLE...
...EITHER WAY...
...UNTIL SOMEBODY COMES ALONG WHO CAN UNDERSTAND YOUR HEART BETTER THAN I CAN, GIRL...
...I'M GONNA PROTECT THAT SMILE OF YOURS.
I'M GONNA CATCH JEANNE NEXT TIME! YOU'LL SEE!

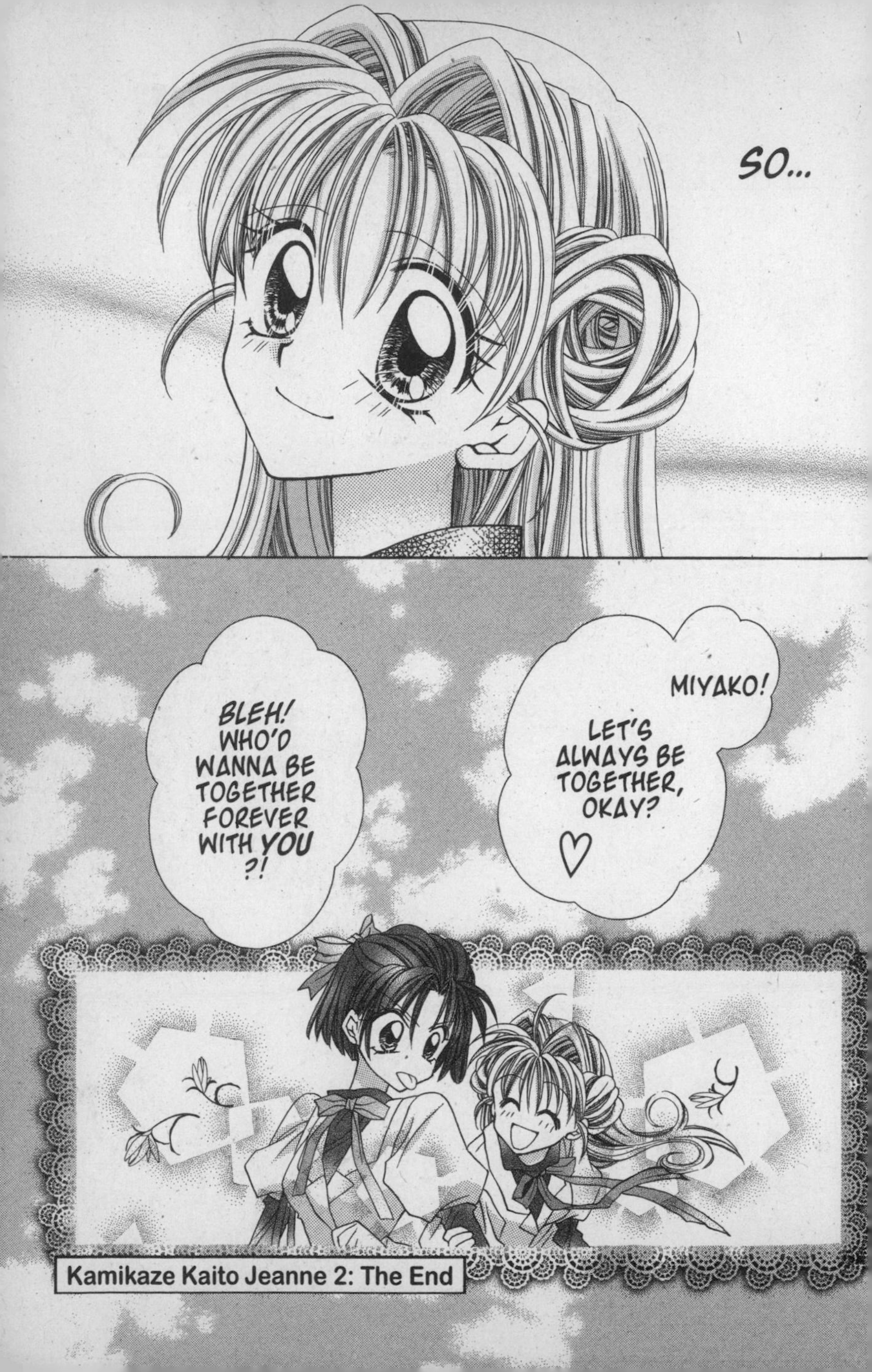
SO...
MIYAKO!
LET'S ALWAYS BE TOGETHER, OKAY? ♥
BLEH! WHO'D WANNA BE TOGETHER FOREVER WITH YOU ?!
Kamikaze Kaito Jeanne 2: The End

Jim Lee
Editorial Director
John Nee
VP—Business Development
Hank Kanalz
VP—General Manager, WildStorm
Paul Levitz
President & Publisher
Georg Brewer
VP—Design & DC Direct Creative
Richard Bruning
Senior VP—Creative Director
Patrick Caldon
Executive VP—Finance & Operations
Chris Caramalis
VP—Finance
John Cunningham
VP—Marketing
Terri Cunningham
VP—Managing Editor
Stephanie Fierman
Senior VP—Sales & Marketing
Alison Gill
VP—Manufacturing
Rich Johnson
VP—Book Trade Sales
Lillian Laserson
Senior VP & General Counsel
Paula Lowitt
Senior VP—Business & Legal Affairs
David McKillips
VP—Advertising & Custom Publishing
Gregory Noveck
Senior VP—Creative Affairs
Cheryl Rubin
Senior VP—Brand Management
Jeff Trojan
VP—Business Development, DC Direct
Bob Wayne
VP—Sales

Sheldon Drzka
**Translation
and Adaptation**

Saida Temofonte
Lettering

Larry Berry
Design

Ben Abernathy
Editor